Fame, Fortune and Sweet Liberty

Fame, Fortune and Sweet Liberty

The Great European Emigration

Dirk Hoerder
Diethelm Knauf
(Editors)

Edition Temmen

Die Deutsche Bibliothek - CIP-Einheitsaufnahme

Fame, fortune and sweet liberty :
the great European emigration / [Hoerder ; Knauf]. -
Bremen : Ed. Temmen, 1992

Dt. Ausg. u. d. T.: Aufbruch in die Fremde
ISBN -3-926958-96-0

NE: Hoerder, Dirk [Hrsg.]

Translations by
Thomas Kozak, New York

With 214 illustrations,
47 on color

© **Edition Temmen**
Hohenlohestr. 21 - 2800 Bremen 1 - Germany
Phone 0421-344280/341727 - Fax 0421-348094

Production: Edition Temmen

ISBN -3-926958-95-2 (German edition)
ISBN 3-926958-96-0 (English edition)

On April 18th, 1872, Heinrich Beck (left) applied for "Bremen citizenship". He listed his occupation as "master brewer". In his wedding documents he had added "from Fort Wain, Indiana". The brewer, Heinrich Beck emigrated from Württemberg in southern Germany to North America, in 1864. He returned ten years later and settled in Bremen. In June, 1873, he was one of the founders of the internationally known brewery Beck & Co. in Bremen. There he developed the characteristic pils beer. Possibly he learned brewing methods in the USA which contributed to the development of Beck's Beer which can withstand long sea voyage through various climatic zones without losing in taste. Today, Beck's has friends on all five continents. "Traces of emigration" can thus be found in the history of Beck & Co.

This book is sponsored by the brewery Beck&CO, Bremen.

The idea for this book had Christiane Harzig, Labor Migration Project, University of Bremen.

Contents

Introduction

Internal European Migration and its Expansion to
the Global Scale
Dirk Hoerder / Diethelm Knauf 9
Migrants, Transients, Immigrants: Towards an
Understanding 10
Ethnic Neighborhoods and Acculturation 13
The Diversity of Migration Processes and Experiences 14
Migration in Preindustrial Times 19
From Local to Global, from Agricultural to Industrial
Migration 23

The European Cultures of Origin

Hallelujah, We're off to America!
Western, Central, and Northern Europe
Agnes Bretting 27
England, Scotland, Wales 27
Ireland 29
France 33
Belgium 34
The Netherlands 35
Luxembourg 36
The German-Speaking Countries 36
Scandinavia 40

Za chlebem - to Bread: Eastern Europe
Dirk Hoerder 48
Poland 48
The Western Provinces of Czarist Russia 52
Finland 52
The Baltic Countries 53
The Peoples of Russia 54
Polish and Russian Jews 55
Czechs, Slovaks, and Magyars 59
The Balkan Peoples 61
Summary 63

Cerca di lavoro - Looking for Work:
Southern Europe
Dirk Hoerder 66
Italy 66
Spain and Portugal 69

The Journey

From the Old World to the New
Agnes Bretting 75
The Emigration Policies of the German States
(1815-1915) 75
Travel Routes and Embarkation Ports in Europe 78
The Emigration Business in Bremen and Hamburg . . 84
Germany as a Transit Country for Eastern Europeans . 87
The Emigration Agents 91
Emigration and Shipping: The Rise of the
Shipping Lines 95
Food and Lodging in Hamburg and Bremen 102
From Sailing Ship to Steamship: The Voyage 106
Arrival in the New World 111
Immigrant Aid Societies 116

The Countries of Immigration

There is no »Kaiser« here: The United States as a
Country of Immigration
Christiane Harzig 123
The First Rural Settlements 123
The Opening of the West: Settlement Migration . . . 129
Political Trends and Restrictions on Immigration . . 131
Industrialization and Urbanization: Labor Migration 136
The Everyday Life of Immigrants 139

Freedom in the North:
Canada
Andrea Koch-Kraft 148
The Rivalry between France and England in the East 148
Upper and Lower Canada 152
The Canadian Pacific Region 153
The Opening of the West and
the Development of the Canadian Mosaic 154
New Immigrants from Postwar Europe 157
The New Immigration Policy: Occupational
Criteria versus Humanitarian Goals 158

To Govern is to Populate! Migration to
Latin America
Diethelm Knauf 160
Early European Expansion 160
Colonization Programs and Labor Recruiting 164
The Period of the World Wars 165
The Example of Brazil 171
Migration and the Receiving Culture 172

The Legendary Southern Continent:
Australia
Diethelm Knauf 176
From Discovery to the Founding of the Colony . . . 176
Convicts and Free Settlers 178
The Myth of the Bush 180
The Gold Rush 182
Populate or Perish - Immigration after 1945 184

»A Working Man's Paradise«:
New Zealand
Diethelm Knauf *186*

»...and divide the spoils«:
Africa
Helga Rathjen 191
The Scramble for Africa:
The Colonial Period 191
German Interests in Africa: A Case Study 191
The Labor Question:
Colonial Labor Migration 194
African Labor Migrants Today 195

Prospects

Migration Processes after World War I: The
German and European Experience
Klaus J. Bade 199
The End of the Mass Transatlantic Exodus from
Germany 200
Emigration from the Weimar Republic, Nazi Germany,
and the Federal Republic of Germany 200
From Emigration to Labor
Importation: Foreign Workers in the German
Empire, the Weimar Republic, and Nazi Germany . . .202
Immigration Processes after World War II 204
Migration and Integration Policy: Future
Tasks and the Historical Experience 205

Credits 208

Acknowledgements 208

District of the City of New York,
Port of New York.

Roll 672
M 237
B 2922

CUSTOMS LIST OF PASSENGERS.

The Passenger Act.
Department Decision s 27.
Regulations, Bureau of Statistics.

I, John G. Cameron, Master of the R.M.S. Teutonic do solemnly, sincerely and truly swear that the following List or Manifest subscribed by me, and now delivered by me to the Collector of Customs of the District of the City of New York, is a full and perfect list of all the passengers taken on board said vessel at Liverpool & Queenstown from which port or ports the said vessel has now arrived; and that on said list is truly designated the age, sex, calling or occupation, the port of embarkation, the number of pieces of baggage, of all the passengers, the date and cause of death of any such passengers who may have died on the voyage, and also a statement, so far as it can be ascertained, with reference to the intention of each immigrant passenger as to a protracted sojourn in this country, and also, in regard to Cabin passengers, the country of which they are citizens, and of passengers other than cabin passengers, their native country, their intended destination or location in the United States, and whether they are citizens of the United States, or not, and the location of the compartment or space occupied by each, as required by the Passenger Act of 1882 and the Regulations of the Secretary of the Treasury. So help me God.

Sworn to before me this 15 day of April 1897.

Thos Dunn
Deputy Collector.

Wm G. Cameron
Master.

† To be used for all passengers.
†† To be used for cabin passengers' only.
❋ To be used for passengers other than cabin passengers.

No.	NAME IN FULL.	Age. Years.	Months.	Sex.	Calling or Occupation.	Country of which they are Citizens. Last Residence	Native Country.	Intended Destination or Location. State or Territory.	State of passengers other than Cabin, whether Citizens of the United States.	Transient, In Transit or intending protracted sojourn.	Location of Compartment or Space occupied forward, amidships or aft.	Number of pieces of Baggage.	Port of Embarkation.	Date and Cause of Death.
1	John McKenna	19		M	Lab	Corleagh	Ireland	New York	No	Permanent	No 2 Upper deck	1	Liverpool	
2	James Connell	25		"	"	Lpool	"	"	"	"	"	1	"	
3	Rose Leddy	20		F	Servant	Drumconda	"	"	"	"	No 5	1	"	
4	Kate "	18		"	"	Guttin	"	"	"	"	"	1	"	10 – 12
5	Patrick Donohue	22		M	Servt Farmer	Killeshandra	"	"	"	"	No 2	1	"	
6	Bessie Wilson	19		F	Servt	Ballyardle	"	Pittsburgh	"	"	No 4 Main	❋	"	
7	Joseph Shanahan	16		M	Lab	Limerick	"	New York	"	"	"	1	"	
8	Samuel Rooney	51		"	"						"	5	"	
9	Jane "	40		F	Wife						"	1	"	
10	Ellen "	15		"	Spinster						"	1	"	
11	Thomas "	12		M	Lab						"	1	"	
12	Dinah "	11		F	Child						"	1	"	
13	Michael Whalen	52		M	Miner	Cleator Moor	"	Butte City Mon			No 2 Upper	1	"	
14	Sarah Jane Mawhan	19		F	Milliner	Cookstown	"	New York			No 5	1	"	
15	George Todd	26		M	Cotton Bleacher	Leeds	U.S.A.	Kearney N.J.	Yes		No 2	2	"	1 – 0
16	Mary Scott	63		F	Seamstress	Liverpool	England	Wassaic N.Y.	No		No 5	2	"	2 – 2
17	Geo. R. Green	40		M	Farmer	Gosbeilin	"	Ithaca			No 4 Main	3	"	
18	Mary "	38		F	Wife	"	"	"			"		"	
19	Thomas "	17		M	Lab	"	"	"			"		"	
20	James Shannon	21		"	"	Glassdrummond	Ireland	New York			No 2 Upper	1	"	
21	Ellen Maguire	16		F	Servt	Swaulinbar	"	Trenton.			No 5	1	"	
22	Bridget Rooney	18		"	"	"	"	Newark			"	1	"	
23	Mary Maguire	19		"	"	"	"	Trenton N.J.			"	1	"	
24	Sarah McGaun	44		"	Wife	Rathfriland	"	New York			"	2	"	
25	John "	21		M	Farmer	"	"	"			No 2	1	"	
26	Michael McDonough	59		"	Ironworker	Bilston	"	Edwardsville Pa.			No 4 Main	3	"	
27	Winifred "	50		F	Wife	"	"	"			"		"	13 – 14 – 7

8

Introduction

Internal European Migration and its Expansion to the Global Scale

Dirk Hoerder and Diethelm Knauf

»If it's Thursday, then this must be Paris« - this stereotype of the traveler, insecure about space and time, has become symbolic of the rapid pace at which distances can be covered in the modern world.

Besides tourism, there is at present a second form of geographic mobility, that of the large number of labor migrants who tread the well-worn paths to distant centers, seeking work. In Germany today they are called »guest workers«; at other times they were called »alien workers«. In some countries they are considered immigrants, while in others they have the status of temporary help (»sojourners«). Labor migrants might be Mexicans heading for the U.S., Italians on their way to France, or Yugoslavs seeking work in West Germany, to name just a few examples.

Were the migrants of the past, and are those of the present really as ignorant as the stereotypical tourist, who follows the tour guide as a sheep follows the shepherd? Weren't the migration routes well known, the destinations vividly described by earlier migrants? In this book, we examine the process of migration in the nineteenth and twentieth centuries and show that, for many migrants, even travel over great distances did not mean a loss of orientation in space and time.

Mobility is not an invention of our times; in fact, great population movements took place in the nineteenth century, from the end of the Napoleonic Wars in 1815 to the beginning of World War I in 1914. In the fifty years after 1820, settlers traveled west to open up the American West. Others traveled east, first to areas in the Balkans and southern Russia, later even to Siberia. Most people emigrated for economic reasons: these distant regions offered an abundance of cheap unsettled land. Others were forced to leave their homes by religious or political persecution; the refugees from the failed revolution of 1848 and Jews fleeing the pogroms of czarist Russia are two examples. But most people, thousands and tens of thousands of men and women, were driven to leave their homes in search of work (or, as they themselves often put it, »in search of bread«) in the industrial centers where those very things - work and bread - were supposedly available.

The seemingly unending stream of migrants in the first sixty years of the nineteenth century then grew in the half century before World War I to what the historian Ferenczi (1929) called the »proletarian mass migration«. The nineteenth century has thus come to be known as the age of migration par excellence. Between 1815 and 1914, 33 million men, women, and children migrated from Europe to the U.S., and 3.3 million more came to Canada. Even greater numbers were involved in migrations within Europe: in the year 1900, more than half of all Europeans no longer lived in their birthplaces.

Although these figures are impressive, it should be remembered that migration had been a part of human life for a long time; the nineteenth century was not preceded by a period of unchanging peasant societies, where families remained in one village not only for lifetimes, but even for generations. Women had gone to other farms to work as servants or to the cities as domestics; men had traveled across Europe as harvesters. Journeymen in the crafts and families persecuted for their religious beliefs had searched for new homes and workplaces; young people had moved away to start families.

In the cultures from which large numbers of people emigrated in the nineteenth century, one spoke of »lost sons« (and, let us add, »lost daughters«); of »exiles of Erin« (since conditions in Ireland were so bad, that people were forced to leave); of »Auslandsdeutsche« (Germans abroad: Germans remained German even outside Germany, while at home people with progressive views were called »men without a fatherland«); and of »Polonia« (the community of Poles scattered over many lands).

On the local level, departures were mourned, but returns were also expected - after the harvest season, after a few months, or after retirement. The emphasis was on bonds; even those who emigrated permanently were bound to their families and friends by letters, gifts, money remittances, and the stories told by those who did return. These bonds were so strong that in 1900 over 80 percent of immigrants arriving in the U.S. stated that they would move in with friends or relatives at first.

The views of the destination countries were varied as well. The U.S. and Canada recruited immigrants and regarded everyone, with few exceptions, who arrived as an »immigrant«, a new permanent resident and prospective fellow citizen. Other countries (Germany, for example) permitted the urgently needed male and female workers to enter only on a temporary basis. These »alien workers« - the term had a negative connotation - were not to be given the traditional rights of immigrants.

Although all of the many and varied migra-

tion patterns involved a search for humane living conditions, there were significant differences among them, depending on the particular historical situation. Compare, for example, the emigration of the Huguenots in the seventeenth century with the transatlantic migration of the nineteenth and twentieth centuries. In this book, we try to develop a differentiated picture of the transatlantic migration process. Besides our own historical interest, we are guided by the conviction that, by evaluating the experience of the turn-of-the-century emigrants to America, we can gain important clues for solving the problems of today's migrants. If we compare the reasons, motives, intentions, and reality of the migrants of 1900 and of today, as well as the assimilation processes they had and have to undergo in their new societies, we can discover many parallels. Even a simple comparison between immigrants, including Germans, in the U.S. and Turkish »guest workers« in West Germany is considered a provocation by nationalistic or culturally self-aware Germans; yet even the terminology used reveals the attitudes of the two receiving countries to the (im)migrating foreigners.

Migrants, Transients, Immigrants: Towards an Understanding

Every country that accepts immigrants has certain expectations as to how these people should be treated. For this reason there are many different names for them, each calling for certain behavior patterns.

Guest workers (*Gastarbeiter*): by using this name, the receiving country emphasizes the idea that these workers are temporary guests. When the (economic) times

Farewell of the emigrants, engraving from 1883

have changed and their manpower is no longer needed, they are supposed to return to their homelands. This recruitment plan was at first in keeping with the intentions of most of the »guest workers«, who wanted to work a few years in a foreign country, earn money, and thereby lay the foundation for a secure existence or even a modest social advancement in their home culture; they did not plan to integrate into the culture of the receiving country.

Earlier, these people were even more strictly segregated. Significant numbers of migrants began entering the German Empire beginning in the 1880s and were called at that time (and until after 1945) »alien workers« (*Fremdarbeiter*). Many of these remained, although originally they had not intended to. The best known example is the case of the Polish miners in the Ruhr area. The term »guest worker« is now increasingly being replaced by the term »alien employee« (*ausländischer Arbeitnehmer*), which leaves out the expectation of return and to some extent even implies the opposite: this status is inheritable. Children born to alien employees in Germany remain foreigners - a characteristic sign of a narrow-minded political culture.

Emigrants seem to have little in common with »guest workers«. The connotations of the two terms are almost exactly opposite, but neither gives a clear picture of the real processes involved. »Emigrating« men and women, one imagines, have decided to leave their homeland forever to settle in a new land and become integrated into its culture. In reality, however, this applies only to a small subgroup, the so-called settler emigrants who sell their homes and possessions (which implies that they belong to a social class with some, if often limited, resources) and emigrate in family groups to areas with cheap land and (presumably) better opportunities. This group includes, for example, the nineteenth-century German emigrants to southern Russia, southeastern Europe, and North America. Even these emigrants sometimes failed in their plans for social advancement in the receiving culture, and so one does find return migrants among them.

Immigrant, the designation used as a matter of course in the U.S. and Canada, assumes like its counterpart »emigrant« the willingness to integrate into the new society. Here, too, the implications of the terminology must be evaluated critically. Those immigrants who do not assimilate quickly are looked down on for being »foreign« and forced into ethnic stereotypes. The unclear terminology has also had consequences for historical scholarship and the social sciences: those who believed strongly in the willingness of the immigrants to assimilate and in the superiority of their own political, social, and economic system simply did not see return migration. The U.S. only began collecting return-migration statistics after 1908, when the majority of immigrants were »racially undesirable« southern and eastern Europeans and there

was strong interest in limiting their immigration or getting them to return.

A different problem of conceptual clarity is also in evidence in more recent U.S. scholarship. Oscar Handlin (1950) spoke of the »uprooted«, made weak and helpless by social changes; after a critical reappraisal of this concept, one now reads of the »transplanted«. This metaphor hints at the involvement of social and economic forces, but still fails to describe adequately the role of the individual (the decision to migrate, the actual journey, and living in the new society).

At the turn of the century, the proportion of return migrants from the U.S. averaged 34 percent; about a sixth of German migrants returned, and among the other ethnic groups the return ratio sometimes exceeded 60 percent of the annual immigration. Of the approximately 33 million immigrants to the U.S. in the period 1820-1914, only about 2 million were farmers; in other words, only 6 percent of the immigrants were permanent »emigrants« by intention (although the family members who accompanied the immigrants should be added to these figures). As early as the 1840s, immigration to the U.S. was made up of only about one-third agricultural migrants, with one-third craftsmen and skilled workers and one-third unskilled workers and domestic servants.

The »emigration to America« does not seem quite so unique, however, if we consider the fact that internal European labor migration, the movement of skilled workers to industrializing areas of eastern Europe and of unskilled workers to large cities all over Europe, was larger than transatlantic migration. Seasonal migration such as that of harvesters, which had for a long time been local or confined to shorter distances within Europe, now also took on a transatlantic character. A well known example is that of the Italian harvest hands, who traveled as far as Argentina in winter and then returned to Europe in the spring. These few examples already demonstrate that the paired concepts »emigration« and »immigration« are insufficient to describe either the historical or the present-day reality. In this book, we differentiate between settler migration and labor migration. In

settler migration, mainly family groups traveled to regions with better or cheaper land and away from areas with poor soil or severe overpopulation, from failed harvests and famines. Labor migrants were mainly individuals, often unmarried and only occasionally joining together in groups; when married, they migrated with the intention of earning enough money to send for their families. They usually arrived without possessions and often migrated further or returned to their home cultures; only after a long stay did they become de facto immigrants. In most cases, men migrated first and women came later; Irish and Jewish women were exceptions, often migrating alone and sending passage money for their sisters and girlfriends as soon as they had established themselves in the receiving culture. These men and women were migrants between cultures, between labor markets, and between stages of economic development.

There are different stages in the sequence of migratory movements: as late as the eighteenth century, workers and settlers were recruited by offering special privileges, or work was brought to the workers (cottage industry or the putting-out system); then there was a period of intensive settler migration; finally, there was a period of labor migration to areas where capital was being invested. It should be noted that migration often involved both peasant and subpeasant classes and led them to industrial jobs via an intermediate stage of mining or construction work. Migration was often only intended to be temporary, to secure or improve one's status in the home culture (enlarging a farm, becoming an independent craftsman or shopkeeper, or acquiring new skills to improve one's position in the factory). This temporary period of unskilled work was and still is done voluntarily (although under economic pressure), with the aim of avoiding or delaying the permanent move into the working class. The migrant's plans to migrate permanently or temporarily had significant consequences for his or her willingness to integrate into the culture of the new homeland. People who only planned to come for a season or a few years had little reason to adopt the institutions of the receiving

In a New York Jewish neighborhood, 1906

their friends and relatives about their experiences, and thereby awakened in people at home the desire to emigrate as well; a so-called chain migration had begun.

The chain-migration phenomenon has played a significant role in all phases and systems of migration. For the history of immigration to the U.S., the Civil War of 1861-1865 is an important cutoff between major chain systems. In the first half of the nineteenth century, most of the immigrants came from central, northern, and western Europe; settlers, skilled workers, and craftsmen were dominant, with unskilled workers and female domestic servants making up only about a third. This population, mainly from Germany, Scandinavia, Ireland, and Great Britain, is known as the »old immigration«. When industrialization in the U.S., as in Europe, went forward with great speed in the years after the war, the migration process changed as well. After the mid-1880s, the most important lands of origin were Italy, Poland, Russia, and Austria-Hungary; i.e., countries in southern and eastern Europe. With the »new immigration«, there were sharp increases in the annual number of immigrants and in the percentage of unskilled workers, needed as manpower for the emerging industries. At the same time, productive land became rarer and more expensive; with the spanning of the North American continent and the end of the wars against the Native Americans in the years between 1870 and 1890, most of the freely available land had been distributed. By the turn of the century, there were hardly any farmers among the immigrants.

For the labor migrants, whether »emigrants«, »guest workers«, or de facto immigrants, it can be said that their labor is welcome, but their culture is not. Even their labor is only desirable in the framework of large-scale calculations of the productivity required to produce a certain economic growth rate. As for their coworkers and other members of the receiving economy, they often ignore the contributions of the labor migrants to the gross national product and judge them in terms of supposed competition for jobs or depression of wage levels. In times of crisis, when labor is - statistically - no longer needed, the labor migrants become completely unwelcome.

society; they were interested only in those which were important for their daily lives, for employment, shelter, and residence permits. Those who had come intending to stay permanently exhibited greater willingness to assimilate. Finally, there was an especially strong bond to the home culture among those who wanted to come temporarily but then delayed their return again and again, thus becoming unintentional long-term migrants. A Hungarian couple, for example, planned to return and sent money home for years to buy land, and yet they remained in America.

Both settlers and labor migrants usually kept up contacts with their homelands, told

Ethnic Neighborhoods and Acculturation

People coming to a new country, where they hope to realize their hopes and ambitions, confront and must learn to deal with a number of different reactions from the government and people of the new society. If we imagine an eastern European Jew from a small village in Galicia coming to New York, or an Irishwoman landing in Baltimore, we can get a feeling for the cultural distance migrants might have had to overcome. Economic structures, political culture, public life, work, housing, and entertainment were all new and strange at first. No wonder then, that arriving migrants were first attracted to places where familiar ways were still to be found, to the ethnic neighborhoods, the parts of a city where some of their countrymen were already settled in. They lived much of their lives within these »quarters«, following their own ethnic traditions and cultural patterns of daily life.

After a community-building period, usually lasting around ten to fifteen years, immigrants began to confront the new society more directly and make greater demands on it. German immigrants became German-Americans, and their children already considered themselves Americans of German extraction - which was natural because they were American citizens by birth.

This process of integration proceeded relatively quickly in some groups, lasting twenty to thirty years, whereas in other ethnic groups (where particular types of work or especially isolated residence patterns prevailed) it could take three generations or longer. In the latter cases, a general pattern can be identified: the first generation remained strongly rooted in the traditions of the home culture; the second generation was extremely open to assimilation (even to the point of denying their origins); and the members of the third generation became integrated members of American society, considering themselves Americans but respecting the cultural heritage of their forebears.

Ethnic neighborhoods in Chicago around 1900

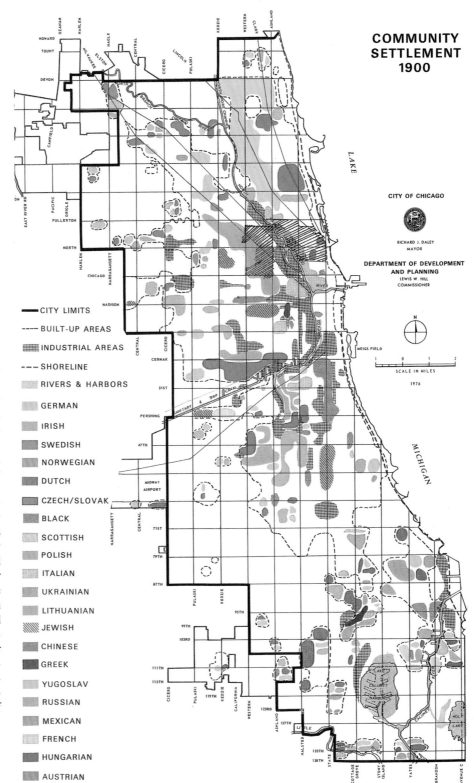

COMMUNITY
SETTLEMENT
1900

CITY OF CHICAGO

RICHARD J. DALEY
MAYOR

DEPARTMENT OF DEVELOPMENT
AND PLANNING
LEWIS W. HILL
COMMISSIONER

SCALE IN MILES

1976

CITY LIMITS
BUILT-UP AREAS
INDUSTRIAL AREAS
SHORELINE
RIVERS & HARBORS
GERMAN
IRISH
SWEDISH
NORWEGIAN
DUTCH
CZECH/SLOVAK
BLACK
SCOTTISH
POLISH
ITALIAN
UKRAINIAN
LITHUANIAN
JEWISH
CHINESE
GREEK
YUGOSLAV
RUSSIAN
MEXICAN
FRENCH
HUNGARIAN
AUSTRIAN

13

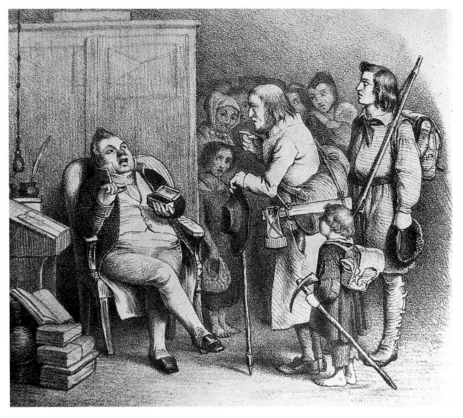

Previously, this process of acculturation was defined as unconditional integration, as symbolized by the image of the melting pot. For a long time it was assumed (and still is today in the public consciousness) that migrants - be they the members of different European ethnic groups coming to the U.S. or the Czechs, Slovenians, and rural Austrians coming to Vienna - were material to be molded, or empty vessels to be filled with new cultural values and customs. This picture is false; there are no historical examples of new arrivals who were able to integrate themselves rapidly and seamlessly into a new culture. Migrants have always brought along their »cultural baggage«, arriving as fully socialized individuals.

At first, immigrants tried to manage their everyday life in the new society by adapting their own cultural practices and values to meet the new demands. They passed through an acculturation process, a kind of second socialization. Acculturation should be understood as a series of mainly voluntary steps toward the new culture, maintaining or further developing elements of the old.

In this process, the neighborhood functioned as a kind of »cultural channel«. Religious institutions, self-help organizations, shops and saloons, language and customs - all of these were »like home« in the ethnic neighborhood. They gave the migrants self-confidence and provided support. Within the established community the new arrivals could learn the new culture one lesson at a time. When the »Anglos« made fun of their accents or tried to limit them to the most degrading kinds of jobs, they found understanding and sympathy in the community; living in neighborhood boarding houses was a practical way to keep the cost of living low. In the neighborhood, helplessness and dependence could be overcome, since there were shops and small businesses offering jobs, and later even middle-class families seeking domestic servants. Gradually a system of political representation developed, facilitated by the liberal provisions of U.S. law. An immigrant could gain the right to vote simply by indicating his willingness to become a citizen at some later date. All that was necessary was an oath renouncing his previous allegiance; there was no requirement that he give up his old cultural values. The appropriate term to describe these integration processes is, as we have said, acculturation; we avoid using the older concept of assimilation because it often implies that immigrants readily abandoned their language and traditions and eagerly accepted everything from their new environment. Integration refers to the measures of governmental, public, or private institutions which provide help without applying pressure; for example, the extension of voting rights or free access to public education. The kinds of integration aids offered depend on a society's image of itself and the public consciousness: either a nation considers itself culturally pluralistic, or else it is a closed circle, to which members of other cultures have no access.

The success and speed of acculturation depend on two main factors: the absence of pressure on the immigrants, trying to force them to give up their cultural traditions and values and adopt those of the receiving society, and the presence of opportunities for active participation in the new society. During this process in which the minority culture moves closer to the dominant culture, the latter also undergoes a process of change, which society and government must recognize and allow to go forward. Society's acceptance of its multicultural status can lead to a more comprehensive self-understanding which guarantees migrants a decent way of life.

The Diversity of Migration Processes and Experiences

The complex patterns of migration are familiar to us from letters, newspapers, oral histories, and biographies. These sources report on the homeland living conditions

Making the decision - Hessian emigrants, around 1860

which led to the decision to migrate and describe the local and regional phases of migration. They tell how people heard the first rumors of America as the promised land of unlimited opportunity, how they obtained more detailed information, how they journeyed to the distant land, and how they were received when they arrived. The sources reveal the process of integration into the new society, complain of conflicts and disappointments, and recount the migrants' economic successes or failures, sometimes leading to a return to the homeland. This kind of complexity can be seen in the following excerpts, from the life stories of the Italian Bruna Pieracci and the Lithuanian Antanas Kaztauskis.

Bruna Pieracci was the daughter of an Italian peasant who came to America from the province of Modena and became a miner. She tells about her family and how they decided to emigrate to the U.S.

Several characteristics which are typical for the labor migration process can be seen in this family history. The Pieraccis are poor peasants who are unable to feed themselves on what they grow on their inferior farmland. For this reason the men of the family join seasonal migrations to seek work in neighboring countries, while the women contribute to the family income by doing sewing work in nearby cities or villages and by working as domestics for wealthy city-dwellers. The children are also put to work, caring for the babies or tending the family's few animals. Bruna's father is the first to experience more distant migration, leaving the village for a longer period and traveling a greater cultural »distance«. He is able to make a modest living in Scotland and sends money regularly to his family. Apparently there is already a small Italian »community« in Scotland, because his first employer there is another Italian. At first he only intends to stay five years, but soon fourteen years have passed; finally family pressures bring him back to his native village. There, however, the economic situation has not improved, and the family still has difficulty feeding itself. At this point the father first hears about America. He gathers information and convinces himself that America is indeed the land of freedom and unlimited possibilities. There, he imagines, he can finally real-

Our home was in the village Frassinoro, meaning golden ash tree, in the province of Modena. The surrounding land was poor and rocky. Its people were peasants who managed to scratch only a part of their living from the unyielding soil. In each winter, the men were forced to emigrate to neighboring countries to find work to support their families. The mothers cared for the babies; the young boys for the few head of livestock; and even the young girls went to the city and worked as domestics in the homes of the wealthy. In spring, the men returned to help sow the small fields and help with many other chores. They stayed until the harvest when they would leave again. My mother, Filomena (Piacentini) was a seamstress and went to neighboring villages to sew for well-to-do families. She and a friend walked from village to village with portable sewing machines strapped on their backs. It was hard work and the pay was small. My father, Orlando Pieracci, was fourteen years of age and not yet a man when he too had to emigrate to earn money to help his family, since his father showed no inclination to leave his native village.

My father emigrated first to Scotland. He was apprenticed for five years to a man, also an Italian, who owned a chain of ice cream stores. The five years soon became fourteen and by that time he was part owner of a »fish and chips« shop. During those years in Scotland he lived in Glasgow and Edinburgh. He worked hard and dutifully sent money home to help support his parents, several brothers and a sister. After such a long absence from his family and native village, he was persuaded to return to Italy. While in Scotland he had learned to speak English and taught himself to read and write it as well. During the years of his absence the village had not changed. It was an ancient village. The church, once an ancient monastery, was 900 years old. Since he still found no opportunity for any profitable employment, it soon became apparent that he would have to emigrate again. He did stay home for several years, however, earning a meager living by going to the city and bringing back supplies of wood and wine for the villagers. The route was over rough and treacherous mountain roads with a large wagon drawn by a pair of mules. He was not happy there and prepared to leave again, planning to return to Scotland. Fate, however, had decreed otherwise.

Since he returned, he had married and, having read and heard so much about America and of the wonderful opportunities and the freedom there, he decided to come to America instead. From the books he had read about this new land and from so far away it seemed to him that it surely must be »the land of beginning again« where he would realize his dream of a better way of life for himself and his children, for by this time there was a baby daughter.

He emigrated to America in the year 1907, which is said to have been the year of the greatest immigration influx in the history of the United States. He had only passage money for himself so he had to leave his wife and daughter behind, with the promise to send for them as soon as possible. His destination was the state of Iowa. There, near the state capital of Des Moines, were several small coal mines. He settled in one of the camps near a mine. It was a small coal field and the coal veins were so low the men had to work on their knees or with bent backs to dig out the coal. Despite his thriftiness, and his sacrifices, it was two years before he could send for his wife and daughter.

The mining camps were quite a contrast to the mountain village in the »old country«. They were all alike: clusters of small boxlike houses made of wood and painted gray, or boxcar red. These immigrants had never seen wooden houses before and they appeared flimsy indeed in comparison to the ancestral homes of stone with walls twenty inches thick. What was even more strange was the absence of trees and shrubbery for this mining camp had been built in the middle of what had been an Iowa cornfield. They were amazed at the flatness of the terrain and among themselves they called it »The Sahara«.

Bruna Pieracci

ize his hopes for a better life for himself and his family. At present, however, there is only enough money left to pay for one passage, his own. He arrives in America in 1907 and goes to work in a mine in Iowa. The differences between these mining camps and his mountain village in the old country are immense. Although he works hard and tries to live as cheaply as possible, it takes him two years to earn enough to send for his wife and daughter. A poor mountain peasant in Italy has become an industrial worker in the U.S.

To summarize: There was a long-standing tradition of migration in the Pieracci-family; Bruna's father had migration experience before he set out for America, migration took place in stages, and the decision to emigrate was strongly influenced by the image of America as the golden »land of promise«, where Bruna's father hoped to achieve his goals of financial security, social advancement, and a degree of independence. The cultural differences were great, and he had trouble adjusting to them; he soon realized that it would not be so easy to make his dreams and wishes come true. He probably imagined that he would keep the mining job only temporarily, until he had earned enough to become independent, by opening a small shop or getting a position higher on the occupational ladder. As time passed, however, it became clearer and clearer that these hopes would never be realized. His wife became ill, remaining depressed after an operation and speaking only of Italy, and the family did not even have enough money to return home. He focused his efforts on making the American dream at least come true for his children, and in this he succeeded: his son became an electrical engineer; two daughters became teachers; and the third kept house for her parents. All four achieved economic success, but what they remembered from their childhood was emptiness and the oppressive cold of the winters. Still, the family had owned its small house and garden, instead of renting them as in Italy.

The American dream was also the mobilizing factor for Antanas Kaztauskis. »Life, liberty, and the getting of happiness, that is what you want!« he had been told again and again by the old cobbler, who made the

Being forced into prostitution was a serious danger for women traveling alone. Warning poster around 1900

rounds of the surrounding farms and played the role of informant and agitator. Lithuania belonged to czarist Russia at the time, and the men were forced to work on road construction and to serve in the Russian army.

The recollections of Kaztauskis, an unskilled worker who ended up in the Chicago stockyards, reveal the extent to which labor migration can be a journey from one culture and stage of economic development to another. The text is an excerpt of

Kaztauskis' autobiography, which appeared in the prounion newspaper »Independent« in 1904, at the time of a militant strike in the stockyards. The text emphasizes the human side of this bloody conflict, telling how a peasant from backward Lithuania learned to survive in the capitalist metropolis. Antanas Kaztauskis fled from his homeland to avoid the Russian military draft. He secretly bought a ticket, bribed the Russian border guards, and made his way, with help from his fellow migrants, to Chicago. But there his ideas of America as the land of freedom, democracy, and happiness were ridiculed as naive by his fellow Lithuanians, old family friends who had been living in the U.S. for several years. They had come to know the reality of America by personal experience: »life, liberty, and the getting of happiness« meant »money«. Kaztauskis began to experience the same sort of disappointment almost immediately - the housing was shoddy but expensive; jobs were available only irregularly and through bribery; the work was hard; and the conditions were beneath human dignity. He came to see his freedom as the lack of any protection whatsoever against the Meat Trust, the group of meat-packing companies which controlled the market and had the power to dictate wages and working conditions.

Here again we have the transformation of a peasant (this time from the backward agrarian society of Lithuania) into an industrial worker in a capitalist economy, living in a city of two million. His compatriots used the role of money as an example to make clear to him how different his new environment was in terms of culture, and he himself described the growing cultural distance he felt during his journey: »I felt everything get bigger and go quicker every day...Everything got quicker - worse and worse..«. In order to overcome these radical cultural differences, or sometimes even to survive, the immigrant needs the help of his more experienced compatriots; this was true for Kaztauskis as well. He found three Lithuanians who had known his father's sister in the old country; they took him in, found him a job, taught him the most important rules of survival, and helped him get past the initial language problems (Kaztauskis knew no English when he arrived). In this way they played the part of the ethnic community, the neighborhood which lends the new arrivals self-confidence and support, so that they can then learn the new culture one lesson at a time. After a few years, Kaztauskis succeeded in finding a better job, one that paid enough so that he could

»You!« cried the shoemaker, and he now threw the boot on the floor so that our big dog lifted up his head and looked around. »It's not you at all. It's the boy - that boy there!« and he pointed to me. »That boy must go to America!«

Now I quickly stopped yawning and I looked at him all the time after this. My mother looked frightened and she put her hand on my head. »No, no; he is only a boy«, she said. »Bah!« cried the shoemaker, pushing back his hair, and then I felt he was looking right through me. »He is eighteen and a man. You know where he must go in three years more.« We all knew he meant my five years in the army. »Where is your oldest son? Dead. Oh, I know the Russians - the man-wolves! I served my term, I know how it is. Your son served in Turkey in the mountains. Why not here? Because they want foreign soldiers here to beat us. He had four roubles ($ 2.08) pay for three months, and with that he had to pay men like me to make his shoes and clothes. Oh, the wolves! They let him soak in rain, standing guard all night in the snow and ice he froze, the food was God's food, the vodka was cheap and rotten! Then he died. The wolves - the man-wolves! Look at this book.« He jerked a Roman Catholic prayer book from his bag on the floor. »Where would I go if they found this on me? Where is Wilhelm Birbell?«

At this my father spit hard again into the fire and puffed his pipe fast. »Where is Wilhelm Birbell?« cried the shoemaker, and we all kept quiet. We all knew. Birbell was a rich farmer who smuggled in prayer books from Germany so that we all could pray as we liked, instead of the Russian Church way. He was caught one night and they kept him two years in the St. Petersburg jail, in a cell so narrow and short that he could not stretch out his legs, for they were very long. This made him lame for life. Then they sent him to Irkutsk, down in Siberia. There he sawed logs to get food. He escaped and now he is here in Chicago. But at that time he was in jail.

»Where is Wilhelm Birbell?« cried the shoemaker. »Oh, the wolves! And what is this?« He pulled out an old American newspaper, printed in the Lithuanian language, and I remember he tore it he was so angry. »The world's good news is all kept away. We can only read what Russian officials print in their papers. Read? No, you can't read or write your own language, because there is no Lithuanian school - only the Russian school - you can only read and write Russian. Can you? No, you can't! Because even those Russian schools make you pay to learn, and you have no money to pay. Will you never be ashamed - all you? Listen to me.«

Now I looked at my mother and her face looked frightened, but the shoemaker cried still louder. »Why can't you have your own Lithuanian school? Because you are like dogs - you have nothing to say - you have no town meetings or province meetings, no elections. You are slaves! And why can't you even pay to go to their Russian school? Because they get all your money. Only twelve acres you own, but you pay eighty roubles ($ 40) taxes. You must work twelve days on your Russian roads. Your kind old wife must plow behind the oxen, for I saw her last summer, and she looked tired. You must all slave, but still your rye and wheat brings little money, because they cheat you bad. Oh, the wolves - how fat they are! And so your boy must never read or write, or think like a man should think.«

Then my fat brother grinned and said to the shoemaker, »You always stir up young men to go to America. Why don't you go yourself?«

I remember that the little shoemaker had pulled a big crooked pipe out of his bag. Now he took a splinter from the basket of splinters which hung on the wall and he lit his pipe and puffed it. His face showed me that he felt bad. »I am too old,« he said, »to learn a new trade. These boots are no good in America. America is no place for us old rascals. My son is in Chicago in the stockyards, and he writes to me. They have hard knocks. If you are sick or old there and have no money you must die. That Chicago place has trouble, too. Do you see that light? That is kerosene. Do you remember the price went up last year? That is Rockefeller. My son writes me about him. He is another man-wolf. A few men like him are grabbing all the good things, - the oil and coal and meat and everything. But against these men you can strike if you are young. You can read free papers and prayer books. In Chicago there are prayer books for every man and woman. You can have free meetings and talk about what you think. And so if you are young you can change all these troubles. But I am old. I can feel it now, this winter. So I only tell young men to go.« He looked hard at me and I looked at him. He kept talking. »I tell them to go where they can choose their own kind of God - where they can learn to read and write, and talk, and think like men - and have good things!«

He kept looking at me, but he opened the newspaper and held it up. »Some day,« he said, »I will be caught and sent to jail, but I don't care. I got this from my son, who reads all he can find at night. It had to be smuggled in. I lend it many times to many young men. My son got it from the night school and he put it in Lithuanian for me to see.« Then he bent over the paper a long time and his lips moved. At last he looked into the fire and fixed his hair, and then his voice was shaking and very low: »We know these are true things - that all men are born free and equal - that God gives them rights which no man can take away - that among these rights are life, liberty and the getting of happiness.«

He stopped, I remember, and looked at me, and I was not breathing. He said it again. »Life, liberty and the getting of happiness. Oh, that is what you want.«

(After having arrived in Chicago):

That first night we sat around in the house and they asked me, »Well, why did you come?« I told them about that first night and what the ugly shoemaker said about »life, liberty and the getting of happiness«. They all leaned back and laughed. »What you need is money« they said. »It was all right at home. You wanted nothing. You ate your own meat and your own things on the farm. You made your own clothes and had your own leather. The other things you got at the Jew man's store and paid him with sacks of rye. But here you want a hundred things. Whenever you walk out you see new things you want, and you must have money to buy everything.«

That night I felt worse. We were tired out when we reached the stockyards, so we stopped on the bridge and looked into the river out there. It was so full of grease and dirt and sticks and boxes that it looked like a big, wide, dirty street, except in some places, where it boiled up. It made me sick to look at it. When I looked away I could see on one side some big fields full of holes, and these were the city dumps. On the other side were the stockyards, with twenty tall slaughter house chimneys. The wind blew a big smell from them to us. Then we walked on between the yards and the dumps and all the houses looked bad and poor. In our house my room was in the basement. I lay down on the floor with three other men and the air was rotten. I did not go to sleep for a long time. I knew then that money was everything I needed. My money was almost gone and I thought that I would soon die unless I got a job, for this was not like home. Here money was everything and a man without money must die.

The next morning my friends woke me up at five o'clock and said, »Now, if you want life, liberty and happiness,« they laughed, »you must push for yourself. You must get a job. Come with us.« And we went to the yards. Men and women were walking in by thousands as far as we could see. We went to the doors of one big slaughter house. There was a crowd of about 200 men waiting there for a job. They looked hungry and kept watching the door. At last a special policeman came out and began pointing to men, one by one. Each one jumped forward. Twenty-three were taken. Then they all went inside, and all the others turned their faces away and looked tired. I remember one boy sat down and cried, just next to me, on a pile of boards. Some policemen waved their clubs and we all walked on. I found some Lithuanians to talk with, who told me they had come every morning for three weeks. Soon we met other crowds coming away from other slaughter houses, and we all walked around and felt bad and tired and hungry.

That night I told my friends that I would not do this many days, but would go some place else. »Where?« they asked me, and I began to see then that I was in bad trouble, because I spoke no English. Then one man told me to give him $ 5 to give the special policeman. I did this and the next morning the policeman pointed me out, so I had a job. I have heard some big talk since then about my American freedom of contract, but I do not think I had much freedom in bargaining for this job with the Meat Trust.

Antanas Kaztauskis

have his bride join him. He became active in the union movement, working to build a broad kind of solidarity and overcome ethnic barriers, prejudices, and animosities. More and more, he considered himself an American, although he still kept in touch with his compatriots and with his relatives in Lithuania.

What would the journey of a typical German labor migrant to the U.S. have been like? Let's go back and look at an example from the 1880s: Germany is in the throes of the so-called foundation crisis (*Gründerkrise*). Hans (we'll call him Hans, because that's what all Germans in the U.S. get called) is the second son of a farmer in northern Germany, not far from the North Sea ports. His father, Paul Schmidt (Americans also seem to assume that all Germans are called Schmidt) has a farm near Osnabruck. It's small, just a few acres of land, but the payments he has to make to the government and the church are oppressive: ordinary taxes, school taxes, and church taxes. Then come the rent to the landlord and, most important, the interest payments on his bank loans. In the 1830s, the farmers' payments in kind (tithes) and annual labor service were abolished, but the cash payments that replaced them were set much too high, so that most farmers were forced to go heavily into debt - now their children and grandchildren are still paying off these loans. Since the family can hardly make a living from farming alone, the women have to do spinning at home to earn extra money, and Hans does hauling jobs for neighboring landlords and better-off farmers. Hans's prospects are discouraging. His older brother, the first-born, will inherit the farm, and his sisters will receive at least a small dowry; there won't be much left for him. Should he work for his brother as a farm hand, or should he get a job as a factory worker or miner in the Ruhr? He still has some hopes of marrying into a farm, and he has also heard about America. He was fascinated by the incredible opportunities people said were waiting there. Agents of the Bremen shipping companies, out promoting emigration to America, said the wages over there were much higher, and that there might be cheap land available - and that anybody could make something of himself in America. After all, Hans is an ambitious fellow; he feels pressed economically, but he still hasn't decided what he should do. Then something unexpected happens: his mother dies, and the family relationships are thrown into disarray. The new distribution of family roles is the reason for Hans to go. He has decided to emigrate to America.

Hans takes a job with a wagon-driver in the village; that way he doesn't have to walk, and the driver also knows the way. Of course, that means his route is predetermined, because the driver is going to Bremerhaven. He arrives there after two days of travel, helps the driver unload his wagon, and looks around for a job on the docks, since he still needs to earn the money to pay his living expenses and his passage to America. Now he's a temporary migrant in Bremerhaven. A few months later, the driver knocks on Hans's door. He's just met someone returning from America, who gave him the address of a friend in Milwaukee, Wisconsin. Hans has saved up just about enough for a passage to New York. On the boat, in steerage, he makes friends with other German emigrants. Most of them come from eastern and central Germany, but there are some other northern Germans, too. Many have relatives and friends who migrated to the U.S. earlier and who may have sent them passage money; at any rate they know where to get in touch with compatriots in New York, who can find them a job and a place to live, or help them travel on to other parts of the U.S. Some of the passengers on the ship are making the trip for the second time. From them Hans learns that not much cheap land is available any more, at least not fertile land. He would need a lot of money to buy a farm, since the railroad companies and rich speculators like Astor and Vanderbilt had bought up all the good land. This is a big disappointment for Hans, and he decides to take a job in New York, again as a dock worker, to earn the money for his journey onward. His experience from Bremerhaven helps him get his bearings in the confusion of the great harbor. Some time later he sets out for Milwaukee, but when he goes to the address the wagon-driver gave him back home, he can't find the person in question, who has apparently moved away. But some other Germans living in the building offer him a bed for the night, and the next day they help him look for a job in town. The tanneries are hiring, and other Germans are already working there, but it still takes Hans two weeks of looking and a bribe to the foreman to get a job; his new neighbors lend him the money he needs. So Hans begins his new life in Milwaukee in debt. In fact, he can only survive because the community supports him. Hans is happy with life in the ethnic neighborhood: here he can buy German food and go to a German tavern; there are clubs and festivals, German churches, and even a German school. Normally Hans speaks German, but he soon learns enough English to get by alone at work or in the city. He adopts American clothing styles, and soon he can no longer be spotted as a »green-horn« by his outward appearance. He joins the workingmen's benefit society, because it provides financial protection in times of crisis, but also because he can make and maintain social contacts at the society's regular meetings. After about two years, Hans gets back in touch with his parents in his old northern German village, finds out that the neighbors' daughter is still un-married, and asks his father to propose marriage for him. When the girl and her

New York labor agency around 1900

parents accept, Hans sends her money and a ticket for the passage to America.

Hans, the farmer's son, passed through several different stages on his journey. In Bremerhaven he was a transient, a temporary labor migrant; in New York, he was a foreign labor migrant; and in Milwaukee he became a de facto immigrant. His migration took place in stages. For someone who could have become a farmer with his own land and farmhouse, ending up as a worker in a tannery would surely have meant a big drop in status; but for a farmer's son with no prospects for his own land, the status of an industrial worker provided a job that paid enough to live on and gave him more independence than he ever could have hoped for as a farm hand.

Other farmers' sons from the village were inspired by Hans's example, whereas his father and the older generation strongly disapproved of his way of life - even though they knew that young men and women had left the village in search of land and work before, within their own lifetimes and as far back as the recorded history of the village extended.

Migration in Preindustrial Times

The great migrations of 1815-1914 were not preceded by a period of static agrarian societies. Previously developed migration patterns influenced the diverse migration processes of the nineteenth century; what follows is a brief overview of these patterns.

One of the dominant factors in the history of Europe was the continuous movement of people on the waterways, over the mountain passes, and along the major and minor trade routes. Goods were transported on horseback or in wagons; soldiers marched through Europe, and their weapons meant power and dominion; ambassadors and diplomats maintained the new ruling power; wandering singers, monks, and agitators spread new ideas and beliefs; and vagabonds, beggars, brigands, actors, and vagrants crowded the roads and market squares. Most important, however, were the people who traveled from town to town and from country to country looking for work - men and women heading for places where they imagined food and shelter were to be found. The travelers carried news and established a communication network which made it possible for others to follow. Migration was thus not a daring venture into the unknown; it was undertaken with particular destinations in mind: those from which pioneers and previous migrants had sent promising reports, those which could be reached by routes and migration systems with long-established traditions.

Preindustrial societies were characterized by a significant amount of geographic mobility. Four main factors influenced the intensive migration of Europe from the fifteenth to the eighteenth century:

1. The development of the cities as trade centers, with a need for male and female workers;

2. the demand for and recruiting of skilled artisans and female textile workers by the European governments in the wake of their mercantilistic policies;

3. the persecution of religious minorities; and

4. the repartition of eastern and southeastern Europe among Russia, the Ottoman and Habsburg Empires, and Prussia (and later the German Empire), resulting in a need for settlers.

Population movements were triggered by political and/or religious pressures or by economic necessity. Such factors shifted parts of the working population across all of Europe, and in this way regions became linked by a web of migration routes. Colonists moved into thinly settled regions; women went to the cities as nannies or cooks. German stone-masons discovered an attractive labor market in Sweden in the sixteenth and seventeenth centuries, as that country reached the zenith of its political power. Both merchants and construction workers headed for newly founded cities.

Migration to the cities took on significant proportions from early on. When looking at the military and tax records of the city of Basil from the 17th century, the number of *temporary residents and persons without full rights of citizenship* cannot be missed. It would have been impossible to man defense installations and the city wall without them. A memorandum from 1757 discussed the topic of why the number of persons without full rights of citizenship was on the increase while the number with

full rights was on the decrease. The reason was to be found in the growing number of factories and workshops. Already in the year 1630, the citizen, Franz Passavant applied to the town council for the permission to employ several foreign workers in his silver factory. He needed workers from outside of the city. There was a considerable demand for unskilled day work in printing and in paper mills. We have complaints from the 17th and 18th centuries made by the guilds and the town council of Munich about the numerous illegal tradesmen. In the year 1782, the number of persons, practicing in all professions without legal permission was as great as the number

Artisans were subject to increasing impoverishment. German cobbler around 1841

of official tradesmen with rights granted by the guilds and the town council. The total number of residents in the original Munich town center who had full rights of citizenship and rights to practice their trade, numbered only 9075 at the beginning of the 18th century. This was only slightly more than one quarter of the total population of Munich at that time. In Hamburg, the yearly income of the city treasury from sources listed under income from foreigners (*Schoßeinnahmen der Fremden*) almost tripled between 1596 and 1626, from 2091 marks to 5820 marks. 51 percent of the residents of the Norwegian city of Bergen be-

tween 1621 and 1630 had been born outside of Norway. Thus, there already existed a long history of people moving into the cities in search of a permanent residence and a secure job, who were excluded from citizenship. In addition, a considerable number of foreigners in several cities did not have the legal status of a »foreign contract« (*Fremdemkontrakt)* nor had they paid the »protection taler« (*Schutztaler*).

The growth of the cities can be attributed to the immigration of artisans and the establishment of trade colonies and commercial enterprises with their personnel on the one hand, and to a general movement of rural populations into the cities on the other. The motto »the town's air makes a man free« had been true since the middle ages; peasants could free themselves from serfdom and their feudal bonds to the land by fleeing to the cities. Town air also brought deadly danger, however: the living conditions were so unhealthy, the death rates so high, that the cities required a steady stream of new immigrants just to remain functional. Aside from the rural-urban migration, there was also an interurban stream, a circulation of middle- and upper-class people among the cities.

Skilled artisans were recruited by many European governments in the seventeenth and eighteenth centuries. In accordance with their mercantilistic economic plans, they sought to increase the artisan population or intensify the production of textiles, thereby augmenting their primary source of income, tax revenues. They also wanted to expand their economic power and eventually gain the upper hand over rival nation states. The same sort of political-economic considerations later led governments to prohibit emigration, to prevent the export of particular skills and capabilities. This ban on the »export of knowledge« is understandable in the context of the times: artisans and laborers still passed the secrets of their trades from father to son or from master to a limited number of apprentices; there were no engineers; and the owners of iron forges could not operate their blast furnaces without the skills of their workers.

Great public projects attracted talent from all over Europe. For example, at the time of Peter the Great (1689-1725), the »artisan

Journeymen had to travel long distances during their apprenticeship. It was the custom to bid farewell to departing companions

on the throne«, there were 20,000 Germans living in Moscow and 30,000 more in St. Petersburg, all recruited by the czar to carry out his ambitious economic modernization program. New cities were founded and enlarged with a pan-European labor force. Gothenburg in Sweden was founded in the seventeenth century with the help of Dutch city planners and German, Scottish, and Dutch merchants. Livorno in Italy was expanded in the late sixteenth century in order to compete with the Spanish ports; English Catholics, Jews and forcibly converted Moors (*Moriscos*) from Spain, and merchants from Marseille sought to profit from the situation. Whenever specialists or unskilled workers were required, there were information channels leading to other areas with people willing to emigrate.

Sometimes, however, these mercantilist economic policies were counteracted by the politics of religious intolerance. By driving out religious dissidents, a country often deprived itself of important economic advantages. The expulsions of the Jews in 1492 and the *Moriscos* in 1609-1614 were important factors in the decline of Spain. When over a half million Huguenots fled from France in 1685, when the Edict of Nantes guaranteeing their freedom of worship was revoked, the economic resources they brought with them proved to be of significant advantage for the lands that took them in, Prussia and the Netherlands. Prussia also profited from the 20,000 Lutherans it took in from the Salzburg

region in 1731-1732, and from the Bohemian Protestants who emigrated to Berlin and elsewhere.

In eastern Europe, enormous population shifts were set in motion by processes of political and territorial restructuring - the development of Russia into a major power after the end of the war between Russia and Sweden (1721), the setbacks suffered by the Ottoman Empire (1683-1699), the resurgence of Habsburg Austria, the rise of Prussia after the Silesian Wars (1763), and the partition of Poland (1792-1795). In the Balkan peninsula, ethnic groups were displaced; members of certain religious confessions were driven out; settlers were called in from distant lands; and craftsmen were recruited. A complex settlement pattern with a mixture of different cultures took shape. Between 1718 and 1799, more than 100,000 Germans settled in the Hungarian plains in three waves, the so-called Danube Swabians (*Donauschwaben*). These privileged immigrants formed a »better« class distinct from the native population, showing how migration can also lead to changes in social hierarchies. Tensions among these ethnic groups later led, along with economic factors, to labor migration to America - from the multiethnic Austro-Hungarian Empire to the multiethnic cities of North America. The emigrants' experiences

from the Old World (the confusion of many languages in the marketplaces, struggles for ethnic autonomy, and multicultural labor unions) also had an effect on their acculturation patterns and political activism in the U.S.

The recruitment of settlers from distant overpopulated agricultural regions also played a significant role in the development of southern Russia. Empress Catherine II (1729-1796) began advertising for colonists to go to southern Russia and the Ukraine in 1763. Within five years, about 20,000 Germans had established settlements there, and a century later the number of colonists and their descendants was estimated as 1.5 million. Then, however, some of their special privileges (exemption from taxation and military service, land grants, etc.) were revoked, and in a new wave of migration 100,000-200,000 of these settlers moved on to America. Russia began to favor colonists from Slavic nations, since they were easier to assimilate, and there were also internal migrations after serfdom was abolished in 1863.

In addition to these four migration processes, there were three other important types of preindustrial population movement: the migration of journeymen, the migration of domestic servants to the cities, and seasonal agricultural migration.

The migration of the journeymen was regulated by the laws of the guilds, which required three to seven years of travel. This search for work outside one's home town served two

Descendants of German immigrants in the Hungarian Plains in their festive dress. Engraving from 1844

benefit associations to help in cases of illness or accident, and to some extent the guilds themselves provided a sort of social security system. For example, a journeyman arriving in a place where his services were not needed still had the right to a subsistence payment or to a few days of work, to earn enough to cover his travel expenses to the next town. Of course, these support structures did not always function as smoothly as in the ideal case described here. In the nineteenth century, as the guild system began to fall apart, the police and city officials began to see journeymen more and more as unwelcome vagabonds.

Domestic servants, mainly women, moved from the land to the cities. This was almost always local migration, not trans-European migration like that of the artisans. The daughters of farmers and farm hands moved to the cities and took jobs in the households of wealthy families. The contrast between the modesty of life in the country and the grand scale and glitter of the cities, especially the capitals with the pomp and luxury of court life, often led these women to imagine that the city streets were paved with gold, and that they could easily make their fortune there, probably by finding a »good« husband. In reality, however, these servants had to put up with miserable living conditions. They had to live in tiny rooms or walled-off corners, often in basements or attics and usually unheated and without sanitary facilities; they had very little free time, and were often victims of sexual exploitation.

The importance of the journeymen's migration for the spread of technology and product design is generally known; by contrast, the role of domestic servants in the education of children and the development of household structures has received very little attention until quite recently. What, for example, would Vienna's famous cuisine have been without the skills of her Czech cooks?

In many areas, both male and female agricultural workers were recruited at annual hiring fairs. This led to the growth of regular migration cycles, at first on a local scale and then, in the nineteenth century, over greater distances. Along with this annual migration of farm hands, there was also a seasonal migration of harvest workers. In

functions. On the one hand, by working in different workshops and in different cultural regions, the journeyman could acquire different skills and gain valuable experience. On the other hand, the travel requirement also prevented the journeymen from setting up shop in their home towns and competing with their former masters and employers. Although learning skills was the original motive for the rules, by the eighteenth century the protection of the masters had become the dominant factor. German became the *lingua franca* of artisanal production, for the guild system had developed in the German-speaking areas of central Europe, and journeymen traveled

from other countries to learn their craft in Germany. Even when they traveled onward, their job experience was often passed on in German. German remained the generally accepted language in the nineteenth century, as skilled workers, coming from the German-speaking regions and traveling the journeymen's routes, played an important part in the spread of new technologies throughout continental Europe.

Stationed along these routes were inns where the journeymen met together and exchanged information. The artisans formed mutual-

Seasonal agrarian workers on their way to Holland, 1865

the beginning these were mainly men, who left their villages (alone, in work gangs, with their families, or in mixed groups) after the harvest there was over and traveled to a neighboring area, often a fertile plain or river valley, where additional workers were needed. Other workers followed the chronological order of the crops, from early-ripening to late-ripening types of grain, or wandered from warmer to colder regions, where the harvests were later. A third migration pattern was an annual trek from unproductive hilly or marshy country to the fertile plains. For example, the farmers who settled in the moors north of Bremen could not make a living off the barren marshy soil; every summer, they left their farms in their wives' care and went to work as day laborers in the Netherlands.

From Local to Global, from Agricultural to Industrial Migration

There was a sort of natural progression from seasonal agricultural migration to the nonagricultural ways of working with the soil, in construction jobs. Building roads, canals, and dams required huge numbers of workers. The first locks were developed in Holland, where a system of canals was built in the fifteenth century. Canals were built in France in the sixteenth century, in England in the seventeenth, in Russia in the eighteenth, and in the U.S. in the nineteenth. In the eighteenth century, workers were also needed for large-scale projects to control the flow of rivers, and the construction of the railroads beginning in the early nineteenth century attracted unemployed and underemployed people from the surrounding countryside, but also labor migrants from much farther away. Once local

workers had been mobilized by these construction projects and had grown accustomed to money wages, they often used the roads and rail lines they had built to journey onward. The distances they traveled increased, and the time away from their farms and homes began to last longer than a season. Finally they found work in the cities and decided to stay there.

In addition to these mainly intraeuropean migration patterns of the preindustrial period, there were others directed to distant continents. As trade in Europe intensified in the early modern period, the need to explore and exploit the rest of the world grew. The new discoveries led to a period of expansion and the conquest of new continents. The lands the Europeans took over can be roughly divided into two classes: those which were thickly settled and had mineral wealth and relatively highly developed economic and social systems, and those with agriculturally usable but uncultivated land and low population den-

23

Seasonal work was an essential part of a family's existence all over Europe. Poland around 1900

were women. All hoped for a better life, although only a few really believed they were going to a »land of unlimited opportunities«. By emigrating, farm hands from east of the Elbe could escape from frequent beatings; South German peasants, from oppressive taxes and arrogant tax-collectors; Italian contadini, from the owners of the large estates; Irish farmers, from hunger and the British colonial government. They were all trying to take »fate« in their own hands, to get bread and work, to gain independence from their families, restrictive customs, and oppression. Their goals were modest - very modest when compared to the myth of the dishwasher turned millionaire - , but these migrants considered them well worth the effort.

References:

Bade, Klaus J. (ed.): Auswanderer, Wanderarbeiter, Gastarbeiter. Bevölkerung, Arbeitsmarkt und Wanderung in Deutschland seit der Mitte des 19. Jahrhunderts. Bd. 2, Ostfildern, 1984.

Bade, Klaus J. (ed.): Deutsche im Ausland - Fremde in Deutschland. Migration in Geschichte und Gegenwart. München, 1992.

Harzig, Christiane: »Ethnische Nachbarschaften: Hemmnis oder Basis für Akkulturation«, in: Hoerder, Dirk; Knauf, Diethelm (eds.): Einwandererland USA - Gastarbeiterland BRD. Gulliver 22, Hamburg, S.45-54.

Hoerder, Dirk: »(Un-)willkommene Arbeitskräfte? Einwanderer - Gastarbeiter«, in: Geschichte, Politik und ihre Didaktik. 15.Jg., 1987, Heft 3/4, S.168-177.

Hoerder, Dirk; Rößler, Horst; Blank, Inge (eds.): Roots of the Transplanted. 2. vol., Northern Illinois Press, forthcoming 1993.

Morawska, Ewa: »Labor Migrations of Poles in the Atlantic World Economy 1880-1914«, in: Comparative Studies in Society and History. 3.vol., no.2, April 1989, S.237-272.

sity. The lands of the first type (for example, the Spanish holdings in South and Central America) were plundered by the soldiers and colonial officials, destroyed culturally by Catholic missionaries, and acquired by merchants and plantation owners. The native populations were forced to work for the new masters, often in regions far from their homes. In order for lands of the second type to be economically productive, large population movements were required. In 1776, about 150 years after the beginning of European settlement, there were approximately three million white and black inhabitants in North America. The colonization of Australia began in 1788, with about one million immigrants (including deported convicts). Between 1860 and 1900, about 750,000 additional Europeans arrived under the »White Australia Policy«, which excluded Asian immigrants.

When the immigrants in one of the colonized or conquered continents needed more workers, these could be supplied by forced migration. Hundreds of thousands of convicts from Europe, many millions of Africans, several million Indians (especially Tamils in the phase of so-called »second slavery« from about 1830 to 1917), Chinese contract laborers, and hundreds of thousands of Melanesians were shipped to where the European masters needed them. Later, in the nineteenth century, workers also came from the peripheral areas of Europe - Ireland, Italy, and eastern Europe.

About fifty million people emigrated from the Old World, most of them between 1815 and 1914. The population of Europe was about 190 million in 1800, 266 million in 1850, and 401 million in 1900. In the twenty years before World War I, almost half of the population of many European countries no longer lived in their places of birth; they had been part of the intraeuropean migrations. Especially England, France, Germany, and Switzerland recruited male and female workers from the periphery.

The focus in this book is on those who left Europe and migrated to the western part of the Atlantic economic region, which stretches from Byelorussia and the Ukraine in the east to the Pacific coast of Canada and California in the west. More than a third of the migrants who chose the North Atlantic route

Emigrants at the Prague Central Railroad Station, 1868

We all know them - the Pilgrim Fathers, who set forth on the Mayflower seeking freedom of worship and religious tolerance. After a long and perilous journey, they landed in 1620 on the New England shore, where they found the freedom they were looking for. This story is one of the fundamental myths on which the American identity is based. To be sure, it was poor navigation rather than a vision of freedom that led the Pilgrims to land south of where Boston lies today. Their Plymouth colony would not have survived the first winter without the help of the native population of »Indians«. We should also note that the English expansion in North America had already begun somewhat earlier, and with much more worldly economic aims: in 1607, the Jamestown colony in Virginia, originally intended as a trading post, had been established by the Virginia Company of London as the first permanent English settlement. The first black slaves had also landed before the Pilgrims, shipped in to Jamestown in 1619.

All of the major European powers participated in the exploration, conquest, and settlement of North America. People from all over Europe served as soldiers in the armies of the colonial powers, cleared the land as farmers, set up businesses, built the roads and cities, and earned their bread as craftsmen. They came by the thousands before 1800; in the nineteenth century, the »century of the great European emigration«, migration truly became a mass phenomenon.

"Give me your tired, your poor, your huddled masses, yearning to breathe free" - welcome to the land of liberty, 1887

The European Cultures of Origin

Hallelujah, We're off to America!
Western, Central, and Northern Europe

Agnes Bretting

Western Europe (i.e., the British Isles, France, and the Benelux states) supplied a large proportion of the immigrants to the U.S. About 44 million Europeans migrated overseas between 1821 and 1915, of which 36 million came to the U.S. Ten million of these came from England, Scotland, and Wales; if the six million Irish emigrants are added to these, the British Isles supplied 37 percent of the overseas migrants. Because of the distinctive economic and historical development of the Irish emigration, however, it will be treated separately below.

England, Scotland, Wales

In addition to England, the United Kingdom of Great Britain included the Duchy of Wales (since the end of the thirteenth century, 1282/1283) and the former Kingdom of Scotland (since 1707). In England, the Anglo-Saxons were the dominant ethnic group. As early as the fifth century, they had driven the native Celtic populations back to a few small areas in Wales and Scotland. The Celtic population of southern Scotland became fully Anglicized early on, but the old Gaelic Scots who came from Ireland and settled in the north in the sixth century maintained their cultural independence and a degree of political autonomy much longer. Beginning in 1018 and for many centuries, a Scottish royal house ruled almost without interruption. The

Scottish national consciousness was strengthened by historical events (and remains strong even today in the 200 clans), and the Scottish Reformed Church remained independent of the Church of England.

In Wales, a very small Celtic-speaking minority survives to this day, but in general the English were successful in suppressing nationalist uprisings. Opposition to English political and cultural dominance manifested itself mainly in the establishment of separate religious institutions, independent of the Anglican church (which had become the state religion in the sixteenth century, under the Tudors). Climatic conditions and geographic features divided the island into various economic regions. The southern part of the island had grain-growing regions to the east and grazing land in the west. Much of the Welsh landscape was desolate mountains, where only small plots could be cultivated, so the raising of cattle and sheep predominated. Large coal and iron-ore deposits began to be mined industrially in the late eighteenth century. Scotland was an area of extremely poor land, especially in the northern Highlands. There large extended families lived on widely scattered farms and raised animals; their life was harsh.

In the seventeenth and eighteenth centuries England developed into the leading economic nation of Europe, replacing the Spanish and Dutch as the rulers of the seas and acquiring colonies on all the continents. Trade flourished with the support of mercantilist legislation. The extensive introduction of new crops and techniques for improving the quality of the soil led to significant increases in agricultural production in England and Scotland. This progress was achieved, to be sure, at the expense of the small farmers; they were squeezed out

as large estates were created by systematic »enclosures« of the land. Independent farmers were bought out and sank to the social status of sharecroppers or farm hands; many were forced to leave the farming regions. This migration, combined with the sharp increase in population which began in the 1830s, produced an oversupply of workers. By early in the nineteenth century, the economic center of gravity in England and Scotland had already shifted from the farms to the mines and factories, where massive exploitation, wages below the subsistence level, and child and female labor were the rule. England thus became urbanized and industrialized sooner than any of the other European countries of emigration. By the end of the nineteenth century, only about 12 percent of all employed persons worked in the agricultural sector; the corresponding figures for Germany and Sweden were about 37 and 58 percent, respectively.

Many migrants left the island in the 19th century. The desire for independence from the owners of the large estates or owners of the factories and the fear of a loss of social status led many to look for work in America rather than in the English cities. Although British industry absorbed large numbers of workers, the emigration rates increased steadily into the 1880s. There was also a tradition of long-distance migration in England; settlers and workers were always being recruited for the overseas colonies. In the seventeenth and eighteenth centuries, the practice of *indentured emigration*, emigration under a work contract, was widespread: before 1870, only about 30 percent of emigrants paid their own passage. This system gave the impoverished hope - even if they couldn't improve their social status, in America there was at least some possibility of a secure livelihood. In

Scotland, where the primitive agriculture of the Highlands could not absorb the population increase of the eighteenth and early nineteenth centuries, it was most often the poorest people who emigrated. By contrast, there were fewer indentured servants from England, where the typical emigrants were not the very poorest artisans or agricultural workers but rather people who saw emigration as the only way to avoid becoming completely impoverished. They were more willing to accept a limited (and hopefully temporary) loss of status in a society where they were strangers than at home.

The government was not opposed to emigration, at least not when it was directed to the British colonies; for some time, this kind of migration was even encouraged. There was the deportation of convicts to Australia, and in addition, the poverty laws in effect between 1835 and 1850 granted government-paid transportation to welfare recipients going to Australia, South Africa, or Canada. To be sure, these emigrants (about 1400 per year) contributed only a trickle to the great stream of emigration from Great Britain in this period.

The majority of British emigrants chose to make their new start in the North American colonies or the independent U.S., because of the favorable settlement conditions

there. Years with poor harvests, high food prices, falling crop prices, and/or crises in particular industries led to periodic ebbs and surges in the tide of emigration: peak years in the first half of the nineteenth century were 1819, 1827, the early 1830s, and 1842. Only after 1860, however, did the movement reach its peak. From 1861 to 1870 the ratio of emigrants to the total population was 2.8 per thousand; it climbed to 4.0 over the next ten years and reached a new high of 5.7 in the decade before 1890. Then an economic recession in the U.S. caused a drop to 3.6, but in the first decade of the twentieth century the figure shot up again to 5.8.

In this period, the migrants came mostly from the large cities, and they continued to work at industrial jobs when they went to America. The causes of the rise in emigration lay in the social environment at home: exploitative working conditions, wages that were hardly enough to live on, and a feeling of helplessness against the ruling class. All of these factors led many to give up the struggle and try for a new beginning in America. The trade unions generally had a positive view of this movement, hoping that a shrinking labor supply might help them negotiate higher wages. Another factor encouraging emigration was the relatively low price of a transatlantic passage in

this period; after about 1890 the *prepaid tickets* sent by friends and relatives in North America played a significant role as well. Between 1860 and 1890, the price for the trip as a steerage passenger dropped by about 40 percent. In 1870, a typical British worker would pay about 5-6 weeks' wages for a ticket, whereas the price for a German or Swedish worker would be at least 3 months' wages.

It was also true that the decision to emigrate at this time was less final than it had been in the days of the sailing ships. Now regular steamship schedules made return migration much more feasible. Young, unmarried working men and women took this possibility into consideration when making their travel plans and took advantage of it in fact: between 1903 and 1931 there were over 200,000 return migrants. In some trades, the transatlantic route even became part of a complex system of seasonal migration. It was reported that British house painters and decorators worked in America in the spring; in Scotland in the summer, when their upper-class customers were socializing in London; and in London in the fall, when rich Londoners went to Scotland for the hunting season.

The overseas migration after 1860 was basically a massive expansion of older migration traditions. There had already been a relatively high proportion of artisans among the settler migrants to the colonies, despite the fact that emigration was often supposed to be illegal for people with such valuable technical skills. More important, however, was the internal migration which affected large numbers of people in the eighteenth century. Agricultural workers from Wales and Scotland came to the more fertile regions of England looking for work, and in the nineteenth century they were replaced by Irish migrants. After 1830 there was movement from the country to the cities all over England, increasing in size just as the overseas emigration did. It is no longer possible to tell how many of the people emigrating from the cities in the 1880s and

Scottish emigrant family 1905

1890s were originally rural immigrants to the cities, but the number must have been high.

Despite its high emigration rates, England was also one of the European nations importing workers in this period. Most of the immigrants came from Ireland, but, beginning about 1750 and increasing in the early nineteenth century, there was an influx of Germans, Lithuanians, and Italians; after 1850 there were also relatively large numbers of Russian and Polish Jews. The Jews settled in London and the other large cities, where there had been Jewish communities since the middle ages. There were also labor migrants from highly skilled trades who were attracted by the opportunity to improve their knowledge and technical qualifications in the advanced English industries. Immigration and emigration, especially overseas emigration, were always parallel phenomena in England, although immigration was not of great importance for the country's economic development.

Ireland

Ireland is the most westerly of the British Isles, lying in the Atlantic and separated from England by the Irish Sea and the North and St. George's Channels. The Celtic Gaels who lived there were converted to Christianity in the fifth century, and in the seventh century Irish monks were serving as missionaries all over Europe. English rule in Ireland began under Henry II in 1171-1172. Later attempts to impose the

Irish misery. A pauperized tenant is evicted by his landlord. Engraving from 1840

Reformation met with failure: in the Republic of Ireland today, 93 percent of the population is Roman Catholic. In Northern Ireland, the character of the population was altered by the immigration of Scottish Protestants in the seventeenth century. Today Catholics are still the largest single group there, but make up only 35 percent of the population, along with 30 percent Presbyterians and 25 percent Anglicans.

From the late twelfth to the sixteenth century, English rule remained limited to the eastern coast of the island. After the bloody suppression of several uprisings (1597-1603, 1649-1651, and 1690), the English

FAMINE SONG

Oh the pra-ties they are small o-ver here, Oh the
pra-ties they are small o-ver here, Oh the pra-ties they are
small and way up in Done-gal We eat them skins and all o-ver
here, o-ver here, And we eat them skins and all o-ver here.

Oh I wish that we were geese night and morn,
Oh I wish that we were geese night and morn,
Oh I wish that we were geese till the hour of our release,
When we'd live and die in peace stuffing corn, stuffing corn,
When we'd live and die in peace stuffing corn.

Oh they'll grind us into dust over here,
Oh they'll grind us into dust over here,
Oh they'll grind us into dust, but the Lord in whom we trust,
Will repay us crumb for crust over here, over here,
Will repay us crumb for crust over here.

The most compelling of reasons caused the great exodus of
Irish people to North America, sheer starvation. The famine
years, culminating in "Black '47", have been often described
elsewhere and there is no need to elaborate on the depth of
human misery created not only by natural disaster but also by
a degree of official neglect that verged on the genocidal. In
terms of this work it might be said that were it not for the
famine this collection of songs would be concerned with a
rather small North American minority, rather than one of the
largest identifiable ethnic groups in the United States.
    This version of The Famine Song was learnt in childhood,
but from whom I cannot remember. Nowadays, in perform-
ance, one more frequently hears the adaptation by Alfred
Perceval Graves.

From a collection of songs by Bill Meek: Songs of the Irish in America

expanded their domain, but never succeeded in Anglicizing the population. In 1801, Ireland was united constitution-ally with Great Britain. At this time there was already a strong Irish nationalist movement, fed by hatred for British policies which treated Ireland as a colony. The enforcement of English anti-Catholic laws in Ireland in effect stripped the Irish of their political rights. Furthermore, English landowners began to organize systematic enclosures, mainly of pasture lands; they gradually gained control of about two-thirds of the land in Ireland and thus deprived the small farmers of their means of subsistence. Irish agriculture was either shut down or made completely dependent on England.

As a result of strong pressure from the nationalists, who favored a free and independent Irish state, Irish Catholics were granted full political rights in 1829. But the economic exploitation of the island continued unabated, and it was only in 1903 that the small tenants were granted the sta-tus of independent farmers. These events led to even stronger nationalist pressure on the English rulers. The *Fenian* movement, founded in 1858, strove for independence via a revolution, while the *National League* (1877) and later *Sinn Fein* wanted to achieve autonomy within the British Empire (home rule) by parliamentary means. In 1916 an uprising aimed at seizing independence by force was quickly suppressed, and its leaders were executed. After years of bitter civil war, the Irish Free State was established as an autonomous Dominion in 1921, excluding the six predominantly Protestant counties of Ulster. The constitution of the independent state Eire was signed in the capital of Dublin in 1937; Eire withdrew from the British Commonwealth in 1948 and became a republic in 1949.

The province of Ulster became Northern Ireland, a part of the United Kingdom of Great Britain, with Belfast as its capital. From the beginning, the Catholic minority felt politically oppressed and economically disadvantaged and strove for union with the Irish Republic. These tensions have led to decades of violent civil war in Northern Ireland, which is now occupied continually by British troops.

Ireland, the »Emerald Isle«, had unusually fertile soil, but the overall agricultural yield was always limited because large areas of lowland and highland moor could not be tilled. Most of the population lived from farming, mainly on subsistence plots, but this system broke down when noblemen, mainly Englishmen, bought up the land. Starting from the eastern part of the island, these landlords introduced rationalized, highly mechanized agricultural methods and at the same time began to acquire more land by means of enclosures; both of these developments contributed to the rapid growth of unemployment among the tenant farmers and agricultural workers. In 1869, more than 80 percent of the tilled land was in the hands of less than 1 percent of the population. Directly below these landlords were the so-called leaseholders, a predominantly Protestant class which made up about 2.5 percent of the population. They leased large farms suitable for raising animals, and the leases could be inherited. Between these two upper classes and the mass of small tenants there was a group of »middlemen«, relatively well-off farmers who leased larger tracts of land and then subleased them in small parcels. They were out for a quick profit and thus granted only short (usually one-year) leases; they were considered the most tight-fisted and unscrupulous exploiters of the small tenant farmers.

By the end of the 1860s, about 77 percent of the population belonged to the class of small tenants. They had one-year leases and were cottagers, living on someone else's land and leasing another small plot to grow potatoes for their own use; sometimes they were farm laborers without a fixed residence, who had saved enough from their irregular work so that they, too, could lease a potato garden. This kind of plot, called a conacre, was leased to the highest bidder every eleven months. The poverty of these tenant farmers was oppressive: with the high rents and the insecurity of the short leases, there was no chance for them to improve their lot. If the land appreciated in value, the landlords profited, yet they had no obligations whatsoever to their tenants. Until 1885 a landlord could evict any tenant from his lands with only six months' notice. The tenant farmers struggled constantly to avoid sinking further, into the great mass of landless farm laborers.

Subsistence farming was becoming more and more impossible, since taxes and other fees had to be paid in cash. For the majority of the population, however, it was getting harder and harder to earn any money; most could just barely afford to live. There was practically no opportunity to switch to industrial wage work in Ireland, nor were there any mineral resources worth mining there. Industrialization was not only not undertaken, it was actively opposed by English industries. In 1824 the protective tariffs for Ireland were drastically reduced, and soon the remaining cottage industries, where tenant farmers or laborers had earned additional income, could no longer compete with the English imports. When duties on grain imports were eliminated in Great Britain in 1846, in the name of free trade, the Irish lost the English market for their grain as well. For a broad sector of the Irish population, it was no longer possible to earn a living.

The result was emigration to areas where work was available. Throughout the nineteenth century, emigration was a part of daily life for the Irish. The creation of large estates and the resulting division of the remaining land into smaller and smaller parcels meant that part of the population had to leave. The landlords favored the tiny plots, because with a larger number of tenants they could improve their voting rights in Parliament; only in the mid-1840s was the law of entailment introduced.

Of the tenants' sons and daughters who did not inherit land, some migrated to the few Irish cities, and even more migrated to England; thousands and thousands emigrated to North America. Emigration to England was at first seasonal labor migration, but often enough the emigrants settled there. Since there was no language barrier (after Cromwell's forced Anglicization in the seventeenth century, only a tiny minority still spoke Gaelic exclusively), the decision to remain was relatively easy. It should be pointed out, however, that Irish emigrants have kept their independent cultural traditions alive to this day. By the middle of the nineteenth century there were already about half a million Irish in England, mainly in London and Liverpool, where they replaced the Welsh and Scots as factory workers. In 1861 there were 180,000 first- and second-generation Irish immigrants living in London alone.

After 1830, there was a constant stream of Irish emigrants heading overseas; by far the most popular destination was the U.S. A trip to Australia cost about four times as much as a trip to New York and lasted three times as long. The prices for Canada were somewhat more attractive, but the trip still lasted longer, and there were fewer opportunities for unskilled workers there.

Emigration to the U.S. took on massive proportions beginning in 1846-1848, when for three consecutive years potato blight destroyed the entire crop and thereby robbed a large part of the Irish population of its very basis of existence, since the potato was their only food crop. A terrible and widespread famine ensued, and the English government did nothing to alleviate it. Over a million people died of starvation. Others tried to escape the catastrophe by

Poverty-stricken Irish peat farmers

emigrating, but hundreds died before they could reach America, and many of those who did arrive in New York were too weak to make a new start. This Irish emigration to escape hunger had consequences for the

laws governing transatlantic migration and for the measures undertaken at the American ports to regulate immigration.

The wave of emigration continued in the following years, now driven not only by hunger but also by recognition of the hopelessness of the general economic situation. In the eight years between 1846 and 1854,

1.75 million Irish men and women (over 20 percent of the total population) decided to seek their future in North America; by the end of the century, the number had reached almost 4 million. In the years between 1876 and 1921, 84 percent of all Irish emigrants went to the U.S., with only 8 percent going to England. Chain migration, especially by means of prepaid tickets, played a significant role in this movement, which began in the provinces of Munster and Connaught in the south and west but soon involved most of Ireland.

In 1860, the ratio of emigrants to nonemigrants was 1:5, as compared to 1:42 for England, 1:34 in Norway, and 1:33 in Germany. After 1880 people thought of the U.S. almost as a part of Ireland - practically

The massive emigration of mainly younger people had serious social and economic consequences for Ireland, which became the only European country in which emigration led directly to a drop in population. Sinking birth rates also played a part, but the fact that the overall population decreased by almost half over a 50-year period is mainly the result of emigration. The population of Ireland in 1846 was over 8 million, but by 1901 it was only 4.5 million. The wave of emigration took away mainly agricultural workers. Farmers had to find less labor-intensive ways of making a living, and so more and more cultivated land was made into pasture to raise animals for meat. This change was promoted by the landlords because the price of beef kept

it to their pasture acreage. In 1841, 80 percent of the farms in Ireland were smaller than 15 acres, but ten years later the figure had fallen to less than 50 percent, and by 1901 only a third of the farms belonged to this small family farm category. This development shows how little chance most Irish farmers had of surviving economically around the middle of the nineteenth century. Nevertheless, there was an overall consolidation of the Irish economy; those who were able to remain had improved chances. For example, the labor shortage allowed the wages of agricultural workers to rise by 57 percent between 1843 and 1844. Of course, only younger people could take advantage of these changes; poverty deepened for people too old to emi-

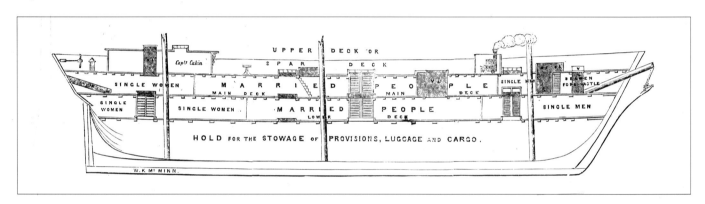

every family had members living there. The emigrants tended to be young unmarried people. Between 1850 and 1887, about 66 percent of the emigrants were between 15 and 35 years old; after that the figure was about 80 percent. Young girls in particular migrated to the large cities in the U.S., where they soon made up a majority of the domestic servants; only there did they have a chance at economic independence. The proportion of women emigrating alone from Ireland was remarkably high, about 50 percent of the total Irish migration in the nineteenth and twentieth centuries. Irish men mostly settled in the East Coast cities, where they could start earning money immediately. They were willing to take on heavy work, and the employment network which soon developed helped get them work in road, canal, and railroad construction all over the U.S.

Section of the emigrant ship »Bourneuf« of Liverpool (1852); showing the arrangement for government passengers to Australia

going up, making cattle raising very profitable. The reasons for this lay in the imposition of high tariffs on the import of grain (1815) and the increasing demand for beef in England, where more and more of the food needs of the rapidly growing population had to be met with imports.

At the same time, the number of small farms in Ireland was decreasing. Subsistence farming was no longer possible; in fact, it was the farmers who had just barely been able to feed their families from what they could grow on their land who were most likely to emigrate. Their land was acquired by the better-off farmers, who added

grate. Since the development of viable Irish industries was impeded by the exploitative policies of the English, migration in search of work always meant migration beyond the borders of Ireland. There were jobs available in English industry, but many preferred a transatlantic voyage to wage labor in hated England.

The large sums sent back to Ireland by emigrants also had significant economic effects. Every year, about a half million dollars flowed from the U.S. to Ireland, especially after the postal money-order system was introduced in 1871. This money was not used only to pay for the passages of additional relatives; a greater part went to rent payments and local investments. Also common was financial support of the national political parties, both radical and moderate, by the »American Irish«; this influence on national politics is still felt today.

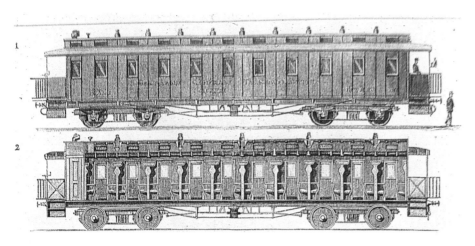

France

The situation in France was quite different. Despite colonial possessions and a liberal emigration policy, France's immigration balance was always positive. Between 1850 and 1910, only about two million people left France. During the peak emigration period (1881-1890), there were only 0.3 emigrants per thousand total population; for England the corresponding figure was 5.7 per thousand. About 20 percent of the emigrants went to the French colonies; the rest went in approximately equal proportions to other European countries and to other overseas locations.

France had only moderate population growth in the eighteenth century and almost none in the nineteenth century. While the population of Germany grew by 45.1 percent between 1800 and 1850 and by 59 percent by 1900, that of France grew by only 29.6 and 11.5 percent in the same periods. The figures for the period 1900-1949 show 68.0 percent growth for Germany and 1.2 percent for France. Various hypotheses have been put forward to explain this unique development: relatively late marriages due to the longer period of military service in France, high tax rates, and laws forbidding children under 15 to work - with the result that people regarded children not as work helpers and sources of financial support in old age, but as luxuries.

The unusually low birth rate led to labor shortages, and many specialized workers were in great demand and traveled from town to town. Internal migration was common in France; about one fifth of all families were affected by it. On the other hand, the availability of work made France the most important European country of immigration. The neighboring countries, where rapid population growth led to shortages, found a veritable escape valve for their problems in France, where a drop in the numbers of both consumers and producers was slowing down the economy. Belgians, Italians, Germans, and Swiss, but also Spaniards, Englishmen, and Russians sought and found work in France. Many of them remained and were integrated into the population.

The nineteenth-century European immigrants settled mainly in the border regions. The majority of Spaniards and Italians were employed in the wine industry of the south; the workers for the developing industries in the north and northwest came mainly from Belgium and Germany, although some Italians worked there as well. Those who went to the cities often lived in ethnic enclaves. In Paris there had been neighborhoods identified with ethnic groups (often concentrated in particular professions) since the middle ages.

In southern France there were radical changes in agriculture as a result of the construction of the first railroads in the 1870s. The opening up of an interregional market led to a single-crop economy based on wine, and the existing family businesses

The interior

gave way to large capitalist operations. This entire development was based on the use of seasonal workers, whose numbers increased steadily until the 1920s.

The immigrants' most important role, however, was in the industrialization of France. About 40 percent of all immigrant workers were employed in industry. Without the work of these immigrants, the rise of French industry would have been impossible. Active recruitment of foreign workers only became necessary in the twentieth century; during and after World War I, workers were recruited from the colonies, and Poles came in ever greater numbers. They worked alongside the Belgians in the mining industry, which took on new economic importance for France at this time.

In 1911, the population of France included over 400,000 working people from Italy, 287,000 from Belgium, 117,000 from Germany and Austria-Hungary, 110,000 from Spain and Portugal, and thousands from Switzerland, Russia, and the Netherlands. There were very few immigrants from the French colonies in Africa; their numbers did not increase until after World War II. Despite these large numbers of foreigners, there were relatively few ethnic conflicts. Latent xenophobia did exist in France, and on the local level there were tensions which sometimes exploded into violence. In Aigues-Mortes, for example, French workers in the salt mines brutally attacked their Italian co-workers, but incidents such as this were the exception. After the Franco-Prussian War of 1870-1871, which for France meant the loss of Alsace and Lorraine, Germans in France were the objects of some hostile action.

The reason that antiforeign sentiments were not often openly expressed was the official government policy of integration for foreign workers. On the whole, the effort to create a multiethnic society was successful. Between 1881 and 1886, immigration to France grew by 13 percent, which threatened to increase the tensions among the ethnic groups. But, although many limitations on the rights of immigrants were proposed in the period before World War I, the law actually passed in 1889 shortened the waiting period for naturalization from five to three

years and granted citizenship to all children born in France. The result of this policy was that labor migrants not only settled in France but also integrated themselves relatively quickly. Even the late-arriving Poles had little difficulty finding a place in the multiethnic French society.

Until the end of the nineteenth century, the Belgians were the largest immigrant group in France, followed by the Italians; in the twentieth century, the Italians passed them by a small number.

Market scene in Brussels, around 1900

Belgium

Belgium freed itself from the Kingdom of the Netherlands by revolution in 1830 and established a constitutional monarchy. It had a tradition of seasonal migration which extended beyond its borders. The migrants were known in France as *Franschmans* and worked mainly as harvest hands or building roads, canals, and railroads. The French-speaking Walloons found this labor migration easier than the majority of the migrants, who came from the thickly settled northern part of Belgium - Flanders, where about 60 percent of the population lived. The relatively thinly populated south,

where rapid industrialization had begun in the middle of the nineteenth century, drew internal migrants from the agrarian north and also immigrants from other European regions. There was work for many people in the coal mines, metal and textile industries, and sugar refineries.

At midcentury about 95,000 foreigners lived in Belgium, and by 1910 their numbers had increased to over 250,000. As in France, active recruiting of workers began only after World War I; before that, the immigrants came spontaneously, looking for work. Many remained in Belgium and were able to integrate relatively quickly into Belgian society. Nevertheless, the number of immigrants was always surpassed by the number of emigrants in the second half of the nineteenth century. Despite its rapid industrialization, the country could not absorb all of the available workers. However, the destination of the emigrants was not usually overseas; for Belgians, migration usually meant labor migration to the neighboring countries. They planned to stay a few years and then return home. Although Antwerp was an embarkation port for thousands of other Europeans, especially southern Germans, going to North America, only a few Belgians followed the procession to the New World as emigrants.

The port of Amsterdam. Colored engraving 1701

The Netherlands

The Dutch also played a relatively minor role in transatlantic migration. The Netherlands came under Habsburg rule in 1477 and were annexed to Spain in 1555; they achieved independence in 1648, after a series of bloody wars. In the following years, the country was in competition with Spain and Great Britain and rose to become, for a short period, the leading trading country and sea power. Merchants, traders, and a few settlers migrated to colonies founded all over the world by the Dutch East India Company (1602) and the Dutch West India Company (1621). In 1624, Dutch migrants established a colony in New Holland, now New York. Forty years later, however, they had to give this colony up to the British; their North American possessions were not economically strong or thickly settled enough to risk a confrontation with their powerful European neighbor. At the time of the English takeover in 1664, only about 10,000 Europeans lived in New Holland, as compared with about 30,000 in New England. In contrast to the British possessions in North America, only a few Dutch emigrants went to »their« colony - the massive recruiting efforts had more success in Ger-

many and Scandinavia than at home. The reason for this lay in the political and social conditions in the Netherlands at this time: the seventeenth century after the achievement of independence was their »golden age«. The rural population could earn a relatively good living from the fertile marshlands, and the enclosure of large areas with new dikes provided living space for the growing population. Cross-border labor migration was also an option, one used mainly by artisans.

After the surrender of New Holland, Dutch emigration to North America came to an almost complete stop. A group of religious dissidents, the Labadists, founded a Christian commune in Maryland in 1683, but it broke up after only five years due to internal squabbling. Between 1683 and 1690 a few Dutch Mennonites (most of whom had emigrated previously to Krefeld or the Palatinate) followed the German Franz Daniel Pastorius and took part in the founding of Germantown in Pennsylvania. Both of these groups together, however, included no more than 300 Dutch emigrants. Since neither religious persecution nor economic distress nor overpopulation was a problem in the Netherlands, settler migration to the other Dutch colonies (Borneo,

Java, the Celibes, Ceylon, and Capetown) also remained limited.

As a result of its turbulent history, the Kingdom of the Netherlands which was established in 1815 had an ethnically homogeneous population which was about equally divided between Catholics and Protestants. Wars with England in the eighteenth century and with France at the beginning of the nineteenth century helped keep the population pressure low. There was internal migration to the slowly developing industries, but this was simply a part of the general European migration from the countryside to the cities. In the border areas, on the other hand, the Netherlands drew seasonal migrants from the neighboring countries; e.g., the German *Hollandgänger*. Like Belgium, the Netherlands also provided embarkation ports for the transatlantic migration.

Nevertheless, there was a »mass migration« from the Netherlands to North America in the nineteenth century, even if the number of Dutch immigrants was almost imperceptible when compared to the other groups in the U.S. The transatlantic migration curve roughly paralleled that for Germany, except that the absolute peak year for the Netherlands was 1847. Possibly the massive transit migration from southern and southwestern Germany was one stimulus for the Dutch emigration. The overall ratio of transatlantic migrants to nonmigrants in the Netherlands was 1:15. Although it is true that members of the Separatist religious community made up an unusually high proportion of Dutch emigrants in the nineteenth century, the reasons for emigrating were mostly economic: inheritance laws had led to the creation of tiny farms which could not support a family; industry could not yet absorb the growing population; and a failed potato harvest in 1845-1846 probably gave many people the final push toward a decision to emigrate. The Separatists tended to migrate in large well organized groups and often sent for other community members later, giving the impression of a religious motivation for their migration. Although the Separatists experienced a small degree of religious persecution in the 1830s, by the 1840s they enjoyed complete freedom; when the liberal constitution took effect in 1848, religious oppression ceased to be a valid reason for emigration. In the U.S., the Dutch settled mainly in Michigan, New York, Wisconsin, Iowa, Ohio, Illinois, and New Jersey.

Luxembourg

Luxembourg experienced very little overseas emigration, but a lot of economically important labor migration to neighboring countries. As a County with a confused succession history, Luxembourg had been ruled by the French, the Spanish, and (as part of the Netherlands) the Austrians; the Congress of Vienna in 1815 made Luxembourg an independent Grand Duchy, but it remained linked by a common monarch to the Kingdom of the Netherlands until 1890. One result of this complex history was that the official language was French, even though most of the population was of German stock. The country was geographically small to begin with, and then in 1839 it lost over half of its territory to Belgium, when the population of the western Walloon region joined in the Belgian revolution. The number of emigrants was negli-

gible, especially in the case of transatlantic emigration: people from Luxembourg usually appeared in the national immigration and emigration statistics under the category of »other nationalities« or were lumped together with either French or German migrants on the basis of language.

The German-Speaking Countries

In central Europe, Prussia and Austria had established themselves as the leading Ger-

Passage contract from an Antwerp broker

man-speaking nations, but there were also 35 small and very small states, numerous free cities, and several Swiss cantons where German was the official language. Despite their common language and despite many historical connections, there was great political, economic, and religious diversity among these entities. The emigration movements from these countries were in some cases substantial, took place at different times, and were set in motion by different kinds of factors.

Like other European states, all of the German-speaking areas still had more or less strictly enforced bans on emigration in the early nineteenth century. Nevertheless, there had always been some migration, within the countries, within Europe, and to some extent even overseas. As early as 1600, for example, almost 40 percent of the population of Frankfurt am Main was made up of »foreigners«. Of about 20,000 inhabitants, several thousand were journeymen; about 3,000 were Protestants who had left

the Spanish Netherlands for religious reasons; and about 2500 were Jews, living in a ghetto under varying degrees of tolerance. The earlier migration movements resulted from either force of some kind, expulsion by government authority, or economic recruiting campaigns; spontaneous individual decisions only rarely played a role. Most important was the intra-European migration of journeymen: in many trades the guild rules required travel as part of the professional qualification process. Journeymen had to travel for 2-3 years, and for this purpose they received from the authorities a Wanderbuch which was also valid as a passport. Every master was obligated to take a journeyman into his shop for a certain period or, if this was impossible, to give him expense money to travel on to the next town. In this way the journeymen helped spread technical knowledge all over Europe, along with information about the living conditions and job opportunities in other areas.

Expulsion by government authorities was the second important cause of migration, striking mainly at religious communities subject to persecution or suppression by the dominant church. Along with the Dutch Protestants who fled to Germany to escape persecution by the Spanish Catholics in the Netherlands, the 500,000 Huguenots who were expelled from France in 1685 were important for the German economy. Many of them were skilled craftsmen or merchants and were welcomed in the German states and cities. The same was true of the 20,000 Austrian Protestants expelled by the archbishop of Salzburg in 1731, who settled in East Prussia (although the majority later emigrated to North America). Group migration driven by religious intolerance played an important role throughout the seventeenth and eighteenth centuries and even into the early nineteenth century.

Thousands of other people were encouraged to leave home by recruiters working for foreign governments. Highly skilled craftsmen were especially sought after at European courts - so much so that many states enacted strict bans on emigration for these occupations. Also active, for the most part illegally, were military recruiters; they were also subjected to especially close control by the authorities. One exception in this regard was Switzerland, where a kind of »enlistment fever«, in which men sold their services to foreign armies, was widespread. During the eighteenth century there were usually between 70,000 and 80,000 young men serving outside the country, so that there were more soldiers on the move than civilian emigrants. Since foreign military service brought significant amounts of money into the country, it was not only tolerated but actually promoted by the government authorities.

Settlers were also recruited from all of the German-speaking areas beginning in the eighteenth century, to go to eastern Europe and North America. The first large-scale transatlantic emigration movements were from the Palatinate in 1709, from Württemberg in 1717, and from Baden in 1737.

In southern and southwestern Germany, the effects of strong population growth and the economic problems brought on by the property-inheritance laws were already strongly felt in the eighteenth century. Because each farm was divided equally among all of the inheriting children of the leaseholder, the land was broken up into smaller and smaller parcels, which came to be called »dwarf farms« (*Zwergwirtschaften*). The number of new families being started increased, leading to even faster population growth. At the end of the eighteenth and the beginning of the nineteenth century, the poorest peasants were granted the status of free men, but this led to increasing indebtedness: for many peasants, the payments owed to the landowners in place of the feudal obligations were so burdensome that any failed harvest or economic crisis could force peasants to give up their farms. Also related to the liberation of the peasants was the privatization of the *Allmenden*, community-owned lands open to general use; this had the negative effect of depriving poorer farmers of a secure source of subsistence for their old age. At the same time, the newly granted freedom to practice the trade of one's choice and the strict protective-tariff policies adopted by many governments made many craftsmen economically insecure as well. There seemed to be no economic chances left for

Germans and Magyars in Hungary 1850

Hessian handloom weaver around 1864

these people, for farmers who had already lost their land or were faced with inevitable impoverishment, and for artisans who were experiencing or foreseeing an economic crisis due to increased competition or a loss of buying power among the general population; for them emigration was a realistic alternative to impending poverty.

In Baden, Württemberg, and the Palatinate; in the western Tyrol and Vorarlberg (the Austrian provinces where the laws called for partible inheritance); and in the parts of Switzerland where the soil was so poor that it was practically impossible to divide a farm, the settlement recruiters found ears eager to hear their message. There was a good travel route along the Rhine for the emigrants, and for this reason the first massive transatlantic emigration came from the south and southwest of the German-speaking area.

In the early years of the nineteenth century, the population there also had to absorb the severe economic damage caused by the Napoleonic Wars. When the harvests failed in several consecutive years, emigration resulted: 20,000 people left for North America in the years 1816 and 1817. After that

the number decreased for a while (for example, there were only 3000 transatlantic emigrants in 1820), but beginning in the 1830s it rose continuously. The primary destination was now the U.S.: 2.9 million Germans went from 1820 to 1879, and another 2 million followed by the end of the nineteenth century. Emigrants to the U.S. made up almost 90 percent of the total German emigration, with the rest going to Canada, Brazil, Argentina, Australia, and South Africa.

The gradual liberalization of emigration restrictions in all of the German-speaking countries and the expansion and technological improvement of transportation routes made people in the nineteenth century generally more mobile. Yet it was the deteriorating demographic and economic conditions that caused mass transatlantic emigration to spread to other regions of Germany, from the south to the north.

In Rhenish Hesse and the areas west of the Rhine, the introduction of partible inheritance came later, as part of the French *Code Civil* during the Napoleonic occupation; this meant that the rapid population growth of the period did not lead to widespread poverty as quickly as in other regions. There was also more industrial development, beginning as early as the 1850s, which was able to absorb at least some of the landless rural population. For this rea-

son significant transatlantic emigration from this area did not begin until the middle of the nineteenth century and remained relatively small.

In Bavaria east of the Rhine, in Tyrol and Salzburg, and in northwestern Germany, impartible inheritance was the rule, so that farms were inherited intact. The typical agricultural operation was larger, and members of the subpeasant class could get by by working as farm hands, although they usually needed supplementary income of some kind (for example, from home work in the textile industry or, in northwestern Germany, from seasonal work in Dutch brickworks). But soon the cottage textile industry was unable to compete with cheap imported English manufactured goods, and after the division of the Netherlands in 1830 seasonal migration to Dutch factory jobs dropped sharply, and was completely forbidden by the Dutch government a few years later. In this situation, day laborers, farm hands, and noninheriting children of farmers - those who owned no land and had no chance to earn any supplementary income - saw themselves forced to emigrate. The conditions were again different in those regions where peasants were dependents of a very small number of estate owners; i.e, in Schleswig-Holstein, Mecklenburg, and Prussia east of the Elbe. In Schleswig-Holstein the peasants had held their farms under inheritable leases since the eighteenth century and were for the most part exempt from performing feudal services. Extensive development of the land made it possible to absorb the surplus population for a relatively long time. Transatlantic emigration from the area began late and did not reach significant proportions.

In Mecklenburg, by contrast, there were hardly any free peasants; most of the rural population was made up of day-laborers and domestic servants working on a small number of large estates. They had no hopes of buying land and did not even own their own homes, receiving instead revocable settlement permits from the estate owners. It was the responsibility of the landlords to care for the poor, but this duty was also dependent on residence; in addition, the landlords could block marriages by denying the

Bremerhaven, the old harbor 1837

right to a homestead, since marriage without proof of a legal residence was not permitted. The peasants' nearly absolute dependence and above all the absence of any hope of freeing themselves from it led to massive emigration of the rural population beginning around 1850.

In Prussia east of the Elbe, there was a sharp increase in population during the first half of the nineteenth century, but it was for the most part absorbed by a rising need for workers as a result of liberal agricultural reforms. In the 1850s, Polish agricultural workers were even recruited on a seasonal basis. The situation changed in the 1860s and 1870s, as the population pressure increased even more. There was a severe general crisis in agriculture in the 1870s and 1880s due to cheap grain imports from

an expanding European market and from overseas. The beginning of pauperism among the rural underclass in these regions soon led to transatlantic emigration, as it did, for similar reasons, in the German-speaking cantons of Switzerland: many of the farms in fertile valleys became unprofitable, and many farmers decided to leave. With the advance of industrialization and the descent of artisans and small businessmen into the urban lower classes, the process of emigration from the entire German-speaking region changed at the end of the nineteenth century. Fewer family groups and more and more single individuals were leaving, including increasing numbers of single women. The advent of the steamship meant that many people no longer saw transatlantic emigration as a final irrevocable decision, but rather as a sort of extended seasonal migration.

Hence three main phases of transatlantic emigration from the German-speaking re-

gion can be distinguished. Before 1865, mainly independent peasants and artisans emigrated; they came for the most part from southern and southwestern Germany and traveled in family groups. In the second phase, between 1865 and 1895, the rural poor of northern and northeastern Germany began to leave home, and more and more of the emigrants left as individuals. In the third phase, from 1895 to World War I, individual men and women emigrated from all parts of the German-speaking area. These migrants hoped to earn a living in America as workers or in domestic service in the cities; rural settlement was feasible for only relatively few emigrants. After the Civil War, the Homestead Act (1864) still encouraged emigrants to settle the land, but by the 1880s at the latest the available land had been taken, and America needed workers to create an infrastructure and man the factories that were being built on a grand scale.

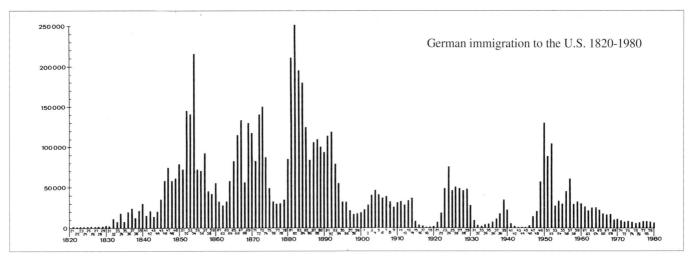

German immigration to the U.S. 1820-1980

But the emigration situation had changed in Germany as well, also as a result of large-scale industrialization. Emigration to North America was now parallelled by intensive rural-urban migration within the cultures of origin. Landless peasants sought employment as factory workers in nearby cities, and young women took positions as domestic servants in urban middle-class households. In Austria, for example, Vienna had an attraction for the rural population much like that of North America: immigrants came by the thousands from Bohemia, Moravia, and Silesia. The situation was similar in most large European cities. Many of the young independent job-seekers later moved on to the U.S., joining others who had decided to go there directly, perhaps with vague hopes that in America they could avoid what they considered a downward step, into the life of a factory worker.

The transformation of the German Empire, in particular, from an agricultural state with a few industrial centers to an industrial power with strong agricultural regions led not only to significant transatlantic emigration and internal migration but also to considerable immigration from eastern and southeastern Europe. The parallelism among these migration movements is most easily seen in northeastern Germany. In the 1860s, despite the prevalence of impartible inheritance, population growth and the small size of the farms made it increasingly difficult for heirs to pay off their nonin-

heriting siblings. When the agricultural crisis of the 1870s further increased the indebtedness of farmers, many reacted by emigrating to America. In the 1880s, however, this emigration decreased, and a swelling stream of migrants flowed toward the German industrial centers instead. The dream of one's own farm could no longer be realized in Germany or America, and industrial work in the U.S. was not much better-paid than that in Germany at this time. In the 1890s, an industrial boom began to take hold in the German cities, lasting until World War I and providing jobs for many people, and thus attracting landless proletarians from northeastern Germany as immigrants.

Emigration from agricultural areas in the northeast even led to an acute labor shortage there. The drop in grain prices and increasing mechanization of agriculture had led many of the large landholders to switch to sugar beets as their primary crop. This labor-intensive crop, however, provided only seasonal jobs. In the winter, unemployment among the resident population grew. Russians and Galician Poles were recruited as seasonal helpers, and soon the agricultural operation could not function without them. Their positions were not permanent, but rather required them to return to their homelands during the winter.

Recruited Poles also worked in the industrial cities of the Rhineland and especially in the Ruhr, but they came mainly from the Prussian part of Poland and could

not be treated as foreigners. About 70,000 foreign workers entered the German Empire each year during the period 1910-1920; despite strong pressure from industry and the large landowners, who desperately needed the non-German workers, the government refused to enact forward-looking immigration policies. While emigration laws were liberalized in Germany at this time, fear of foreign influences led to protectionist immigration laws. This policy was continued after World War I, and its consequences are felt even today.

Scandinavia

Sweden and Norway occupy most of the Scandinavian peninsula in northern Europe, but Denmark, Iceland, and Finland are generally included in the term Scandinavia because of geological and cultural connections. The economies of these countries were all based on farming, fishing, and lumber. The Scandinavian population is almost completely Protestant, and the languages, except for Finnish, are so closely related that people can understand each other when necessary. The countries' histories touched at many points, although those of Finland and Denmark were strongly influenced by the interests of their powerful neighbors, Russia and Prussia.

Finland acts as a bridge between western and eastern Europe, not only geographically, but also ethnically and culturally. The original Lapp inhabitants, driven northward by Finns moving in from the Baltic area in very early times, became a nomadic, politically insignificant minority. The Finns soon came under the influence of Sweden, both politically and culturally (when they converted to Christianity); Finland was part of the Kingdom of Sweden until the nineteenth century. Starting in the middle ages, Swedes settled on the Finnish coasts, and Finns lived in northern Sweden and Norway. Swedish was spoken as the official language in some parts of Finland, although the majority of the population always spoke Finnish, a language completely unrelated to the other Scandinavian tongues. In the eighteenth century, Finland had to give up territory in the southeast to Russia, and in 1808 Czar Alexander I brought all of Finland under his control, albeit as a semi-autonomous grand duchy. At this time a national consciousness began to grow among the Finnish population. The attempt to preserve and promote Finnish culture led mainly to the rejection of Swedish influences on language and customs. When the Russian government tried to force Finland to give up its special political status at the end of the nineteenth century, a fierce struggle against all foreign domination began. After World War I, Finland became an independent republic.

In Sweden, a long series of unsuccessful attempts by the Danish kings to annex the land had come to an end by the fourteenth century. Under the Vasa kings, Sweden grew strong, and by the end of the seventeenth century it was the leading power of northern Europe. Its population was homogeneous, and Protestantism was the official religion. From 1814 to 1905, Sweden and Norway were ruled by the same kings.

Norway, previously under Danish rule, had almost autonomous status under the Swedish kings. Each country had its own parliament, with a separation of powers and the elimination of most noble privileges. Norway also had a Protestant state

church, which had an even more conservative influence than that in Sweden.

Denmark, occupying a cluster of islands and the Jutland peninsula, formed the geographic bridge between northern and central Europe. Until 1814, the king of Denmark was also king of Norway and duke of Schleswig and Lauenburg. Iceland was also part of the Danish kingdom, and remained Danish even after it was granted an autonomous constitution in 1903. As part

of the »reorganization« of Europe at the Congress of Vienna in 1815, Denmark had to give up Norway to Sweden and Lauenburg to Prussia, but it received Swedish Pomerania in return. In 1846 the Danish king declared Schleswig to be his hereditary possession, and Prussia intervened militarily. Years of negotiations, in the course of which Russia and Austria also made demands, led to the Peace of Vienna in 1864. Denmark lost 40 percent of its

Emigrant agent from Frankfurt, Michigan, advertising in Sweden

A letter from America being read to a Swedish peasant family

territory: Schleswig and Lauenburg to Prussia and Holstein to Austria. The Treaty of Prague in 1866 placed all of these territories under Prussian administration, and a Germanization program was undertaken to make the annexation permanent. North Schleswig was returned to Danish rule in 1920. These changes in government in Schleswig and Holstein were one reason why people decided to emigrate: they resented having to use German as an official language and especially hated service in the Prussian army. In the other Scandinavian countries, by contrast, conflicts of loyalty played no significant role as a motive for emigration.

In Sweden and especially in Norway, the inhospitable land, with its forest-covered mountain ranges and poor soil, made farming very difficult. Fishing was thus economically important, along with farming and lumbering. Even in 1850, less than half of the available land in Sweden was cultivated, or only 0.58 hectare of land per inhabitant. In Norway three-quarters of the land was agriculturally worthless, and even the cultivated land was heavily forested.

Nevertheless, most of the population lived from farming: the Swedish labor statistics for 1870 show 72 percent engaged in farming, lumbering, or fishing, with 13 percent in industry or the trades and about 5 percent each in commerce and transportation, government jobs, and domestic service in the cities. In Norway in 1865, about two-thirds of the population lived from farming, lumbering, or raising animals, with 15.4 percent in mining and industry and the rest of the employed population divided among fishing, commerce, and shipping. This occupational structure changed only slowly, so that in 1891 48.65 percent of the population was still in agriculture, with 23.04 percent in mining and industry. In Denmark, the flat fertile land favored grain growing, but a shift to cattle-raising and dairying began in the 1860s. The profitability of the larger farms depended on rural wage workers, and so Denmark, too, had about 70 percent of its population living in the country until 1900. There was almost no industrial development in Finland in the nineteenth century, and the basis of the economy remained exclusively farming, lumbering, fishing, and shipping.

The farmers were thus the most important class, economically, in all of the Scandinavian countries. Although serfdom had been abolished since the eighteenth century, in many cases the farmers' political

position did not match their economic importance. The strongest and most independent group was that of the landowners, the so-called *bonder*, of Norway. In 1845 they made up 58 percent of the total population. They had the right to vote, and in 1837 they had even won local autonomy; they could actually be called a kind of peasant aristocracy. Despite their privileges, of course, the *bonder* were not always wealthy. As in southern Germany, repeated partitions of the land had produced »dwarf farms« in many parts of Norway. The number of farmsteads grew from about 79,000 in 1802 to more than 135,000 in 1860, with the biggest jump between 1820 and 1845 (from about 93,600 to almost 113,000). Only a very small part of this increase was the result of clearing previously uncultivated land, land partition was the main reason. The number of dependent farmers, day-laborers, tenant farmers, and hired hands grew rapidly; in the thirty years from 1825 to 1855 it rose by almost a third, from 48,571 to 65,060. Since most Norwegian districts were very isolated, migration was difficult, and more and more of the nominally free farmers became economically dependent on large landowners.

Agriculture in Denmark was characterized by large farms, and partition was prevented by the introduction, in 1819, of a minimum legal size for farms. For a long time, the large estates specialized in labor-intensive grain production, providing employment for many tenant farmers and day-laborers. Then a widespread shift from grain to dairying and cattle-raising, completed by the 1880s, helped Denmark withstand the agricultural crisis which struck many European countries when cheap imported grain (mainly from the U.S.) flooded the market. Although this type of agriculture also required many workers, they could more easily be replaced by machines.

Until 1866, only landowners had real political rights in Denmark. The struggle for parliamentary democracy had given the dependent wage-earners, the landless day-laborers and tenant farmers, the right to vote. Because of their absolute economic dependence, however, they could be forced not to use this right by the conservative estate owners, who feared the growth of the liberal party. Male and female farm workers were very poorly paid: the average wage was 100-150 kroner per year, whereas the budget for a four-person household was estimated as 230 kroner. Servants had no voting rights; they were required to carry a certificate of good conduct from their employers; and there were strict governmental restrictions on their freedom of movement as well. For many, escape from this shamefully dependent and socially hopeless situation was only possible through emigration. Noninheriting sons and daughters of small farmers had to take work as farm hands and maids, since there were no other jobs. These people had little chance for social advancement in their homeland.

In Sweden, where land was also inherited by the oldest son alone, this problem had already begun to appear at the end of the eighteenth century. A land-reform law enacted in 1827 legalized the division of farmsteads, but with the primary aim of creating large connected areas for cultivation and working against the breakup of the fields - a breakup which made subsistence farming barely feasible. Nevertheless, a large part of the rural population could not avoid becoming wage earners; many farmers' sons became cottagers or day-laborers. In 1860, almost half of the male population of Sweden (48 percent) belonged to this lowest social class.

In Finland as well, inheritance laws led to a rapid rise in the landless rural population in the first half of the nineteenth century. Since there was no industry to absorb the noninheriting children of farmers, this social problem was an important motive for emigration throughout the nineteenth century.

As in other parts of Europe, an enormous general population growth in this period accelerated the development. This was especially noticeable in Sweden and Norway: in Sweden the population rose by more than 10 percent per year between 1815 and 1865, increasing from 2.6 to 4.1 million; in Norway the population almost doubled from 1801 to 1865 (from 883,038 to 1,701,756). These figures then continued to rise; in Norway, for example to 2,097,328 in 1895 and 2,309,860 only 10 years later.

Scandinavia also faced the problem of feeding these increasing numbers of people. Agriculture could not provide jobs for the larger population, and there were no large industrial centers in any of the four countries. In Sweden in 1850, there were only four cities with population greater than 10,000 (Norrköping, Karlskrona, Gothenburg, and Stockholm), and even in 1880 only 15 percent of the population lived in urban centers. Despite the gradual development of industry, mainly in metal-working, this proportion increased only slowly, to 26 percent in 1913 and 33 percent in 1930: two-thirds of the Swedish population still lived in the country.

The situation in Norway was similar. At the beginning of the nineteenth century, 10 percent of the population lived in urban areas, and this percentage only increased to 15.37 percent by 1860 and to 28.02 percent by 1900 - still below the one-third mark. A relatively slow industrialization, mainly in wood- and metalworking, began only in the second half of the nineteenth century.

Denmark had a higher proportion of urban population, 31 percent in 1870 and 40 percent at the outbreak of World War I, mainly in Copenhagen. Here, too, the pace of industrialization was generally slow.

The country most dependent on agriculture was Finland, where there was virtually no developed industry before World War II; aside from Helsinki there were only small regional capitals like Viipuri (Vyborg), Pori, or Jyväskylä. Workers found jobs mainly in lumber or shipbuilding.

The results of this situation were well developed internal migration, emigration to neighboring countries, and movement from the land into the small towns of the region. Despite restrictive emigration policies (which were enforced more loosely, as in Germany, only after about 1840, cities in the Netherlands had drawn emigrants from Scandinavia in the sixteenth and seventeenth centuries. London, Hamburg, and St. Petersburg also attracted immigrants from all directions. In the nineteenth century, Norwegians sought work in the iron industry of Sweden or on the large estates of Denmark and northern Germany, where many Swedes were also employed. Swedes also took jobs in Norwegian fisheries or as workers in the Lübeck area, and Swedish domestic maids found positions in Hamburg and Copenhagen. Finns moved from the countryside to Turku and Helsinki, but

Emigrating peasants on their way to Gothenburg 1872

Gothenburg harbor

also to join the fishing fleets of Norway or Russia or to become workers in St. Petersburg or in the Swedish woodworking industry. The Scandinavian population had been relatively mobile for centuries, with fully developed internal and seasonal migration. Many of these job-seekers, who had originally planned to stay in the city a few years and return home to the country with some working capital, later decided to take the more daring step of starting over in America.

Transatlantic migration on a large scale began relatively late in Scandinavia. Aside from a small group of Swedes and Swedish Finns from Värmland who founded the successful colony of New Sweden in Delaware in 1638, and from individual Norwegian and Finnish sailors who jumped ship in American ports, there was

no significant Scandinavian transatlantic migration before the nineteenth century. The movement began in Norway in the 1820s, grew to a steady stream by the 1850s, spread to Sweden and Denmark about ten years later, and reached Finland in the 1880s. Transatlantic migration in this case meant almost exclusively North American migration. The peak period was between 1880 and 1900, except for Finland, where the transatlantic migration pattern resembled that of eastern Europe more than that of the other northern European countries.

As might be expected from the structure of the Scandinavian population, the great majority of the emigrants came from the countryside; for the nineteenth century as a whole, agricultural workers with no hope for advancement, tenant farmers in danger of losing their land, and noninheriting farmers' sons made up the greater part of the migrants to America. Land ownership was generally very important in the rural-agricultural societies of Scandinavia; it provided economic security and a chance

for advancement. For this reason family emigration with the aim of homesteading remained dominant for much longer in Scandinavia than in other (western and eastern) European countries; in Denmark, for example, settler migration still accounted for half of all emigration in 1870 and for 25 percent in 1890. The available supply of uncultivated land in the U.S. was already dwindling at this time, but Scandinavian farmers often had enough capital to buy a farm or could work as farm hands to earn the money. Only after 1880 did a gradual structural change set in: the number of unmarried individual migrants under age 25 increased. Young men and women, as a rule well informed about conditions in the American labor market, sought wage work in cities on the East Coast. They, too, came mainly from the country, but had often traveled first to a Scandinavian city to look for work; this step migration was especially typical of young women. Increasing internal migration and transatlantic emigration were chronologically parallel phenomena. Improvements in ship transporta-

Cleng Peerson, leader of the first Norwegian Quaker emigrant group

tion during this period also led to an increase in the rate of return migration, although for Scandinavia this was generally not very high. In Sweden, for example, a total of 1,150,000 emigrants left between 1851 and 1930, and 200,000 returned. On the other hand, years of economic decline like 1894 and 1898, when the return migration suddenly shot up to 70 percent of the emigration rate, show clearly how quickly these labor migrants could and did react to unfavorable changes in economic conditions.

Norway had the earliest and strongest emigration, relative to its population density. In 1825, a group of 50 Norwegian Quakers and Pietists led by a certain Cleng Peerson, who already knew America from personal experience, had settled near Rochester, New York. The motive for their emigration was mainly the intolerance of the official Norwegian Lutheran church, but economic considerations also played a role. Although only a few more Norwegians followed them across the Atlantic in the next ten

years, this first Norwegian settlement in North America marked the beginning of an ever-increasing movement. Only 300 emigrated in 1840, but three years later the number was already over five times greater, 1600. These early migrants often belonged to organized groups, sometimes under leaders who had made the transatlantic journey several times and were consciously instigating and maintaining a chain migration process. Between 1856 and 1865, the first wave of mass migration from Norway began, with 39,350 emigrants going to the U.S. In the following decade the number of emigrants rose to 119,545, and by 1900 320,476 more had gone, including 105,704 between 1880 and 1885; between 1900 and the beginning of World War I, an additional 235,410 Norwegians left for America. The destinations were almost always the U.S. and Canada, with hardly any migration to other non-European countries.

The first mass emigrations were caused by a combination of factors: a growing population, the increasing partition of farms, and years of poor harvests. In 1838, the failure of the potato crop, a basic foodstuff for wide sectors of the population, led to a serious famine which drove many people to emigrate, although their decision may have been made easier by encouraging reports

from the emigrants of 1825. Chain migration was very important in Norway until the middle of the nineteenth century. The geographic isolation of many Norwegian districts encouraged the evolution of particular traditions and dialects which stood in the way of communication with Norwegians from other areas; for this reason, settlements in the U.S. were often of people from one region.

Mass emigration from Sweden began late, with no organized travel to America before 1845. In that year only 65 people emigrated, but among them was a group of 25 who founded a »New Sweden« in Iowa which attracted hundreds more of their countrymen in the following decades. The desire to own their own farms was the main motive for most of these people. Many other Swedes left home because of conflicts with the strict and authoritarian Swedish Lutheran church; the number of independent churches grew rapidly in the 1840s and 1850s. The feeling of religious oppression was thus a second major factor, alongside economic considerations, in the decision to emigrate.

About 14,500 people left Sweden before 1854, and only about 4,000 more followed in the next five years - a temporary stagnation related to an economic crisis in the U.S. Between 1863 and 1867, when the

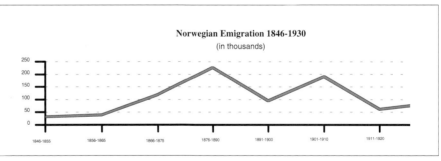

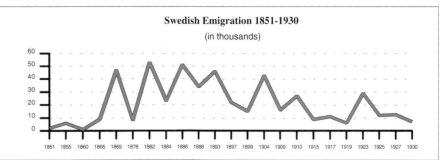

U.S. economy had recovered and workers were again in demand, an additional 12,000 Swedes carried out their emigration plans. Probably many Swedes dreaming of owning their own land were encouraged by the enactment of the Homestead Act (in which the U.S. government made land available to all settlers on very attractive terms) and the offers of land for sale by the American railroad companies.

Severe crop failures in Sweden in 1867 and 1868 caused an abrupt jump in the number of emigrants. If »pull« arguments such as religious freedom, the separation of church and state, and above all the availability of cheap land had driven emigration before, now oppressive economic hardship pushed people out of Sweden. Between 1868 and 1873, 103,000 emigrants left for America, 32,000 in the year 1869 alone. Even at this time there were still many organized religious groups, but there was also a steadily increasing number of individual families and even single young people leaving Sweden because they saw no economic future there. After 1874 about 3,500 people left each year, with a peak in the period 1879-1893, when 493,000 emigrated.

This peak at the end of the nineteenth century was based on the emigration of single young people looking for work. An economic crisis that struck all of the principal industrial sectors (wood products, metalworking, and wheat production) caused a surge in the number of emigrants, to 12,800 in 1879 and to an absolute peak of 46,500 in 1887. At this time the emigrants to the U.S. were mainly farmers, who saw their living threatened by falling grain prices, and young unmarried metalworkers; they found jobs in the construction industry and in factories. In the 1890s and in the twentieth century, there was a clear relationship between the annual emigration rate and conditions in the Swedish and American labor markets. Planned labor migration spread to other regions and social classes, and the destinations also became more diverse. Smaller waves of emigrants headed for Latin America, mainly Brazil. Canada also became a more important destination.

Emigration from Denmark started latest of all, and the total numbers were not very

high. Out of a population of about 2 million, about 300,000 left for America before World War I. Despite the late start (at the end of the 1860s), the shift from family migration to individual migration (with an especially high proportion of women) took place in the 1880s, as in the other countries. Economic conditions led to regional differences in the emigration rate, with about two-fifths of the emigrants coming from Jutland, one-fifth from the city of Copenhagen, and the remaining two-fifths divided among Fünen, Lolland-Falster, Bornholm, and Seeland outside of Copenhagen. Bornholm, for example, experienced a high seasonal immigration of Swedes, which depressed wages so much that many Danish agricultural workers saw no other choices but the poorhouse and

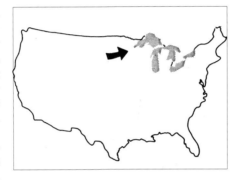

Main areas of Norwegian settlement in Minnesota, Iowa, North and South Dakota, Illinois, Wisconsin

emigration. The situation in Lolland-Falster in the 1890s was similar, with female agricultural workers from Sweden and Poland working the sugar-beet fields, often under the direction of German supervisors, from May to November. Here, too, many of the Danish men left, either for the cities or overseas; only a few were satisfied with the poorly paid jobs in the local sugar refineries.

By comparison with Sweden and Norway, relatively few farmers left Denmark, only 4 percent of the total emigration. Although the proportions varied from year to year, the bulk of the transatlantic migrants was always made up of workers (including, to be sure, agricultural workers). From a high of almost 70 percent in 1870, the percent-

age decreased slowly to about 35 percent at the outbreak of World War I. Only a few people went directly from the countryside to North America; step migration, with an intermediate stop in a Danish city, played the dominant role.

Many workers emigrating from Denmark were members of the socialist movement. In the 1870s, the Danish socialist party actively promoted emigration from the cities, although their plans for a closed settlement in Kansas met with failure. In 1877 the leaders of the socialist movement, L. Pio and P. Geleff, suddenly emigrated to America, without informing their fellow party members of their decision. It was later learned that they had been given money for this purpose by the police, who hoped their departure would help bring an end to the strikes which were taking place in those years. This calculation proved correct: it took decades for the Danish socialist movement to recover from this blow.

Religiously motivated emigration was especially important in Denmark, as in the early phases of transatlantic migration from the other Scandinavian countries. Denmark had the highest rates of religious emigration, relative to the total population, of any country in Europe in the nineteenth and twentieth centuries. Although it was less strict and conservative than the Lutheran churches in Sweden and Norway, the Protestant church in Denmark lost many members to various revival movements and sects in the 1820s. Of these, the Baptists and Mormons in particular emigrated to America. While the Baptists, relatively small in number, left home mainly to escape persecution, the Mormons considered settling in Utah almost a religious duty. The Mormons began missionary work in Denmark in the 1850s and won many converts, especially among the Baptists. They financed the emigration of their members on credit, so that the proportion of very poor people among the Mormon emigrants was relatively high. Between 1850 and 1904, 46,500 Scandinavians converted to Mormonism, including 23,443 Danes, 16,714 Swedes, and 6340 Norwegians. About 50 percent of the total number (and about 54 percent of the Danes) emigrated to America.

Emigration from Iceland was atypical due to the geographic isolation of this Danish possession. There was no significant emigration from Iceland until well past the middle of the nineteenth century. When the British Inman shipping company announced the opening of direct steamship service from Iceland to America in 1873, about 1,000 people, or 1.4 percent of the total population, immediately booked passage. In the following years (until 1930), about 14,000 Icelanders decided to seek their future in America; the reasons included agricultural problems due to changes in the climate, an epidemic among the island's economically important sheep herds, and the eruption of a volcano which totally destroyed several villages.

In absolute numbers, by far the largest group of emigrants from Scandinavia came from Sweden (1,105,000 as compared with 754,000 from Norway and only 309,000 from Denmark for the period 1840-1914). Norway, however, experienced the largest emigration relative to its population (and hence the strongest effects on the home culture), not only among the Scandinavian countries but in all of Europe, with the exception of Ireland. In the peak emigration years 1880-1885, for example, Ireland had 15.83 emigrants per thousand population, while Norway had 11.05, England had 5.71, and Germany had only 3.82. The emigration to America marked an economic and cultural turning point for the Scandinavian cultures of origin: within a short period of time, large parts of a relatively small population decided to leave home.

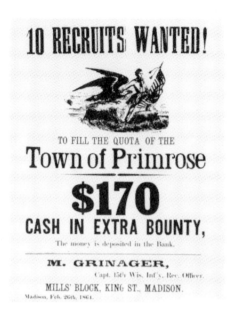

A recruiting poster for the Norwegian Regiment during the U.S. Civil War

References:

Bade, Klaus J.: »German Emigration to the United States and Continental Immigration to Germany in the late 19th and early 20th centuries«, in: Hoerder, Dirk (ed.): Labor Migration in the Atlantic Economies. The European and North American Working Classes During the Period of Industrialization. Westport, Conn., 1985, S.117-142.

Baines, Dudley: Migration in a Mature Economy. Emigration and Internal Migration in England and Wales 1861-1900. Cambridge, 1985.

Berthoff, Rowland Tappan: British Immigrants in Industrial America 1790-1950. Cambridge, Mass., 1953.

Blegen, Theodore C.: Norwegian Migration to America 1825-1860. Northfield, Minnesota, 1931.

Carlsson, Sten: »Chronology and Composition of Swedish Emigration to America«, in: Norman, Hans; Runblom, Harald (eds.): From Sweden to America. A History of the Migration. Minneapolis, 1976, S.114-149.

Diner, Hasia R.: Erins Daughters in America. Irish Immigrant Women in the Nineteenth Century. Baltimore, 1983.

Erickson, Charlotte: Invisible Immigrants. The Adaptation of English and Scottish Immigrants in Nineteenth-Century America. Coral Gables, 1972.

Green, Nancy L.: »Filling the Void: Immigration to France before World War I«, in: Hoerder, Dirk (ed.): Labor Migration in the Atlantic Economies. The European and North American Working Classes during the Period of Industrialization. Westport, Conn., 1985, S.143-161.

Hoerder, Dirk: »An Introduction to Labor Migration in the Atlantic Economies, 1815-1914«, in: ders. (ed.): Labor Migration in the Atlantic Economies. The European and North American Working Classes During the Period of Industrialization. Westport, Conn., 1985, S.3-31.

Hvidt, Kristian: Flight to America. The Social Background of 300.000 Danish Emigrants. New York, 1975.

Kero, Reino: Migration from Finland to North America in the Years between the United States Civil War and the First World War. Turku, 1974.

Kurgan-van Hentenryk, Ginette: »Belgian Emigration to the United States and Other Overseas Countries at the Beginning of the 20th Century«, in: Kurgan,G.; Spelkens,E.: Two Studies on Emigration through Antwerp to the New World. Brüssel, 1976, S.9-49.

Lee, Lynn Hollen: Exiles of Erin. Irish Migrants in Victorian London. Ithaca, N.Y., 1979.

Lehmann, Sylvia: Grundzüge der schweizerischen Auswanderungspolitik. Diss. Bern, 1949.

Marschalck, Peter: Deutsche Überseewanderung im 19. Jahrhundert. Stuttgart, 1973.

Norman, Hans; Runblom, Harald: »Migration Patterns in the Nordic Countries«, in: Hoerder, Dirk (ed.): Labor Migration in the Atlantic Economies. S.35-68.

Schrier, Arnold: Ireland and the Emigration 1850-1900. New York, 1958.

Wabeke, Bertus Harry: Dutch Emigration to North America 1624-1860. Freeport, N.Y., 1944, repr.1970.

Wulff, Reinhold: Die Anfangsphase der Emigration aus Schweden in die USA, 1820-1850. Frankfurt/Main, 1987.

Za chlebem - to Bread: Eastern Europe

Dirk Hoerder

The areas east of the Elbe and Morava rivers and of a line from Bratislava to Triest remained agrarian throughout most of the 19th century. This covers the eastern parts of Prussia; the Polish ethnic territories (at that time incorporated into Prussia, Russia and Austrian Empires); in the Czarist realm the Finnish, Baltic, Byelorussian, Ukrainian and Ruthenian territories; in Austria-Hungary the Czech, Slovak, Ruthenian, Magyar and South Slav territories; further in the Southeast the independent South Slav states and the Roumanian and Greek territories.

These Northeastern, Central and Southeastern European areas were dominated by remnants of feudal structures and backward empires, with large landholdings, e.g. the East Elbian areas of Germany, the northern parts of Poland and the Hungarian Plain, and peasant smallholdings elsewhere, e.g. in Galicia and Slovakia. Before the 19th century, economic development toward commercialization and industrial production had begun only in Bohemia and - east of the area under consideration - in St. Petersburg. In the 1860s, it began in the Warsaw, Lodz and Budapest areas; industrializing islands in agricultural regions. In the whole of these areas migration began only in the 1880s and 1900s. The one exception was Bohemia from where the Czechs migrated into Western Europe and to the United States beginning in the 1850s, with an advance guard of Fortyeighter refugees.

East of the ethnic territories described, along a line from Lake Peipus to Smolensk and down the Dnjepr to Odessa, another migration system oriented to the East exerted its pull: settlers to the South Russian plains and Siberia, workers to St. Petersburg, Moscow and the mining basins. Only the Jewish transatlantic migration came from areas beyond this line.

Poland

During the 18th century Poland was partitioned by the three surrounding Empires, Russia, Austria and Prussia, for the third and final time in 1795. Briefly reorganized by Napoléon as the »Duchy of Warsaw« (1807 - 1815) the great powers established the »Kingdom of Poland« in 1815, also called »Congress Poland« which jointly with the earlier occupied nine western *gubarnijas* came under Russian domination. Russia held the largest share of the Polish territories, but most of these were inhabited by non-Polish ethnic groups. Austria ruled over the poor and populous Galicia while Prussia had taken the smallest but most developed part including much of the Silesian area. As a political entity Poland reappeared on the map after World War One.

As a result, statistics about Polish migration have to be collated from those of the three partitioning powers and Jewish migration has to be deducted.

Given the political domination by the three partitioning powers, the first major emigration from Poland was political exile: After the Polish national uprising of 1830 - 1831, about 10,000 persons left, followed by thousands more after 1848. Most of them went to France and were at first supported by the French government. These emigrés found work in the professions or as artisans and workers. After the 1863 uprising for independence and social reform, another 10,000 persons went West, consisting to about one third of artisans and skilled workers. Some political exiles went to other European countries or the United States. Starting in the 1880s, socialists and social-democrats had to flee the Russian-ruled territories. They, too, went to the United States or the West European Polish exiles' colonies. Furthermore the forced migration of the deportees under the Czarist government has to be noted. After 1863 tens of thousands of Poles of which two thirds were workers, one third professionals were brought to Siberia.

During the 19th century, demographic growth and economic development varied considerably in the Polish ethnic territories. The abolition of serfdom, land reform

and pauperization of those peasants with tiny landholdings took place in the Prussian section from 1807 to the middle of the century, in the Austrian section after 1848, and in the Russian section between 1861 and 1864. At the end of the century, the large landowners who constituted between 0.5 and 1.4 percent of all landowners, held between 35 percent (Silesia) and 45 percent (Russian section) of all the land. On the other hand, the smallholdings of up to five hectares - about half the size of a subsistence plot for a family - amounted to from 35 percent in Upper Silesia to 79 percent in Galicia of the total number of the independent peasant holdings. The abolition of serfdom and the »land reform« meant, to take the Prussian case as an example, personal liberty, security of property, equality before the law (1807). But the 1811 compensation edict gave manorial lords one third of the peasants' land in recompense for the villenage labor that had been due to them. Dwarf holdings under two hectares were abolished altogether, only farms of more than 12.5 hectares were permitted to exist independently. As a result, manoral holdings increased in size and the landless, agrarian population in numbers. In Galicia (Austrian section), peasants had to pay indemnities to their former owners into the 1890s. In the Russian section, tiny lots of land were allocated to the landless and some of the lands seized by the manorial lords after 1846 were restored to the peasants, but the result was the creation of an agrarian underclass that had to rely on seasonal labor, temporary and longterm migrations. Thus the abolition of serfdom also abolished means of agrarian sustenance for the large part of economically marginal peasants and tenants. Land reform did not establish stable peasant societies, it laid the foundations for capitalist agriculture and the worldwide migration of a landless rural proletariat.

To these economic changes the natural population development added another push factor. Population growth during the second half of the 19th century averaged 70 percent throughout Europe. In all of the Polish lands the population grew by 105 percent and in some areas the population tripled or quadrupled. To take one example,

Recruiting emigrants in Poland before World War I

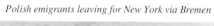

Polish emigrants leaving for New York via Bremen

Pottery market in Krakow, Poland, 1907

Warsaw and Lodz and their infant industries began to attract workers in the middle of the century. Warsaw became the main railroad exchange between Russia and Western Europe, Lodz, a center of textile production, supplied most of the Russian Empire and was one of the most rapidly expanding towns in the Atlantic economies during the last quarter of the century. Even though Congress Poland was among the centers of Russian industrial development and even though production increased tenfold in the two decades of the 1870s and 1880s, its factories could not absorb those parts of the population in need of employment.

Seasonal migration between the three sections, particularly from Galicia to Congress Poland, and from both into the German-occupied areas began in the 1880s and increased after the 1890s. After the turn of the century, France and Denmark also began to attract Polish labor, at first in small numbers. The main labor importing country was Germany. By 1913 about 500,000 Polish workers, mainly unskilled, from the Austrian and Russian sections worked in Eastern agriculture and in the mining and iron industries of the Ruhr District. A similar number of Polish workers from the Congress Kingdom had migrated east to Russia in search of work. These were predominantly skilled workers, ar-

in Galicia the population increased from 6.6 million in 1890 to about eight million in 1910 (net growth after out-migration) while industrial employment during the same period increased only from nine to 9.3 percent, i.e. by about 150,000 persons. All the others had to be fed from the overcrowded land. The frantic efforts to increase landholdings to a size sufficient to feed a family resulted in a tripling of land prices from 1870 to 1900 in some parts of Galicia. The building of railroads tied Polish agriculture closer to the world market.

Polish society was divided into the nobility (*szlachta*) accounting for 8 percent of the population - from minor nobles with no more than a peasant holding to manorial lords ruling over vast territories -, the clergy, usually closely allied with the nobles, the town population with little economic and political influence and the vast majority of peasants and landless laborers. No indigenous politi-

cal institutions could develop an investment policy that would benefit the labor reserves and provide jobs to feed the surplus population. The imperial governments favored their own territories.

In this situation migration was the only solution to chronic food shortages, un- and underemployment, dependency on local officials and aristocrats, cultural repression from German, Austrian and Russian governments.

Street life, Alexandersquare, Warsaw

tisans, clerks and professionals. There was little migration from Galicia to Austria, except for the Austrian-occupied part of Silesia.

Overseas migration began as a trickle of political refugees in the 1830s. Their numbers were reinforced by new arrivals after 1848 and 1863. The first economic migrants, a few settlers, came in the 1850s. They established a catholic parish in Texas, others later settled in Wisconsin and Minnesota. From the late 1850s to the early 1890s, migration came mainly from the German-occupied area. In these forty years, about 380,000 migrants arrived in the United States, according to the most reliable estimates, with only another 50,000 coming during the next twenty years. The peak was in the 1880s. Migration from the Russian and Austrian sections began only in the early 1890s, with the »Brazil fever« sending several thousand Poles to South America after the Brazilian government had offered free passage. Disenchantment with conditions there soon brought an end to this movement and North America became the main receiving society. From the Austrian-held territories, a total of 800,000 persons came between 1890 and 1914, with about 400,000 each coming before and after the turn of the century. Those coming from the Russian territories numbered about 800,000, too, but only 170,000 coming before 1900. The total of all migrations before World War One reached three million, when the whole Polish population amounted to about 25.5 million in 1910. After the United States, Brazil, Canada and Argentina were the most important destinations outside of Europe. More than 90 percent of the migrants came from villages, were farmhands, (former) owners of dwarf holdings and the sons and daughters of small farmers.

Much of the landed gentry opposed emigration since it reduced the supply of tenants and local labor. Ironically, communication and class feeling in this two-tier society was such that the warnings of the elites and their intellectual and religious mouth-pieces about the difficult living conditions in America (even though sometimes realistic) only served to strengthen the peasants' determination to leave: Whatever the elite said was understood

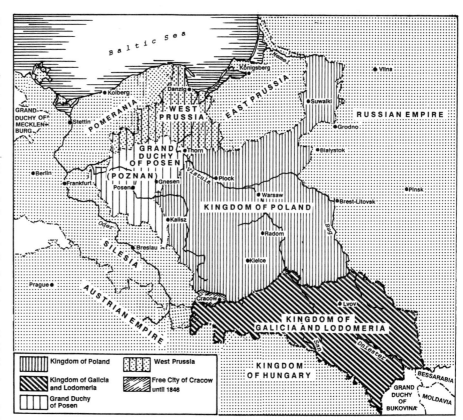

Poland after the Congress of Vienna 1815

by the lower classes as determined exclusively by their own interest, and its sudden concern for the well-being of the peasants was understood as nothing but a trick to keep the poor peasants within reach of the elite's influence.

The legal and political framework of emigration also varied between the three sections of Poland. Emigration from Russia had to proceed secretly for young men, subject to the draft. All others had to comply with complicated passport formalities. In the Prussian area emigration was viewed with pleasure by the bureaucracy bent on Germanization, but with mounting concern by the »Junkers« who saw their cheap and exploitable labor walk off. Austrian regulations were the most liberal.

The precarious existence of many families with below-subsistence plots led to intra-familial social tensions that could be relieved only by emigration. Parents were forced to send children off. These kept their right to a part of the inheritance and kept an eye on it. A lot of hard feelings developed because grown

sons with their families had to share their parents' small plots, because siblings mistrusted each other as to equal division of the parents' land. Tensions also developed because expectations of money from America could often not be met by the migrants, because money was sent to some kinspeople but not to others, because prepaid tickets were sent to kin and to friends who were expected to »make it« in America, but not to closer relatives who expected to be brought over to America.

Outside of their home territories Polish migrants began to develop the notion of being a diaspora that kept its ties with the old culture and remained part of the Polish nation, the concept of a worldwide Polonia.

Wilna, Totalansicht.

View of Vilna, Lithuania, 1917

The Western Provinces of Czarist Russia

More than half a dozen peoples lived between the Polish and the Great Russian ethnic territories. At the turn of the century they joined the westward Atlantic migration system. Smaller numbers moved east into the Russo-Siberian migration system: to the cities, to the South Russians Plains or later into mining and industry. All of these territories were part of the Czarist Empire. They stretched from the Finnish settled areas north of the Gulf of Finland to the Estonian, Latvian and Lithuanian peoples and included the White and Little Russians (Byelorussians and Ukrainians) to the Black Sea and, finally, along the Carpathian Mountains, the Carpatho-Rusyn on both sides of the Russo-Austrian border. Independent statehood had been achieved and lost by some of these peoples far back in history, the multi-ethnic states of the Kiev Rus (10th to 12th century) and the Lithuanian (14th to 15th century).
The Enlightenment which emphasized nat-

ural rights and romanticized ethnic or national folk cultures had reached the Poles, Czechs, Slovaks and Magyars in the revolutionary decades from 1789 to 1849, and spread further east in the second half of the 19th century. An awareness emerged that the dominating languages, the Russian of the rulers and administrators, the German of the burghers in the towns, could be replaced by ethnic languages. Languages that had never been developed into written form, except for religious tracts, were codified. From these »vernacular« languages literatures emerged drawing their inspiration from the oral folk traditions. Peasant cultures became the foundation from which the small intelligentsias, mainly priests and teachers, drew their inspiration. But once cultural norms were codified, they became the »property« of the slowly growing middle classes.
Economically these areas remained agrarian. Large landowners dominated huge areas, others were inhabited by peasants on dwarf holdings. Serfdom was abolished in most of Czarist Russia only between 1861 and 1864, at the time when slavery was abolished in the United States. No land reform to establish viable farms followed. Distribution of some lands in some parts of

the empire satisfied some of the craving for land, but the plots did not even guarantee subsistence for a family. Land and local self-administrative (*zemstro*) reforms during the years from 1856 - 74 (reform era under Alexander II.) and the economic take-off prepared the scene for the massive exodus of peasant-workers. These were peasants or agricultural laboreres who began to spend more and more time in factories: At first seasonal migrations permitted returning to the land for the spring sowing and autumn harvest. Then migrants stayed in the towns for a year, two years or longer, only visiting their families during Christmas and other holiday seasons. The peasant workers became worker-peasants, then workers of peasant background and finally they joined the urban proletariat. For some this happened in Riga, St. Petersburg, Lvov or Odessa. For most the big change came with the move to North America. We will take a closer look at this development, starting with the northernmost people, the Finns.

Finland

The Duchy of Finland had been transferred from Sweden to Russia in 1809. At that time the society was ruled and much of the land was owned by the Swedish upper class. Finnish settlers had been attracted to central Sweden during the 15th and 16th centuries while Swedish settlers had come to the coast areas of the gulfs of Bothnia and Finland. Since the 1820s, a struggle to gain recognition for the Finnish language and culture as equal to the Swedish was under way and finally successful - only to meet with a determined russification drive at the end of the century. The Russian language became the only official administrative language. Finnish autonomy was abolished. Young men were threatened with the danger of conscription into the Russian army. Popular opposition brought the cultural oppression to a temporary stop during and after the Russian Revolution of 1905. Twelve years later, in 1917, Finland became an independent republic.
The Finnish population had increased to 2.6 million by 1900, 12 percent of which

and Vitebsk, and 60,000 Estonians from the province of Estonia. Lithuania, once independent, had been joined with Poland in 1569, its nobility had been polonized and Polish had become the official language. The Latvian and Estonian ethnic territories had early come under German domination, later under Swedish rule and finally fell to Russia. Throughout the period a strong Baltic-German nobility and a German town patriciate dominated over the indigenous populations. After the abolition of serfdom the redemption payments weighed heavily on the peasantry. It temporarily brought them into an alliance with the Russian government against their former owners, the polonized Lithuanian and the German-Baltic nobility.

The three Baltic languages had been reduced to the »*vernacular*« of the peasants and some members of the urban underclasses. The centralizing tendencies of the Russian administration led to the imposition of the Russian language, to attempts to

The interior of a Russian peasant's cottage with oven, wooden floor, icons, cradle; romantic picture from 1805

lived in cities. Textile factories and the lumber industry had been developed under Russian rule. But in rural areas prospects remained dim. The rural population grew by 60 percent from 1850 to 1900 but even though the government initiated a policy of consolidating landholdings, the percentage of peasants among the rural population declined from one half in 1800 to less than one quarter in 1900. The number of tenants and landless laborers had increased correspondingly. The urban development of Turku, Tampere, Helsinki and Viipuri could absorb only a small part of the increase in the neighboring countryside.

During the 18th and 19th centuries, Finnish migration went first to Stockholm, then to other destinations in Scandinavia as well as to St. Petersburg. Emigration toward the United States began with a mere 3000 during the 1870s but soared to 67,000 from 1880 to 1893 and to 261,000 during the two decades from 1894 to 1914. The migrants came largely from the rural areas outside the pull of the cities and those coming from urban areas often were recent in-migrants from the countryside

The Baltic Countries

From Finland's southern neighbors, the three Baltic ethnic territories, about 300,000 Lithuanians migrated before 1914 from the Russian provinces of Kovno, Suwalki and Vilna, about 10,000 Latvians from the provinces of Courland, Livonia

convert the catholic Lithuanians and Lutheran Latvians and Estonians to the Russian Orthodox church, to the settlement of Byelorussian peasants among the »natives«, to a comprehensive system of conscription into the army starting in 1874. In all areas socio-demographic and economic pressures, huge magnate-owned territo-

Farmers from Livland, present-day Estonia and Latvia, engraving from 1850

The Peoples of Russia

From among the three Russian peoples - Byelorussians, Great Russians, Little Russians or Ukrainians - migration to North America was limited. Most of the migration from their areas of settlement was Jewish. Few Great Russians came: Their migration went to the industrializing cities and areas eastward or to homesteads in southern Russia and western Siberia.

For the Byelorussian provinces of Vilna, Grodno, Minsk, Mogilev, estimates of emigration to the west vary between 20,000 and 250,000. Figures clearly below one hundred thousand seem to be realistic. Their ethnic territories had long been under Polish-Lithuanian rule and they belonged to the catholic (20 percent) or orthodox churches (80 percent). The nobility had been polonized and remained so until Poland was divided off the map by the great powers in 1795. Thereafter a russification movement began: The name »Byelorussia« was replaced by »Northwestern Region«, Russian became the official language. Under these conditions an ethnic consciousness emerged late. Even after the turn of the century Byelorussian peasants identified themselves by religion or simply as *tuteishyia*, local residents. The territories achieved a brief independence in 1918.

Most of the Ukrainian ethnic terriories lay within the boundaries of Czarist Russia. Only a small part belonged to Austria (in the provinces of Galicia and Bukovina) and Hungary (Transcarpathian region), however, 85 percent of the transoceanic migrants came from the Austro-Hungarian section. The rest came almost exclusively from the western section (Volhynia, Podolia, Kiev) of the territories that extended north of the Black Sea to the Don and beyond. At the turn of the century the common name for the Ukrainians was Ruthenians, which subdivided into a number of regional groups. Of these the Carpatho-Rusyns (Red Russians) began to consider themselves a separate group during the later 19th century while the others merged into a common Ukrainian ethnicity. A total of perhaps 250,000 people came from both groups. The Carpatho-Rusyns belonged to the Uniate Church

ries, divison of inherited land, disastrous harvests in the late 1860s, the world-wide agrarian depression of the late 1870s and 1880s combined to force the lower classes to consider out-migration. Several thousand Estonians went to homestead in thinly settled areas of Russia. Lithuanians migrated to England and Scotland, to Latvian towns (45,000), to St. Petersburg, Moscow and Odessa (39,000).

Mobilization took place in consequence of labor demand during railroad construction and the subsequent better opportunities to travel. Few Lithuanians - of Lutheran faith - left from the German province of East Prussia. From all three ethnic groups large numbers of migrants left after the defeat of the revolution of 1905. Activists went into exile - labor unions and social democratic or socialist parties had come into existence during the 1890s - but for the whole of the peoples all hopes for improvements under Czarism were destroyed. Most of the migrants - of peasant origin - joined the American labor force as unskilled workers, a few went into farming.

while many of the others followed catholic or to a lesser degree orthodox rituals. The areas from which they came were characterized by small landholdings and high population pressure: a pauperized surplus population tried to alleviate its position by temporary migrations within Europe, multi-annual migration as far as England, and finally, migration overseas, usually intended for a few years only, to Argentina, Brazil, Canada and - to more than 90 percent of the total - the United States.

Of the Russian migrants to the United States 88 percent were unskilled workers, agricultural laborers, peasants and servants; almost 40 percent were illiterate and their possessions in ready cash upon arrival in Ellis Island amounted to less than $20 on the average. About one third of them returned after a temporary stay overseas. In the areas of origin the migration had two kinds of economic impact: the remittances of the migrants became an important part of the regional economies, and cheap agrarian labor became scarce, at least in the view of the landowners.

Emigration of the peoples in the Russian Empire, including the Finns, »Congress Poles« and the Jews, amounted to 4.5 million from 1860 to 1914. One quarter of them left during the three decades to 1890, three quarters in the 25 years to 1914. In the decades before the reforms of Alexander II in the 1860s, only a total of about 30,000 migrants had left. The share of the migrants going to the United States increased from 75 to more than 90 percent from the 1890s to the 1900s. The figures for the period 1899 - 1914 (2.8 million) indicate that Jews and Poles accounted for more than two thirds of the emigration (68 percent). Byelorussians, Ukrainian, and, to a much smaller degree, Great Russians accounted for 11 percent, the Baltic peoples for 9 percent, Finns for 7 percent and Russian-Germans from the South Russian plains for five percent. The latter had migrated there starting in the 1760s, priviliged by Catherine II.. Later, Slavic migrants became the preferred settlers for the homesteads in South Russia since they could be assimilated more easily. When German-Russians and a number of small religious groups lost their priviliges, many

Finnish emigrant family

Misery in Russia. People leaving their village, around 1890

of their members migrated for a second time: in a transoceanic rather than transcontinental move they went to Canada and the United States.

East of the dividing line between the Atlantic and Russo-Siberian migration systems millions moved to the industrializing cities and areas, more millions into the agrarian areas along the Transcaspian railroad and about ten million into western Siberia - called »the other America« by contemporaries - between 1815 and 1914.

Polish and Russian Jews

Jewish emigration from Europe has its roots in the bitter experiences of this people throughout about 800 years of European history. From the Middle Ages to the modern period, Jewish culture never was a homogenous whole but was always influenced by those peoples among which the Jews lived. The major distinction between Jews was language: the Spanish- and Portuguese-speaking group, the *Sephardim* and their North African and Southeast European descendants; and the Yiddish-speaking groups of central Europe, the *Ashkenazim* and their East European descendants. Yiddish, a language derived from

An emigrant son sends New Year's greetings to his parents in Poland

Middle High German, was enriched by terms from local languages, especially Polish. Christian Europe confronted Jews with hostility for religious reasons and forced them into occupations that Christians regarded as inferior, demeaning, forbidden. Thus the image of Jews as socially and economically undesirable emerged.

The period of Jewish migrations within Europe began around 1100. Pogroms against the Jewish population of the Rhine valley were perpetrated during the first crusade in 1096; from England Jews were expelled in 1290; from France in 1394, with restrictions dating back to 1306. In Germany they were made scapegoats and brutally persecuted during the spread of the »Black Death«, 1347 - 1354. From Spain and Portugal they had to leave or undergo forced baptism in 1492 - 1496. Of the *Sephardim* most left for North Africa, others for Italy and the Ottoman Empire. The West and Central European Jews, later joined by *Sephardim*, began to settle in Poland and Lithuania starting in 1150. Most of the religious refugees possessed skills and capabilities that made them sought-after

subjects for many monarchs. Just as the Huguenots were well received in England, the Netherlands and Germany, the Jews were attracted by the Polish crown which needed their commercial experience for international trade, their financial abilities for tax collection, their business acumen and artisanal skills for the development of the realm. By 1600, half a million Jews lived in Eastern Europe and about a quarter million remained dispersed over Western and Southern Europe.

The East European Jewish community created a social-political self-government, the *kehillah*. It was able to lease agricultural lands, and developed its own educational system and social security institutions. The strong emphasis on Talmudic prescriptions as regulations for everyday life gave form and cohesion to the community but prevented development. The small towns, *shtetl*, became symbols of a functioning community life. But from the middle of the 17th century onward the situation deteriorated. During the Ukrainian revolt against Polish domination in 1648 Jews were massacred in large numbers. The Polish Lithuanian Commonwealth, that had welcomed the migrants disintegrated under the pressures of the Russian, Prussian and Habsburg Empires (final partition 1795). It could no longer protect the Jewish community and governmental lev-

ies pauperized large parts of the Jewish population and the economic function of Jews as middlemen between rural and urban societies made them vulnerable to popular fury about deteriorating or merely changing economic conditions. Stratification within the community between the leaders, the *Zaddikim*, and the masses as well as a religious division between a pietistic revival movement, *Hasidism*, and an enlightened reform movement, the *Haskalah*, endangered community cohesion. By the 19th century, Jews in Prussia were subject to assimilation. In Russia they were confined to the Pale of Settlement (the 15 western and ten Polish provinces), were subject to selective service in the army - which lasted for 25 years -, suffered abolishment of self-government, and lived under pressure to convert. At the same time the so called *demographic transition* reached the Jewish population in the Pale: It increased from 1.5 million in 1800 to 6.8 million in 1900.

Jewish emigration from Europe had begun early. Some of the *Sephardic* Jews, when expelled from the Iberian Peninsula, as well as *Ashkenazi* Jews had gone to the thriving port towns and commercial centers of the Netherlands and Great Britain. They followed the worldwide trade routes of these empires just as the British, Dutch, as well as the French, Spanish and Portuguese merchants and traders, did. This was the period of the colonial trade-post migrations involving merchants of all nationalities, sailors, soldiers and colonial administrators. In the North American colonies the migrants of the two culturally and religiously divergent Jewish groups soon merged.

From the French Revolution to the middle of the 19th century the position of Jews in Western Europe changed. Emancipation from various legal restrictions began in France in 1790 and was achieved in Prussia in 1850, in England in 1858 and in Austria-Hungary in 1867. Prejudices remained. The assumption of the dominant cultures was that emancipation would mean assimilation. Many Jews accepted the challenge of modernizing their customs and improving their social and economic condition at the same time. One of the consequences was migration to the United States, and by 1880 about 180,000 Jews had left. Most came from the German Southwest and South, traditionally high emigration areas, where the agrarian structures under both population and modernizing pressures underwent a crisis aggravated by bad harvests. Jewish traders were dislocated and widespread suffering brought a rise of anti-semitism. Others came from the Prussian occupied parts of Poland. Smaller, mostly highly educated groups, came from other European states. Thus the social composition of these migrants was one of professionals, artisans and traders, moving in family groups when means permitted or as single young men where restrictive legislation concerning marriage and civil liberties were still in force. Within the United States the Jewish immigrants followed the expanding westward trade routes and established themselves in a number of manufactures and industries. They established a community of homogenous religious sites and were economically integrated. This community was joined since about 1880 by Jewish mass migration of East European Jewish newcomers. After the abolishment of serfdom in Russia, the building of a railroad infrastructure, the beginning of industrialization and the modernization of agriculture for export, many Jewish merchants, peddlers, millers and artisans found themselves displaced from their precarious economic existence. Even before this period, the struggle for survival had been so difficult for some that the term *luftmensh* had been coined: a person living merely of the air, i.e. by borrowing, clinching a deal here and there, never knowing where the next meal would come from.

The new policies after the assassination of Czar Alexander II (1881) introduced mob and governmental persecution of the Jewish communities. 1881/82: pogroms against more than 200 Jewish communities and further violence up to World War One; 1882: the »May laws« or »legislative pogroms« introduced a period of systematic pauperization. Jews were banished from villages and rural centers in the larger towns, their trades were restricted; 1887: quotas for entry into institutions of second-

ary education; 1889: legal profession closed to Jews; 1891: banishment of Jews from cities outside of the Pale, first Moscow and later from St. Petersburg, Odessa and Kharkov; 1903: Kishinev pogrom, encouraged by police and troops, with more than 300 dead; 1904: further pogroms after defeats in the Russo-Japanese War; 1905: October Manifesto blaming Jews for the uprising and flight of radical Jews into exile. Within the twenty-five years, Jews had been condemned as wealthy exploiters or as proletarian revolutionaries or as racial kinsmen of the Japanese, whatever the situation demanded. By the early 1890s, governmental decrees had forced 1.5 million Jews to migrate within the Pale. By the beginning of the 20th century, in some provinces one quarter of the Jewish population was on relief - provided by the Jewish community only - and on the average in the whole of the Pale one in twelve depended on charity. In the decade before 1880,

United States. By 1914 about one fifth of the East European Jewish population had migrated off: 75 percent of the migrants left from the Russian Empire, another 18 percent from the impoverished Austrian provinces of Galicia and the Bukovina or Hungarian districts, another four percent from the equally hardpressed and governmentally exploited Romanian districts.

The emigrants were young men and increasingly women who usually helped other family members to leave once they had established a foothold in the new society. Women accounted for 44 percent of the migrants. The societies of origin, mainly Russia, suffered a severe drain of skilled labor. Among the Russian Jews 40 percent were skilled workers, among the

Greeting card showing Cernowitz, Poland, 1903

30,000 Jews had migrated to the United States. In the single year after the first pogroms 13,000 left and numbers increased ever after, reaching figures of more than 100,000 annually before World War One, about 2.5 million (according to other estimates 3.5 million) leaving altogether, one tenth of them going to other destinations, especially Paris and London, Argentina and Canada, the other nine tenths to the

Jewish migrants arriving in the United States 64 percent were skilled workers, the mercantile trades on the other hand were underrepresented among migrants (31 percent among the Jewish population in Russia, 5.5 percent among the migrants to North America). A majority of the skilled workers, male and female, were in the clothing trades. The Pale of Settlement with the cities of Lodz, Warsaw, Vilna,

Bialystok under Jewish initiative had become the clothing centers of the Russian Empire. The migrants established production centers in Paris and London and above all in New York.

Czechs, Slovaks, and Magyars

Migration from the Central European areas of the Czech (Bohemia and Moravia), the Slovak and the Magyar peoples followed different but related and interconnected patterns. The Czech territories belonged to the Austrian part of the Habsburg monarchy. Economically they were the most developed areas (after Lower Austria) within the Dual Monarchy, furthest on the road towards capitalist production. Socially and culturally the emerging middle class set the tone. The Slovak territories in the Hungarian part were cut off from economic development through the political border between Austria and Hungary and from the north through the Carpathian mountain range. The Magyars lived in the area from the Great Plain to the hilly Transylvanian areas. On the Plain the lands were owned by magnates, but were touched by liberal reform attempts beginning in the 1830s. The migrations of the three groups were interconnected because the Slovaks were tied culturally and linguistically to the Czechs but politically to the Hungarian government which in the 1860s began a massive magyarization program. The Magyar and Czech migration were comparable in the earliest stages, because refugees from both groups left for the United States after the failure of the 1848/49 revolution and established an ethnic foothold on which later migrants could build. The Slovak areas remained isolated from new currents of thought since even a new intelligentsia had to emerge after the old upper class had been absorbed by the hegemonial cultures. Both the Czech middle-class elites and some of the Magyar nobility participated in the development of

Persecution of the Jews in Russia - emigration of Jews from a Podolian village

Enlightenment and romantic thought. All of these areas were multi-ethnic: Germans in Bohemia and Moravia; South Slav and Romanian peoples, the Transylvanian and German-speaking groups in Hungary. Slovaks moved into the Hungarian lowlands down to Croatia. These peoples sometimes lived in separate territories, in other places in mixed or neighboring villages or interspersed in town and cities. Since the growing feeling of ethnic identity led to a growing separation between the groups, we will deal with them separately. In Bohemia and Moravia the Czech population increased rapidly. So did the much smaller German population. As everywhere in Europe, migration antedated this population pressure. After the religious

Business card of Hapag emigrant agent Josef Pastor

wars of the 17th century the forced re-catholicization as well as the strengthening of German influence and Habsburg rule, sent many thousands fleeing from the Czech lands. The Moravian Brethren, about 150,000, had to leave in the 1620s, comprising almost the whole Czech cultural elite. A middle-class and peasant emigration followed between 1650 and 1680 and numerous other »waves« of peasant emigration have been discerned before the Austrian Edict of (religious) Toleration of 1781. About 60,000 persons had left in the half century preceding the edict. Some of the religious migrants went as far as Georgia and Bethlehem, Pennsylvania. From the 1760s to the 1820s, Czechs also migrated into the Balkan areas that were being resettled after the Habsburg armies had pushed back the frontiers of the Ottoman

Empire. The poor harvests after 1816, the depression after 1815 and the resulting poor living conditions and underemployment forced skilled workers, especially drapers and weavers, to leave the growing textile industry in Russian-ruled Congress Poland, to jobs available elsewhere in the Austro-Hungarian monarchy or in Western Europe. On the other hand, manpower with particular skills was lacking in Bohemia so that a constant in-migration of German artisans and skilled workers took place at the same time. This led not only to a transfer of technological knowledge but also to a transfer of class organizations. The social-democratic and socialist thought that had developed in Western Europe in the 1830s was carried in the heads of labor migrants to the Czech lands, discussed there and modified to meet local conditions and merge with local social thought. These migrations were made possible by the abolition of serfdom in 1781 and of manorial labor in 1848.

Beginning in the middle of the 19th century, the mass migrations began. In the 1840s about 55,000 persons emigrated from the Czech lands. Thereafter emigration figures rose almost continously to reach 282,000 in the decade 1901 - 1910. About on half of these migrants remained within the Dual Monarchy, the largest number going to Vienna. The Viennese cuisine derived its specific character in good measure from the in-migration of Czech women into domestic service. While female migrants in general and persons in domestic services usually are classified as »unskilled«, at least cooks should be included among skilled migrants. Czech migrants also went to other European destinations. Those going overseas went - with few exceptions - to the United States. A community of political refugees emerged there after 1848/49, reinforced by trade unionists and blacklisted strikers in the 1880s. Settlers went to the Midwest. United States' statistics counted 160,000 Czechs arriving between 1899 and 1924. The figures of the 1910 U.S.-census - including arrivals before 1899 - were higher: about 230,000 Czechs born abroad and a community of 540,000 including their American-born children. Even though Bohemia, after Lower Austria, was the most industrialized part of the Dual Monarchy, the factory and mining jobs could not absorb the surplus population. Austrian policies also favored economic development of the region around Vienna over that of Bohemia. Within Bohemia, emigration came less from the most impoverished areas in the northern Bohemian mountains, where the decline of cottage textile industries had brought the population close to starvation. The people were trapped since they could no longer raise funds to move overseas. Most of the migrants came from southern and southwestern Bohemia where there was no industy. Railroad construction brought no investments but facilitated the outward movement. Individuals, but often whole families, left from the large holdings of the nobles or from the tiny family plots that could not be subdivided any further. These areas could not intensify agricultural output and were marginalized during the late nineteenth-century worldwide production increases and changed trade patterns. Manorial labor was replaced by wage labor. Three peaks of migration may be discerned: 1853 - 57, when food prices were

Market town in Galicia, 1915

highest in the century and mobilization for the war against the Ottoman Empire, Crimean War (1853 - 56), exacerbated social tensions; 1866/67 to 1873, the years after the Prussian defeat of Austria and the reconstruction of the empire that brought self-government to the Magyars but defeated all Czech aspirations to self-rule; 1880 to early 1890s, during the worldwide agricultural crisis. While up to 1871 emigration from the advanced Bohemian lands accounted for 75 percent of the emigration from the Habsburg lands to the United States, its share fell to around five percent only twenty-five years later. Absolute numbers remained almost stable, but the spread of the money economy and of the hope that migration permitted escape from economic dislocations brought about the mass exodus from the territories further east.

Adjacent Slovakia, part of the Hungarian half of the Dual Monarchy began to send migrants in the 1880s, first from western Slovakia and soon also from the most impoverished section, eastern Slovakia. This late start explains why only 166,000 Slovaks born abroad were listed in the 1910-U.S.-census, 285,000 including their American-born children. In Slovakia remnants of the same dismal feudal conditions prevailed that were common in most of eastern Europe: At the turn of the century,

one percent of the landholders owned half of the agriculturally usable lands, 48 percent of the land was left for 98 percent of the peasants. Famines added to the sociodemographic strains. Customary rights of the nobles, e.g. to distill their grain and force their peasants to buy the spirits, did nothing to improve the health and economic conditions of the dependent agrarian population. Industrialization came to these distant areas at such a slow pace that even after World War One only about 11 percent of the wage-earning population was in industry or public service, while 71 percent were peasants, day laborers and servants. To the dismal economic situation, the magyarization program of the Hungarian government initiated in the 1860s added problems. The Slovak higher education - a total of three high schools for a population of about three million - was abolished, the number of primary schools decreased from 1,800 in 1870 to 250 in 1905. The Slovak language was codified in its definitive form only in the 19th century. For a while a catholic western and a central written Slovak competed with each other and with Czech as the language of the protestant elite. Administrations had never used the »vernacular«. Even the development of a national leadership was difficult: Foreign domination for centuries had brought acculturation pressures on the existing upper classes that had weaned almost all of them from their native Slovak culture and in the nineteenth century attracted them to the Magyar culture. The Magyars who emigrated at the same time were little better off than their Slovak neighbors. Even though governmental policies favored Magyars over all other nationalities, this hardly meant that there was any trickle-down effect to the peasant masses. If, once again, we look at the U.S. statistics first, 230,000 Magyar-speaking foreign-born persons were enumerated, 321,000 counting their American-born children. Within Hungary their geographical origins were the areas bordering on the Slovak settlements, the northeastern districts. The 1890s were a period of »activation«, in which people were mobilized to emigrate, mass emigration came during the fifteen year span before World War One. But over this period the ratios of Slovaks

Stryj — Rynek — Ringplatz

and Magyars in the total Hungarian emigration became almost equal: 26.8 percent Slovaks, 26.3 percent Magyars, then Croats/Slovenes and Germans with 15 percent each and half a dozen other ethnic groups.

Only about 30 percent of the Hungarian peasantry could live off their plots and feed their families, 15 percent held below-subsistence plots, the rest were day-laborers. In these years, more than two thirds of the migrants came from rural areas and occupations, but in North America nine tenths of the migrants went into mining, iron industry and other industrial production.

But in the 1860s and 1870s composition of the migrants had been different. The »pioneers« were economically secure German-speaking Hungarians, looking for better opportunities, soon to be joined by German-speaking merchants and craftsmen who, despairing of getting a secure income from their work in the old society, sold their small possessions to raise the capital for the trip and a new existence. Miners from northern Hungary were recruited through agents and by oral reports summarizing emigrant letters to the Galician coal- and salt-mining districts from where migration had started earlier. Next came a wave of craftsmen, ruined by the developing manufactory and factory production.

And finally, also connected to the lowering of the cross-Atlantic transportation costs, agrarian daylaborers and smallholding peasants moved. Skilled workers on the other hand were underrepresented since they could find employment in the slowly growing number of local factories. Demand was sufficiently large that Bohemian, Austrian and German skilled workers were attracted to Budapest as well as to industries elsewhere.

The economic division within the Dual Monarchy assigned production of foodstuffs to Hungary, a highly seasonal industry which for unskilled Magyar workers (and those of other ethnic groups) meant chronic unemployment. Of the mobile surplus labor in Hungary, only one fifth was absorbed by local industry from 1900 to 1910 (about 250,000) while another 1,000,000 had to find jobs by migrating out of Hungary, a large part of them overseas.

Emigrants took their belongings in bundles, trunks and chests. This chest found its way back to Europe

The Balkan Peoples

In the southernmost regions of the Austro-Hungarian Empire and on the »Balkan« (the Turkish word for wooded mountains), lived several peoples in ethnically mixed settlement patterns. Some had ancient migratory traditions. They were transhumant herdsmen who undertook annual migration with their livestock into the mountains in summer and down to the coastal pastures in winter. These wanderers had a cultural impact on the linguistic affinities between a number of Balkan languages. Another cultural impact concerns the deepseated distrust of settled populations against passers-by, of the peasants against migrating herdsmen, a distrust that turned the geographical designation »Walachians« into a synonym for wanderers, undesirable strangers, thieves.

Large-scale migration occured in these areas because of the westward expansion of Ottoman rule till the 16th century and the eastward expansion of Habsburg rule after 1683. Populations were displaced, fled with retreating imperial armies, moved into

areas that were being resettled. The eighteenth-century German peasant migrations into the area, and the settlements of soldiers and their families along the Habsburg military border zone created checkered ethnic patterns. The distribution of the Serbs between Austria, Hungary and their own semi-autonomous state and of other peoples over large territories are explained by these imperial power struggles.

In the 19th century, these regions were inhabited from west to east by the South Slav peoples: the Slovenes within Austria, the Croats in a separate administrative unit within Hungary, the Serbs partly in Austria-Hungary, partly in their own territory under Ottoman influence and further to the south and east the Macedonians and Bulgarians. In Transylvania and east of the Hungarian border lived the Romanians. And lastly, we come to the Albanians and Greeks.

In 1815, when the Congress of Vienna had completed its reactionary reordering of Europe, the Ottoman Empire still bordered directly on Austria-Hungary and Russia, with Serbia as a tributary state and a tiny independent Montenegrin state. Greece became independent in 1829. After the Russian-Ottoman War, in 1878 (Congress of Berlin), Serbia, Montenegro and Romania became independent. Bulgaria was a semi-independent state tributary to the Ottoman Empire. Bosnia and the Herzegowina became territories to be administered by the Habsburg Empire which annexed them in 1908. The other south Slavic territories and Albania achieved political independence from the Ottoman Empire before World War One but fell under Habsburg economic influence. Their economic development was dependent on the influx of West European capital. State boundaries did not coincide with ethnic dividing lines and because of mixed settlement patterns in many cases they could not coincide. While the Ottoman Empire, now practically reduced in Europe to a Turkish ethnic state, was considered the »sick man of Europe«, the other three empires, Russia, Austria-Hungary and the German Reich were politically about as sick, all industrialization not withstanding. In 1848/49, the Viennese government had rejected plans for changing the empire into a federation of

ethnically homogenous territories developed by Czech political leaders. The ethnic consciousness of the peoples in the decaying Habsburg imperial structures developed aspirations for separate nation-states. The Habsburg's annexation of Bosnia and the heavy-handed pressures on Serbia led to an Austro-Serbian conflict which the empires used as a pretext for World War One. It became a war of liberaton for most of the smaller peoples.

Migration from these territories began in the 1890s or early 1900s and for most of them remained small. The Slovenes, the Serbs and the Croats were the three south Slavic peoples that sent the most emigrants from the Balkan areas.

The Slovenes, the northernmost of the Yugoslav peoples, lived in the Austrian provinces of Carniola, Gorizia and Carintkia and in the Hungarian district Prekmurje. This area was the »entrance« to the South Slav lands. Thus Slovenia always accomodated commercial thoroughfares, including the Vienna-Triest connection, even though most of the people lived of the land as small peasants (73 percent by 1900). This socio-economic dualism was also an

ethnic dualism: foreigners, especially German-speaking people, made up the upper class, much of the urban population and much of the intelligentsia. The weak Slovene middle class remained subject to foreign economic dominance. The ratio of Slovene to foreign investment capital was 1:10. Emigration from rural Slovenia passed through the port of Triest (Trst), a multi-ethnic city in the border area of Slovene settlement which was the main Adriatic port of the Habsburg Empire.

Croatia consisted of Slavonia, Croatia proper and Dalmatia, the latter long under Italian-Venetian influence. In the Slovene-Croatian-Dalmatian territories first attempts to develop a joint South Slav culture came to the fore in the 1830s and 1840s. The Illyrian movement looked back to Roman traditions and tried to integrate the Venetian and the Dubrovnik past with a mythical folk culture that was probably the creation of an Italian monk inspired by South Slav folk culture. In the later attempts to bring the South Slav peoples together, emigrants played an important role since they could act outside of Austro-Hungarian pressures. In the 19th-century

Croatian society, the percentage of the population living on the land was even higher than in Slovenia. The middle classes consisted of Croatians only on the lower rungs. Many of the landowners, the governmental bureaucracy, the newly rich bourgeoisie, consisted of members of the old nobility, a few entrepreneurs and to a large part of - mainly German-speaking - foreigners. In Zagreb, one fourth of the population was of non-Croatian origin. Politically the »Compromise of 1868« made Croatia dependent on Hungary, the government of which decided among other things on the allocation of all revenues collected in Croatia. The peasants remained outside of the body politic and were mostly illiterate. Agricultural implements remained simple, the wooden plow was being replaced by iron plows on a larger scale only starting in the 1890s. At that time cheap foreign grains were pushing the production of family holdings not only of the world market but even of local markets.

The Croats and the Serbs speak pratically the same language, but the latter had been under a totally different hegemonial culture for centuries. The Byzantine influence explains why much of the Serbian population was orthodox and the language was written in cyrillic letters. The Croats had remained under West Roman influence, were catholic and wrote in Latin characters. Mercantile life in the Serbian areas had been dominated by Greek and to some degree Italian influences, the Ottoman rule had imposed oriental ways of life. However, conversion to Islam occured only among Bosnian people. Since Serbia was first granted an autonomous status and then became independent almost a century before the Croatian and Slovene lands, it had better opportunities to develop a distinctive culture. Independence from the Ottoman Empire meant increasing economic influence of the powerful northern neighbor, Austria. Though Belgrade became the center of the South Slav lands with a population of 40,000 by 1850, a figure Zagreb

Immigration to the U.S. from the Balkan

	Immigration	Remigration		Foreign born	Foreign stock
	1899-1924	1899-1924	in %	1910	1910
Slovenian	537.500	262.500	48.8	123.600	183.400
Croatian				105.700	129.300
Serbian	165.00	148.400	89.9		
Bulgarian				18.300	19.400
Roumanian	148.251	97.861	66.0	42.300	51.100
Greek	500.400	241.900	48.3	118.400	130.400
Abanian	-	-	-	2.300	2.300
Turkish	-	-	-	4.700	5.400

These tables exclude the categories »other«, »unspecified«, »unknown«. The Serbian figures include Montenegrins for the 1899-1924 period, the Croatian figures include Dalmatians, Bosnians and Herzegovinians in the 1899-1924 period. Half of the Turkish immigrants came from the European part of Turkey.

was to reach only in 1890, only just above one percent of the whole of the population of 1.2 million were craftsmen. An attempt to create viable peasant holdings by law in 1873 came to nothing. The size of the land holdings, about three hectares on the average, was too small. These and middle-sized holdings accounted for 96 percent of the peasant-owned land. Only every sixth peasant family owned a plowshare and every fiftyth a cart.

Over the whole of the Serbo-Croatian areas, the peasant economy was changing in one important aspect. The traditional extended family household, the *zadruga*, in which all members cooperated for the economic benefit of the whole kinship unit, were slowly replaced by individual holdings of nuclear families. As a result larger units of land tilled cooperatively were parcelled out among smaller families. Thus family farms were established at a time when elsewhere in the world concentration of landholding was proceeding rapidly and when the double impact of mechanized large-scale farming with seasonal migrant workers in the Americas and Australia and of cheaper transportation facilities overwhelmed family production with imports from distant continents. The cooperative *zadruga* form of living was carried by mi-grant laborers to North America. The common living arrangements in steel and mining towns in some ways resembled the *zadruga* but usually were not based on kinship. This way of life did not simply mean boarding for pay, a pure money relationship, but one with shared work and with accounting at the end of each week.

Summary

In order to place the migration of the East, Central and Southeast European peoples in relation to each other a look at the numbers leaving the main areas is warranted. The total of 415,300 foreign-born migrants from the Balkans listed in the 1910 census compares to 624,300 from the Magyar, Slovak and Czech peoples, to 344,000 from the Russian territories, including Finns, but excluding Jews (Lithuanian, Lettish, Russian, Ruthenian, Finnish), but to 943,800 Poles and 1,051,800 Jews. It is obvious that the areas furthest away from industrialization and penetration of a money economy, the areas east of Poland and the areas southeast of Austria-Hungary sent the fewest migrants. For all of them the mi-gration was not only one between continents but also between widely differing jobs, and depending on how social stratification is designated, perhaps between classes. People from the rural underclass in Europe joined the North American proletariat. From The point of view of their consciousness they may not have belonged to an »international proletariat«, but they belonged to laboring classes between Moscow and San Francisco which had to be internationally mobile to earn a living. Most of them did not go to North America to stay permanently. As temporary immigrants they hoped to earn a sufficient amount of money to be able to return and live a better life in the culture of origin. Many of them did return and the returners often did not go back to the land but joined the landless underclasses »at home« or in the Atlantic world, depending on the point of view.

Serbian country folk, engraving from 1850

References:

Adamic, Louis: Laughing in the Jungle: The Autobiography of an Immigrant in America. 1932, repr. 1969.

Anderson, Barbara A.: International Migration During Modernization in Late Nineteenth-Century Russia. Princeton, N. J., 1980.

Bobinska, Celina; Pilch, Andrzej (eds.): Employment-Seeking Emigrations of Poles Worldwide, XIX and XXth Centuries. Krakau, 1975.

Dubnow, Simon M.: History of the Jews in Russia and Poland. 3 vols., New York, 1975.

Eterovic, Francis H.; Spalatin, Christopher (eds.): Croatia: Land, People, Culture. 2 vols., Toronto, 1970.

Gartner, Lloyd P.: The Jewish Immigrant in England 1870-1914. London, 1960.

Gilbert, Martin: Jewish History Atlas. London, 1969.

Goren, Arthur A.: »Jews«, in: Harvard Encyclopedia of American Ethnic Groups. Cambridge, Mass., 1980, S.571-598.

Govorchin, Gerald G.: Americans from Yugoslavia. Gainesville, Fla., 1961.

Green, Nancy L.: The Pletzl of Paris. Jewish Immigrant Workers in the Belle Epoque. New York, 1986.

Greene, Victor R.: »Poles«, in: Harvard Encyclopedia of American Ethnic Groups. Cambridge, Mass., 1980, S.787-803.

Howe, Irving: World of Our Fathers. New York, 1976.

Kero, Reino: Migration from Finland to North America in the Years between the US Civil War and the First World War. Turku, 1974.

Kubijovic, Valodymyr: Ukraine: A Concise Encyclopedia. 2 vols., Toronto, 1971.

Kuznets, Simon: »Immigration of Russian Jews to the United States: Background and Structure«, in: Perspectives in American History. 10, 1976, S.95-124.

Leslie, R. F.(ed.): The History of Poland since 1868. Cambridge, 1980.

Melville, Ralph: »Zwischen definitiver Emigration und grenzüberschreitender Migration auf Zeit...1861-1914«, in: Studi a Historiae Oeconomica. Bd. 18, 1983, S.79-90.

Obolensky-Ossinsky, Valerianovic: »Emigration from and Immigration into Russia«, in: Ferenczi, I.; Willcox, W. F. (eds.): International Migrations. 2 Bde., New York, 1929-1931, Bd.2, S. 521-580, auf der Basis eines Buches in russischer Sprache, Moskau, 1928.

Prpic, George J.: The South Slavic Immigration in America. Boston, 1978.

Puskas, Julianna: From Hungary to the United States (1880-1914). Budapest, 1982.

Thomas, William I.; Znaniecki, Florian (eds.): The Polish Peasant in Europe and America. 2 vols., Boston, 1918-20, stark gekürzte einbändige Ausgabe, 1984.

Vakar, Nicholas: Belorussia: The Making of a Nation. Cambridge, Mass., 1956.

Mother and children arriving at Ellis Island. Immigrants often wore their Sunday best

Cerca di lavoro - Looking for Work: Southern Europe

Dirk Hoerder

The Mediterranean basin, once the economic center of Europe, had lost its position to the northwestern Atlantic seabord in the 17th century. The emergence of Atlantic trade ousted Italy from competition, the inability of the Iberian governments and ruling classes to develop administrative and commercial structures suited to the demands of the worldwide trade operations permitted the Dutch and British to occupy the first ranks among the world powers of the West. Emigration from these areas was related to the changing position of Italy, Spain and Portugal in the world economy as well as to internal political developments and to demographic factors.

Italy

Migration of Italians during the 19th century was a migration out of a »nation« only in the statistics. Regional and local attachment predominated over national feelings. The powerful and wealthy city-states of the north (14th and 16th centuries) with Venetia dominating the east of the Mediterranean world, Genova the west, had lost their influence and changing small states, especially Savoy (starting in the 17th century), took their place. The division of the Italian peninsula into three sections emerged: the north divided into varying territories under varying princes, in the center the papal territories and in the south a feudal area that was dominated for most of the time by foreign rulers, the Houses of Habsburg of Spain and Austria. The movement for unification, begun after the French revolution with the *Carbonari* (named after the charcoal burners of Calabria), increased in impact under the ideas and leadership of Mazzini (1805 - 1872) and achieved success as the movement »*Il Risorgimento*«, which led to Italian independence in 1861. Dominance of the Piedmontese (Savoy) interests in the new nation

and the maintenance of feudal structures in the south led to a dualism persistent to the present, with the central provinces inserted in between.

During the century from 1876 to 1976 about 26 million men, women, and children left their native villages and towns, »perhaps the most significant social phenomenon« in Italian history, says Italian historian Anna Maria Martellone. Italy's whole population amounted to 29 million in 1881 and increased to 35 million by 1911. In Europe, only industrialized England, Belgium, and the Netherlands had a higher population density. During the main period of emigration from unification to Mussolini's anti-emigration policies 17.7 million left (1870 - 1930). Of these, 70 percent divided between Europe, Africa and South America. Those who could afford the passage to Latin America went there: prospects were better, language problems smaller, cultural adjustment easier. Those with little money went to the United States: tickets were cheaper, industrial jobs offered quick cash income and rail and road construction offered seasonal employment permitting return home for the harvest. Others, often skilled masons, annually followed the traditional routes to France and Germany. Some went to Africa and beginning in the 1880s to the new African colonies, (Eritrea, Abyssinia, and Somaliland starting in 1881/89, Tripolitania starting in 1911 - 12). Italians belonged to the migrants with the highest rates of return. »Birds of passage« they were called, sometimes derisively. They came to the United States in spring and left in fall, or using the inverted seasons of the southern half of the globe, left during the European winter to harvest grain in Argentina for a few months and be back for the tilling of their own land in the northern spring season. Others returned after a few years. To take the example of the United States about five of every ten Italian migrants returned: During the first decade of the 20th century 230,000 Italians left for the U.S. annually on the average, 120,000 returned. During the next decade the relationship was 160,000 to 80,000. Variations in the general pattern depended on economic cycles and harvest conditions. After the general strike in Italy

of fall 1904, its loss, and the killing of workers by the police, 320,000 Italians reached the U.S. while only 77,000 left that year, but three years later when the 1907 depression had wrought havoc in the American economy 240,000 Italians left the U.S. in 1908 while only 131,000 arrived.

In Italy the areas of origin were the industrializing north from which two thirds of the migrants went to European countries during the last quarter of the 19th century (3.4 million). In contrast few migrants came from central Italy, a mere 284,000 during the quarter century. From the south, the Mezzogiorno, Sicily, and Sardinia, 1.5 million left. Before the 1840s only one seventh of them moved to transatlantic destinations. Thereafter the majority crossed the ocean leaving through the ports of Genova and Naples. Triest, another port of emigration, belonged to Habsburg Austria at the time and only few Italians left from there. The differences between the sections concerning out-migration can be explained by the state of agriculture. Productivity was inferior to that of other European countries. Few mineral deposits could be exploited and exported while capital and technological innovations had to be imported. Before the 1880s agriculture was backward throughout much of the north, sharecropping systems survived, particularly in Venetia. In Lombardy and Piedmont capitalist conversion of farming had begun, especially in rice growing and cereal crops. Mulberry growing provided the basis for the silk-industry in Lombardy. In central Italy (Tuscany, Umbria, La Marche, Lazio) diversified farming prevailed under a sharecropping system supplemented in the mountainous regions by sheep-breeding. Temporarily employed daylaborers and shepherds migrated through these areas. In the Mezzogiorno much of the land, the *latifundia*, was owned by absentee landlords. The small peasant holdings yielded so little that the owners were compelled to work on the *latifundias* or lease additional plots

Section of an Italian emigrant ship on the route Europe - South America

"DUILIO" "GIULIO CESARE"
I DUE MAGGIORI VAPORI
in servizio tra
L'EUROPA E IL SUD-AMERICA

SEZIONE   TRASVERSALE

27.000. Tonnellate di dislocamento
194. Metri di lunghezza · ·
23. Metri di larghezza · · ·
29. Metri di altezza · · · · ·
20. Nodi all'ora di velocità ·

67

View of Naples

from the estate managers. For many of the impoverished peasants brigandage or emigration were the only alternatives.

By the 1880s production on the scale of American cereal agriculture and the faster and cheaper means of transportation led to an invasion of American wheat on European markets and in consequence to an agricultural crisis. The earlier profits from agriculture in Italy had neither been used to modernize agriculture nor to invest in other sectors of the economy. Rather they had financed, through taxation or government bonds, the administrative organization of the country, unified since 1861, as well as the army and navy and railroad construction. Modernization of agriculture came slowly starting in the late 1880s in productive areas of the North with the help of protective tariffs.

Since little industrialization had taken place, ships, locomotives, and railroad tracks had to be imported up to the end of the 1870s. While the textile industries - cotton, wool and silk - could draw on long historic traditions the semi-finished products were mainly processed in foreign factories. An industrial take-off occured only after

the world-wide economic crisis of the early 1890s ended in 1896 and most of it remained concentrated in the Milan, Turin, Genova triangle. At any rate it could not absorb the large amount of agrarian surplus labor. The cheap imported goods accentuated the need for changes. In view of falling grain prices employment opportunities and wages of the landless laborers decreased, in view of declining cloth prices home production of cloth was abandoned by women. As a result a cash crisis forced tens of thousands of families to look for income elsewhere. The emigrants remittances were an important economic factor. They permitted Italy to maintain a favorable balance of trade during the 1907/08 and the 1913 economic crises, the latter compounded by the war in Libya. While some of the remittances went to immediate aid for relatives, much of it was deposited in banks and used to finance the industrialization of the north.

Agricultural hands and unskilled laborers made up the vast majority of the Italian migrants (between 74 and 90 percent of the migrants to the United States), less then one percent were professionals and the others ranged from semi-skilled to skilled workers and from artisans to technicians. Many migrants were illiterate. At the time of unification illiteracy in the south remained high, reaching 75 percent). Italian emigration originally was mainly male. During

the last three decades of the 19th century the percentage of female migrants to the United States climbed from 15 to 19 to 21 percent of the total. Women followed or migrated on their own during the 1920s and 30s with a 28 and 40 percent share respectiveley.

Starting in the 1890s industrial workers and political activists left, too. Sicilian radicals and anarchists from all over Italy went to where they could adhere to their notions of a more just society. Like newcomers of all other groups, they realized that the new worlds were far from ideal: They continued their struggles for improved conditions there.

If we look beyond the statistics few migrants came from the urban poor. They had nothing to sell and thus could not raise the cost of the passage. Landless laborers who had at least a hut to sell left, while the day-laborers of the *latifundia*, could not move either because of their extreme poverty. With the exodus of the agrarian population some of the local artisans and barbers had to follow. The Italian historian Martellone found out:

>If a poor farmer lost his land, whether because of a bad crop, accumulated debts, the oppressive capacity of larger landowners or of the greedy and tyrannical petty bourgeoisie who busied themselves in the extortion of money from the peasants through usury and legal harassment, he was fated to spend his life as a wretched daylaborer. It was better to sell when one still owned something, and to leave.

As an old Calabrian peasant put it:

>Here we have a god who, when it rains, sweeps us to the sea, and when it doesn't rain, dries up the world. You can't live here. The Lord doesn't send us any luck. I planted a bushel of seeds and I harvested half of it. I am old and it takes me four hours to get to a piece of land I work on. It is the bitter mountains here, it isn't the flat country. I think it is better to look for charity (and work) all over the world than to stay here«.

It would be »dishonest« to one's family to remain in Italy.

The large-scale emigration led to an increase in the wages of field laborers because a shortage of hands emerged. In the

Europeans lived in the colonies, at the beginning of the 20th century, just above 3,000 white officers with 7,000 native-born soldiers controlled the empire. The largest concentration of European in-migrants was in Angola: a mere 12,000. Starting in the 1830s, the government made repeated attempts to encourage migration to the colonies. But the distribution of land to orphans in Mozambique in 1838, the creation of a fund to promote overseas migration in 1852, a colonization scheme for southern Angola in 1884 - all came to nothing.

Migrants from Portugal and from Spain during the 19th century left for the Americas, with the former colonies in South and Central America receiving the main share. Here societies had been created by the conquerers and earlier migrants that promised life in a cultural and lingusistic environment where ways of living from the old country could be integrated into the new. Brasil's Portuguese-speaking community and the Spanish-speaking communities of the rest of South and Central America - a division going back to the papal division of the world - continued to attract in-migrants. Portugal's population increased from three million during the first two decades of the 19th century to more than five million in 1900 but stagnated at six million from 1911 to 1920 because of emigration. Social division in this society was heavily lopsided: an upper class of about one percent of the population, a bourgeosie accounting for 15 percent and the rest of the population lower class. Three quarters of the population lived in the countryside. Of the important towns, Lisboa and industrializing Porto housed 629,000 in 1911 - almost one half of the whole urban population. The university town of Coimbra remained small but was a vital intellectual center. While there was no shortage of employment, there was a decided shortage of land and grain harvested. The »bread question«, as the contemporary political debates about wheat imports were

south, land prices rose as money sent from America and returnees savings were used to increase the landholdings or build larger houses. However, little or no agricultural innovation was introduced by returnees. On the other side the ties to a region and a village led to a mentality among the migrants that prevented a formation of one »Italian« ethnic group, but rather to clustering according to region (and dialect) of origin and to a continous exchange of information with friends and kin in the old world (*campanilismo*). In the old world villages, the world was annexed. Villagers talked about their friends and kin, as if they lived around the corner - even when they were in Chicago or Buenos Aires.

Spain and Portugal

On the Iberian peninsula the expansion overseas and with it migration had begun in the 15th century. In 1494, the two crowns under the auspices of the pope divided the world among themselves. The exploreres who mapped the world for them were - interestingly - mostly highly professional labor migrants: Italian seafarers who found no outlet for their talents in the declining Mediterranean power. Even though Spanish and Portuguese tradeposts and colonies soon covered considerable parts of the world known to Europeans, out-migration was limited. In the case of the Portuguese, colonial migration remained small as concerns Africa and Asia. By the beginning of the 19th century, about 10,000 called, was one of the decisive reasons for people to leave. In agriculture and industry, large numbers of women and children were employed and wages were abominably low. While in the southern region of Alentejo new agrarian laws improved settlement conditions, in the North and Northwest population density was another major push factor.

Emigration from Portugal achieved sizable proportion with the ending of the slave trade to Brazil and the end to slavery there (1888) led to a demand for cheap European workers. In the 1880s, less than 50,000 people had left, from 1870 to 1900 more than half a million left, from 1900 - 1911: 300,000, from 1911 - 1920: 450,000, and in the decade after World War One another 270,000. While originally most went to South America, the North American share reached 15 percent in the early 20th century. While all occupational groups were represented among the migrants, illiterate peasants and rural laborers predominated. Even with the end of the monarchy in 1910 and during the short life of the Republic (1910 - 1929), the literacy rate improved only slowly. In 1911, it stood at 60.8 percent for males, 77.4 percent for women over seven years of age. Most of the migrants came from the densely populated Minho and Douro regions in the North. Of the total migrants only about five percent returned, but remigration from the United States stood at 32 percent in the period from 1899 - 1924.

As in other countries with a sizable out-migration, the home economy relied to a considerable degree on emigrant remittances and these came only from migrants in the Americas. The improvement of land and creation of even the basics of infrastructures prevented remittances from Portugal's small number of colonial migrants. Thus the failure of the attempts to direct migration to the colonies may have caused a loss in imperial prestige but the sensible decisions of the migrants to go to the developing economies of Brazil and the United States turned out to generate economic benefits on a national scale. It also helped to increase wages in Portugal, since labor was scarce and since the labor movement was weak. During the two years

Portuguese sporting club in Toronto

of political change, 1919/1911, about 250 strikes were counted, but in the years thereafter, they dropped to less than 20 per year. The first major national union was formed in 1912. Of the total industrial labor force of 130,000 in 1917, 35 percent were women and 15 percent minors, another indication of the low-wage scales and of the need to combine several incomes to feed a family.

Throughout much of the 19th century, a considerable part of the migration had come from the islands: Madeira, the Azores and Cap Verdes. Population pressures had pushed people across the Atlantic almost from the period »discovery«. The North American whaling fleets were manned by men from the Portuguese islands and later they moved to California and Hawaii. By the turn of the 20th century, inhabitants from the mainland also fled the rigid social structures and the stagnating economy. Emigration from Spain was also related to its early colonial expansion but achieved

larger proportions than that of Portugal because the western half of the world which the Treaty of Tordesillas had left with Spain could not be exploited commercially as the Portuguese possessions in the eastern half could (e.g. trade in spices). Mining required overseers, skilled miners and transportation networks. Agricultural production on the *encomiendas*, large estates with bound labor, followed upon the in-migration of a Spanish propertied, administrative and managerial upper class. A colonial Spanish-South American society emerged. Two and a half centuries later, this population used the Napoleonic Wars to liberate itself (with the exception of Cuba and Puerto Rico) from dependence on Madrid. Spain's relative economic position within the European system had declined and during the 19th century, several civil wars were fought between liberals and conservatives. The first attempt to install republican governmental structures in 1873, after the deposition of Queen Isabelle (1868) came to naught and a period of restoration set in (1875 - 1899). Economic growth was marked from 1877 to 1891, but the 1890s were a period of depression. Another steady expansion followed from about 1900 to 1914. The country remained overwhelmingly agricultural, mining and textiles were the main industrial economic sectors. But no strong competitive economy developed. Catalan textile production was intended for the tariff-protected internal market and for Cuba. Iron ore and copper were exported in large quantities. Among agricultural products wine and olive oil captured part of the world market. On the other hand, grain production remained low and could not compete with foreign imports. More and more marginal land was taken out of production. Urban industrial and rural grain producing interests combined to defeat liberal economic attitudes and enacted a high protective tariff in 1891. French, Belgian and especially British capital was invested in Spain starting in 1877. The Spanish bourgeoisie and *grandes* preferred consumption to investment.

The population increased from 16.6 million in 1877 to 18.6 million in 1900, but emigration increased at the same time.

Poster from an Italian transatlantic shipping company

About one million persons left between 1882 and 1914, mainly from the Canary islands and the northern coastal regions. The main areas of destination were Argentina and Brazil. Migration to the United States remained below 1000 per year during the decades from 1850 to 1900 with a total of 35,000. The peak of emigration came during the next 30 years: 124,500 migrants came, almost 70,000 of them during the years immediately before World War One. Thereafter, emigration to North America remained low, with the exception of the 1960s.

The agrarian masses in Andalusia and Estremadura had distributed some land of the large landowners during the uprising of 1874, but no agricultural changes followed. The poverty in the areas of *latifundia* continued. The position of the peasants further deteriorated because those lands held in common were opened by law for sale and reluctant municipalities were forced by ever stricter control measures to execute the legal provisions. Large landowners and local political henchmen of the conservative regime (*caciques*) profited by buying land at bargain prices. Finally, the small leaseholds protected by customary law were endangered by a new code of 1889. As a result, peasants and landless laborers revolted through numerous individual acts of resistance and by organizing.

The police reported to have found evidence of a secret Andalusian rural organization called »Black Hand« with tens of thousands of members and branches in the areas around Barcelona, in Madrid and even in Lisboa. Severe repression followed, even though substantial proof of the existence of this organization was never adduced. Militant, secret, direct action as well as rural strike movements continued, often motivated by sheer hunger, as in 1883, 1890, 1898, 1905. To take one example, a large strike of rural workers began in 1902, but once again could not improve general

living and working conditions. The landowners fuelled the movement by declaring that they would burn crops and harvests rather than paying living wages for harvesting them. Landowners with government support sometimes chased off whole villages of leaseholders. The government

argued in 1907 that there was no reason to solve rural problems in Spain when Ireland faced the same problems and the English Government did not act. It acknowledged the magnitude of the problem by adopting a program to »colonize and resettle« Spanish agrarian regions to help poor people and to

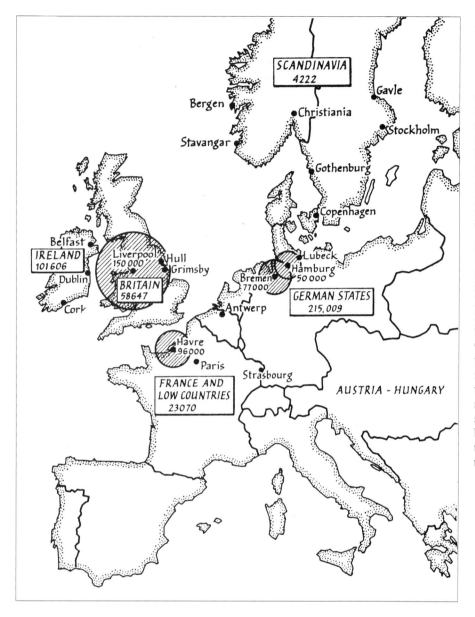

SCANDINAVIA
4222

IRELAND
101 606

BRITAIN
58647

GERMAN STATES
215,009

FRANCE AND
LOW COUNTRIES
23070

AUSTRIA - HUNGARY

of high unemployment after the loss of the Cuban market), a general strike in Barcelona in 1909 (after mobilization for military intervention in the Spanish colony Morocco), all ended in street fighting in which workers were able to inflict heavy damages but in the final outcome were put down by police and army. And once again a period of repression followed.

The modernizing regions in which a bourgeoisie began to develop were the Catalan and Basques provinces, both of which were areas with a sentiment of separatism from the nation. Accordingly, their elite had only limited influence on the political decisions in the capital. Furthermore, the Catalan textile industry was hard hit by the loss of the Cuban market. While Spanish banks began to play a more important role, capital was missing for extension of railroad construction, for the conversion of shipping from sail to steam and for improvements by small landholders in rural areas. Thus 1912 became the year of mass exodus with more than 134,000 persons leaving. From 1912 to 1916 more than half a million emigrated.

reduce emigration. The means allocated, however, were exhausted after 447 homesteads had been established.

Urban workers - sometimes acting jointly with rural laborers - had founded the anarchist Federation of Workers of the Spanish Region in 1868 only to see it dissolved by the government in 1870. They reorganized it in 1881. The Spanish Socialist Workers Party emerged in 1879, and the trade unions combined into a federation in 1888. Finally, the National Confederation of Labor was founded in 1910. While even a cabinet member had admitted in the 1890s that 15 million of the 17 million Spaniards belonged to the peasant and urban lower classes, their organizing efforts brought about an increasing number of strikes but no noticeable progess. The entrenched concentrated wealth and its use of the army prevented any constructive solution to the »social problem«. Strikes of the 1880s and 1890s, an uprising in the Catalan capital Barcelona in March 1902, a series of major strikes in 1903/04 (a period

References:

Baily, Samuel L., »The Adjustment of Italian Immigrants in Buenos Aires and New York, 1870-1914«, in: American Historical Review 88, 1983, Pp.281-305.

Brezza, Bruno (ed.), Gli Italiani fuori d'Italia, Milano, 1983.

Bruguera, F. G., Histoire Contemporaine d'Espagne 1789-1950, Paris, 1953.

Cinel, Dino, »The Seasonal Emigrations of the Italians in the Nineteenth Century: From Internal to International Destinations«, in: Journal of Ethnic Studies 10/1, 1982/83, Pp.43-68.

Clark, Martin, Modern Italy 1871-1982, London, 1984.

Conde, Alexander de, Half Bitter, Half Sweet: An excursion into Italian-American History, New York, 1971.

Martellone, Anna Maria, »Italian Mass Emigration to the United States 1876-1930: A Historical Survey«, in: Perspectives in American History, n.s. 1, 1984, Pp.378-423.

Oliverra Marques, A. H. de, History of Portugal, 2 vols., New York, 1976.

Payne, Stanley G., A History of Spain and Portugal, 2 vols., Madison, 1973.

Rosoli, Gianfausto (ed.), Un secolo di emigrazione italiana: 1876-1976, Rome, CSER, 1978.

Sari, Ercole, L'emigrazione italiana dall 'Unita' alla seconda guerra mondiale, Bologna, il Malnio, 1979.

Tomasi, S. M.; Engel, M. H. (eds.), The Italian Experience in the United States, Staten Island, N.Y., 1970.

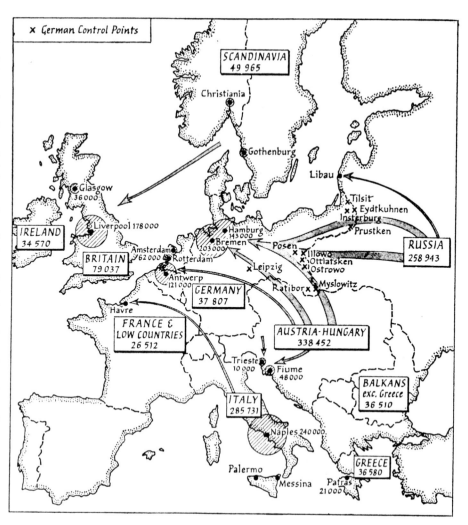

European emigration to the U.S., 1907

Poster from North German Lloyd, Bremen 1928

The Journey

From the Old World to the New

Agnes Bretting

The Emigration Policies of the German States (1815-1915)

For centuries, the German-speaking countries had very restrictive emigration policies. Prohibitions were the prominent feature, with the sole exception of emigration for religious reasons after the end of the Thirty Years' War in 1648. And people who wished to exercise that right had to pay a special tax for the privilege. Throughout the seventeenth and eighteenth centuries, people who wanted to emigrate for any other reason - political, economic, or personal - had to get special permission, and this was a long, complicated, and often costly procedure. In the nineteenth century the right to emigrate gradually became accepted, following the French constitution of 1789, but for a long time limitations and obstacles remained common. Only in the second half of the century, facing the fact that mass emigration could not be prevented by prohibitions, did governments pass laws to protect the emigrants.

The princes, counts, and archbishops who ruled the small German states in the seventeenth and eighteenth centuries, like the leading political thinkers of the time, saw emigration as disloyal (in Absolutist terms) but also as a loss of capital (in Mercantilist terms) and of military strength (in terms of *Realpolitik*). Despite this governmental attitude, hundreds of thousands in the seventeenth and eighteenth centuries, primarily from the south German states, were driven to emigrate by religious persecution; wars followed by pillage, plunder, and famine; economic instability; and political unrest. Peasants, agricultural workers, and craftsmen tried to escape imminent impoverishment, due to overpopulation and the ravages of war, by moving to other German states, or they were lured by the seductive accounts of the colonial recruiters and went to other European countries, to the Netherlands, Spain, Russia, France, Hungary, or Great Britain. For these Germans emigration was a realistic alternative to unbearable conditions at home.

Starting in 1683, North America began to gain in importance as a destination. In this year a group of religious migrants (13 Mennonite families from Krefeld) responded to a call for settlers from William Penn and founded the town of Germantown near Philadelphia. Their successful settlement and the encouraging reports of other groups that followed them stimulated further emigration to North America, so that soon there was a small but steady flow of emigrants in this direction. Legal prohibitions of emigration apparently had only little effect, and the authorities seldom asked about the possible social and economic causes of this migration. Instead, it was the recruiters and agents, the »sellers of souls« and »newlanders«, whom they blamed for enticing their gullible subjects to leave. The rulers passed both specific laws prohibiting recruitment (sometimes punishable by death), and laws punishing not only the emigrants but all those who aided them in their undertaking. In the kingdom of Württemberg, for example, there were no fewer than 18 laws against emigration to North America issued between 1709 and 1815; in the Palatinate there were ten between 1724 and 1779. But not even the imperial edict of Kaiser Joseph II (July 7, 1768) severely punishing any emigration to foreign lands, could stop the exodus.

The very number of laws and edicts barring subjects from leaving shows that the flow of emigration continued. As far as the actual enforcement of the laws was concerned, most rulers followed a laissez-faire approach, at least as long as the number of emigrants remained small. Most periods of high emigration before 1800 were also of short duration. In »normal« times, the emigration policy was driven by financial considerations: the poor were always allowed to leave, and applicants were often granted

Newspaper advertisement for transatlantic voyages departing twice a month from Bremen to North America

Regelmässige Schifffahrt
zwischen
BREMEN und NORDAMERIKA.

Wir expediren fortwährend am 1. und 15. jeden Monats große, gekupferte, dreimastige Schiffe **erster Klasse** nach **Newyork** und **Baltimore**, vom 15. August anfangend, auch nach **Neworleans** und den texanischen Häfen **Galveston** und **Indianola**. Auswanderer belieben sich zum Abschluß bündiger Contrafte an unsere Herren Agenten oder an uns direkt zu wenden. Wir besorgen gleichzeitig Speditionen und Affecuranzen und stellen Wechsel auf alle Häfen der Vereinigten Staaten aus.
Carl Pokrantz & Co.
Comptoir: Langenstraße Nr. 116.
Bremen, Juli 1852.

Höchst billige und schnelle Reisegelegenheit für Einwanderer von
Baltimore nach
Cumberland, Pittsburg, Wheeling, Cincinnati, Louisville und **St. Louis.**
Der Unterzeichnete hat mit der Baltimore- und Ohio-Eisenbahn und der Pittsburger Transportations-Linie eine Anordnung getroffen, wonach Passagiere täglich nach den obigen Plätzen befördert werden können.
Die mit dieser Linie reisenden Einwanderer kommen durchaus nicht auf den Canal. Wegen Passage melde man sich im Comptoir bei
Baltimore, 1. Mai. **Aug. C. Teitman,**
127 Thames-Str.

Da der Unfug der geheimen Werbung fähiger Handwerker und Landleute, zur Bevölkerung entfernter Colonien, und zum Anbau wüster Länder, jetzt mehr als jemals, wieder einzureissen anfängt, und viele Ununterrichtete, im Taumel grosser Erwartung, sich verleiten lassen, als Colonisten, ein vermeintliches Glük in öden Gegenden aufzusuchen; ohne zu bedenken, daß bei dem Zwek und bei den Bedingungen ihrer Anwerbung und Einschiffung, nur eine eben so drückende, als langwierige Dienstbarkeit ihrer daselbst erwarten kann; und wahrscheinlich Mangel und Elend ihr Loos seyn muß; so sieht sich E. H. Rath genöthigt, unter Beziehung auf die, gegen dergleichen verführerische, und in so vieler Rücksicht schädliche Colonisten-Werbung ergangenen Reichs- und älteren hiesigen Verordnungen, allen Bürgern und Einwonern dieser Stadt und deren Gebiets; wie auch allen unter der Stadt Hoheit und Gerichtszwang stehenden Schiffern, und sonstigen Fremden, nachdrücklichst zu verbieten:

weder heimlich noch öffentlich unter irgend einem Vorwand, für auswärtige Colonien zu werben, und dabei mit zu würken; oder zur Werbung und Einschiffung der Angeworbenen auf irgend eine Art behülflich zu seyn,

mit der ernstlichen Warnung, daß im Betretungs-Fall, Jedermann, ohne Unterschied, mit der, in den gedachten Reichs- und älteren hiesigen Verordnungen vestgesezten Strafe, unab-bittlich werde belegt werden.

Actum & decretum in Senatu Hamb. publicatumque d. 7 Maii 1792.

Decree forbidding the recruiting of settlers, Hamburg 1792

official permission to emigrate in order to reduce the pressure of excess population. Russia, Austria, and the British colonies in North America were thus able to gain many settlers through officially sanctioned recruitment campaigns in southwestern Germany.

In the nineteenth century, influenced by the liberal ideals expressed in the French constitution, some German states began to recognize a right to free emigration, either in a constitutional form or in specific legislation. Baden was the first in 1803, followed by Württemberg in 1815, Prussia in 1818, Hesse in 1821, Saxony in 1831, and finally by Bavaria in 1868. The constitution of the German Confederation in 1815 had established the right of free migration between the member states, but the restrictive measures adopted to enforce these incipiently liberal policies meant that many citizens still had to leave illegally. The requirements for an exit visa included time-consuming inquiries into personal matters, ob-

ligatory consultations with officials who were opposed to emigration, and payment of a 10-percent tax on all property taken along; young men also had to prove that they had fulfilled their military-service obligations, and all had to establish that they owed no debts. If the emigrant would leave behind a family without financial support, or if the husband did not give permission for his wife to leave, the exit visa was not issued; a married woman could only obtain an emigration permit if she could prove she was joining her husband. And when the visa was finally granted, the applicant lost all the rights of citizenship; the government regarded the emigrant as stateless, as *persona non grata*, and feared it would have to pay for the support of family members left behind. The aim of the policies was thus to protect the government, not the emigrants. This was the situation in southwestern Germany when the first really large wave of emigration to North America suddenly took shape in the second decade of the

nineteenth century. Acute famine as a result of two successive catastrophically failed harvests forced tens of thousands to emigrate, and some regions were faced with almost total depopulation. Hundreds of emigrants who had made their way to Amsterdam were unable to board ship immediately and soon became destitute, burdening an unprepared Dutch welfare system; many tried to beg money to pay their way back home. It became clear that not prohibitions, but rather legislative and administrative measures to monitor, organize, and regulate emigration were desperately needed. The emigration policy of the German states became more standardized, except for minor details, as the governments reacted to this new situation, but a characteristic negative attitude toward emigration remained. The only exceptions were the city-states of Bremen and Hamburg, port cities where the financial opportunities opened up by the new phenomenon of mass migration were quickly recognized.

In all of the other states, the administrative bodies tried to solve the new problems posed by mass migration by renewing, reworking, or intensifying the existing regulations. At least now the emigration agents were no longer viewed as deceivers of the masses but rather appreciated as skilled providers of needed organizational services. The profession of emigration agent was recognized, and agents were licensed; they were kept under official observation and required to keep careful records and to submit contracts and recruitment brochures for approval. Still, the granting of an agent's license was at the discretion of the government and not a legal right. The authorities still hoped to control the number of emigrants by limiting the number of licensed agents.

Of great significance was the new requirement that agents assume responsibility for the welfare of the emigrants before boarding ship: agents had to deposit a specific sum with the government to guarantee this. The effect of the laws governing emigration agents was that, by about 1840, emigrants could obtain relatively reliable information about prices and travel routes, offers of farm land, or the situation in the U.S. labor market. In this way they were able to plan their trip in advance and for the most part protect themselves from fraud. The laws regulating the emigration agents, enacted to protect the government financially from the social consequences of unplanned emigration, in the end benefitted the migrants as well.

The beginnings of organization in the emigration movement and the first protective measures for emigrants were the result of public pressure. In the 1830s and 1840s, the growing nationalistic movement in Germany not only worked for a united German nation but also favored the creation of German colonies abroad, to which the flow of emigrants could eventually be diverted. Why, it was demanded, should thousands of Germans endure the great personal hardships of emigration and let other countries profit from their hard work, when it was possible to help the emigrants and strengthen the German economy at the same time? Philanthropic, nationalistic, and economic motives overlapped in this kind of argument. Although the idea of governmental-sponsored colonization had prominent supporters, the authorities still preferred to stifle all encouragements to emigration - which included, in their view, any attempts at active control. At any rate, the migrants themselves preferred to select their own destinations, mainly the U.S. at this time.

In times of economic crisis it sometimes happened that governments, again fearing the social unrest that might arise from poverty and need, temporarily reversed their policy and promoted emigration. In the 1840s and 1850s, for example, several states in southwestern Germany used public funds to subsidize the emigration of impoverished subjects; other »undesirables« such as criminals and political activists were offered financial encouragements to emigrate. Many of these programs were poorly planned and ended in disaster for the participants; a notable example was the so-called *Großzimmern Affair* of 1846, when 647 impoverished residents of the parish of Großzimmern, subjects of the Archduke of Hesse-Darmstadt, emigrated to the U.S. at government expense. They were transported in the cheapest way possible, and above all they received no money to help them get started in the New World. Almost all of them ended up in the city poor house in New York soon after their arrival. This

Main building of North German Lloyd in Bremen. The building was torn down in the 1950s

case aroused great indignation in the U.S. press and led to the passage of a stricter immigration control law. The law regulating transatlantic passage, passed in 1847, marked the beginning of a long-term trend toward more restrictive U.S. immigration legislation.

Many political leaders believed that emigration could be a safety valve in societies where overpopulation was leading to increased social tensions. Others regarded the rapidly increasing emigration of the 1840s as a national loss, but one which could not really be prevented. Representatives of both views saw rational solutions for this problem in state control of emigration and support of the emigrants, and in the establishment of German colonies or homogeneous German settlements. The latter concentrations of German immigrants, it was argued, could well be located in the U.S. All over Germany, organizations set up by private individuals promoted the purchase of large tracts of land in the American west, which would then be sold to German settlers. The development of the German shipping lines, the improvement of German harbors, and the subsidization of poorer emigrants were all seen as part of this program of controlled national emigration, as were the construction and financial support of German churches and schools in the U.S., which would preserve and strengthen patriotic feelings among Germans living abroad.

The cooperative efforts of the German emigration groups and German associations in the U.S. provided many benefits for the migrants, but on the legislative level they could not even bring about agreement among the German states on the emigration issue. Hopes for a new national law establishing a liberal emigration policy were shattered when the revolution of 1848-1849 collapsed, and emigration policy remained under the jurisdiction of the individual states. When the North German Confederation was formed in 1866, the

Emigrants' joys

Emigrants' sorrows

value of an emigration law for the nation was recognized in principle, but again very little was done about it. In 1867 the need for an official grant of permission to emigrate was finally abolished, and only proof of military service was required after 1870; this situation was not changed by the establishment of the German Empire in 1871. When the national emigration act was finally passed in 1897, superseding the laws of the individual states, it did provide clear regulations regarding the conditions of transportation, food, and shelter for the emigrants. Each emigration agent now had to deposit the prescribed security payments with the Imperial Commissioner for Emigration, and his license still strictly limited his range of options with respect to ports of embarkation and countries of destination. This provision can again be seen as an attempt at governmental regulation of emigration, this time in the context of an imperialistic policy of expansion. Since, however, most German emigrants at the turn of the century had firm plans as to their destination - many traveled with prepaid tickets sent by relatives or friends who had emigrated previously - this policy was doomed to failure. The emigration advisory office set up in 1919 by the government of the

Weimar Republic had a similar lack of success in influencing the direction of emigration movement. The emigration act of 1897 remained in force until 1975; on March 26 of that year the Federal Republic of Germany passed a new law establishing the principle of freedom of travel for all citizens and rejecting any restrictions of this right.

Travel Routes and Embarkation Ports in Europe

Anyone who had decided to emigrate, with or without official permission, was faced with a number of practical problems; one of these was how to organize the actual journey. By the second half of the nineteenth century a complex network of railroad lines covered the European continent, but before that time the only available transportation was by river boat, coach, or on one's own two feet. A long-distance trip was often exhausting and fraught with difficulties. Before 1800 there were only a few roads that could be used by coaches, and therefore most of the freight traffic used waterways.

Most of the emigrants could not afford the fare for the mail coaches; they had to travel

on foot, get their own wagon, or ask a coachman or teamster to take them along. In any case, travel was slow, and the trip took a long time. There were many borders to cross and customs fees to pay - in the eighteenth century, for example, there were no fewer than 29 duties to be paid between the city of Mainz and the port of Rotterdam; from Strasbourg to the Dutch border or on the Weser river above Bremen the number was 32. If the emigrants traveled on a freight barge, there would be additional stops to transfer the baggage to another ship, since many towns enforced their *Stapelrecht* (a medieval privilege which required goods being transported through a town to be unloaded and offered for sale for a certain time) or tried to increase their transit fees by forcing the shippers to take the longest possible route.

The emigrants' arrival at the port did not, however, mean the end of their travel expenses. Before about 1840 there was no regularly scheduled transatlantic ship traffic, and thus the emigrants often had to wait for days or weeks in the port city. Many emigrants had underestimated the costs for food and lodging on the trip and were already in poor financial condition by the time they arrived in the port city. Especially during periods of heavy migration, when the numbers of emigrants surpassed the carrying capacity of the ships, the waiting period in the port could lead to total impoverishment and the end of the journey for many would-be emigrants. This is clearly seen in the years 1816 and 1817, when war and famine in three south German states (the Palatinate, Baden, and Württemberg) triggered a sudden mass emigration. Thousands of Germans succeeded in reaching the harbors of Amsterdam and Rotterdam, but the shipowners there were taken by surprise and unable to accommodate the large numbers of passengers. Many people were literally left on the docks; their money soon ran out, and they filled the hospitals and poorhouses of the cities, went begging in the streets, or tried to find some way to return home. For the Dutch government, the only way out of this situation was to close the borders to impoverished emigrants and expel any foreigners who had no means of support.

The easiest way to get to a port remained the river boat, and so the emigration routes of the early period followed the large rivers in most cases. The settlement of parts of Russia by German farmers, on the invitation of Catherine the Great, would not have been feasible without the Danube as an ideal travel route for potential emigrants from Baden. The Rhine, with its highly developed boat traffic and its connections to the emigration centers in southern and southwestern Germany, was the natural route to the harbors of Antwerp, Rotterdam, and Amsterdam. The only competition faced by the harbors at the mouth of the Rhine in the eighteenth and early nineteenth centuries was from Le Havre, which emigrants from southern Germany, Switzerland, or Alsace-Lorraine could reach easily by freight wagon or on foot. At this time the numbers of emigrants embarking from the German ports of Hamburg and Bremen were still very small.

Before 1783, the British *Navigation Act* forced all ships coming from or going to America to visit an English port; London, Bristol, and Liverpool thus became the most important ports of embarkation for European transatlantic emigrants. Liverpool, founded in 1207, experienced a peak

in harbor activity during the eighteenth century. The prosperity of the city was based on privateering and the so-called triangular trade: exchanging cheap goods, weapons, and rum for slaves in Africa; selling the slaves in America; carrying tobacco, sugar, cotton, and other raw materials back to England; and exporting finished goods from England to the colonies, Europe, and the rest of the world. The strong trade links between Liverpool and

Hamburg port of emigration, second largest in Germany

North America made that port the preferred European destination of the American transatlantic shipping lines that developed in the nineteenth century; London and Bristol were gradually eliminated as competitors. The foundation of the government-subsidized *Cunard Steamer Company* in 1840 and the establishment of the *Mersey Dock Board* in 1857, to coordinate harbor improvements on both banks of the river (Liverpool-Birkenhead) eventually made Liverpool one of the largest ports in the world, and this position was maintained until World War I. The transport of emi-

grants was a source of profits for the Liverpool shipping companies, but never the most important one. Until the end of the 1860s, about 20,000 Irish emigrants left via Liverpool every year, and Liverpool was the embarkation point for about 4.75 million of the 5.5 million emigrants who left Great Britain during the period 1860-1900. Only after the *Navigation Act* was revoked in 1783 did the English harbors have any significant competition from the continental ports. Antwerp had played an important part in transatlantic emigration from the continent since the sixteenth century, and became a serious competitor for Liverpool, despite interruptions in its economic development due to wars (as when Antwerp became part of Belgium in 1839).

Amsterdam and Rotterdam profited directly from Antwerp's political difficulties. Rotterdam was especially well suited as a transatlantic emigration port, lying close to the Atlantic and connected via the Rhine with an extensive hinterland. Amsterdam, on the other hand, had been well known as a trading port for a long time. To be sure, it lacked a deep-water harbor, making necessary the construction of a costly system of locks. The transportation of emigrants still played a significant role in the city's trade in the eighteenth and early nineteenth centuries, but in the long

Emigrants in Bremerhaven waiting for departure, ca. 1866

run Amsterdam lost its importance as an embarkation point.

On the basis of their existing trade relations with North America, three other continental ports were able to develop successful emigration industries despite poor land-transport connections: Le Havre, Bremen, and Hamburg. The improvements in transportation during the nineteenth century meant that an emigrant planning his journey had access to several embarkation ports and could take other factors into consideration in making the choice: Did the ships sail directly to America? How often did they sail? How much did a passage cost, and what kind of service was provided?

The port of Le Havre, close to the Atlantic and with deep water open year round, became an important embarkation point because travelers had few customs stations to pass on the way there and because there were several transatlantic departures per week, even relatively early on.

When failed harvests in northern Germany caused a sudden surge in emigration during the 1830s, many of those leaving embarked

from Bremen. Amsterdam was limiting the development of the emigrant transportation trade at this time, and Hamburg even forbade it. Thus Bremen got a chance it would not otherwise have had, considering that it lagged behind Amsterdam, Hamburg, and Antwerp in the competition for Atlantic trade. The Weser did not provide particularly good access to the city, and the hinterland was industrially undeveloped. The harbor had been silting up since the sixteenth century, so that ships had to put in at smaller harbors downstream. But now the shipowners seized the opportunity and began, with support from the city Senate, to develop the emigration trade as a real industry. The seaport of Bremerhaven was established at the mouth of the Weser in 1827, and policies designed to protect and care for the emigrants increased Bremen's attractiveness. The price the city had to pay for the success of this strategy was total economic dependence on trade with North America.

Bremen's Hanseatic sister, Hamburg, was in a somewhat more favorable situation. Harbor development had begun in the fifteenth century, when Hamburg surpassed the previously dominant Baltic ports, and in the sixteenth century Hamburg merchants gained from Antwerp's political problems. Hamburg was connected by the Elbe and its tributaries to an industrialized hinterland and had become a center of world trade by the eighteenth century. Trade with North America was significant but never the main source of revenue, unlike in Bremen. Still, it was Bremen and not Hamburg that attracted the emigration traffic and became the most important embarkation port in Europe by the end of the nineteenth century. This was the result of intense efforts by Bremen merchants and the Bremen Senate, who worked hand in hand to develop this industry. Laws that protected emigrants during their stay in Bremen and while on Bremen-based ships proved to be an effective way to establish and maintain the city's good reputation as an emigration port.

The further development of the transportation network meant that the journey to the port city became less important for emigrants deciding on a travel route than the conditions for the sea voyage. In the 1840s and 1850s, the towed river boats were replaced with steamboats, and the construction of railroads began: it became possible to calculate travel times. The trip from Strasbourg to Mannheim on the Rhine, for example, which had taken several days, now took exactly twelve hours, while that from Mainz to Cologne lasted ten hours. From Cologne there were rail lines to almost all of the European embarkation ports. Emigration travel centers soon developed in towns where railroad lines crossed or where travelers could change from ship to rail - in Mannheim, Frankfurt am Main, Cologne, Leipzig, and Berlin the

Bremen made it its buisiness to care for the safety and well-being of emigrants very early. Poster warning of thieves and tricksters

travel were required. From Cologne there was also a connection to Le Havre: the railroad trip to Paris took 22 hours, and after an overnight stay another train took the emigrants directly to the quay in seven hours. From Deutz, across the Rhine from Cologne, travelers could reach Bremen in 20 hours by rail. Bremen was also linked with Leipzig (24 hours by train), whereas

emigration business blossomed, and emigration agencies opened up.

In the informative brochures distributed by these agencies in the 1850s, Cologne was mentioned most often as a starting point for the journey overseas. From there one could reach Antwerp in ten hours by rail or by Rhine steamer, or Rotterdam in two days by steamer. From Rotterdam there were connections to London or by ship and rail to Liverpool; in either case two more days of

Hamburg was directly connected with the transportation hub at Berlin.

The expansion of river-boat and railroad lines meant increased competition for all of the European embarkation ports; Bremen demonstrated what an important factor the treatment of passengers in port and on the sea voyage could be in this competition. For a long time the ships leaving from Liverpool had a bad reputation, with reports of epidemics, starvation among the steerage passengers, and rough treatment of emigrants by the captain and crew. The Liverpool merchants, who were not economically dependent on the emigration business and were also quite sure of getting the profits from transporting the British emigrants, did little to alleviate these problems. In Britain the government had been subsidizing the emigration of impoverished or »undesirable« people for hundreds of years, and keeping the cost of transportation low had always had priority over any proposals for protecting the emigrants. The few laws that there were regulating the conditions on passenger ships were not strict enough and above all were not enforced.

Despite all the warnings by the German

passage to America (i.e., via England), the other European ports soon copied the idea. Emigrants were transported across the channel to Hull and then by train to Liverpool. This Hull-Liverpool route was also used by many Scandinavian emigrants. Only after scheduled service on steamship lines became available to emigrants in all the major ports (and the prices became comparable) did this transit migration of non-British emigrants cease to be profitable.

Belgium, which was also a transit country for many emigrants, had attempted to bring the passenger transportation industry under legal control in 1843, just as Antwerp was connected to the European railroad network. One regulation required emigration ships to

and the *Holland-America Line* (Nederlandsch-Amerikaansche Stroomvaart-Maatschappij) started weekly operation between Rotterdam and New York one year later. France was also a transit country, especially for emigrants from southern Germany, but showed no interest in expanding the business; neither the land journey nor the sea voyage were legally regulated. Because of earlier bad experiences with transit migrants, the Dutch government was less interested in protecting the emigrants than in protecting itself from emigrant-related liabilities. The law there made the transport company, the shipowner, and the travel agent responsible for the proper treatment and safety of the passengers. By far the most effective protective laws were those of the German ports; there

governments, and despite numerous negative reports from emigrant aid organizations about the English ports and about Liverpool in particular, many German emigrants undertook the difficult journey to take advantage of the very cheap passage prices available there. Even German local officials, when required to subsidize the emigration of poor people, sometimes chose Liverpool as the embarkation port because of these low prices. When Hamburg merchants offered a so-called indirect

carry enough food for 90 days. But neither Antwerp nor Rotterdam was able to prevent the loss of much of the emigrant traffic to the German ports. Government decisions to support the emigrant transportation industry came too late: regular transatlantic service was only introduced in the 1870s, ten years later than in other ports. The Belgian *Red Star Line* (actually called the Société Anonyme de Navigation Belge-Américaine because it had American stockholders), began scheduled service in 1872,

Ruhleben near Berlin - chief control station for eastern European emigrants on their way to Bremen and Hamburg

the most powerful of the shipping companies, *Hapag* (standing for *Hamburg-Amerikanische Packetfahrt Actien-Gesellschaft*) and the *North German Lloyd* (*Norddeutscher Lloyd*), took the welfare of the emigrants seriously and used this policy to establish them-

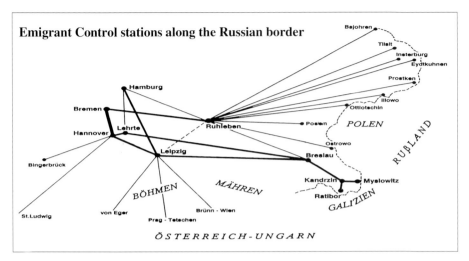

Emigrant Control stations along the Russian border

selves as the leaders in the emigrant-transportation industry.

By the 1870s, the overseas voyage was generally well organized, and people were familiar with the routes to the embarkation ports. When mass emigration from eastern and southeastern Europe began, the ports of Liverpool, Le Havre, Antwerp, Rotterdam, and especially Bremen and Hamburg were the natural choices as points of embarkation. Since the emigration business was highly profitable, there was fierce competition among the railroad companies and steamship lines. The most important factor in the fight for a share of the emigration market was the rate charged, which was evaluated in terms of both the ticket price and the services included in the package. What discount was offered for children, and what were the age limitations on it? How much baggage was transported free, and how much was charged for baggage over the limit? Would there be compensation for financial loss if the arrival was delayed, and were meals included in the fare? These were the questions that interested emigrants when they compared the available options.

It was also in the 1870s that the steamship companies began to offer so-called through tickets which covered both the rail trip to the port and the transatlantic voyage. Later even the land journey in the U.S. could be booked in advance. Through this scheme the shippers were able to offer the emigrants significant price reductions on the rail trips, since they bought blocks of tickets on a regular basis. In

the 1880s special emigrant trains were established on all the main lines. In 1884, for example, the French *Compagnie Générale Transatlantique* arranged an emigration train from Basel to Le Havre: this direct train took 21 hours, and during the journey German-speaking attendants looked after the passengers and sold food and milk at reasonable prices. With time this line became a serious threat to the German ports, and in 1902 the German steamship companies introduced special emigrant cars, attached to the express trains, to permit direct travel from Basel to Bremen or Hamburg in 24 hours. These cars offered third-class service for the price of fourth class.

In 1892, when the government of Prussia closed its borders to transient passengers from Russia because of an epidemic there, the railroad companies protested vociferously - the income from the sale of rail tickets to emigrants traveling from the border to Hamburg or Bremen had reached 2,200,000 marks in 1891, with an additional 500,000 marks for passages to Rotterdam or Antwerp. However, the establishment of health inspection stations, financed by the Hapag and Lloyd lines, permitted the borders to be reopened, and business could continue. The inspection stations were set up at points where the Russian and Prussian railroad lines met, and all emigrants were required to use the special trains or cars, which were now often uncomfortable. The transit passengers were not allowed to leave the train until it

arrived in the port city - a measure designed to protect the German population from epidemics, but one which also had economic advantages for the German railroad and shipping lines: by keeping the passengers together and under constant supervision they could put their competitors at a disadvantage.

This policy was true for the return migrant traffic as well: many migrants from southern and southeastern Europe considered themselves temporary labor migrants and planned to return home with the money they saved in America. Not all were willing or able to make good on these intentions, but others were forced to return when their efforts to gain an economic foothold in America met with failure. There are no accurate data on return or multiple migration, but the proportion of returnees was around 34 percent on average and as high as 60 percent in some ethnic groups. These migrants provided an additional source of profit for the steamship companies. Since many eastern Europeans emigrated illegally, however, it was often very difficult for them to return. Once again strict supervision and transportation in special trains were required to make sure these migrants would not remain in Germany. During 1907, for example, a total of 104 special trains left Bremen with migrants returning to Russia and Austria-Hungary. For the transit passengers, the routes were set and the journey was regulated and monitored from start to finish. The large shipping companies in the six major European emigration ports had business under tight control.

There were a few smaller ports which also profited from emigration: Hull in England and Dublin in Ireland; Stockholm, Gothenburg, and Copenhagen in Scandinavia; and Libau (Liepája), Trieste, Fiume (Rijeka), Genoa, Stettin, and Danzig on the continent. Although some of these ports received government subsidies for nationalistic reasons, their share of the emigration market was negligible. At the end of the nineteenth century, the German Hanseatic cities of Bremen and Hamburg were by far the leading ports in this industry.

The Emigration Business in Bremen and Hamburg

Although overseas trade was the primary source of income for both Bremen and Hamburg, the governing Senates of the two cities took different approaches to emigration. Until 1836, Hamburg's policy was like that of most of the other German states, which discouraged the emigration of their subjects; in Bremen, on the other hand, it was already recognized that emigration represented a great economic opportunity for the merchants. Because of good personal, religious, and economic relationships between Bremen merchants and William Penn, the Quaker founder of the Pennsylvania colony, a small number of German emigrants had set sail from Bremen for Philadelphia as early as the seventeenth century. To be sure, most overseas migrants at this time left from Amsterdam or Rotterdam; in 1709, when a wave of emigration carried thousands of people from the Palatinate to Pennsylvania and Carolina, the emigrants followed the natural route, down the Rhine to the Dutch ports.

Since emigration from Bremen was only a sporadic phenomenon in the eighteenth century, nothing was undertaken to promote it. If emigrants came to the town, they were accepted; the Senate ignored the existing anti-emigration laws of the other German states, including the edict issued by Emperor Joseph II in 1768. In 1784 a merchant named Johann Friedrich Amelung was recruiting glass craftsmen in the north-German states, hoping to found a glass factory in North America; Bremen shipowners were quite willing to provide transportation to Baltimore, ignoring the requests of neighboring states to deny the emigrants passage. Amelung was again able to count on the help of the Bremen merchants when he returned two years later to recruit more workers for his factory in New Bremen, Maryland. The factory finally failed and was closed in 1795; the glassblowers became farmers in the U.S.

This early phase of Bremen's history as an emigration port shows the principle the city followed: the laws of other states could be ignored where there was a profit to be made. This principle meant, however, that

First page of an emigrant handbook

Business card in Czech

the free will of the emigrants themselves could also be ignored, as was all too clearly seen in 1776, when about 12,000 Hessian soldiers, often recruited by force, embarked from Bremen to fight in North America.

In the eighteenth century, Bremen merchants themselves began emigrating to America, where they founded their own firms or, more frequently, the American branches of Bremen trading companies. These economic ties grew stronger after the British colonies declared their independence and the *Navigation Act* was repealed: Bremen merchants could now outfit their own ships to sail directly to North America. In 1782 the first ship flying the Bremen flag sailed to America without making an intermediate stop in England. Emigration was already one part, albeit a rather insignificant one, of these closer trade relations.

Then, in 1816 and 1817, a new mass emigration from southwestern Germany began, and some of the emigrants found their way to the Hanseatic ports. While these people were accepted by the Bremen Senate (although with no particular enthusiasm), Hamburg closed its doors to them and renewed its ban on the transportation of emigrants. That did not mean, however, that Hamburg merchants did not sell passages to emigrants when they had the chance. In 1792, for example, a man named William Berczy was recruiting people to settle in New York state, in an area on the Genessee River near Lake Seneca. He set up an office in Hamburg, and the people he signed up embarked from there as well. The Senate feigned ignorance of his activities for as long as possible, despite the vehement protests of the neighboring German states, especially Prussia. But events such as this remained the exception in Hamburg. In 1827 the two Hanseatic cities signed a treaty agreeing to equal trade relations with the U.S., at a time when their overall trade balance was at a low point. Bremen was especially lacking in export goods, because its hinterland and transportation network were underdeveloped; since emigrants could make up for this lack, the Bremen merchants began a concerted effort to increase their share of the emigration trade.

In the same year the Bremen Senate purchased from the Kingdom of Hanover a strip of land at the mouth of the Weser, where just three years later the port of Bremerhaven, a deep-water port open to large ships all year round, began operation. In 1832 the Bremen Senate passed the first detailed legal regulations regarding the conditions for transatlantic voyages. The main provisions were a minimum amount of steerage space and a minimum amount of food per passenger for ships carrying emigrants. Whereas the space rule simply copied the American regulations of 1819 (no more than two emigrants per 5 tons of a ship's registered tonnage), the rule regarding food represented a significant new step: at most European ports the steerage passengers had to provide their own food for the trip, a practice which sometimes led to starvation on the steerage deck or to the outbreak of diseases caused by poor-quality, spoiled, or insufficient food. The Bremen law required the captains and shipowners to provide the food: although the emigrants on Bremen ships still had to cook for themselves, the controls on the amount and quality of food on board prevented shortages during the voyage. Any ship leaving Bremen for North America had to carry provisions for 90 days, whereas the average trip took about six weeks. The law's other requirements, that ships be inspected for seaworthiness and carry passenger lists, meant a greater degree of security for the emigrants, but it was the elimination of the need to bring one's own food that established Bremen's reputation as

Waiting hall for steerage passengers in Bremen 1907

port where emigrants were properly cared for. The law was modified slightly in 1834, and in the following years the number of emigrants departing from Bremen grew steadily.

The Hamburg merchants had to react to this situation if they hoped to remain competitive. Yet even in 1832, when over 10,000 emigrants departed from Bremen, large groups of emigrants were turned away by the Hamburg Senate, which feared possible social repercussions. The issue became urgent in 1836 when, despite all prohibitions, 2870 emigrants arrived in Hamburg seeking a transatlantic passage. Finally a majority of the senators recognized that emigration was too profitable a business to be conceded to the Bremen merchants. For years, Hamburg merchants had been leasing ships to Bremen brokers for use in transporting emigrants; now, in September 1836, the Senate presented to the Chamber of Commerce (*Kommerzdeputation*) the draft of a law which would regulate emigrant transport more strictly than the existing laws of England, the U.S., or even Bremen. These more particular controls were deemed necessary because Hamburg ships were carrying emigrants not only to the U.S. but also to Australia and South America (especially Brazil), countries with no laws protecting immigrants.

Although the members of the *Kommerzdeputation* in principle welcomed the new initiative, they did not approve the draft proposal. They themselves had demanded the repeal of the prohibition on emigrant

transport, but the detailed regulations, such as a requirement that each company leave a security deposit with the police to guarantee honest business practices, were deemed an insult to every honorable Hamburg merchant - especially since there were no such requirements in Bremen. The requirement that a ship's doctor and a very large amount of food be carried by all ships with more than 25 passengers would, they claimed, significantly lower the competitiveness of the Hamburg shipping companies. Despite these objections, the law took effect on February 27, 1837, at first for a trial period of five years. Continuing protests then led, on August 11, to less exacting police inspections and the elimination of the security deposit.

There was one weak point, however, that the Hamburg legislators failed to take into account: the so-called indirect emigration, where passengers were taken to England and then embarked from there for the transatlantic voyage. This system was not affected by the new regulations, except for the requirement that passenger lists be compiled, and even that was repealed in 1839. Emigrants sailing from England were poorly protected by the British laws, and the continual complaints which arose from the unregulated indirect system damaged Hamburg's reputation as an emigration port. In the kingdom of Bavaria, for ex-

Business card

85

ample, there was a period when no licenses were granted to emigration agents working for Hamburg shipping companies. The problem was finally addressed on May 21, 1851, when a new ordinance required »indirect transporters« to make the usual security payments. After March 21, 1853, the English partner firms had to be licensed in Hamburg as well.

In the 1840s, there was a general upswing in the emigration business. In Bremen the merchants, emigration brokers, shippers, and Senate joined together (many of the senators were themselves involved in the emigration trade) to promote this industry. The brokers were especially active in organizing this effort and were able to improve their initially questionable professional reputation as a result. Soon Bremen's economy became dependent on the emigration trade, and, eventually even the American merchants had to yield to the financial power of the Bremen merchant shipowners. A law passed on April 9, 1849 stipulated that licenses for the transport of emigrants could be granted only to citizens of Bremen, who had to pay a security deposit for the privilege. Some of the other regulations, such as those regarding food

for the voyage, were amended to reflect current standards, so as not to fall behind Hamburg in this regard. Instead of the police, a broker inspection system was set up to make sure the laws were enforced.

Due mainly to the slow pace of the legal initiatives and the incompleteness of the regulations, the emigration trade in Hamburg grew only slowly; at first it even shrank. While the number of emigrants embarking annually from Bremen increased by 68 percent between 1836 and 1844 (from 11,811 to 19,863 emigrants), in Hamburg the number decreased from 2870 to 1774 emigrants - although only passengers taking the direct route were counted. Pressure from the shipowners led to the passage of some improved laws, such as the adoption of the Bremen regulations regarding outfitting and provisions for the steerage deck in March 1842. No other regulations were deemed necessary, although the law of 1837 had expired in the meantime. On March 26, 1845 the Senate passed a new set

In front of Bremen's central railroad station awaiting transfer to Bremerhaven 1910

of rules drawn up by the *Kommerzdeputation*, with significant improvements - this time prior to Bremen's. The transport firms had to pay a security deposit; the passengers had to be insured as part of the contract; and the shipowners were obliged to assume financial responsibility for the passengers if the departure was delayed. The numbers of emigrants, especially to Brazil, began to rise. In 1847, Hamburg agents were again granted permission to operate in Bavaria. Regulations designed to keep Hamburg in step with Bremen were passed in 1848 and 1850. There, however, an ambitious merchant had already opened a spacious emigrant residence in Bremerhaven with city support, and Hamburg had nothing comparable to offer. The *Kommerzdeputation* had proposed such a measure in 1846, but this was rejected due to a lack of funding.

Because the numbers of emigrants were increasing and because land transport in the German states was improved (both Bremen and Hamburg were part of the railway network after 1847), more and more emigrants came through the Hanseatic cities. Questionable business practices also became more common, with complaints of fraud by competing emigration agents, innkeepers, store owners, and money changers. Since this kind of activity threatened the reputations of both cities, information agencies were opened in 1851 as a step in alleviating the problem. In these offices, emigrants could find out the average prices for food, travel needs, and lodgings as well as the exchange rates. The offices also negotiated contracts with innkeepers, who agreed to run their establishments in an orderly fashion and above all not to overbook their rooms. In Hamburg the office was funded by the »Emigrant Protection Association«, whose members were mainly merchants involved in the emigration trade; in Bremen the shipowners and shipping companies financed the office, but the employees were approved by the Senate. This made it possible for them, unlike their colleagues in Hamburg, to go beyond mere advice and exercise policelike functions at train stations, inns, and currency-exchange offices. Both offices proved to be very effective in controlling fraudulent transactions with emigrants. In 1854 both cities set up official offices to monitor the entire emigration process, the deputations for emigration affairs. These organizations were made up of Senate and Chamber of Commerce members and worked closely with the police to enforce the laws, but they also acted as arbitrators when there were disputes. The introduction of these governmental controls helped the reputations of the two Hanseatic cities among emigrants and established them as the leading European emigration ports.

These laws were adapted over the years to meet changing conditions. The change from sails to steam power made some requirements feasible and eliminated the need for others. On July 9, 1866, a new set of regulations replaced those issued in 1849. Agents were responsible for their passengers as soon as they arrived in Bremen; passengers had to be transported to Bremerhaven by rail or steamboat; and the number of lifeboats on the ship had to be documented. Hamburg passed a law on April 4, 1864 which specified the contents of the ship's apothecary and required medical examinations for all steerage passengers prior to embarkation. Medical examinations were also introduced in Bremen on November 27, 1868. Hamburg ships had to carry someone to care for sick passengers, but it did not necessarily have to be a doctor, although both Hapag and Lloyd ships were carrying doctors as a general practice by this time. Pressure from the deputy of the North German Confederation, who supervised the transport of emigrants in both Hanseatic cities after 1869, led to a rule calling for the separation of sick and healthy passengers in steerage in 1870.

On January 14, 1887, the Hamburg Senate passed a comprehensive emigrant transportation act that in effect combined and brought up to date all 15 laws and regulations enacted over the preceding 50 years. The stipulations governing the conditions in steerage were stricter and more detailed than those for Bremen ships. The Bremen Senate did not issue such a comprehensive law, considering the regulation of 1866 with the various supplementary measures to be sufficient. Both sets of legislation

were replaced by the national law passed in 1897, which met the needs of the German shipowners by maintaining most of the provisions of the Hanseatic laws. The Hapag and Lloyd companies opposed the empire's limitations on the destinations for which transport licenses were granted, but had no success, since the government wanted to use the law to channel emigration as part of a plan to advance colonial ambitions.

These legal provisions governing the transportation of emigrants established the Hanseatic cities' reputation for taking care of migrants and assuring them honest treatment. Of course, these regulations were more the result of concrete financial calculations than humanitarian motives; but for the emigrants the motivation was less important than the feeling that they had been dealt with fairly. There was still some fraudulent activity at all emigration ports, and not all captains fulfilled their contracts, especially after the ship left port; but compared with other European embarkation ports, the merchants and political leaders of the Hanseatic cities provided relatively good conditions for emigrants.

When mass emigration from eastern Europe began in the 1880s, Bremen and Hamburg

were the leading ports, and the Hapag and Lloyd companies had a monopoly on emigrant transport and were obviously interested in attracting as many of the new emigrants as possible to their ports. The good reputation the companies had established in organizing the mass migration from Germany helped them achieve this goal. Soon the political leaders had to decide how best to handle the arriving masses of transit migrants. New problems were posed, and the Hapag and Lloyd companies cooperated with the government in addressing them.

Germany as a Transit Country for Eastern Europeans

After 1870, German emigrants in steerage met more and more eastern Europeans. People in Russia and Austria-Hungary were leaving home to look for a better future in the U.S.; others emigrated to Canada, Argentina, or Brazil; some even chose more unusual countries to make a new start. Since there were no emigration ports in their own countries, they followed the established routes to Hamburg and Bremen for embarkation; in Germany, they were classified as transit migrants.

Since there were no unified laws governing emigration in Germany at this time, the border states of Prussia and Saxony were forced to deal with the problem of transit migration. Their primary policy concern

The pier in Bremerhaven: To the left an arriving emigrant train - to the right departing express steamer Kronprinz Wilhelm ca. 1904

was to prevent undesirable immigration, especially in Prussia. Although thousands of Galician Poles were employed in Prussian mines and factories and in agriculture east of the Elbe - not counting the Poles with Prussian citizenship working in mines in the Ruhr - the government was anxious to keep these people classified as seasonal workers. Their residence permits were valid only from March 1 to October 15, and the police carefully monitored their return home for the winter. A further problem was the immigration of Jews: cities like Berlin had a relatively high proportion of Jews, and antisemitic political movements were gaining strength in the 1870s and 1880s, even finding parliamentary spokesmen. When thousands of Jews were driven out of Russia by pogroms after the assassination of Czar Alexander on March 11, 1881, there were growing fears that Jewish influence in Germany would become too great.

Most of the eastern Europeans crossing the German border had the clear intention of emigrating overseas. Naturally a few tried to stay in Germany, and some were left there when they ran short of money for the transatlantic passage. In 1877, the Senates of Hamburg and Bremen had to admit impoverished Russian and Galician Jews, who actually wanted to go to Brazil and the U.S., to the poorhouses. Returning these people to their homelands was difficult, not only because of the travel costs but because the Russian government had closed its borders to returnees without valid passports. This type of passport was expensive to obtain, and only 10-15 percent of those wishing to emigrate were in possession of such a document. To avoid diplomatic incidents, the imperial Foreign Office had already (1877) issued orders that all trains coming from Russia be inspected by Prussian officials at the border, to assure that no passengers entered Germany without the means needed to continue their journey. The North German Lloyd sent its own representative to the main entrance point for Russian emigrants, Eydtkuhnen. It was at this time that nativists in the U.S. were first successful in their efforts to limit immigration by legislation. Before 1882, the U.S. had basically followed an open-

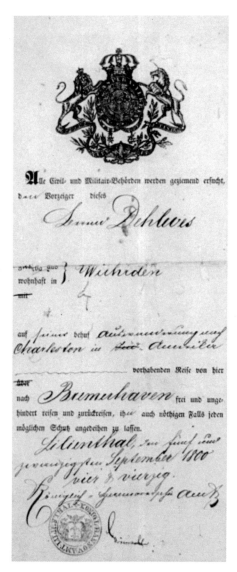

Emigrant passport

door policy; in 1864, when the Civil War led to a noticeable labor shortage in all of the states, a »Law to Encourage Immigration« was even enacted - although it was repealed only eight years later. Although individual states actively supported further settlement by European migrants, those who favored a more restrictive (or more accurately, selective) immigration policy were becoming more influential. The law

of 1882 imposed a tax on each person entering the country and barred certain groups (convicts, the mentally retarded, and anyone who might put demands on the U.S. welfare system).

The fact that these »undesirable aliens« could now be excluded gave the transport firms and government agencies in Europe to reconsider their policies as well. When a Hapag steamship was not permitted to land its Russian Jewish passengers in New York in 1884, the Prussian authorities began to run »poverty checks« on the transit migrants. Beginning in 1886, a family had to have 400 marks for each adult migrant and 100 marks for each child; the only exception was made for emigrants who presented an official guarantee of support from the Jewish Central Committee. Along with these provisions, the German shipowners agreed to pay the return passages of any migrants turned back; after 1887 they were required to do so by U.S. regulations. Nevertheless the shipping companies found the regulations too restrictive, since too many of the potential emigrants could not put together such a large sum in cash. The economic survival of the firms now depended on emigration, and the owners realized that the emigrants from Russia and Austria-Hungary not only took the places of Germans, who were leaving in ever smaller numbers, but represented a new business opportunity with great potential for expansion. The shipping companies' profit interest thus stood in direct opposition to the interest of the state, which desired above all to protect itself from the costs of caring for the hapless transit migrants.

Only a few transit migrants were able to meet the Prussian requirements, and large-scale efforts to get around the border checks were the result. The »smuggling of emigrants« reached unimaginable proportions, and the agents - including employees of the German shipping companies - were actively involved. They loaned the emigrants money to show to the border guards; they gave their clients passports »borrowed« from people who had some professional or business reason for crossing the border; and most of all they bribed Russian border guards, who allowed hundreds of migrants at a time to cross the border without checking. More and more emigrants began to choose the route through Saxony to Antwerp and Rotterdam, and the German shipping companies turned to the government in Berlin for relief. Their argument was that their position vis à vis the foreign competition was weakened by the Prussian regulations, and this convinced the authorities: beginning in 1887, all passengers in possession of a Hapag or Lloyd steamship ticket and a railway ticket were allowed to pass without proving they had the necessary amount of cash. The same rules were put into effect at the border between Saxony and Austria-Hungary in 1888, marking the beginning of a policy in which the government supported the German steamship lines in their fight against foreign competition.

The situation changed, however, when a cholera epidemic broke out in Hamburg in 1892. Outbreaks had been reported at various locations in Russia in July, and the first cases in Hamburg appeared in August. The city was stricken severely, with 16,757 cases and 8605 deaths in a population of about 500,000. It was assumed that the epidemic was imported into the city by Russian transit migrants, and the Hapag company reacted immediately, accepting no more steerage passengers from Russia after August 26. The Lloyd company followed suit, and the government closed the border to migrants with steerage tickets. The transatlantic emigration traffic from the German ports came to a virtual standstill, and in November the U.S. government ordered a 20-day quarantine for all eastern European immigrants; Canada halted immigration completely. Emigrants continued to leave eastern Europe nevertheless, although in smaller numbers. The emigrants traveled by ship from Libau or Riga to Antwerp or Rotterdam, or they tried as before to smuggle themselves over the German border.

Only a short time passed before the German lines began to regard the closing of the border as too restrictive. Instead of prohibiting transit migration, they argued, the government should make the shipping companies responsible for guaranteeing the health of the passengers. The steerage passengers were already (since 1868) given a medical examination before em-

barkation, and now the companies tried to save as much as they could of the emigration business by evading the strict government procedures as soon as the situation had eased somewhat. The North Atlantic Steamship Association (*Nordatlantischer Dampferlinienverband*, NDLV), which included all of the major companies and regulated prices and market shares, introduced a new fare, the »second-class lower cabin« class, which had the same price as steerage. In this way the ships arriving in the U.S. carried only »cabin« passengers. Despite all limitations, the number of passengers soon began to rise again, even in Hamburg, where strict controls remained

barkation. As in the case of the impoverished, the U.S. tried to shift the burden of weeding out unhealthy migrants to the European countries. Closing the Russian-Prussian border was the easiest way to avoid this responsibility, but this would have had disastrous economic effects on the Hapag and Lloyd shipping lines and on the state-controlled Prussian railroads. The solution proposed by the shipping lines in July 1893 was to reopen the borders, but to gather the transit migrants at certain control points and give them a preliminary medical examination. If they were healthy, they could travel on to the embarkation ports in special guarded trains.

Newspaper advertisement for steamship passage from Bremen to New York with timetable and pricelist

in effect until 1893. When the transportation of Russian steerage passengers was prohibited completely in March, although the U.S. had in the meantime lifted the quarantine and Canada had reopened its borders, the Hapag agents began to sell their passengers special cabin-class tickets, which were then traded for steerage tickets on board. In this way it was possible for 100-150 Russian emigrants to leave Europe each day, mainly from Hamburg.

The U.S., however, now demanded improvements in the medical examination of emigrants in the European ports of em-

After some hesitation, the government accepted this proposal, and by the end of the year emigrants were being processed at five border stations (Eydtkuhnen, Bajohren, Ottlotschin, Illowo, and Prostken), followed by additional stations soon after. The construction and operation of the stations were financed by the Hapag and Lloyd companies, at an annual cost of 40,000-80,000 marks.

The stations followed a simple system: arriving emigrants were divided by sex and brought to waiting rooms, where their papers and tickets were checked; then they had to strip and take showers while their clothing and baggage were disinfected. After the medical examination their clothes were returned, and they could proceed to the »clean« part of the station. Passengers who failed the examination had to stay in the medical area of the station for observation or treatment, or else they were sent directly back to Russia. Those who came through boarded a special train which took them to Ruhleben, near Berlin, where there was also a facility (set up in 1891) for transit migrants who had managed to avoid the border procedures when they entered Prussia. At Ruhleben the »healthy« emigrants had to undergo a second medical examination, after which they could board a special train to the embarkation port - a train no one was allowed to leave during the trip. At the German-Austrian border health checks were not mandatory, but were carried out on a case-by-case basis. The German shipping lines operated so-called registration stations at Myslowitz and Ratibor (and later at other points); from there the migrants were taken by special train to Ruhleben.

This method offered an efficient solution to the problem of financial and medical controls. Because the German lines were interested in maintaining good relations with the U.S., a group of American doctors was permitted to visit the border stations in 1893 and gave them a very positive evaluation. The German lines also derived more direct benefits from the stations: they could often force emigrants to give up tickets already purchased from Cunard or other shipping lines and buy new ones. They tried to book as many passengers as possible and used the border stations to make a profit, clearly at the expense of the emigrants. If the station officials had the slightest suspicion that a migrant intended to travel to London and board a Cunard ship, they would reject him for reasons of bad health or poverty and send him back. With the help of the stations the German lines not only survived the business losses incurred as a result of the cholera epidemic but took over the lead among the European emigration ports. This was possible because the German government had granted them almost complete control of the emigrants at the borders. Foreign shipping companies protested in vain against these practices; they could, with certain restrictions, obtain licenses to operate in Germany under the national emigration law of 1897, but it was not easy for all lines to obtain the same privileges, and the way the

stations functioned clearly favored the domestic lines.

In 1903, the British Cunard line broke its contract and withdrew from the NDLV, opening a new route from Fiume to New York with the support of the Hungarian government. The Hapag and Lloyd companies began to use the border control stations to exert pressure. The competition for passengers proved costly to both sides: at the previously unheard-of steerage prices offered by Cunard, a Russian emigrant could travel to London for 10 rubles and from London to New York for 20 rubles more, whereas with a German line the trip would have cost 64 rubles. But since Cunard made no profit using this method, and since the German lines could not afford to lose their share of the emigration market, a new agreement among all the large North Atlantic lines was reached in 1904. The British company had at least been successful in curbing the power of the German lines; Hapag and Lloyd remained ahead in the competition, but they were no longer able to shut out their rivals completely.

But it was not economic factors alone which caused the German side to give ground - there was also the pressure of public opinion, which began to question the practices of the control stations. The migrants themselves had always resisted the regulative procedures, especially the financial inspection, but the health stations were especially detested. In keeping with the American requirements, emigrants with trachoma or similar eye infections, skin diseases, tuberculosis, syphilis, smallpox, measles, or feeble-mindedness were turned back at the border. But the decisions were arbitrary, and there was no appealing the judgement of the doctors. Since they were paid by the shipping lines, the doctors could not risk letting through emigrants who would be rejected by the American immigration authorities. Thus diagnoses such as »pregnancy« or »unmarried and pregnant« were sufficient for rejection. About 11,000 emigrants per year were kept from leaving Europe for health reasons, and many were stopped at the German border. From the perspective of the shipping companies, the officials had done a good job: the number of passengers rejected at Ellis

Island dropped significantly after the opening of the stations.

Such statistics say nothing, however, of the human suffering caused by the decisions of the inspectors. Since healthy passengers were not permitted to remain in the stations, groups were frequently broken up. Sometimes small children were held back while the rest of the family went on - unless they all wanted to go back. There were also protests against the fact that only steerage passengers had to undergo examination and disinfection; cabin passengers and even seasonal workers entering Germany for the summer were excused from the procedure. The treatment of the steerage passengers was often inhumane and callous. Passengers were cargo, but the transit migrants found it insulting to be treated openly as such. The protests were repeated a thousand times, but went unheard, at least until the spectacular price war between Cunard and the German lines drew public attention to transit migrants and the conditions they were subjected to. In 1904 a reporter from the Social-Democratic paper Vorwärts disguised himself as a transit migrant and reported on the stages of the journey. His »inside report« shocked the German public. Although part of the press »supported the unjust treatment or rather maltreatment of the Russian emigrants in Prussia by simply ignoring it or even trying to defend it«, wrote the Berliner Zeitung on October 22, 1904, »the continuous criticism of the Social-Democratic, democratic, and consistently liberal press was enough to cause serious trouble for Mr. [Albert] Ballin and Mr. [Heinrich] Wiegand« (the directors of Hapag and Lloyd, respectively). This pressure led to somewhat more humane treatment for the emigrants; bathing and disinfection, for example, were no longer obligatory, but only required if ordered by the doctor.

Up to World War I the stations followed the procedures agreed upon by the NDLV in 1904, and the Hapag and Lloyd companies were usually able to take care of problems - as when the Prussian government ordered stricter checking of Russian return migrants in December 1910. Neither line was interested in again becoming the object of national or international criticism. On

August 1, 1914, the German lines stopped operations and closed the border stations; after the war, Article 368 of the Treaty of Versailles stipulated that transit migrants be allowed to pass the border with only the customary passport check.

The Emigration Agents

The eastern European emigration was a profitable business for the shipowners - as shown by their investment of thousands of marks in stringent transit controls, by the intense struggle for market shares, and by the intervention of government agencies. Emigration agents played a significant role in this development, as they had since the seventeenth century, acting as middlemen between the potential emigrants, the shipping companies seeking passengers, and the American landowners looking for new settlers. The job of emigration agent began as unscrupulous fortune-hunting and gradually became a recognized, government-regulated profession.

Emigration agents have existed since emigration began, always functioning both as middlemen between emigrants and ship's captains and owners and as recruiters of emigrants. In the seventeenth and eighteenth centuries, recruiters working on a commission basis traveled back and forth across Germany looking for soldiers and colonists. The Netherlands, Great Britain, and France needed all sorts of people to build and defend their new overseas pos-

Passport holder advertising Friedrich Missler shipping agency, Bremen 1905

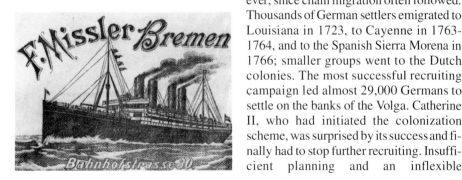

sessions, but Prussia, Austria, and Russia were looking for settlers as well. Generally these recruitment campaigns did not use professional agents; those who had already made the decision to emigrate were offered inducements such as special privileges in their new homes to convince friends and relatives to come along. Yet there were also recruiters in the eighteenth century who made a living from this activity. They worked for foreign governments, landowners, or ship captains or without a contract, at their own risk. These traveling agents were outlawed by the governments, especially if they were recruiting soldiers. Winning new colonists was of greater importance for the foreign countries, however, since chain migration often followed. Thousands of German settlers emigrated to Louisiana in 1723, to Cayenne in 1763-1764, and to the Spanish Sierra Morena in 1766; smaller groups went to the Dutch colonies. The most successful recruiting campaign led almost 29,000 Germans to settle on the banks of the Volga. Catherine II, who had initiated the colonization scheme, was surprised by its success and finally had to stop further recruiting. Insufficient planning and an inflexible

The hotel »Stadt New York« in Schweinsberg, Hessen, was a Missler sub-agency and sold passages to America

bureaucracy allowed the emigration permitted by the German authorities to get out of control; the result was that an imperial edict in 1768 made all emigration illegal. Before the beginning of the nineteenth century, most German emigration was directed eastward, but after 1800 America became the more attractive destination: taxes were low or nonexistent; cheap, fertile land was readily available; there was no obligatory military service; and above all there was freedom of religion. Large groups of religious dissidents, traveling mainly to Pennsylvania, had helped lay the foundation for the new emigration business in the eighteenth century. The introduction of the so-called redemptioner system had made it possible for the emigration movement to reach mass proportions at this time: emigrants with little or no money could obtain a ticket for the transatlantic passage by means of a labor contract that was finalized only after their arrival in America. Many

Switzerland. Here wars and failed harvests had brought about economic crisis, and it was relatively easy for people to travel on the great waterways, the Rhine and Danube. The owners of large tracts in North America had sent agents to southern Germany as early as the beginning of the eighteenth century to recruit settlers. Exact figures are not available, but the number of these agents was not insignificant. Many of them were honest merchants who conscientiously fulfilled their contracts with government permission. Others, however, probably the majority, were unscrupulous profiteers who were paid a small sum by captains or shipowners for each passenger »delivered«. Their recruiting methods ranged from gross exaggeration to outright lying; they tried to convince the ignorant peasants that America was a paradise where the land was fertile and easily tilled and where land was available to all at very low prices or for the asking. Reports of fraudulent dealing by these so-called »sellers of souls« or »newlanders« (most of whom had never set foot on the »new land« themselves) were widespread, and most people should have heard about them. Returning migrants and letters from settlers to their families in Germany also began to provide more accurate information. Nevertheless, the hopes of naive and ignorant people led them to believe the accounts of the recruiters and to set out for the New World without the necessary knowledge and planning. The mass emigration of 1816-1817 revealed how far this recruitment system could lead: as we have seen, thousands of emigrants were stranded in Dutch and North American ports because there were too few ships to take them across the Atlantic or too few prospective employers to buy up their redemptioner contracts. The business of the »sellers of souls« was recruiting the emigrants; what happened to the people afterward did not concern them. This kind of uncontrolled and unorganized recruitment of emigrants had to be ended.

saw this procedure as a chance to make a new beginning, and even at the turn of the nineteenth century about a third of all steerage passengers were traveling as redemptioners. Although this opportunity was the immediate reason for many decisions to leave home, we must look to the living conditions of the prospective migrants to understand their motives for even considering emigration in the first place.

The main centers of activity for the emigration agents were the principalities of Württemberg, Baden, and the Palatinate and the area of the Rhine, as well as Alsace and

In the port cities some began to realize (in Germany Bremen merchants were the first to do so) that organized emigration could be good business, and soon Bremen agents were at work all over southern Germany. As the numbers of emigrants grew, the three registered Bremen brokers (no more were legally permitted) began to organize the emigration business on a grand scale: they chartered ship space and then filled it with the emigrants whom their agents had recruited in the south and who were now on call, waiting to leave. In this way the emigration business became less dependent on the shipowners and captains, and the role of the brokers, which had been a subordinate one before, became much more important. In other ports business was conducted without registered agents; in Hamburg, for example, any merchant could make himself a broker. By the end of the 1830s, however, a three-layer system had developed in the emigration trade: transport companies or brokers in the harbor cities, their agents in the large cities of the interior, and subordinate agents in the villages. The traveling recruiters of the eighteenth century were replaced by professional emigration agents with a fixed business address. The principal agents were usually merchants who regarded the emigration trade as one business activity among others. Subordinate agents, on the other hand, came from all sorts of backgrounds, including trades-

men, mayors, innkeepers, barbers, teachers, and preachers and sacristans - people who were known in their area and had contacts among the people. Subagents were paid according to the number of contracts negotiated, whereas the principal agents were paid a fixed salary plus commission. About twenty years passed before this system had become fully established. The continued existence of some dishonest agencies and the fear that agents were encouraging people to emigrate meanwhile led the governments to pass new laws: by the end of the 1850s emigration agents were subject to some sort of official regulation; they had to apply for a license and pay a deposit to guarantee honest business practices. This procedure had already been introduced in Great Britain, although there emigration was not only accepted but often even encouraged. In Scandinavia an inland network of emigration agents developed only at midcentury, so that licensing requirements were not imposed until the 1860s. By the turn of the twentieth century the emigration agents of western Europe were only involved in organizing the business; recruiting was taking place in southern and southeastern Europe.

The Missler-Hallen in Bremen providing accomodation for emigrants, 1907

The introduction of steamships and regular transatlantic service from all major ports led to a normalization of travel costs and conditions, and this left the agents very little latitude for increasing their profits. In addition, more and more prepaid tickets were being sent by relatives in America. In the Hanseatic cities, the shipping companies had meanwhile set up separate departments for the passenger business, distinct from freight forwarding, and the brokers had lost most of their influence. Since there was no difference between a ticket purchased from Hapag for emigration and one for a pleasure cruise, the domestic emigration offices had essentially become travel agencies. Nevertheless, there were always at least a few recruiters active throughout the nineteenth century. Brazil and Argentina needed settlers and tried to make their countries more attractive to Europeans by offering free passage tickets and financial support for making a new start - although cooperation between the European agents and these governments was poor, and many settlers were left to fend for themselves when they arrived. The conditions encountered by German settlers in the south of Brazil were so harsh that the Prussian government prohibited all emigration to this region on November 3, 1859, and this »von der Heyd decree« remained in force until June 1896. Even the U.S. government actively recruited settlers from northern and western Europe in the second half of the nineteenth century. The 1864 *Act to Encourage Emigration*, which was repealed after only four years, still marked the beginning of a pro-immigration stance for many states. The government itself was

Critical view of German emigration agents in Poland before World War I

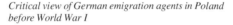

less interested in attracting new settlers than in luring badly needed workers for the rapidly expanding industrial sector. American recruiters traveled through Germany, Sweden, Norway, and Great Britain offering employment contracts and paying the travel expenses as an advance on the wages to be earned.

Elsewhere in Europe there were also German recruiters seeking workers: Prussian employers were hiring thousands of Polish agricultural and mining workers as seasonal help every year. When the first transatlantic migrants from eastern Europe began to arrive in Germany in the 1870s, emigration agents from the shipping lines immediately appeared in the villages of their homelands. The firms hired by the German lines included Louis Scharlach, Karesch & Stotzky (both from Hamburg), Morawetz, and especially Friedrich Missler (Bremen). In order to open up the new market in a systematic way, they began hiring subagents (as usual mayors, innkeepers, preachers, etc.) to sell ticket vouchers for them in Russia and Austria-Hungary. Since emigration was not legally regulated in either country, these subagents were not licensed. In Austria-Hungary most of the new emigration came from Croatia, Galicia, and Bohemia. Although any type of advertising to attract emigrants was strictly forbidden, the shipping companies paid such high commissions that hundreds were willing to take the chance and work illegally as recruiters.

In Russia emigration to North America began when harsher oppression of Jews forced them to leave home. After the first brutal pogroms of spring 1871 large groups of Jews left Odessa for America, choosing Hamburg as their embarkation port. In general the route via Hamburg or Bremen was considered the most advantageous. Although after 1888 there was service to the Baltic ports from Odessa or Libau, embarkation from Russia was not financially feasible for most emigrants because an expensive passport was required there. The journey from Fiume or Trieste to North America lasted three weeks, and transit through Germany was necessary to reach Le Havre or the Dutch ports. The Hanseatic cities had many advantages, including

direct rail connections to the border stations (after about 1880), a shorter transatlantic passage, and regular departures (at least twice per week).

The almost total economic dependence of the steamship lines on the emigration trade and the entrepreneurial opportunities offered by the new eastern European market made for fierce competition, even between the two principal German companies. In Russian villages agents of the Hapag and Lloyd lines distributed brochures accusing each other of fraud and inflated ticket prices. The Bremen agent Friedrich Missler, one of the sharpest businessmen in this field, rewarded his subagents with small presents which were decorated with the company name and often his own picture. In this way handkerchiefs, snuff boxes, change purses, beer mugs, and even church clocks ended up in Hungary and Croatia: people there may not have known the North German Lloyd company, but they knew that Friedrich Missler could get them to America. When the government-subsidized British Cunard line »Austro-Americana« tried to break into the German-dom-

Jewish shipping agent's card

inated market with extremely low prices in 1904, the Bremen and Hamburg company headquarters practically ordered the agents to increase the use of illegal recruitment methods; the Senates of the two Hanseatic cities allowed this without comment despite strong protests from Vienna and Moscow.

The assignment of the agents was to recruit passengers for a particular shipping line and then assist them during the journey to the embarkation port. In Russia, however, hardly any of the emigrants could afford the high fees for a passport; this meant that, if agents wanted to earn a living, they had to help people emigrate illegally. The 1911 report of the Dillingham Commission, appointed by the U.S. Senate to investigate mass immigration problems, concluded that there would be virtually no emigration from eastern Europe to the U.S. without the advertising activities of the emigration agents and their help in evading restrictive laws. Although this way of looking at the situation ignores the fact that emigration was a result of miserable economic, social, and political conditions in the homeland, it was doubtless true that the work of the emigration agents in eastern Europe was more like that of the »sellers of souls« of previous centuries than like that of the professional agents of western Europe.

In 1889-1890 two Hapag agents who operated an office in Auschwitz (Oswiecim) were on trial for continuing fraud; the case gives us an impression of the unscrupulous tactics used by the agents in eastern and southeastern Europe. Jacob Klausner and Simon Herz had given generous bribes to railroad conductors, officials, customs agents, and even policemen. In their office, decorated by a German imperial eagle and a portrait of the Kaiser, they had a »telegraph« system (made from an old alarm clock) with which they claimed to book accommodations in Hamburg, arrange jobs in the U.S., or even communicate with the »Kaiser« of America on behalf of their clients. Policemen, respected and feared by the emigrants, were paid to report that America could only be reached via Hamburg. Anyone who bought a travel voucher for a line other than Hapag was urged or sometimes compelled to let it expire and

Passage contract of the Red Star Line (1909) in different languages, issued at Eydtkuhnen on the Prussian-Polish border

buy a »proper« voucher from the agency. Since the emigrants believed - or were told - that their journey was illegal, and since many young men wished to avoid the military draft, they did not resist these tactics. If anyone did, they would be arrested, imprisoned, beaten, and otherwise harassed by paid-off policemen until they gave in and followed the »advice« of the agents.

Of course, this agency, which sold about 12,400 transatlantic travel vouchers per year, was an especially crass example of ruthless business practices. But we must ask ourselves how such a situation could even arise. One reason for the way this agency operated was naturally the widespread corruption of the Russian and Austria-Hungarian bureaucracy: without the cooperation of magistrates, police officers, railroad employees, and customs guards, the agents would not have had a chance. On the other hand, the vast majority of the emigrants were helpless when confronted by the closed ranks of the emigration agents; they came from small villages and could neither read nor write. For these poor peasants America was the only hope for a better life in the future - they knew nothing about the U.S., but because so many of their dreams were connected with the country they were prepared to believe almost any stories, especially the good news. It was total ignorance of U.S. geography, for example, combined with childhood training to respect authority and trust unconditionally in information from government sources, that led to a tragic epi-

sode in 1899-1900. A group of 400 emigrants who booked passage to Canada were taken to Hawaii and sold to plantation owners. The highly specialized and strictly government regulated system of professional emigration agents which had developed in western Europe was not carried over into the eastern European market. Unscrupulous agents controlled the business there - a business on which the German steamship companies were becoming more and more dependent.

Emigration and Shipping: The Rise of the Shipping Lines

Mass overseas migration was almost exclusively emigration to North America, and hence the most important part of the journey for most emigrants was crossing the Atlantic. The first of the so-called »Atlantic packet« companies was the American *Black Ball Line*, founded in 1818, which operated *liners* (ships traveling the same route on a regular schedule) between Liverpool and New York, carrying mail and a few cabin passengers. In 1822 it was followed by the *Red Star* and the *Swallowtail* (both New York-Liverpool) and the *Black X Line* (New York-London), and more connections were added in rapid succession. All of these lines were operated by American firms. In the European countries, the shipowners tried to build up their companies again after the Napoleonic Wars and break into the transatlantic trade. Bremen

quickly became the leading contender on these routes, surpassing its strongest competition, Le Havre, by the end of the 1840s. As steamships replaced the sail-powered postal ships in the second half of the nineteenth century, the German ports of Hamburg and Bremen and their shipping companies, Hapag and North German Lloyd, respectively, were already by far the largest European lines operating on the North American routes. They were the most important shippers for the millions of emigrants going to the U.S., and thus we can characterize the rise of the shipping lines to great economic power by following the story of these two companies.

In Bremen the brothers Caspar and Hermann Heinrich Meier, who had business offices in both Bremen and New York, had begun offering regular direct service between the two cities in 1828. They identified two of their ships as postal liners, departing on the same day of every other month. Six postal trips per year did not seem significant compared to the large numbers of ships crossing the Atlantic on an as-needed basis, but merchants were attracted by the fact that these ships did not wait in port for a full cargo of freight or passengers but sailed on the appointed day unless prevented by really serious bad weather from doing so. The Meier brothers' line was a success, and in 1837 monthly

Der Norddeutsche Lloyd

von 1857 bis 1882.

for a ship to be ready to sail was both unpleasant for the emigrants and a source of problems for the city - as well as a clear indication that the economic possibilities of the emigration business were not being fully exploited. Building a sailing ship for regularly scheduled service, with space for steerage passengers, was not a great financial risk; the cost could be amortized in only four or five years. The shipbuilding industry expanded; there was more cargo space available; and shipowners could cover part of their expenses by selling passenger tickets to emigrants and thereby offer cheaper freight rates: the Hamburg and Bremen shipping trade prospered.

In 1845 some New York merchants were planning to start a new steamship company to compete with the government-subsidized British Cunard line, which had been operating nine paddle-driven ships since 1840. The U.S. government supported this new venture by granting it a contract for mail delivery to and from Europe. As to the decision as to its European destination, Bremen was able to win out over all rivals, both its Hanseatic sister city Hamburg and foreign competitors from England, Portugal, France, Belgium, the Netherlands, and Denmark. This victory was achieved by granting the new line cash advances - $100,000 from the Bremen Senate, the same amount from the Prussian government, and $89,000 from other German states. The new *Ocean Steam Navigation Company* began operating two ships, the »Washington« and the »Hermann« between New York and Bremen, with an intermediate stop at Cowes, England. This enterprise was of great economic importance for Bremen because it advertised the city's trade ties with North America all over Europe. Nevertheless, the line was unsuccessful: over the years, high coal costs, low freight and passenger income (the cost was too high for most emigrants), and technical problems (leading to frequent delays for repairs) made the line a money-losing enterprise. The American investors gave up in 1857, and the German financiers had to absorb a substantial financial loss.

It was at this point that the Bremen merchant H.H. Meier, Jr. and a few other busi-

service was initiated. Other companies initiated regular service as well: by 1849 there were 16 liners of Bremen ownership sailing the North Atlantic route on a scheduled basis. Eleven of these sailed to New York; three went to Philadelphia; and two went to New Orleans. In 1835 the Hamburg shipowner Miles Sloman began operating his first Atlantic liner, which had no significant competition until the foundation of the Hapag company in 1847.

The importance of the Atlantic routes grew rapidly, and Bremen's economy in particular became highly dependent on it. Hamburg had close commercial ties to England and also extensive trade with South America, Africa, and Australia. But in Hamburg, too, the increasing numbers of emigrants made regular routes to North America necessary. For one thing, a long wait at the port nessmen founded the *North German Lloyd*, recognizing that the economy of their city would be severely affected by the loss of a regular transatlantic steamship connection. Undaunted by the failure of the American venture, they used from the start only steamships on this line. The Hapag company in Hamburg had been operating steamships with steerage space for emigrants along with its regular sailing-ship service since 1856, reacting to the success of other lines in Liverpool, Antwerp, and Le Havre, where postal vessels were available to emigrants. Their strongest competitor, the Cunard line, had also been offering this service since 1853.

In the Hanseatic cities, merchants had waited a relatively long time before founding stock companies to finance transatlantic lines, and many of the transatlantic lines operated by private companies had gone bankrupt, lacking sufficient funds. The Lloyd company was actually the first stockholder-owned firm in the history of the Bremen shipping business. But the construction of steamships was significantly more expensive than that of sailing ships: the Hapag company, for example, paid more for its first two steamships than for six sailing ships built between 1847 and 1854. The foundation of the steamship lines led to a total reorganization of the financial structure of the shipping business: single individuals as shipowners, the so-called merchant shippers (*Kaufmannsreeder*) which had been typical for the Hanseatic cities, were replaced by companies with a broad economic basis, and soon a complex network of international financial links developed. The new lines offered cargo space as well, but the main focus was on the passenger trade. There were various classes of passenger comfort available, with steerage as the least expensive. Both Hapag and Lloyd had financial difficulties at first, and for both it was the thousands of steerage passengers who finally assured

their success. The Lloyd line in particular was dependent on the emigration trade, since the New York route was the economic foundation of the entire enterprise. The American lines soon lost their importance in the shipping traffic with Germany: 82 percent of the ships in the North Atlantic trade were American-owned in 1840, but the number sank to 60 percent in 1860, 35

percent in 1870, 12 percent in 1890, and less than 10 percent by 1900. From 1792 to 1912, American firms were required to have their ships built at American yards, and this rule made competition with their European rivals much more difficult. American capital went more and more to railroad construction, until at the end of the nineteenth century the railroad companies

Hapag poster from the 1870s

began to exert their growing influence on the European shipping business.

The sailing ships could compete with the powerful new steamships until about 1870. The older technology had a chance because the steamship passage was somewhat more expensive and because not all American ports were served by the new lines as yet. But the advantages of steamships for transatlantic crossings were evident: despite the greater number of passengers, the significantly

Captain Heinrich Wieting, known as the father of emigrants. He carried emigrants across the Atlantic for over 30 years

cantly shorter duration of the trip made it possible to bring along more abundant and above all fresher food and drinking water; illness on board was reduced; and the trip was less dangerous. While only about a third of all passengers traveled by steamship from Bremen in 1866, by 1871 it was 84 percent, and by 1874 98 percent. In Hamburg the last sailing ship with emigrants bound for North America left port in 1879. The number of passenger steamships increased so rapidly that in 1882 a Bremen newspaper, the *Bremer Handelsblatt*, demanded the establishment of »Atlantic sea lanes« and a speed limit in fog because there were purportedly too many collisions. Sailing ships were still used for freight, however, until the end of the century.

By 1876 the Lloyd company had no competition in Bremen, and Hapag achieved the same status in Hamburg by 1881. Technological improvements such as the propeller and later the double propeller, iron and steel hulls instead of wood, and more powerful and durable engines made it possible to build larger and faster ships. The Lloyd company introduced so-called high-speed steamships in 1881, three years after the British Guion Line became the first to build such ships and six years before the Hapag company followed suit. These ships were relatively small but especially fast, with a top speed of 16 nautical miles per hour instead of 12. They were preferred by better-off passengers, especially the growing numbers of American tourists, and therefore the number of steerage spaces available was small. For example, the Hapag ship »Deutschland« built in 1900 could carry 300 passengers in steerage, 420 in first class, and 332 in second class. Enormous ships were built for combined freight and passenger use (i.e., east-west travel with emigrants and cargo and west-east travel with mainly cargo). The shipowners calculated that the east-west trip should cover about two thirds of the total cost of a round trip, with the emigrant tickets covering over half of this amount.

In effect, the freight income was almost pure profit if all of the passenger places on a steamer could be filled. The first steamships had room for 500 passengers, which was already twice as great as that of sailing ships, but only 50 years later the steerage capacity had tripled. The Hapag steamship »Kaiserin Auguste Victoria« built in 1905 had room for 1800 steerage passengers as well as 900 in the cabin classes; the steerage deck could be reconfigured to hold cargo for the return voyage. The sailing ship »Deutschland« built in 1848 would have had to make two to three trips per year for six years to carry the cargo transported on one trip by the passenger steamship »Pennsylvania«, built in 1897 for the Hapag company.

Competitive pressure led most of the large companies to give the prestige factor more importance than economic calculation in making decisions. The Blue Riband awarded for the fastest Atlantic crossing

was very influential, turning every voyage into a race to be won regardless of cost. For the same reasons the ships' furnishings were selected with care and tended to be quite lavish. Since four-fifths of the profit came from the sale of steerage tickets, the extravagance of the upper decks was in effect being paid for by the poorest passengers. The trend towards ships of increasingly greater size, speed, and luxury made investment in new construction a more risky proposition. The number of steerage passengers remained the same, but immense amounts of coal were burned, and hundreds of firemen, stokers, stewards, cooks, and other personnel were employed in order to outdo the competition and win well-to-do passengers. Within the Hapag line, for example, the sailing ship »Deutschland« needed a crew of 17 to care for 220 passengers in 1848, while the steamship »Deutschland« needed 543 for 1000 passengers in 1900 and the »Kaiserin Auguste Victoria« used 600 crew for 2700 passengers in 1905. The gigantic »Imperator Class« of ships introduced in 1913 required a crew of over 1180, one third to one half of whom worked in the engine room. Faced with the fact that a twofold increase in speed used three times as much fuel, the director of the French *Compagnie Générale Transatlantique* (CGT) once complained that coal for the engine was now costing more than caviar for the first-class passengers.

In the 1890s Albert Ballin, the director of the Hapag company, decided to offer winter cruises in order to make use of the ships' capacity year round. This idea turned out to be quite profitable, and other lines soon copied it. The acceptance of these pleasure trips, which were soon offered on a smaller scale for a middle-class clientele, shows that sea voyages were no longer considered uncomfortable or dangerous. Since passenger travel was no longer completely dominated by emigrants, the decrease in the number of emigrants in the twentieth century did not threaten the economic existence of the shipping lines.

The leading firms in the emigration business were Hapag (1847) and Lloyd (1857) in Germany, Cunard (1840) and White Star (1869) in Great Britain, the CGT (1869) in

France, the Red Star Line (1872) in Belgium, and the Holland-America Line (1873) in the Netherlands. Many of these companies only survived economically because of government support: Cunard, for example, could not have begun the first transatlantic steamship service without government funding, and the CGT also needed regular subsidies.

In southern and eastern Europe, national steamship lines were maintained for political reasons, so that the governments could at least get some economic advantage from emigration. The Russian line from Libau to New York, for example, was established only in order to participate in the emigration business, but had little success. The Italian emigration law of 1901 attempted to protect the national shipping companies from the competition of the powerful foreign lines by regulating the price of steerage tickets. And when the Hungarian government signed an agreement with Cunard in 1904, opening a new line from Fiume to New York, it was in the hope that having an embarkation port would bring in some income from emigration, even without a national shipping company. None of these supported and subsidized shipping companies had a real economic chance, however, against the large northern European lines, especially the German lines.

In Germany, the economist Friedrich List had tried to convince the members of the German Customs Union of the advantages of a national steamship line in 1841. But the lack of a central authority which could forge compromises among the conflicting interests of the German states meant that such proposals could not be realized. Neither Hapag nor Lloyd received state money, not even after the unification of Germany in 1871 - a fact which the directors often noted with pride. To be sure, they neglected to mention the indirect support both companies profited from, such as the 1885 law subsidizing postal ships at up to 4,000,000 marks per year, provided that »if possible« the ships were built at German shipyards. Previously most of the steamships had been built in England, where the newest technology was available at advantageous terms.

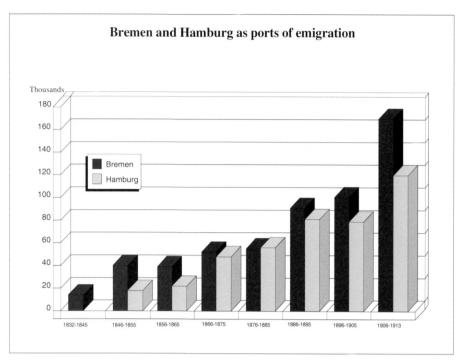

Bremen and Hamburg as ports of emigration

National pride and prestige and the high profits to be made in the emigration trade led to the appearance - and often the rapid disappearance - of many smaller lines. The Hapag company in particular had to defend itself again and again from the incursions of new competitors. In 1872 Robert M. Sloman's Transatlantic Steamship Company (*Transatlantische Dampfschiffahrtsgesellchaft*), known as the *Adler Linie*, began operation with three ships on the Hamburg-New York route, and only two years later there were eight ships. The success of this company was based on very low prices, achieved by reducing the services provided to steerage passengers to a minimum. The Hapag company was forced to reduce its prices, and in summer 1874 a ticket to New York cost 30 Taler instead of 55. But the economic crisis of 1873-1874, which was also felt in the U.S., ruined Sloman's plans. Despite high commissions for emigration agents and despite low prices, the number of emigrants fell: no one wanted to risk a new start in a country shaken by crisis. Sloman was prepared to sell, and the Hapag company, despite its own financial difficulties, saw a takeover as the only way to be permanently rid of this

competitor; the agreement was signed in May 1875, and Hapag gained seven steamships, six freight barges, a landing dock in New York, and several warehouses. The company's financial reserves were drained, however, and it had to fight for its life when the crisis dragged on into 1876. The situation became so precarious that one crossing had to be canceled: hardly any cargo and only seven steerage passengers had been booked. It took three years for the Hapag company to recover its strength, three years which its competition, the Lloyd company, used to its advantage.

After only a short time, Hapag was confronted with a new rival. The number of emigrants had just reached a new high when Edward Carr, one of Robert Sloman's former partners, founded a Hamburg-New York line which carried only freight and steerage passengers. Hapag reacted by using more of its ships on this route, but the price war that broke out in 1882 had a serious effect on the company, as reflected in the sinking dividends paid to stockholders - 9 percent in 1882, 4 percent in 1883, and zero in the two following years. The price competition soon touched other lines as well, and the transatlantic fares fell every-

Poster of the leading French shipping company 1935

where. In 1885 the market collapsed, and a cooperative effort involving all the affected lines was necessary. The Hapag company convened a meeting in Cologne on July 1, 1885, involving five major shipping companies, Hapag, Lloyd, Union, Holland-America, and Red Star. They signed the first agreement setting uniform passenger fares. CGT and Cunard refused to cooperate, but otherwise this approach showed promise: Carr offered to sell out to Hapag, although a price could not yet be agreed on. In 1886 Carr merged his company with Sloman's *Union Line*, which had signed the Cologne agreement, and in May of that year Hapag and Union established a cooperative booking agency for steerage passengers, ending the ruinous competition in emigrant transportation. This new department was headed by Albert Ballin, who had worked for Carr and later was director of the Hapag company for many years. Ballin was a leader in the fight for international cooperation among transatlantic lines. Fundamentally, the lines had a common interest in preventing such catastrophic price wars. They met again in Cologne in the late 1890s, when Hapag, Lloyd, Red Star, and Holland-America founded the North Atlantic Steamship Association (NDLV), which constructed a complex set of treaties regulating the transport of steerage passengers in detail. Not only fares and agent commissions were set, but also the market shares of the member companies. A member was not allowed to increase its share at the expense of another member, and these quotas, calculated on the basis of tonnage for each line and regularly updated, were the most important part of the agreement. If a company exceeded the limit by transporting more passengers than was permitted, it had to pay a certain amount of money to a fund which compensated other companies for financial losses incurred when they failed to reach their quotas. A permanently employed NDLV official monitored the process, collected the monthly payments, and prepared a yearly financial statement which was the basis for any quota adjustments required; disputes among the member lines were settled by an arbitration commission. All the lines had monopoly rights in certain ports, and their shares in the transport of mail and cargo were also determined. In 1892 the fares for crossings from America to Europe were made part of the agreement as well.

Although not all lines were included (the important British lines did not want to give up their national independence), the NDLV was a success for its members. A supplementary treaty, the *British Continental Contract* of September 1895, made the British lines temporary members of the NDLV (for three years), while at the same time extending its provisions to the cabin classes. The CGT joined the group in 1903, followed by the *Canada Pacific Company* and the *Austro-Americana* in 1904 and finally by the *Russian America Line*.

At the beginning of the twentieth century, serious competition for the NDLV began to emerge in the U.S. American shipping companies had played only a minor role in the transatlantic market for many years, and neither the *International Navigation Company* (founded in 1891 in a merger of the America and Red Star lines) nor the *Atlantic Transport Line* (founded in 1898) was able to cut into the profits of the European shippers significantly. But when J. Pierpont Morgan bought the *Southern Railway* in 1901, he gained control of the rail lines serving the southern Atlantic and Gulf coasts, except for New Orleans and Galveston. This meant that, when the shipowners wanted to negotiate for the transfer and transport of freight, they had to deal with a powerful company which could dictate terms. Morgan also seized the opportunity and founded his own transatlantic steamship line. In rapid succession he bought up existing companies - the Leyland and White Star lines in Great Britain, the International Navigation Company and Atlantic Transport Line in the U.S., and the Dominion Line in Canada. These purchases had exhausted his financial reserves, so he was looking for partners. Hapag and Lloyd were interested in this possibility, and the German Kaiser himself urged them to explore it, wishing to avoid competition between German and American lines. In 1902 the parties signed an agreement delineating their spheres of influence. This made it possible for Morgan to buy the Holland-America Line and begin

A last good-bye - lighthouse »Roter Sand« in the Weser delta, 1898

negotiations for the CGT as well. When his new company, the *International Mercantile Marine Company* (IMMCO), began operations in 1903, it was linked loosely to the NDLV through its agreements with Hapag and Lloyd.

The Cunard line pursued its own interests and tried to work against the NDLV. It accepted the invitation of the Hungarian government to open the route between Fiume and New York in exchange for financial support. Hapag and Lloyd were strongly opposed to this arrangement because they saw it as a threat to their dominance of the eastern European migration business. The most disastrous price war in the history of the NDLV followed. Emigrants profited from the events, which

drove steerage fares to new lows, and freight tariffs were reduced as well. The NDLV members fought back by opening new routes in areas, traditionally served by Cunard: Hapag now offered a new service between Scandinavia and New York. The economic losses resulting from this price war were immense, about 20 million marks for the members of the NDLV, according to its estimates. When the situation for the shippers worsened dramatically as a result of the economic crisis of 1907, the competing groups met for negotiations which led to the establishment of the Atlantic Conference in June 1908, one of the most important organizations in the history of the shipping industry. The agreements reached regulated the transatlantic transport of steerage and cabin passengers and cargo and included all the members of the NDLV, Cunard, IMMCO, and the Canadian lines. They came just in time to blunt the effects of a serious economic recession in the U.S. which, like all such crises, produced a sudden drop in the number of European emigrants. The Conference controlled the transatlantic traffic until shortly before World War I.

The treaty provisions constantly had to be checked, modified, and adapted and were thus very unstable and subject to objections from the members. In 1913 the shipping lines and the major railroad companies met in Berlin to discuss disagreements involving the Canadian group. There were unresolvable differences with respect to the calculation of tonnage between the two German shippers, Hapag and Lloyd, the key members of the NDLV. Hapag withdrew from both the NDLV and the Conference; the Atlantic Conference broke apart. Difficult negotiations followed, with some hope of a positive outcome, but the outbreak of World War I made further cooperation impossible.

Despite constant competitive struggles, the shipping companies made huge profits from the emigration trade. A few large companies dominated the national markets and developed the strategy of international cooperation. For the emigrants the introduction of this »pool policy« made conditions and prices more stable, but on the other hand competition was stifled, and fewer advantageous offers were available. For the lines the allocation of routes and market shares was worth its costs, and cooperation made it easier to defend themselves against new competition and undertake expansion at lower risk. In this environment of relative security Hapag and Lloyd, for example, were able to extend their routes on a grand scale. The companies united in the pools controlled the events in the emigration business; the emigrants themselves often became mere pawns or trading chips in confrontations between powerful economic interests.

Food and Lodging in Hamburg and Bremen

At the beginning of the nineteenth century emigrants arriving at the port usually could not board their ships immediately to prepare for the transatlantic voyage; even in the 1850s, the stay in the port city often lasted several weeks. Even when steamships took over, the emigration agents made sure the emigrants arrived several days before the sailing date to allow time for the required medical examinations and other formalities. Businesses in the Hanseatic cities quickly adapted to this new group of customers, who primarily needed food, lodging, and equipment and provisions for the voyage. People leaving Europe to seek a new life were not rich, but generally they had sold everything they owned so as to have some money to get started in America; the only really poor emigrants were those whose passage was being paid by their homeland governments. The merchants of the Hanseatic cities thus had reasonable hopes of making a profit from the transit migration.

These profits were so lucrative, in fact, that traders and peddlers of all sorts tried to get into the business, and fraud, deception, and exploitation of inexperienced migrants became more and more common. The increasing number of customers also made

the competition among innkeepers, money changers, and shopkeepers more intense, but this did not work to the advantage of the emigrants: hardly anyone tried to lure customers with lower prices or better service; on the contrary, the offices, shops, inns, and exchange agencies tried to increase their business using special employees (called *Litzer* in Bremen and *Buttjer* in Hamburg) who were paid a certain sum for each customer they brought in. For a long time no one paid much attention to the methods used by the *Litzer* and *Buttjer* to attract customers, even when it was well known that these commonly included lies, false promises, threats, and even violence. In both Hamburg and Bremen, numerous emigrants fell into the hands of these agents and their employers.

The government authorities and honest businessmen soon recognized that this sort of activity endangered the reputation of their cities and that something must be undertaken to control it. In 1851, so-called emigrant information agencies were opened for this purpose. These were a purely private institution in Hamburg, whereas in Bremen they had a half-official character, supervised and staffed by the Senate. In both cities, employees of the agencies met emigrants arriving from Berlin at the railroad station and took them to

their offices, where they were give free information about the average prices for food and lodging, travel needs, and baggage transportation; about money exchange rates; and about their travel options. They were advised about what to expect when they arrived in the U.S., warned about the tricks played by the swindlers (*runners*) who were active there, and given the addresses of the German consulates, German societies, or other aid organizations for immigrants. Aside from policemen and the employees of the information agencies, no one was allowed on the platform when an emigration train was arriving.

Naturally this procedure made it much more difficult for the *Litzer* and *Buttjer*, and so honest businesses tried to cooperate with the information agencies. The agency in Bremen negotiated a contract with the innkeepers' association and issued licenses to certain establishments, which then had to follow certain rules. Beginning in 1879, innkeepers in Hamburg submitted price lists to the agency for approval. The agencies then booked emigrants for these inns, even trying to accommodate their special needs - when possible, for example, they sent Jewish transit migrants to a hostel operated by a Jewish innkeeper. The emigrants could choose lodgings in three price classes, depending on the availability and

The hotel »Stadt Warschau« in Bremen, ca. 1910

quality of meals and rooms, which ranged from a mattress in a large dormitory to one's own bed with linens in a multibed or single room. On July 1, 1868 the Bremen Senate issued regulations for the operation of lodgings for emigrants. The innkeepers had to live on the premises, and the number of guests was limited in that each person had to have at least 9 cubic meters of space (12 cubic meters in hotels). Every establishment was inspected once a month by officials of the health department, with no warning and often at night - to check, for example, that men and women were sleeping in separate dormitories.

This system of licensing and control of lodgings functioned very well, but other sectors of the emigration business were much more difficult to monitor. Emigrants needed all sorts of items for the transatlantic journey - extra food (beyond that required to be carried by Hamburg and Bremen ships), cooking and eating utensils, mattresses and bedding, and a few dollars in cash for the first few days. Tobacco, alcohol, tools, and weapons were also bought by many emigrants, and there were also useless items that migrants were talked into buying as souvenirs. It is difficult to say how much the merchants of the Hanseatic cities made on such sales, but it was certainly not an insignificant amount. Estimates indicate that eastern European emigrants spent about 500,000 marks per year in Hamburg during the 1880s, and after 1900, when the number of emigrants increased, the amount was probably higher. These Russian transit migrants, however, were not permitted to leave the emigrant hostels where they were housed, which was a serious disappointment for the small shopkeepers. Bremen and the villages along the Weser were already earning about 1 million Taler per year from emigration business in 1840, and the profit for the city of Bremen alone was 4.5 million Taler between 1832 and 1855. It was estimated that each person expended 50-70 Taler on the way to his new homeland, of which about 10 percent was spent in the embarkation port. In 1873, an unexpected drop in the number of emigrants due to economic recession left many merchants in dire economic straits.

The emigrants' house in Bremerhaven, 1850-63

The question was how to monitor all of these diverse kinds of economic activity. The information agencies handed out lists of average prices for various articles; they warned emigrants about shopkeepers who were known cheaters; and they offered help to emigrants who had been taken in. These measures did not completely eliminate the duping of emigrants, but did reduce it. Overall, the information agencies did much to spread and maintain the good reputation of the Hanseatic cities as embarkation ports. With the railroad lines completed and steamships in use for the transatlantic

The interior of a third-class emigrant house 1882

voyage, it became possible for travelers to calculate departure and arrival times in advance and thus spend less time waiting in the harbor; but during such waits they were glad to take advantage of the information agencies.

In Bremen before about 1850 the situation was somewhat more difficult than in Hamburg, because the city had to transport the emigrants from town to the actual harbor in Bremerhaven. They were put on board open freight barges and taken down the Weser, which was very uncomfortable and lasted two or three days - or even longer if the water level was low or the barge stuck on one of the many sandbars. Since the departure of the sailing ships could be delayed by wind and tidal conditions, emigrants often had to wait for weeks more in Bremerhaven or the nearby villages; finding lodging for hundreds of transit migrants was a continual problem. Many shipowners brought the passengers directly on board, which was very unhealthy, and in 1847 regulations were issued requiring that the housing provided in Bremerhaven be no worse than the steerage deck. Many emigrants left in 1848, and the numbers seemed to be growing; the Bremen merchant Georg Claussen therefore decided the time was right to build a special residence for emigrants, the *Auswandererhaus*. The Bremen Senate supported this plan by providing a site at low cost, and the building was finished in 1850. The large dormitories had room for up to 2000 people, and the kitchen could feed as many as 3500. The building also housed an infirmary and a chapel, in which Protestant and Catholic services alternated. This home, privately managed but state-controlled, was very effective in winning emigration business for Bremerhaven. One of the factors leading to its construction had been growing competition from nearby villages such as Lehe and Geestemunde. The enterprise was a great success, and soon the *Auswandererhaus* was providing lodging and especially meals not only to emigrants but also to nonlocal dock workers and sailors.

In 1854 it was made illegal to house emigrants aboard ship for more than one day prior to sailing, and during this year a daily average of 244 emigrants lived in the

In 1851 Bremen established an agency for the protection of emigrants

Auswandererhaus. After that the number went down, however, partly due to a general decrease in the number of emigrants and partly because waiting times after arrival in Bremerhaven were shortened due to technological advances. Steam-powered vessels had replaced the Weser barges, which were banned from carrying emigrants after 1864. There was a rail connection between Bremen and Bremerhaven after 1862, making it possible to calculate travel times exactly. Merchants in Bremen were no longer willing to share the profits to be earned from the emigrants with Bremerhaven, and despite vehement protests from businessmen and innkeepers in the smaller harbor town, the shipping companies began to keep their passengers in Bremen until one day before the ship sailed. This had a noticeable effect on the Bremerhaven economy, and the *Auswandererhaus*, which had already been struggling financially since about 1858, had to close in 1860. The building was later used as a barracks, as a military hospital, and as

a brewery, and today it is used by a Bremerhaven educational institution.

The measures taken in Bremen to regulate emigrant housing were modeled after those in Hamburg: there, too, the migrants could choose between two classes of inns, with prices and services agreed upon by the information agency and the innkeepers' association. In 1868 the inns in Bremen were inspected by a commission from the North German Confederation, which was impressed by the quality of the lodgings but complained that the prices were often somewhat excessive. The commission also commented that emigrants could have been housed just as well and at lower cost in the Bremerhaven *Auswandererhaus*, but by this time Bremen operators had succeeded in diverting the transit migrants away from the harbor town. With respect to protection of emigrants during the transatlantic voyage, Bremen had a model policy; with respect to protection in Bremen, however, the Senate seemed more interested in the well-being of the merchants than in that of the emigrants. This became especially clear after 1890, when the city's inns were overfilled almost year round. The steady stream of migrants forced the authorities to open emergency shelters in barns, theaters, dance halls, and unused factories, and people were lodged in the railroad stations as well. These shelters lacked sufficient sanitary facilities, and in 1890 one reporter wrote of about 1300 people crowded together like cattle on the floor of a factory building. Still the city did not do anything to change these conditions until 1907; the idea of lodging at least some of the emigrants in Bremerhaven was not even considered.

In the late 1880s, when there were still many Germans leaving and the emigration from eastern and southeastern Europe was beginning to grow, Hamburg also had difficulties housing such large numbers of people. After 1891 the Hapag company used mothballed steamships as houseboats, holding as many as 1000 migrants each, and public buildings were also used as shelters. In contrast to Bremen, however, the Hamburg Senate did take action to alleviate these intolerable conditions. In 1892 Hapag was given the task of constructing emigrant barracks and given free land next to the *Amerikaquai*, where its ships docked. These barracks were opened for operation in July 1892 under the control of the police and provided dormitories, common rooms, and dining halls for up to 1400 transit migrants, who were brought directly to the barracks by train. In the beginning emigrants were allowed to leave the barracks and seek lodging in the city as before, once they had completed the various entry procedures; but when cholera broke out in August, a veritable quarantine was imposed on Russian transit migrants, who were falsely accused of introducing the disease. The innkeepers of the city protested vehemently against this action because it cut drastically into their business, but the authorities refused to compromise. This imposed housing strategy and other measures (like the closing of the Russian-German border) led to a noticeable reduction in the number of emigrants, and many innkeepers had to close their establishments. There were 52 proprietors licensed to house transit migrants in 1886, but by 1901 only 13 remained, and by 1913 there were only eight such inns.

The emigrants were well cared for in the barracks, and numerous improvements were introduced over the years, usually after criticism in the media. When the city needed the land at the *Amerikaquai* for expansion of the harbor in 1901, the Hapag company planned in detail and constructed an »emigrant village« near the harbor, in the Veddel section of the city. The emigrant trains traveled without making any intermediate stops to the Veddel shelter, which was surrounded by a wall and divided into two sections, an »unclean« area for arriving transit migrants and a »clean« area for those who had completed the medical examination, disinfection, and bathing procedures and were ready for embarkation. There were an infirmary and a medical observation station, and each dormitory was designed for a maximum of 22 persons. The total capacity of the shelter was 3000 emigrants, and two hotels located inside the Veddel complex offered smaller rooms for those who wished to pay extra for more comfortable lodgings. The emigration village included large common rooms and dining halls, numerous washrooms and

showers, Catholic and Protestant chapels, and even a music pavilion. All of the buildings had central heating and electric lights, and the village provided separate living quarters and kosher cooking for Jewish migrants. Contemporary accounts describe these accommodations as exemplary, and they served as models for other facilities. The innkeepers of the city found it hard to compete with this centralized housing: only Russian emigrants were required to live there, but because comfort was offered at quite low prices few emigrants chose to take lodgings in the city.

In Bremen, as we have seen, the Senate placed the interests of the merchants and innkeepers above those of the emigrants for a relatively long period. Transit migrants

station. Still there were 52 licensed emigration hotels with a total of 3537 beds in Bremen in 1904.

But the periods of total overfilling, with hundreds of emigrants housed in emergency shelters with inadequate sanitation, became more and more frequent and became a health risk for the city. The public health authority demanded a solution along the lines of what was being done in Hamburg, and the authorities finally reacted in 1906, when the housing capacity for transit

Emigrant hunters and luggage thieves

had to find private lodgings before 1907, and since most of the transportation business was in the hands of two large firms, Morawetz and Friedrich Missler, there was a similar financial concentration in the lodging sector. Friedrich Missler, emigration agent for the North German Lloyd, also operated the two largest emigration hotels in Bremen, the »City of Warsaw« and the »Slavic House«. In 1903 he also opened an inexpensive restaurant, which also offered kosher meals, near the train

migrants was exceeded 35 times. Working in cooperation with Friedrich Missler, the North German Lloyd finally built emigrant quarters - in 1907 there were eleven halls with room for 3400 people, in addition to the 1100 private beds still available from licensed emigrant innkeepers in the city. No one was forced to live in the emigrant quarters, and all migrants were free to come and go in the city. For several years Russian transit migrants were more frequently lodged on the outskirts of the city, in houses soon referred to as »Russian quarters« by local people. The pattern that developed later was that the somewhat better-off German emigrants took private quarters, while the transit migrants from eastern and south-eastern Europe chose the more economical emigrant shelters. The latter cannot be compared with the highly organized facilities in Hamburg, but now at least Bremen had reasonable housing with satisfactory sanitary conditions to offer the arriving emigrants.

Perfect organization, however, also implied assembly-line-like processing of the emigrants, who often felt demeaned by such treatment, and the underlying motivation for improved care of the emigrants was always to increase business. On the other hand, it should also be pointed out that institutions such as the information agencies and emigrant shelters provided significant benefits for many emigrants. The problems faced and in most cases solved by the embarkation ports were repeated on the other side of the Atlantic; in many destinations, especially in the U.S., similar regulations and facilities were established to control the business of immigration.

From Sailing Ship to Steamship: The Voyage

Overseas tourism seems natural to us today, and it is hard to imagine that a crossing of the Atlantic was a dangerous and uncertain voyage 150 years ago. The most important factor for the emigrants was the decision to leave home and make a new start in an unknown foreign land. The realization of this decision was often hard, but the voyage itself was the most strenuous and hazardous part of the emigration process. On the journey to the embarkation port and on the way to their final destination after landing in America, the emigrants were faced with numerous problems, but in these situations they could at least choose for themselves who their agent should be, what means of transportation they should take, where they should stay at night, and what they should buy. Aboard a transatlantic ship, on the other hand, they had hardly any choices and

could only hope for continued good health and an uneventful voyage.

In the age of the sailing ship, before about 1850, the crossing was so exhausting and dangerous that few people wanted to make it a second time; the steamship made it feasible for more migrants to consider a return visit to their old homelands. Sailing ships were completely dependent on the wind and weather, and thus it was practically impossible to predict the duration of a voyage. In addition, captains and owners regarded emigrants more or less as cargo and provided only the bare necessities as far as food and accommodations were concerned. Steerage was a makeshift passenger space built between the upper deck and the cargo hold; it could easily be removed again so more cargo could be loaded on the return voyage from America to Europe. A series of rough double bunks, each designed to hold five persons, was built against the walls of the ship, and sometimes also in a row along the beam. The shipowners allowed each adult a strip of space about a foot and half wide; children got half of this amount; and very small children were not included in the calculation at all. These bunks, however, were not just sleeping places - they were basically the only space available to the emigrants for the entire duration of the voyage. Most of the baggage was stowed in the cargo space below the steerage deck, but all the boxes and chests that held what people needed during the trip were piled up between the bunks. Many captains also stored cargo in the steerage area, and no tables or benches were provided.

The emigrants were supposed to bring their own mattresses, bedding, and cooking utensils; for a long time they had to bring food as well, but later in Hamburg and Bremen this important part of travel planning was shifted to the shipping companies. There were a few toilets on the upper deck, and a tub of sea water was heated for washing. Cooking stoves were provided only on the open deck, since fires in steerage were strictly forbidden. Since all emigrants (and that usually meant the women) wanted to prepare a warm meal every day, the number of stoves was never enough, and cooking was a constant problem. Those who were

unable to expend the energy and fight for a cooking slot on deck usually had to go without a hot meal that day. Many captains tried to help by organizing cooking groups and designating cooking times for each group, but only the good will of the captain and the degree of discipline among the emigrants determined whether this kind of organization would make the trip more bearable or not.

Steerage passengers were a motley crew, with men, women, and children of all ages and of differing nationalities and religions packed together in a tiny space for weeks at a time. They came from all occupations and social classes and traveled as families, as groups of friends, or alone. They had to get along with each other for a relatively long time - six to eight weeks in the eighteenth century or five to six weeks with a sailing ship in the nineteenth century. Inclement weather, storm-induced damage to the ship, or even a long period of calm could make the trip even longer, with voyages of up to 100 days not uncommon.

The trip lasted for weeks, with poor sanitation and insufficient, unfamiliar food; these conditions continually caused problems for the steerage passengers. If they had to supply their own provisions, emigrants often purchased food that was lacking in quality or quantity - because of ignorance, lack of money, or the bad advice of unscrupulous merchants. Captains always had extra provisions on board which they could sell the emigrants, but many took advantage of the emigrants' misfortune and charged exorbitant prices. Hunger became a regular passenger on the emigrant ships. The drinking water which shipowners were required to provide was also mentioned in many complaints. Usually the water was taken from a river shortly before sailing, but it was stored in whatever barrels were available (which may have contained sugar, vinegar, turpentine, or petroleum), and there was no way to keep them cool on board. Soon after sailing it began to have a musty taste, and on many trips it became undrinkable. Captains tried homegrown remedies such as adding vinegar or molasses to the water, but these were of very questionable value. Spoiled drinking water was one of the main causes of illness, which

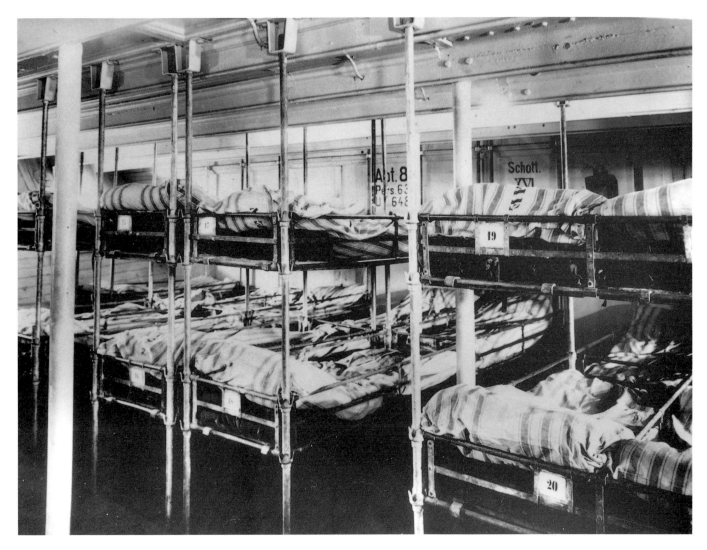

Steerage, in its customary form, on a North German Lloyd emigrant ship between 1890 and 1914

could become an epidemic and spread quickly through the steerage deck, aided by poor sanitation and the fact that air and light reached the steerage deck only through hatches from above (which had to be closed in rough weather). There was no way to isolate sick passengers, and no doctor was available to care for them; sometimes the captain had simple remedies to give them. In the half-darkened, poorly ventilated steerage deck hundreds of emigrants ate, slept, and all too often became seasick, so that the health of many deteriorated as the trip progressed. It was very difficult to maintain even minimal personal cleanliness under these primitive conditions. Passengers were urged to go up on deck as often as possible, and if weather permitted

they took their bedding up for airing or washing. At these times the steerage deck was thoroughly cleaned and disinfected with vinegar, and to combat bad odors buckets of hot tar were taken below to evaporate. This method was very risky on wooden ships, however. In 1858 a bucket on the sailing ship »Austria« tipped over and set the ship ablaze; only 79 of 542 passengers survived.

Accidents such as fires, sinkings, and shipwrecks were infrequent, but when they occurred there were many fatalities. Every emigrant who boarded ship had heard of

such incidents, but the danger of becoming ill during the voyage was much greater than that of dying in an accident at sea. The number of passengers who never reached their destination or died soon after landing was relatively high. Between 1854 and 1858, for example, the average percentage was 1.8 percent for passengers on Hamburg ships and 0.4 percent for ships from Bremen. Nevertheless, millions of people reached the New World after a journey that was strenuous and uncomfortable, but which presented no particular problems outside of boredom. Some even took with them pleasant memories of the voyage, and contemporary illustrations even showed emigrants dancing and enjoying themselves on deck.

Dinner time in the steerage, engraving from 1882

Storm, engraving from 1886

Yet catastrophe was always possible, and the emigrant could do little to lower the risk. That was especially true during periods of peak migration, when ships were frequently overloaded. In 1816-1817, when thousands of Germans crowded into Amsterdam and Rotterdam to embark for America, every shipowner took on passengers, regardless of whether his ship was suited for such use. The »April«, for example, took 1200 passengers into its makeshift steerage area, and over 400 died before the ship even reached the Atlantic. When thousands of Irish emigrants fled starvation between 1846 and 1850, so-called »Irish fever ships« began arriving in America and were quarantined by the authorities. Between June and November 1847 alone more than 10,000 Irish immigrants died at the quarantine stations. Friedrich Kapp, a fugitive from the German revolution of 1848 and later a Commissioner of Emigration for the state of New York, reported:

»On the 8th of May, 1847, the *Urania*, from Cork, with several hundred immigrants on board, a large proportion of them sick and dying of ship-fever, was put into quarantine at Grosse Isle. This was the first of the plague-smitten ships from Ireland which that year sailed up the St. Lawrence. But before the first week of June as many as eighty-four ships of various tonnage were driven in by an easterly wind; and of that enormous number of vessels there was not one free from that taint of malignant typhus, the offspring of famine and of foul ship-hold. This fleet of vessels literary reeked of pestilence.«

The actions of the captain during the crossing were often of vital significance. Most of them were honest and responsible men, and newspapers of the time often carried advertisements paid for by passengers, publicly thanking the captain and crew of a particular ship for care and kind treatment. But there were also captains who took bad care of their »human cargo«. Friedrich Kapp told of cases such as that of the British sailing ship »James Foster, Jr.«, whose crew forced the steerage passengers to work because the captain had hired too few trained hands. Young emigrants were badly abused; »some arrived so exhausted that they were hardly able to leave the ship

Clipper Italiano Cosmos Detto Pilota di Connellati 3... 'Costruito in Legni Remati nel Cantier da Costruttor Fratelli Cadenaccie
Armator Fratelli Bagnalli Genua

Italian sailing ship in service on the Genoa - Montevideo route

unaided«. Physical mistreatment and the failure to fulfill contractual obligations were hard to prove, and emigrants had little hope that such abuses would be punished by the legal system.

This fact and the frequent epidemics on board, which were correctly attributed to poor nutrition and generally poor conditions, led the U.S. government to act. In contrast to the German states, which for the most part did not approve of emigration and therefore did little to ease the plight of those who left, the U.S. authorities had to deal directly with the consequences of unregulated transatlantic crossings. Their welfare agencies, hospitals, and poorhouses had to take in and care for immigrants who arrived half-starved, sick, and impoverished.

The first federal legislation regulating the transatlantic traffic was passed in 1819, as a result of the overcrowded and completely underequipped emigrant ships from the Netherlands, which had aroused vehement public debate about the care and treatment of emigrants. The German societies in America in particular called for legal control measures. The new law stipulated that no more than two passengers could be transported for each five registered tons of the ship, that the shipowner had to provide a minimum amount of food, and that each arriving captain had to present a list of all passengers (with age, sex, occupation, birthplace, and date of arrival for each) and a separate account of all passengers who had died on the way. The introduction of the passenger list had important consequences for later historians, but not for the emigrants of 1819. Nor did the other provisions have the hoped-for effect: provisions could only be checked on outgoing ships, and the limitation on passenger numbers was ineffective because the calculation was based on total tonnage rather than the space actually available in steerage. Thus a large ship would be allowed to carry many passengers even though its steerage deck was very small or crowded with cargo.

Still this first law must be seen as an honest attempt at overseeing the transatlantic crossing and making it safer for the emigrants. In the Hanseatic cities of Hamburg and Bremen this example was followed (in 1832 and 1837, respectively) in detailed regulations for the voyage. Here, too, humanitarian motives were probably less important than a desire to limit the social costs of uncontrolled emigration for the governments. In the 1840s, as emigration rates began to rise significantly (reaching an absolute peak in the twentieth century), thousands of completely destitute, half-starved Irish immigrants started to arrive in

Express steamer »Kaiser Wilhelm II.« arriving at Bremerhaven

New York. It was clear that the law of 1819 was insufficient, and on February 22, 1847 a new law was passed establishing a minimum amount of space for each passenger in steerage, 14 square feet per adult, with bunks no shorter than 6 feet and no narrower than 18 inches; children less than 8 years old were not included in this calculation.

Many political leaders in the U.S. considered even this law insufficient, and in May of the same year the state of New York passed its own law, creating Commissioners of Emigration. To be sure, this commission was only responsible for the welfare of the immigrants after their arrival, and the crossing itself remained the hardest part of the journey to control. Secretary of State James Buchanan sent a representative to Europe in 1827 to gather information on the embarkation and transport conditions in different ports, in preparation for further

legislation. This delegate, Dudley Mann, inspected harbors in England, Ireland, France, Belgium, the Netherlands, and Germany and prepared a detailed report on his findings to be sent to Washington. In most countries, he found, no one protected the emigrants; except in the German ports they were at the mercy of brokers, shipowners, and captains. The regulations

adopted in Hamburg and Bremen were considered ideal, and Bremen in particular was singled out for praise. But since Mann had been U.S. representative in Bremen for many years and had good relations with Bremen merchants, his description was not really unbiased in this respect. Mann's report was the basis for amendments to the U.S. legislation - the *Act to Provide for the Ventilation of Passenger Vessels, and for other Purposes* of May 17, 1848 and the *Act to Regulate the Carriage of Passengers in Steamships and other Vessels* of March 3, 1855. The latter law was especially designed, as suggested by Dudley Mann, to improve the lot of steerage passengers, pre-

vent starvation, and make it possible to prosecute shipowners or captains for breaking contracts or mistreating passengers during the voyage.

Thus both in Europe and in the U.S. there were efforts at making the risks of the crossing more bearable for emigrants, and each of these efforts had some positive effects. But often business interests stood in the way of enforcement of the laws. For example, the U.S. law of 1847 was strongly rejected by European emigration agents and shipping companies. The space requirements drastically reduced the number of steerage passengers in many cases, shrinking profits. Higher fares were one result, and many agents tried to collect the higher prices even for tickets sold before the new regulations were passed - even though the shipping companies had been granted a three-month transition period. Bremen businessmen declared that the new law would ruin them, but naturally this did not prove to be the case in the long term; the highly profitable emigration business did not come to a stop. Even if the profit margin on each ticket decreased, the merchants had no trouble making up the loss and more by raising prices.

It was technological progress, however, rather than laws that eventually made transatlantic travel less unnerving. Many things changed for steerage passenger when steamships replaced the sailing ships, a process that was complete by the late 1870s on the North Atlantic routes, and some problems simply disappeared. With steamships the voyage lasted less than three weeks (17 days on average), and the high-speed ships built in the 1880s and available to steerage passengers in the 1890s made the trip in only 9 days. The advantages of a shorter travel time are obvious: fresher and more abundant provisions improved passenger meals, and illness was less life-threatening than on voyages lasting several weeks. Furthermore, emigration was now an important business in its own right, so that passengers were no longer seen and treated as replacements for freight. The new steamships were built expressly for passenger service, with carefully designed sanitary facilities such as washrooms, separate dormitories for men and women, special sections for families and groups, several kitchens, and cabins for sick passengers. Later there was even some degree of comfort offered the steerage passengers - a special cook was hired for this group, and in the 1880s tables and benches were even provided. By 1900 there were separate dining halls for steerage passengers, with kosher meals provided for Jewish migrants. Mattresses, bedding, and dishes were now supplied by the shipping lines. Steerage passengers on steamships - few emigrants could afford cabin-class tickets - did not have a luxury cruise across the Atlantic, but their voyage was no longer really comparable to that on sailing vessels. They, too, were crowded together with strangers in a small space, and many still became seasick or ill, but such experiences were merely discomforts which lasted a few days; the mortal danger of earlier journeys was gone. The late nineteenth century also saw more young unmarried labor migrants, men and women, on the transatlantic routes; they did not have families to worry about and could put up relatively easily with a few days of discomfort.

In the 1920s the steamship lines introduced a new third class of service, simply furnished four-bed cabins, which gradually led to the elimination of the steerage deck. After various attempts at legal regulation of the emigration process, cooperation between the lands of origin and destination - both with strong motives for making sure mass migration was well organized - gradually succeeded in putting an end to many abuses, especially during the ship journey itself. Shipowners, agents, and brokers wanted to make a profit in the business, and the U.S. was eager for new settlers and later for factory workers; these economic factors were always dominant, although humanitarian concerns doubtless played a role as well. In the final analysis, however, it was technological change and its application to ship travel that stripped the transatlantic voyage of its terrors.

German postal ship which also carried passengers to East Asia and Australia

Arrival in the New World

The stream of transatlantic migrants followed the trade routes, and thus there were European emigrants arriving at ports all over the world, on freighters. Colonists settled in British, Dutch, Portuguese, and Spanish possessions in Australia, South America, Africa, and Asia; but the only mass migration was between Europe and America. The numbers of migrants going to other destinations may have been significant for the populations of those countries, but they were small on the global scale.

Emigration to Australia seemed for a time to be a potentially profitable business for British and German shipping companies. The continent was thinly populated and needed farmers, agricultural workers, and artisans to develop its economy. Beginning in 1837, relatively large groups of German Lutherans of the so-called »old confes-

At the pier in Trst, southern Europe, around 1900

sion« began leaving from Hamburg for Adelaide, and the settlements they founded in the Barossa valley thrived. Their success attracted new emigrants, and in 1844 Bremen businessmen began advertising for passengers to Adelaide; the demand was not great enough, however, to justify regularly scheduled service. Since trade with Australia was not very profitable and quite risky for the shipowners due to the great distance involved, shipping on this route was never as highly developed as that to America. Still Germans made up about a fifth of the population of European extraction in Australia in 1844.

More profitable was the trade with South America, to the La Plata, to the Brazilian ports Rio Grande, Port Natal, and Rio de Janeiro, and to smaller ports in Chile and Peru. The primary ports serving these destinations had been Genoa and Marseille, but in the nineteenth century the great ports of northwestern Europe, mainly London and Hamburg, became dominant here as well. For the most part it was Spaniards, Portuguese, and Italians who emigrated to South America, but the number of Germans who decided to try a new beginning there was not insignificant; recruiters traveling

Deutsche Reichspostdampferlinie nach Australien.

Abfahrtszeit:

Alle **3 bis 4 Wochen** geht Mittwochs ein Dampfer von **Bremen** nach **Australien** ab.

Die Abfahrtszeiten in den einzelnen Anlaufhäfen sowie die Dauer der ganzen Reise lassen sich annähernd aus folgendem **Bei-spiel** ersehen:

Bremen	. . . . . ab	13. Juli,
Antwerpen	. . . »	17. Juli,
Southampton	. . »	18. Juli,
Genua	. . . . »	26. Juli,
Neapel	. . . . an	27. Juli,

about Germany in the 1820s had no diffi-culty attracting farm workers for Argentina and Brazil. Yet South America remained far behind the U.S. as land of immigration in the popular imagination, and scheduled ship service never developed. The econo-mies of the South American countries were based on the plantation system, and condi-tions were not favorable for small farmers. The Germans who were recruited to settle in Brazil found it so hard to make a start there and were so badly exploited by the plantation owners, that the Prussian government abruptly stopped all emigra-tion to Brazil - a prohibition which re-mained in effect until 1896. After the ad-vent of steamships the companies set up postal connections covering the globe; for example, the North German Lloyd operated regular service to Brazil after 1875 and to Australia after 1885. These postal ships

took passengers, but not many of them were emigrants. The bulk of European overseas migration was dierected to North America, which mainly meant the U.S. There were various reasons for this development: a transatlantic passage was relatively cheap, and many ships were available because trade with North Amer-ica was substantial. In the U.S. there were also broad expanses of unsettled, fertile land being offered to settlers at attractive prices, and after about 1850 Europeans were also drawn by the great demand for factory workers in America's rapidly grow-ing industrial sector. Canada was less in-viting for European emigrants, but many settlers did go there, especially from Great Britain. Exact emigration figures for Canada are hard to obtain for much of this period because a significant number of those landing at Halifax, Montreal, or Que-

bec traveled on to the U.S.

By far the greatest number of emigrants in the Colonial period arrived at Philadelphia; of lesser importance were New York, Bos-ton, Baltimore, and New Orleans, at the mouth of the Mississippi. Philadelphia played the decisive role for German emi-grants, because the »redemptioner market« for the entire east coast was there. After the Revolution, some American merchants profited from the almost catastrophic trade reductions at European ports due to the Napoleonic Wars, but this brief upswing was cut short by the outbreak of the War of 1812 between the U.S. and Great Britain. New York was able to resume trade imme-diately after peace was restored in 1814, by selling British goods that had been in storage there during the war at a profit. A further factor helping make New York the leader among the competing east coast ports in this period was the opening of the Erie Canal in 1825. New York could now offer a direct route to the west, where European immigrants could find the large unsettled tracts of land they wanted.

The growth in trade soon made New York the leading destination for immigrants as well, and before the Civil War New Orleans was in second place, especially attractive to poor immigrants because of very low fares charged by the Mississippi river boats. Of course, the immigrants had to put up with very slow travel and a rather high risk of accident - in addition to the danger of yellow-fever epidemics, which broke out frequently during the hot summer months in New Orleans and claimed many victims among the newly arrived immigrants, weakened by their long transatlantic journey in steerage. In the long run New York was the best choice as a port of arrival for immigrants.

The other North American ports with trade connections to Europe also handled part of the stream of immigrants, even those further south like Charleston, South Carolina. San Francisco was only an important port for Europeans during the Gold Rush of the 1850s, whereas Galveston received German settlers going to Texas even before it joined the Union in 1845. Construction on the American railroads began in the 1840s, and forty years later most of the states were connected by a relatively dense rail network. This increased competition among ports for freight, but the immigrant traffic stayed mainly on the established routes. The railroad companies made a good profit on the immigration business, reaching agreements with the shipping lines to coordinate train and ship schedules and offer immigrants reduced fares; shipping agents could often sell combined tickets for transatlantic crossing and rail travel in the U.S. In some cases railroad companies participated in setting up new ship connections: in 1867, for example, the Baltimore & Ohio Railroad invested more than 50 percent of the money needed by the North German Lloyd to open a new line connecting Bremen and Baltimore. In 1887

the Hapag company decided to offer service to Philadelphia because especially advantageous opportunities for selling rail tickets were available there. As in Europe, special trains or railroad cars for immigrants were set up, beginning in the late 1870s; at first the trains were terribly uncomfortable and traveled very slowly, but increasing competition among the companies eventually led to improvements.

All of the major shipping lines served New York, where about 75 percent of the millions of immigrants who arrived in the second half of the nineteenth century (and even more in the twentieth century) set foot on land for the first time. Most traveled on immediately for points farther west, via Chicago and St. Louis, which became hubs of immigrant traffic. The city of New York, however, did not simply make a profit from the immigrants; it also bore all the negative consequences of mass immigration. Years before the federal government accepted these problems as a national priority, the city administration was forced to react. Just as regulation of the emigration business was necessary in the European embarkation ports, there was a need to deal with swindlers and greedy merchants in the ports of arrival. So-called *runners*, often immigrants themselves, took advantage of the helplessness and inexperience of the arriving Europeans: innkeepers, money changers, employment agents, and land dealers employed them. Questionable brokers and agents sold worthless or overpriced railroad and riverboat tickets and untillable or even nonexistent pieces of farmland somewhere in the west. The abuses escalated so rapidly in the 1840s that the city began to take action. Citizens of like nationality or religion joined together in aid societies, and people with liberal or philanthropic views founded welfare associations. But the government also felt obligated to care for the increasing numbers of sick and impoverished immigrants. Both human sympathy and political foresight demanded measures to assure that arriving immigrants became useful citizens and not welfare recipients.

In 1847 the office of Commissioner of Emigration of the State of New York was created; these Commissioners were charged »to pro-

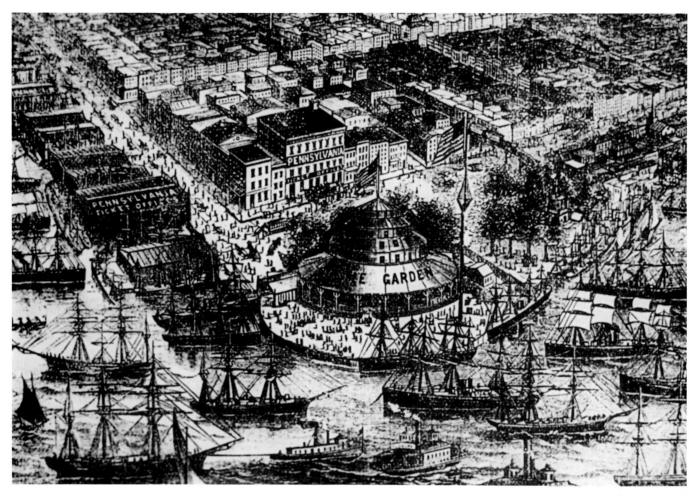

Castle Garden, the first immigrant control station in New York

tect the newcomer, to prevent him from being robbed, to facilitate his passage through the city to the interior, to aid him with good advice, and, in cases of most urgent necessity, to furnish him with a small amount of money«, as German-born Friedrich Kapp, himself a Commissioner of Emigration, stated. The six Commissioners included the mayors of New York and Brooklyn and the presidents of the Irish and German Societies, whose members had long been concerned with the plight of their newly arrived countrymen. The work of the Commissioners was unpaid, their costs being covered through a fee paid for each arriving immigrant by the shipping lines - who then passed the expense on to the immigrants themselves in the form of higher ticket prices. At first the fee was one dollar per person, despite vehement protests from the shipping lines. In 1876 the U.S. Su-

preme Court ruled this practice unconstitutional, thereby jeopardizing the work of the Commission. The shipping companies themselves now recognized that the work of the Commissioners was absolutely necessary and volunteered to pay the Commission 50 cents per arriving passenger. In 1882 the matter was finally settled when a federal law was passed calling for collection of so-called commutation money from immigrants; the amount became one dollar in 1893, two dollars in 1902, and four dollars in 1907.

The major reason for the positive evaluation of the Commission's work on the part

of the shipping lines was the fact that in 1855 it had succeeded in establishing a central landing facility in the Castle Garden building (formerly used for public events and entertainment). The main problem was overcoming the objections of several citizens' groups, whose members opposed the presence of so many immigrants in their neighborhood. Not until Castle Garden was opened was it possible for the Commission's work to protect the immigrants to really have an effect. The steerage passengers landed directly at Castle Garden, which was accessible from the water on one side, and were thus kept away from the various *runners*. Officials helped the immigrants and advised them with respect to further travel, finding work, and changing money. No immigrant had to go into the city unless he decided to himself, and even then he was given the addresses of reliable inns, and it was also possible to buy railroad tickets in Castle Garden itself. Although there seem to have been cases of corruption in the Castle Garden management from time to time, the Commissioners of Emigration and above all the opening of Castle Garden brought to an end the most shameful abuses against the immigrants. In other immigration ports such as New Orleans, Baltimore, and Philadelphia, business was easier to monitor. Since there were fewer new arrivals, no central landing dock was needed; state and later federal government and public-health officials went aboard the arriving immigrant ships.

In 1892 Castle Garden was closed, and a new and larger federally operated landing facility was opened at Ellis Island. The number of southern and southeastern European immigrants had taken on undreamed-of proportions, and nativists all over the U.S. were stirring up fears of growing foreign influence. The land in the West was now settled, and it was no longer possible to buy a farm at a low price. Large ethnic ghettos arose in the cities, many of them slumlike, and strikes and economic crises became more frequent. The immigrants themselves were often blamed for the miserable conditions in these areas, and they also dominated the market for unskilled labor. Ethnic groups that had immigrated earlier considered them unwanted competitors, while employers took advantage of their ignorance, using them as strikebreakers and to depress wages. People spoke of »undesirable immigrants«, and the word »alien« took on a strong negative connotation. The majority of Americans were convinced that their country could not tolerate uncontrolled immigration any longer, and restrictive immigration laws were the result. Ellis Island was created as an instrument to enforce these new laws, and thousands of Europeans ended their journey to the New World here, without ever setting foot on American soil.

The problems posed by dishonest *runners* and profit-greedy businessmen in the nineteenth century were now replaced by problems involving immigration regulations, which became more and more complex over the years. Emigrants were in need of advice and assistance against exploita-

Ellis Island, around 1900

The Great Hall, 1900-1913

tion and arbitrary officials on both sides of the Atlantic, and various private organizations were founded to help them.

Immigrant Aid Societies

Most migrants had to depend on their own resources from the moment they left home; they could no longer count on direct help from relatives or friends and were dependent on the honesty and good will of the agents and officials they encountered. There were always some merchants, however, who thought only of their own profits and did not care what happened to the emigrant. Legal regulation of the emigration traffic came relatively late and was never fully successful in eliminating abuses. Private individuals concerned about the fate of the migrants tried to make up for these insufficiencies by founding migrant aid societies.

Before the 1840s most Germans paid little attention to the plight of their fellow countrymen who emigrated. Governments were trying to prevent emigration or make it more difficult, and thus the only legal actions taken were to regulate the activities of the emigration agents, beginning in the late 1830s. The liberal middle-class press did not comment on the problem for many years, but as years passed it was no longer possible for the public to overlook the growing number of cases in which emigrants in transit were robbed or swindled and ended up in misery. Since government authorities offered no help, citizens felt called upon to do something, seeing in emigrant aid a private path to greater political participation. Private groups sprang up all over Germany in the politically turbulent 1830s and 1840s and were one way for citizens to express their dissatisfaction with feudalistic governmental structures. Many of these initiatives were solely concerned with the emigration problem.

Two general types of society should be dis-

tinguished: settlement societies and »aid« societies in the proper sense of the word. The former were business ventures in which stockholders invested money in a piece of land and then tried to recruit emigrants to settle there by offering cheap passage tickets and help in getting started. The members of these settlement societies realized on the one hand that emigration could not be stopped and was at least in part a necessary social safety valve, but on the other hand they considered mass emigration a national, cultural and economic loss for Germany; in the settlement societies ethical, idealistic, and economic motives coalesced.

Two of the best known settlement societies were the so-called Texas Society (*Texas-Verein*) and the Hamburg Colonization Society (*Hamburger Kolonisationsverein*). The Texas Society was formed in 1842 on the initiative of two German noblemen and became notorious for the completely incompetent planning and organization of the proposed settlement: a large number of emigrants ended in death or misery in Texas. The Hamburg society was founded in 1849 by a group of ambitious businessmen who hoped to promote trade with Brazil by founding a German colony there. The colony, »Donna Francisca«, was es-

tablished, and the emigrants managed to make a new start there, but the venture was not the commercial success the merchants had hoped for. Dozens of other settlement societies were founded all over Germany, but most were simply small groups of emigrants who wanted to reduce their individual risk by spreading it among the members of an emigration company. When German emigration rebounded after World War I, self-help organizations of this type again sprang up.

The second group, the true aid societies, did not try to recruit emigrants for settlement overseas, trying instead to help them solve the problems which they encountered during the journey. They first arose at crossing points of the emigration routes, at Frankfurt am Main, Cologne, and Darmstadt and above all in the harbor cities Hamburg and Bremen, where the poor treatment of emigrants appeared most clearly. Some of these emigrant aid societies were nothing but profit-oriented emigration agencies, and in these the mixture of business and an unselfish desire to help meant that emigrants had to be especially careful, even if the agents were really trying to help them and give them good advice. In Koblenz, for example, an emigration agent who was well known as a swindler called

Women denied admission to the United States, 1903

116

his business the »Office for the Protection of Emigrants to America and Australia«. Yet there were also offices that really tried to help emigrants, even though national or economic motives played a role as well. They distributed pamphlets with information about travel routes and prices and descriptions of the climate and economic conditions in various destination countries and regions. They often ran public counseling offices, helped migrants who had been cheated in legal fights for compensation, and brought cases of fraud to the public's attention. The National Society for German Emigration and Settlement (*Nationaler Verein für deutsche Auswanderung und Ansiedlung*) was founded in 1848 and soon had local sections in most southern German states, where emigration was heavy at this time. The Berlin Society for the Centralization of German Emigration and Kolonization (*Berliner Verein zur Centralisation deutscher Auswanderung und Kolonisation*) was founded in 1849 and opened a branch in Hamburg in 1850; this office operated Hamburg's version of the Bremen information office for emigrants beginning in 1851. There were many other societies of this type, but most were short-lived and of only local importance. For the emigrant in transit, however, each of them represented a place of refuge in time of need.

The institution that seemed predestined to be the primary agency helping homeless, lonely, and despairing emigrants was the church; but both Lutheran and Catholic organizations waited a long time, until the 1870s, before deciding to take on the care of these people. At first they argued that only rootless people with no true faith in God would leave their homes, that God-fearing Christians should stay at home, but this position gradually changed as more and more requests for German-speaking pastors arrived from German settlements abroad. In 1837 the Protestant *Langenberg Society* (or Evangelical Society for Germans of Protestant Faith in North America) was founded with the express purpose of training pastors for service in America. Before about 1860, Catholic Germans had to join already existing parishes in the U.S.; these were mainly dominated by Irish immigrants, and ethnic conflicts often arose.

The office of the St. Raphaels-Verein, Bremen, with small church

German emigrants also wanted religious support during the trip, however; active Christians in the embarkation ports recognized this need and began distributing Bibles and pamphlets to the steerage passengers. In the Bremerhaven Auswandererhaus there were Protestant services twice a week and Catholic masses every two weeks. These services were paid for by a group of Bremen merchants, with support from the steamship companies after about 1860.

As mentioned above, the reaction of the official church to the needs of the emigrants came only relatively late. In 1870 a Lutheran pastor for emigrants in Hamburg and Bremen was appointed, followed by a Catholic chaplain in 1871. A society of Catholic laymen was active in Le Havre beginning in 1854, but it took fifteen years for these active Christians to convince the church hierarchy of the need to help the emigrants. Peter Paul Cahensly, a merchant familiar with the problems of emigrants in Le Havre from his own experience, worked tirelessly to help them. In 1871 he obtained official authorization to establish the *Raphael Society* to aid emigrants, and by 1877 there were officials of this society at work in Bremen, Hamburg, Le Havre, Liverpool, London, and Rotterdam. Their work was financed with the contributions of members and in part with Church funds. Lutheran missionaries in ports also received support from business circles, and in Hamburg they even sold steamship tickets for the Hapag company, using the profits for their religious work.

Over time the work of the missionaries took on an increasingly practical character, especially when transit migrants from eastern and southeastern Europe, many feeling completely helpless in a foreign environment, began arriving in the Hanseatic cities. These people were in a critical situation: their home countries refused to offer any help or assume responsibility for them, so they were dependent on their own

meager resources - most could neither read nor write, knew no German, and had no travel experience. The shipping lines tried to ameliorate these conditions by hiring interpreters, but the increasing numbers of emigrants clearly represented a challenge to those in authority in the churches - especially the Catholic Church, since almost 90 percent of the non-Jewish transit migrants were Catholic. Yet it was not until 1888 that a Slavic-speaking priest was appointed for Hamburg and Bremen. More priests followed, and their work mainly involved translating, helping fill out official forms, and acting as a trustworthy agent for bank transactions - the priests transferred the emigrants' money to the U.S. or received and delivered prepaid passage tickets from American relatives or friends. Both churches had good connections to America because they operated similar institutions in the North American port cities. Cahensly himself crossed the Atlantic and founded an American branch of the *Raphael Society* in 1883. Both Lutherans and Catholics employed partner organizations in the ports of embarkation and landing: missionaries in New York looked for brightly colored tags attached to hats or clothing to recognize »their« immigrants.

In the U.S. as in Europe, the official churches were late to react to the immigrant situation, and a schism made it harder for the

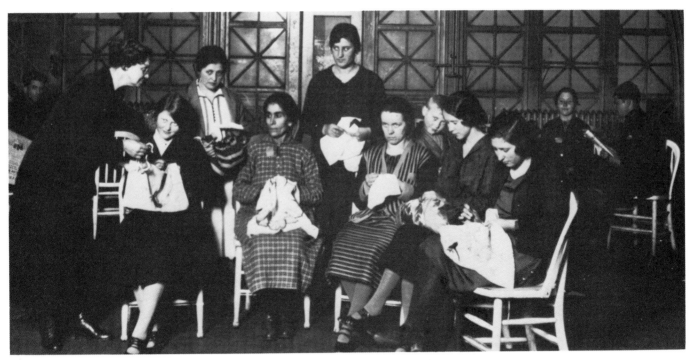

Lutheran church to make a useful contribution. Catholic immigrants were well cared for since the foundation of the American *Raphael Society*, and by the end of the nineteenth century both of the major confessions were operating immigrant housing facilities in New York. The Lutheran immigrant house opposite Castle Garden was opened in 1873 and offered low-cost shelter for about 400 people. For German Catholic immigrants there were similar facilities in the *Leo House*, which was opened in 1885 and still exists today, and there were also centers for immigrants from other ethnic groups and immigrant missions set up by numerous Protestant groups, such as the Baptists and Methodists. At the beginning of the 1880s the Jewish aid societies in Europe were faced with roughly the same problems as the churches. Since many Jewish emigrants, especially from Russia, had been forced to leave home, often fleeing brutal persecution, they had not been able to plan their journey carefully. In 1881 thousands of Russian Jews running from the pogroms arrived penniless in the border town of Brody in Galicia; they could not travel on, yet they dared not return home. The Jewish re-

ligious communities had always had a strong feeling of responsibility for their fellow Jews, with ethnicity only a secondary factor. Emigrants in transit could always depend on the help and support of fellow Jews living in cities along the way. Confronted with the situation in Brody, German and American Jews joined together to establish a massive aid program. They organized and financed transatlantic passages for thousands - 14,000 for the *Hebrew Emigrant Aid Society of the United States* (HEAS) alone - and carefully checked to be sure that those who emigrated possessed the skills and good health needed to make a new start in America. They also negotiated with the Russian government so that the others could return home. These aid societies remained active after the Brody crisis, and in 1892 there were 25 groups helping Jewish emigrants at the border control stations set up by the Prussian government, on the transit-migrant trains, and at the embarkation ports.

Another wave of Russian Jewish emigration was loosed by the so-called Kishinev pogrom of 1903, and the Berlin Aid Society of German Jews (*Berliner Hilfsverein der deutschen Juden*), founded in 1901, reacted by opening the Central Office for Jewish Emigrant Affairs (*Zentralbüro für jüdische Auswandererangelegenheiten*) to coordinate aid measures. There were separate groups for Jews from Rumania and Galicia, for example the Israelite Aid Society for the Homeless (*Israelitische Unterstützungsverein für Obdachlose*) in Hamburg. Officers of all these organizations were concerned with finding cheap lodgings, arranging for kosher meals in port and aboard ship, making financial guarantees to allow Jews to pass the border stations, and helping Jews who had been cheated.

The Jewish aid societies in Europe also had partner groups in the U.S. The most important society there after 1870 was the *Hebrew Emigrant Aid Society of the City of New York*. After 1881 all work was coordinated by the national organization, HEAS, and in 1903 the eastern European immigrants founded their own society, the *Hebrew Immigrant Aid Society* (HIAS). There were numerous local welfare groups which were often a significant help to individual migrants, putting them in touch, for example, with the *Industrial Removal Office* which could place them in jobs at locations all over the U.S. The success of the latter organization was limited, however, by the fact that most Jews arriving in the U.S. wished to live and work in cities.

Other ethnic groups looked out for their arriving countrymen as well. In the nineteenth century there were societies for Irish, Swiss, French, and German immigrants, and later there were groups for Poles, Hungarians, and others. The first German association specifically devoted to the welfare of arriving immigrants was the *German Society of Philadelphia*, founded by citizens of German extraction in 1764 when they saw the miserable conditions faced by arriving German redemptioners. Similar organizations were formed in other harbor cities with German communities: in Charleston in 1765, the *German Society for Maryland* in Boston in 1783, and the New York society in 1784. The latter soon became by far the most important group because New York was where the most Germans were arriving. These aid societies helped immigrants find housing and employment, located relatives, and changed and transferred money, but they perceived their primary function as aid to German immigrants in need - including those who had been living in New York for some time. A committee reviewed requests for financial aid and provided it to people who had gotten into difficulties through no fault of their own. The German societies (and later the groups founded by eastern Europeans) saw themselves as guardians of national honor, and many of their activities seemed overly nationalistic to other Americans, provoking hostile reactions.

Private welfare associations were a traditional part of American society, and it so was natural that they played a role in organizing immigration. The majority of the ethnic societies were integrated into the network of aid organizations, and the German Society of New York in particular worked closely with the Commissioners of Emigration and after 1892 with the officials at Ellis Island. Toward the end of the nineteenth century societies were also formed to oppose the restrictive immigration laws demanded by nativists. The *Immigration Protective League* was formed in 1898 by German-Americans, and the *League for the Protection of Immigrants* founded in 1902 was especially concerned with growing racist prejudice against eastern European immigrants. Many of these groups believed that rapid Americanization of the immigrants was the best way to avoid prejudice and hostility. There were even societies with Americanization as their primary purpose, the best known of which was the *North American Civic League for Immigrants*, founded in 1908. These groups were generally unsuccessful, however, because many migrants in the twentieth century did not intend to remain in America and become citizens, and because many of the programs were based on feelings of American superiority.

It is difficult, if not impossible, to evaluate the success of the various emigrant aid societies on both sides of the Atlantic. But the large number of groups established itself shows how badly they were needed; they performed functions that were neglected by government and business. Many migrants needed advice, consolation, and support in crisis situations and got them from the aid societies, which existed because of the unselfish endeavors of their members.

References

Armgort, Arno: Bremen - Bremerhaven - New York. Bremen, 1992.

Bickelmann, Hartmut: »Das Abenteuer der Reise«, in: Zeitschrift für Kulturaustausch. 32, 4/1982, S.330-335.

Bickelmann, Hartmut: Deutsche Überseeauswanderung in der Weimarer Zeit. Wiesbaden, 1980.

Bowen, Frank C.: A Century of Atlantic Travel 1830-1930. Boston, 1930.

Bretting, Agnes: »Auswanderungsagenturen in Deutschland im 19. und 20. Jahrhundert: ihre Funktion und Bedeutung im Gesamtauswanderungsprozeß«, in: Moltmann, G. (ed.): Von Deutschland nach Amerika. Band 4, Wiesbaden, 1989.

Coleman, Terry: Passage to America. A History of Emigrants from Great Britain and Ireland to America in the Mid-Nineteenth Century. London, 1972.

Engelsing, Rolf: Bremen als Auswanderungshafen 1683-1880. Bremen, 1961.

Erickson, Charlotte: American Industry and the European Immigrant 1860-1885. Cambridge, Mass., 1957.

Gelberg, Birgit: Auswanderung nach Übersee: Soziale Probleme der Auswandererbeförderung in Hamburg und Bremen von der Mitte des 19. Jahrhunderts bis zum Ersten Weltkrieg. Hamburg, 1973.

Howe, Irving: World of our Fathers. The Journey of the East European Jews to America and the Life They Found and Made. New York/London, 1976.

Just, Michael: Ost- und südosteuropäische Amerikawanderung 1881-1914. Stuttgart, 1988.

Just, Michael: Die Transitwanderung der »New Immigration« in Deutschland und ihr Eintreffen in den Vereinigten Staaten von Amerika. Wiesbaden, 1988.

Ottmüller-Wetzel, Birgit: Auswanderung über Hamburg: Die Hapag und die Auswanderung nach Nordamerika 1870-1914. Berlin/Hamburg, 1986.

Szajkowski, Zosa: »Sufferings of Jewish Emigrants to America in Transit through Germany«, in: Jewish Social Studies. 39, 1977, S.105-116.

Native American village, around 1840

»Gazing toward Manhattan«

The Countries of Immigration

There is no »Kaiser« here: The United States as a Country of Immigration

Christiane Harzig

The U.S. is a country whose history and society have been and continue to be shaped by immigrant women and men. For over 300 years people have been coming there to live, work, and build a future for their children, bringing with them the traditions, customs, desires, fears, and dreams that make up the fabric of American culture. This process is continuing—the new immigrants bring their cultural baggage with them as always, and immigration questions are as pressing as ever. If the immediate advantage of immigration for American society is not as apparent now as it was 300 years ago, when the first men and women began to settle on the east coast, establish an agricultural base, and found the first cities, still the U.S. can only benefit by maintaining an open attitude to newcomers.

The First Rural Settlements

The century of great discoveries was over; the contours of the continents on the globe were mostly known; and Spain, Portugal, and the Netherlands had founded and fortified their trading posts in North and South America and Asia as, in 1607, three ships with English colonists landed in Virginia. The passengers of the »Sarah Constant«, »Goodspeed«, and »Discovery« were not the first Europeans to set foot in this part of America, but they were the first English people to found a settlement (Jamestown) on the North American continent with the intention of remaining there. More migrants followed, settling at Plymouth in 1620 and Massachusetts Bay in 1630.

These settlers from England were not seeking easily accessible raw materials which could be mined for a quick profit, as was the case in the Spanish colonies in South America. Instead North America offered fertile land which could be farmed on a long-term basis, and thus the new settlements were stable and capable of further development, in many respects reproduc-

ing the social structures of the homeland. At first the newcomers were dependent on the help and knowledge of the Native American population, from whom they learned to grow maize and eat wild turkey; the Thanksgiving holiday still commemorates the settlers' thankfulness for this help, without which they would not have survived the first years. It soon became clear, however, that the settlers' hunger for land and more advanced technology would clash with the Native American way of life. What followed was a long and painful history of military conflicts, deceitful negotiations, and broken treaties, ending with the complete oppression and almost total annihilation of the Native Americans.

Attempts at exploiting native population of North America for the white settlers' purposes, as happened in South America, did not succeed. The settlers in the first colonies on the east coast soon realized that they would need more people for the further economic and social development of the colony, for trade with the homeland, and to

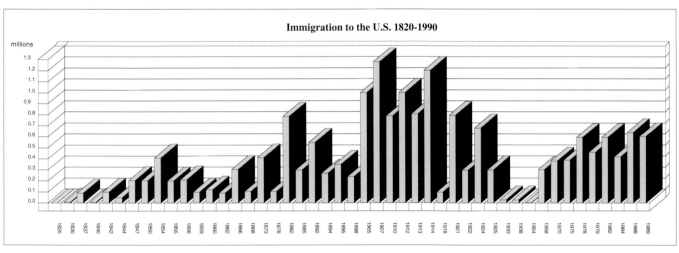

Immigration to the U.S. 1820-1990

Daniel Boone, pioneer of the Kentucky wilderness

pp. 124-125:
View of Manhattan, 1907

sell their own products, but also to fight with the Native Americans. At first it seemed there would be enough indentured servants, men and women working under contract, to meet the need for workers. People who did not have the money for a passage but still wanted to try their luck in the New World committed themselves to work for several years in America in exchange for the transatlantic fare. The employer paid for the ticket and then had a worker at his disposal for a few years.

The fate of these contract workers was often no better than that of the black slaves; like them these white workers could be abused and poorly fed and housed, and like them (for the duration of their indenture) they could be sold to another master. The newspapers in Baltimore and Charleston were full of such advertisements, including, for example, one offering the remaining five years of a »well-fed German serving maid«.

This way of increasing population was practices mainly in the middle colonies of Maryland, New Jersey, and Virginia; in 1625 about 43 percent of the population of Virginia consisted of indentured women and men. A primary advantage of this system was that members of the poorest classes could emigrate from the Old World to the New. The probability of achieving economic and social success after these years of contract servitude decreased, however, as the colonies developed further. By the beginning of the nineteenth century the indentured-servant system collapsed, in part due to new British legislation limiting the number of passengers per ship. The alleged purpose of the new laws was to regulate the transport conditions, but the result was that the fares increased and fewer people could afford to emigrate. During this time England needed workers at home. But the immigration of intentured servants was not enough to satisfy the need for labor in the expanding agricultural sector of the southern colonies, which was primarily based on monoculture on large plantations. In 1619 a Dutch ship with 20 black slaves on board landed in Virginia. Historians have determined that at first the status of these African blacks was not perceived by the colonists as significantly different from that of the indentured servants, and that they, too, could achieve freedom and the right to own property after several years. But this situation changed after only a few decades, due to the evident growth of racism among the whites and to economic conditions in tobacco agriculture, where more and more cheap labor was needed. Now there was no thought of slaves' earning their freedom; instead the next two centuries saw the abduction, enslavement, and brutal exploitation of hundreds of thousands of blacks. They never shared the opportunities offered to voluntary immigrants coming from Europe to the New World.

Besides the English colonies and settlements there were Swedish, Dutch, and French colonies in North America at the beginning of the seventeenth century. The Dutch were involved in the fur trade along the Hudson River, under the aegis of the Dutch West India Company. The French were interested in founding settlements, but the government in Versailles tried to reproduce the feudal type structure of the homeland by imposing strict regulations on the colonists in Quebec. Neither group was able to prosper for long following these strategies: only about 10,000 people emigrated to Canada during the 150-year period from 1610 to 1760, and the separate existence of New Netherland soon had to yield to the English military presence in the area.

That did not mean, however, that the still »new« continent did not attract non-English Europeans. In the period between about 1650 and 1800, shiploads of Europeans, admittedly few in number, were landing at the harbors of New Orleans, Baltimore, Philadelphia, and New York. Some remained in the already settled coastal areas, but many others moved on into the interior and began to open up land of the New York and Pennsylvania colonies.

The foundation of the Pennsylvania colony in 1682 was immediately followed by an influx of political and religious refugees from Europe. Pennsylvania had originally planned to accept only Quakers, but instead religious freedom was granted to all Christian communities, and this made the colony one of the most attractive areas of settlement in the eighteenth century, especially for Protestant sects. New arrivals for the most part avoided Puritan New England because of its perceived religious intolerance.

One who came to Pennsylvania in search of religious freedom was Franz Daniel Pastorius, who journeyed to Pennsylvania in 1683, via Rotterdam and England, to prepare for the establishment of a new settlement. Then, on October 6, 1683, thirteen German Mennonite families from Krefeld landed in Philadelphia and founded a village nearby, Germantown. Like the English founders of Jamestown 75 years earlier, these Krefeld families were neither the first nor the only emigrants from Germany, but they were the first Germans to found their own settlement on the North American continent. During the eighteenth century, about 2000 German immigrants came to Pennsylvania each year.

The broad extent of the Pennsylvania colony made it possible to build settlements which were to a great extent ethnically homogeneous and which, isolated far from the dominant English culture, could maintain their identity and independence, and their often pacifistic way of life. It had already become clear in the past century that the English welcomed the new immigrants from Europe, as much-needed workers and settlers, but expected them to become Anglicized as rapidly as possible. To break down the cultural and linguistic independence of some settlements, Anglicization societies were even established to send »missionaries« to the German areas. Most Germans, however, rejected the schools set up by groups such as the *Society for the Propagation of Christian Knowledge among the Germans.*

The agricultural and building methods used by the settlers in the German-speaking areas were surprising to their neighbors in the New World. They placed a high value on fertile land and chose it rather than land close to the rivers, which made markets more accessible. They used cooking and heating stoves instead of open fireplaces, in order to save wood; they treated the cattle with greater care; and they remained for the most part where they were, while farmers from other groups were more likely to move westward.

About three decades later than the Germans, immigrants from the northern part of Ireland (Ulster) began to arrive in large numbers in Philadelphia. Emigration was

Colony of Mecklenburgers (Germany), near Milwaukee, 1861

no new experience for these *Scotch-Irish*, as the Americans called them: at the beginning of the seventeenth century they were brought over from Scotland to northern Ireland to settle the land there. Economic misery now drove them to emigrate again, and about 40,000 of them came to the thirteen colonies between 1770 and 1775 alone. These Scotch-Irish immigrants were Protestant (Presbyterian), and at home they had been in continual conflict with the official Anglican church because of church taxation; in the New World, however, they had fewer problems with the English. They spoke their language and had an easier time fitting into the Anglo-Saxon way of life in the British colonies than the Germans did. They often became pioneers, journeying to the western edges of the colonies to settle.

Another group, however, provoked protest among many colonists by their very existence: all measures possible were undertaken to prevent the immigration of Roman-Catholic settlers, no matter what their ethnic origin. Many Protestants had been subject to persecution and oppression by the Catholic Church in their homelands and considered even the French settle-

ments in Quebec threatening. Although none of the thirteen colonies made Catholic immigration illegal, they used laws and regulations to make it difficult to practice the religion or limit the political rights of Catholics. Even the Maryland colony, where the immigration of Catholics was expressly permitted, the tolerance law was repealed in 1654. This widespread and ingrained prejudice especially affected Irish immigrants in the nineteenth century.

When the movement for independence from the British crown began to grow stronger and stronger in the colonies during the second half of the eighteenth century, the idea of freedom spread equally through all immigrant groups. No particular group was united for or against the Revolution; instead, each settler's stance was determined by his or her particular interests and experience. Those who, like the Scotch-Irish settlers at the western edges of the colonies, were often in conflict with the British authorities because of their restrictive settlement policies, were among the most vocal supporters of independence. Some German colonists, too, were ready to fight against their hated Loyalist landowners. Others, for example newcomers who were insecure and unfamiliar with conditions in the New World or those who enjoyed the protection of the British government, joined the Loyalists. After the Revolution, the Crown rewarded many for their loyalty with grants of land in Canada. On the other hand, the 30,000 Hessian soldiers used by the British in the war had not been asked whether they were for or against independence. They had to fight for the British, but after the war about 5000 remained in America as settlers.

The rebels, on the other hand, expected that their participation in the Revolution would give them a say in the political future of the new nation. They refused to let themselves be turned away by the dominant Anglo-Americans.

By the end of the eighteenth century the original British colonies had formed a new nation with its own political vision of the future, and members of many ethnic groups had found their home there. The English had determined the political character of the country with their language, laws, and political traditions, but they were now only barely a majority of the population. They were dominant in New England, especially Massachusetts, but in some of the southern states they were outnumbered by the black slaves. The Germans were the second-largest white group, and in Pennsylvania their population was only slightly smaller

Settlers crossing the plains, 1880

than that of the English, with the Scots and Irish in third place.

Although the new nation had just begun to develop, the general contours of the new society were already delimited at the time of the Revolution. The Anglo-American culture had established its dominance; the Native American inhabitants of the east coast had been conquered; the blacks who had been forced to immigrate were being oppressed and exploited; and the European immigrants had for the most part been successful in establishing themselves.

In the first few decades after independence relatively few immigrants came to America: only about 4000 came each year, for a total of 200,000 by 1820. Laws prohibiting emigration in Europe and above all the Napoleonic wars kept people from leaving home. In the 1790s, thousands of Frenchmen fled the revolution in their homeland to the U.S., although, as some historians emphasize, those who emigrated had mainly been supporters of the French Rev-

County sheriff was a greatly coveted elected office. Pictured here is Norwegian-born Otto K. Olson (1874-1933), who served as sheriff in Laona, Wisconsin

olution in its early stages; the supporters of the ancien régime went mainly to England and to the German states. During the period of restoration in Europe, after the Congress of Vienna in 1815, the number of emigrants began to grow gradually, with no dramatic increases. In 1819 the U.S. Congress found it worthwhile to begin taking statistics on immigration and passed the first immigration law, which also contained regulations governing the transatlantic voyage.

In the years 1803-1867 the new nation took action to increase its geographic extent—in other words, it adopted a policy of expansion to the west. Already in 1803, when the Louisiana Purchase was completed, it was being predicted that the U.S. would eventually extend to the Pacific coast. In this agreement, President Thomas Jefferson bought the vast territory between the Mississippi River and the Rocky Mountains for the sum of 15 million dollars from Napoleon, who had acquired it from the Spanish. The next important step was the exploration and mapping of the northern Great

Plains, Rockies, and Pacific Northwest by Meriwether Lewis and William Clark. This area was opened up to settlement later, as the Native Americans were defeated and driven away. In 1818 the border between Canada and the U.S. was defined; in 1819 Florida was bought from the Spanish; in 1835 Texas applied for membership in the Union; and in 1848 the Mexican War ended with the annexation of the southwest (what later became the states of California, Arizona, New Mexico, and Nevada). With the purchase of Alaska from Russia in 1867, the country had attained its present borders on the North American continent.

By the 1830s the U.S. was the most popular destination for emigrants. Democratically organized and with a population which was primarily of European origin, it seemed to offer Europeans great advantages over the British colonies to the north (Canada) and the Latin American countries. The climate was more familiar; the land was fertile; and along with agriculture there were growing signs of industrial development. Those who had immigrated earlier did their part by writing enthusiastic letters home and inviting friends and relatives to join them.

The Opening of the West: Settlement Migration

Social and economic conditions in Europe, including a population explosion, crises in agriculture, famines, relaxed emigration restrictions, and improvements in transportation, helped make the stream of emigrants grow to unheard of proportions in the 1830s and 1840s. About 300,000 immigrants landed at American ports in the years 1835-1839 and about 400,000 in 1840-1844, but in 1845-1849 the number was over one million. Many remained in the cities, but the majority moved on to the interior. Before 1870 it was mainly the land east of the Mississippi that was settled, but later the immigrants pushed on farther west, and the middle-western states of Wisconsin, Illinois, Minnesota, Missouri, and Iowa began to advertise, trying to make their states attractive for new settlers.

In the early 1850s, for example, the state of Wisconsin had a commissioner of emigra-

Czech immigrants in Colfax, Nebraska

tion working in the city of New York; he was to inform newly arriving Europeans about the advantages of the state. This agent soon decided, however, that this job had to be done in Europe. Newspaper advertisements and brochures were used to recruit settlers for the midwest.

One of the most important preconditions for settlement in the west was the construction of roads and other transportation lines. At the beginning of the nineteenth century Congress voted funds for the extension of the roadway network, especially to estab-

lish a land route to Illinois. Private companies built thousands of unrestricted and toll roads in New England and the Midatlantic states. In the 1820s the emphasis was on waterways, both naturally existing rivers and canals, which were developed with the labor of Irish and German immigrants. Without the Erie Canal, which was opened in 1825 and connected the Hudson River with Lake Erie, the industrial growth of the northeast would have been much slower. New York City was now linked with the Great Lakes, and this provided an attractive travel route for immigrants heading for the midwest, soon making New York the leading immigrant port of entry. Over 3000 miles of canals had been built by 1840, but

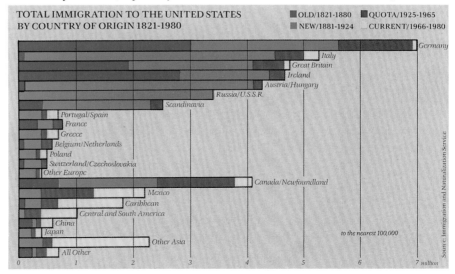

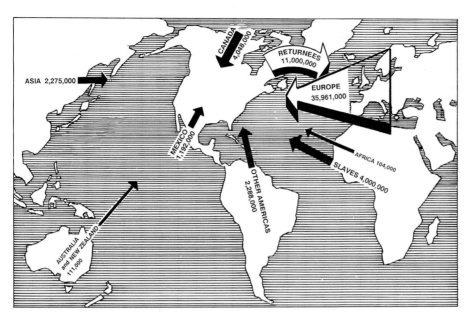

ASIA 2,275,000

CANADA 4,048,000

RETURNEES 11,000,000

EUROPE 35,961,000

MEXICO 1,192,000

AFRICA 104,000

SLAVES 4,000,000

OTHER AMERICAS 2,288,000

AUSTRALIA and NEW ZEALAND 111,000

not all of them were as successful or important as the Erie Canal. At any rate, the function of canals was soon taken over by railroads, which after about 1845 began to spread over the country like a spider web, with Chicago as the center.

The many private railroad companies which hired immigrant laborers to build thousands of miles of rails in a relatively short time, had a strong economic interest in immigrants, who were not only paying passengers but also potential buyers of the hundreds of thousands of acres of land (on either side of the rail lines) which the government had granted to the companies for construction. They also sent recruiters and agents to Europe to sell this land to future settlers. The immigrants not only bought land from the railroads, they later became steady customers, since they had to use the railroads to ship their produce to market.

The Homestead Act, passed in 1862, was a further encouragement to settlement of the west. This act provided that the government would make land available to settlers under certain conditions. Once the homesteader had lived on and worked the land for five years, it became his property for a very low price. Although this law was often taken advantage of illegally by land speculators, it still helped thousands of European immigrants make a new start in

the midwest. In the 1890s, the opening up and settling of the land was declared finished.

The mass immigration which began in the 1840s and 1850s continued in the second half of the nineteenth century, with a brief interruption during the Civil War between the northern and southern states. The number of arriving immigrants was 1.4 million in the 1840s and 2.8 million in the 1850s, fell to about 2 million in the 1860s, increased again to the prewar level of 1.7 million in the 1870s, and reached a new peak of 5.2 million in the 1880s. People came from all parts of the world, but Europeans made up about 80 percent of the immigrants.

The total number of emigrants from the German states to the U.S. for the period 1820-1890 was 4.4 million, and the Irish were the second largest group with about 3.4 million, this time mainly Catholics from the southern part of the island. The third largest group was made up of immigrants from England, Scotland, and Wales, in all 2.7 million. Their assimilation was relatively easy because they were culturally near the Anglo-Americans, because they shared the language and religious and political customs of the Americans, and because of the job skills they brought with them from the Old World. The fourth largest European group consisted of about 1 million men and women from Sweden,

Denmark, Norway, and Iceland, and only about 660,000 people came from the other European countries combined.

At first the greatest number of the immigrants settled in the port cities, New York, Boston, Philadelphia, Baltimore, New Orleans, and San Francisco, where about 18 percent of them were living in 1860. Relatively large numbers were also absorbed by the cities' hinterland, New York State and Pennsylvania, the New England states, the Ohio valley (easily reached from Baltimore), and the states which could be reached by water (on the Mississippi or the Great Lakes). The southern states, on the other hand, were for a long time less attractive to Europeans.

Rapid industrial development began before the Civil War, and was stimulated by it. The postwar years brought full economic expansion. This produced an ever growing need for workers. Since the need was now in the large cities and industrial centers, there were fewer immigrants seeking farmland and more looking for a well-paying factory job. This they found in the steel works of Pittsburgh and Homestead, the textile mills of Lawrence, the slaughterhouses of Chicago, and the sweat shops of New York.

By 1910 the U.S. had 47.3 million inhabitants, and 13.5 million or 28.5 percent were foreign-born. The Germans and Irish were still the largest ethnic groups in the nation, but the immigration authorities had long since noted that immigrants were coming from different countries of origin. In 1910 slightly over 1 million immigrants were registered; of these only about 3 percent were German, while 25 percent came from Poland and other central European states (including many Jews), 18 percent came from Russia, and 21 percent came from Italy.

In the large cities immigrants from eastern and southern Europe began to dominate the scene on the street. The population of New York, for example, included 341,000 immigrants from Italy, 484,000 from the Russian Empire, and 267,000 from Austria-Hungary in 1910. In the cities of the midwest, in Chicago and especially Milwaukee, the proportion of German immigrants remained relatively high, 23 percent in Chicago and 58

You can't come in. The quota for 1620 is full

percent in Milwaukee, but the »new wave« of immigration was noticeable here as well.

Political Trends and Restrictions on Immigration

The framers of the American Constitution had already considered the political role of (male) citizens born abroad. To make it impossible for foreign leaders to be voted into power, Article 1 provides that prospective Representatives and Senators must have been U.S. citizens for at least seven and nine years, respectively, before taking office; Article 2 stipulates that both the president and the vice-president be U.S.-born. A second level of restriction was that on who could vote: the *Naturalization Act* of 1792 made it possible for anyone who was white to apply for citizenship after living for at least two years in the U.S., making it clear that citizenship was based on a voluntary agreement between two parties (the state and the individual) and was not an inheritable natural right or connected with a national culture.

Influenced by news of the French Revolution and fearful that representatives of foreign powers (e.g., England and France) could influence political events in the U.S., Congress passed the *Alien and Sedition Acts* in 1798. The President was given the

power to deport foreigners in peacetime and hold them in internment in wartime. In addition, any publication judged injurious to the President or government was forbidden. The important thing about these laws was not their effects, but the atmosphere they created or the ideology they reflected: for one thing, it was clear that conservatives often tended to doubt the loyalty of immigrants; for another, this was the first time that internal conflicts had been projected overseas—trying to blame foreign powers for them. These patterns would prove to be characteristic of American attitudes toward immigrants.

The first three decades of the nineteenth century, when relatively few immigrants arrived from Europe, were used by the government to consolidate the new nation. The dream of some Americans, that a new society could be built on the North American continent to prepare for the millennium or a Christian golden age, became more important. In addition, a feeling of national consciousness and national pride was established under the cultural hegemony of the Anglo-Saxon population. The Native Americans, who had once been synonymous with »America«, were being denied any room to exist on the North American continent; the Mexicans were being oppressed in the name of »freedom« in the west; and people in both north and south considered blacks to be inferior—they were not seen as human beings and were thus not treated as such, and racism became firmly established as a part of »American« thought. European immigrants were tolerated and sometimes thought to enrich the nation, but sometimes—especially if they were Roman Catholic—they were considered a

Ellis Island in Russian is called the »Island of Tears«, and in every way it merited the name. We all cried. Every immigrant who was sent to the island spent at least the first day in tears. We cried because of fear and disappointment. We had come a long way: we had sold everything we had and spent every cent, and now we were afraid of being sent back. We had much to be disappointed about. We were treated like prisoners and with as much sternness and contempt. We marched to bed and we marched to eat our supper; and as we marched, we were counted by people who evidently did not know how to smile. All the way to America, we were scrubbed, cleaned, and examined by physicians and now dirt and squalor seemed everywhere. We had no sheets of any kind and the blankets we used we found piled up on the floor; there was no place to take a bath, wash.
As for the people in charge of us, they seemed to regard us as some sort of inferior beings.

L. Schwartz, Immigrant voices

threaten ing obstacle on the way to the golden age.

In the 1840s and 1850s, however, antipathy toward immigrants among the »native« American population threatened the very foundations of the political system. The terms »Know-Nothing« and »nativism«, the first denoting a political movement and the second an ideology, became established in this period. For the following decades they can used to characterize social and political opinions and actions that were directed against anything foreign and in particular against immigrants. Capturing the mood of the time, the American Party, originally known as the »Native American Party«, was founded at the national level in 1854 and after elections in 1854 and 1855 it was able to send 75 Representatives to Congress. The members of this party were

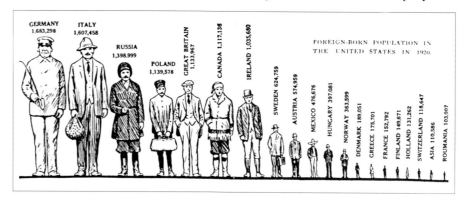

*»The only way to handle it«
Caricature from 1921*

called »Know-Nothings« because they refused to reveal anything about secret rituals which were part of their meetings and organization, always answering »I know nothing«. Small businessmen, doctors, lawyers, and teachers who considered themselves cultural guardians of their communities and artisans and workers who felt that competition from the immigrants threatened their workplace autonomy were the supporters and members of the Know-Nothing movement.

In Congress the Know-Nothing Representatives were ineffective: none of the laws they proposed (for example, one establishing a 21-year waiting period for naturalization) was adopted. Their ideology, however, took root as »nativism«. This concept, perhaps best understood as xenophobia, was examined in detail by John Higham in his book »Strangers in the Land«. He identifies three main components of this ideology: anti-Catholicism, antiradicalism or antisocialism, and racism or Anglo-Saxon chauvinism; all of these elements were to be found among the White Anglo-Saxon Protestant (»WASP«) ruling elite.

Fear of the global influence of the papacy and its affect on U.S. politics was an element of nativism that remained relevant at all periods. The structures of Catholic thought and church organization seemed incompatible with the individualistic, profit-oriented Protestant spirit of American democracy. There was also the feeling that the U.S. had been in conflict with Catholic powers earlier, during its expansion as a Protestant Republic (by annexing Mexican territory), and that Rome would now somehow gain power and influence in America through the Irish immigrants. This had to be prevented at all costs.

The second element, a tendency to attribute all internal conflicts and social unrest to the presence and agitation of foreigners and to blame European ideological movements for them, was a common pattern during the following 150 years. People like the refugees from the Paris Commune, the Haymarket martyrs of Chicago in 1886 (almost all of whom were German), the Swedish-born Joe Hill (who organized for the International Workers of the World), and the Italian immigrants Sacco and Vanzetti all seemed to fit this way of interpreting events and became its victims. The conservatives and nativists seldom recognized that the causes of these conflicts were to be found in social injustice in their own country; they seldom allowed that American working men and women might have many good reasons to fight for improvement of their living conditions.

The Civil War of the 1860s, fought to reunify the nation and to do away with slavery, brought both obstacles and opportunities for European immigrants. Because of rapid industrialization and declining immigration the need for workers had risen so sharply that employers even reverted to the use of work contracts similar to the indentures of the Colonial period. New arrivals were welcome at this time, although isolated incidents like the 1863 draft riot in New York did produce xenophobic reactions. When members of an Irish volunteer fire brigade received orders to report for service in the Union army, they rioted, attacking police, soldiers, and the Draft Office armory; i.e., the local manifestations of the hated war. Then the rioters turned on their black neighbors—as whites they felt superior to the blacks and yet feared their competition in the unskilled-labor market, and they believed they were being sent to fight for the sake of black slaves. They burned an orphanage, leaving over 200 black children homeless, lynched several black men, and beat and abused countless others. The intervention of additional militia troops finally brought the riot to an end, but these events aroused antipathy against Irish immigrants, who for a long time had

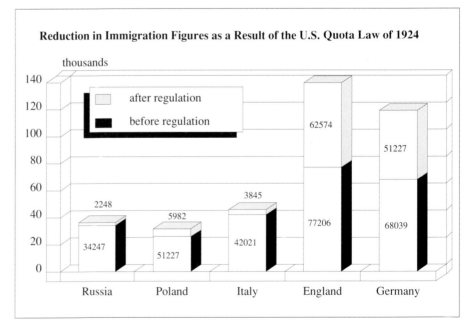

132

the reputation of being disloyal to their new country.

People at this time forgot all too soon that many Irish-born Americans, like the German-Americans, did fight on the Union side in the Civil War, often in their own ethnically homogeneous units. Instead, the Know-Nothings and nativists felt that their hate of immigrants was justified. Another factor they overlooked was the class-specific aspect of the Civil War draft: unlike rich and middle-class Americans, working-class Irish-Americans did not have the $300 in cash needed to buy exemption from military service.

After the war little time was taken for healing the nation's wounds; instead work on the rapid expansion of industry continued. The following twenty years brought the so-called Gilded Age, or as Higham calls it the Age of Confidence. The economy expanded; money seemed to grow—at least for some—on trees; workers were in short supply; and every male or female immigrant represented a positive economic value that could be calculated in dollars and cents. There was still confidence in the ability of the »American way of life« to assimilate foreigners. People were familiar with the cultural peculiarities of the Irish, Germans, and Scandinavians and could apply various handy stereotypes to immigrants, but these characteristics were hardly seen as threatening now. Thus Germans were thrifty, honest, and orderly, knew how to work hard, but also felt they had a right to amuse themselves in the beer garden on Sundays. Puritanically minded Americans considered the latter an affront, but many others saw beer gardens as an interesting new way to spend their leisure hours. The Irish were still seen as the Pope's agents on American soil, but by the end of the 1880s their economic status had improved and the second generation disappeared into the mainstream of American society. The stereotype of the Irish working man remained: he could do the work of two men, but he was also a brawler and a drunkard.

On the west coast new conflicts arose because of Chinese immigration. The *Chinese Exclusion Act* of 1882 was the first law which specifically limited immigration, forbidding all immigration of Chinese workers for ten years. This law was renewed in 1892 and 1902, and in 1904 a permanent prohibition was enacted which remained in effect until 1943, when it was replaced by a quota system—which allowed only 105 Chinese to enter each year. About 180,000 Chinese immigrants arrived on the west coast during the period 1854-1877, hoping, like so many others, to make a strike in the gold fields of California. Because hardly any of them had the money for a passage ticket, however, most arrived in debt or as contract laborers. In addition they had to pay a special tax for prospecting rights, even though in the gold-mining camps they were only allowed to do the most menial work. Later they found work in railroad construction, but again only in the most poorly paying jobs. When the transcontinental railroads had been built, the need for workers dropped sharply and this kind of division of labor between whites and Chinese broke down: both were now competing in the same job market. Because Chinese workers were paid very poorly, white workers began to hate them because they kept overall wage levels low. In this atmosphere, efforts to pass a national law against Chinese immigration were successful.

Even before the Chinese Exclusion Act there had been a series of attempts at the state level to limit immigration, but the Supreme Court rejected these laws as unconstitutional because international affairs are the responsibility of the federal government. There were state laws banning the immigration of certain individuals, and in 1875 prostitutes and criminals were excluded, and in 1882 this ban was extended to include the mentally retarded, the mentally ill, and anyone perceived as a potential burden on the welfare system. In 1885 the importation of contract laborers was prohibited, although this issue was no longer relevant by this time: with the number of immigrants arriving in the U.S. growing constantly, it was no longer necessary for employers to recruit workers in Europe. In 1891 more groups were excluded, including people with »loathsome and dangerous« diseases, polygamists, and persons who had been found guilty of »moral turpitude« (whatever that was supposed to mean). More precise definitions of undesirable immigrants were incorporated in 1903: epileptics, professional beggars, procurers, anarchists, and advocates of political violence. Above all it was the exclusion of sick people and the addition of a financial-means test that significantly affected the emigrant transport industry in Europe. The law of 1891 provided that steerage passengers, and only those immigrants, be examined by immigration officers, as soon as they landed in the U.S. They had to provide information about their national origin and current status and undergo a medical examination. Foreseeing the consequences of such regulations, the law places the legal and financial responsibility for transporting rejected passengers back to Europe in the hands of the shipping lines. As a result, control points were set up in Europe (along the transit routes in Germany and in the port cities) to separate out any potential rejects before they boarded ship. In addition, the captain of each arriving ship had to present a list of all foreigners on board, with their nationalities, last addresses, and destinations.

The immigration law of 1891 was a turning point in the history of immigration policy in the U.S. The federal government took over legal and political responsibility; the office of the Superintendent of Immigration was established in the Treasury Department; and the state-owned immigrant processing center at Ellis Island was built. Before this time immigrants had arrived at Castle Garden, but this old structure was no longer adequate for the large numbers involved. Ellis Island was opened in 1892 and will always have an important place in the history of European immigration to the U.S. Angel Island was the processing center for the west coast.

From the standpoint of the bureaucracy, these new regulations had little effect on the raw numbers of immigrants arriving. Since the selection process now took place in Europe before departure, only about 2 percent of those arriving at Ellis Island were turned back because of disease or »moral« objections. Within this statistical 2 percent, however, there were painful individual stories. Some aspects of the new law had an especially hard impact on women, and the »moral objections« clause opened the way for the application of a double standard which affected mainly unmarried pregnant women. If a woman had decided to emigrate to avoid mockery and persecution in her home village because of her illegitimate pregnancy, Ellis Island could become a dead end street, because she would be rejected and sent home again. The same was true in cases where local laws had prevented marriage in the home village: even though the father expressed to the immigration officer his willingness to take responsibility for wife and child, only he could leave Ellis Island for the mainland, and the woman and child were threatened with return to Europe. Only the intervention of the *Immigrant's Protective League* and other private aid societies could sometimes stop serious miscarriages of justice.

What was viewed by social reformers as a protective measure, to put an end to the illegal trade in young women, turned out to be an additional immigration hurdle for women traveling alone. In contrast to men, the female immigrant was interrogated about her exact destination address: if it did not meet the moral standards of the authorities—if it seemed to be the address of a house of ill repute or a single male relative, immigration could be refused. Often women were not allowed to leave Ellis Island without male »protection«. The reformers were proud of this new rule, unaware of the problems it created for many women.

The exclusion clause regarding mental retardation could also be interpreted arbitrarily, but for the most part it was rejection due to infectious disease that provoked fear and insecurity among the immigrants. The result of the medical examination seemed unpredictable. If a child contracted measles during the transatlantic trip, the family was usually faced with a long stay in the quarantine station on Ellis Island; in the worst case the mother would have to return to Europe with the child, ruining the family's plans. The father was left with the rest of the family in New York, and the passage money for the wife and child had been spent in vain. How long would it be before such a sum became available again?

Political, economic, and social events in

Showers for arriving immigrants on Ellis Island

the late 1880s and 1890s kept the question of banning further immigration on the public agenda, and the American Protective Association had its greatest success during the economic crisis of the mid-1890s. This group was founded in a small town in Iowa in 1887, with priests and nuns as the primary targets of its attacks; the property of the Catholic Church should be seized, they argued, and the potential voting rights of new immigrants (especially Catholics) should be restricted. The APA saw the Republican Party as its political home, and although the direct political power of the organization remained small, it did succeed in planting certain ideas and lines of argumentation in people's minds. Anti-Catholicism became stronger; the more radical demands of the labor movement were attributed to foreign influences; and for a long time ethnic and cultural questions played an important role in politics. The Democratic Party gradually began to speak out for the cause of the immigrants.

Working-class people had to deal with the problem of xenophobic sentiment on two different levels. On the one hand the trade unions followed the logic of the Chinese Exclusion Act and loudly demanded further restriction of immigration after the economic depression of 1893; in 1896, for example, the American Federation of Labor came out in favor of a literacy test for immigrants. On the other hand, the labor movement itself was changing due to the increasing radicalization of the working class. In the great railroad strike of 1877 and the fight for the eight-hour work week in 1886, the movement increasingly came under attack by nativists, who claimed the unions had fallen prey to foreign agitators and un-American elements and influences; i.e., radical immigrants.

Another group that took up the theme was the *Immigration Restriction League*, an association of elitist bluebloods from New England whose goal was to keep »uneducated« and »underdeveloped« elements in Europe out of the U.S. They started a publicity campaign and political program to impose the literacy test on immigrants. The legislation was passed but vetoed by President Cleveland in 1897, but the League bided its time, hoping for the election of a

president who was more open to the idea of a literacy test.

A few years later, after further restrictions on Chinese and Japanese immigration had been enacted, it was decided to conduct a thorough investigation of European immigration. At first it was the opponents of restrictions who called for the establishment of an immigration commission composed of three Senators, three Representatives, and three academic experts, plus a large staff. Headed by Senator William P. Dillingham, the commission attempted to find out how well the immigrants were being assimilated into American society. Their 40-volume report was published in 1911 and covered all aspects of immigrant life, from their labor in the different branches of industry to the fertility of immigrant women.

The Immigration Restriction League and its politically influential allies saw to it that the results of the commission's very detailed and scientific analysis were never developed into an appropriate program of political action. For although the data collected affirmed that the immigrants could indeed be acculturated, the final conclusion of the report was that the eastern and southern Europeans, unlike previous im-

Some immigrants had to have their intelligence tested

migrants, did not enrich American society but rather represented a threat to its welfare. These immigrants, they claimed, were less skilled in the trades, came to the U.S. only for economic reasons and not for political and religious freedom, and did not usually intend to remain in the country, considering return migration instead. Even a relatively weak historical analysis should have brought out the fact that all of these arguments had been used fifty years earlier against the migrants of the previous wave. The outbreak of World War I brought immigration from Europe to a temporary halt, but the debate over immigration continued. Now it was the loyalty of the »hyphenated Americans« that was in question, especially for the Germans but for the Irish as well. Many German-Americans, proud of German cultural and also military achievements under Kaisers Wilhelm I and II, hoped that the U.S. would remain neutral since the war was at first restricted to Europe. But soon they had to face the fact that these kinds of links to Germany were

German immigrants in a Harper's Weekly caricature, 1872

meaningless compared with the strong cultural and economic connections linking the American ruling class to Great Britain. The pressure on German-American communities then grew even stronger when the U.S. entered the war in 1917.

But it was not only German-Americans who experienced oppression due to growing Anglo-American chauvinism; members of other ethnic groups faced increasing pressure to assimilate. Americanization programs for new immigrants were strengthened, and immigrants were expected to learn English quickly and apply for naturalization as early as possible. But less humane measures were contemplated as well: the American Protective League did not hesitate to carry out semi-legal raids under the pretext that immigrant organizations were engaged in subversive activities.

In the years after the war, social conditions developed which were even more favorable to the growth of anti-immigrant sentiments. The strikes of 1919 were attributed to the activities of southern and eastern European immigrants, and there was fear of an imported Bolshevik revolution. Constant propaganda about the »red menace« and the raids carried out by Attorney General A. Mitchell Palmer (which resulted in the deportation of over 1000 alleged radicals) soon shattered the last of the

liberal politicians' arguments against the legal restriction of immigration.

Because the immigration rate increased drastically in 1919 and 1920 to over 50,000 per year, a temporary restriction was enacted at the beginning of 1921, limiting immigration from each ethnic group to 3 percent of its population in the U.S. in 1910, with an overall maximum of 357,000 immigrants. It soon became clear, however, that this law did not achieve its intended goal of reducing southern and eastern European immigration because those groups had already grown to significant proportions by 1910. Therefore the Immigration Act was rewritten to admit 2 percent from each ethnic group, but now calculated on the basis of its foreign-born population in the 1890 U.S. census. This system gave the so-called old immigrant groups high quotas while keeping those of the Poles, Italians, and Jews low. This law did not take effect until 1929, so that its consequences coincided with those of the Great Depression.

Industrialization and Urbanization: Labor Migration

Between 1830 and World War I the United States changed from an agrarian country with apparently unlimited farmland available to the leading industrial power of the modern world. Its population began to shift from rural to urban during the same period, and by 1920 more people lived in towns of 2500 or more than on the land.

At the same time the lands of origin of the immigrants changed in two respects: the centers of mass emigration shifted from northern, western, and central Europe to eastern and southeastern Europe, and far-reaching modernization took place within the European homelands. The latter process definitely led to differences in the cultural baggage the immigrants brought with them to the U.S. The lives of the immigrants in the U.S., their opportunities and experiences, their successes and failures, were determined to a great extent by when they arrived, the stage of social development the receiving culture was going through at the time,

where they settled (in the country or in the city, on the unsettled western frontier or in the ethnic neighborhoods of the large cities), and whether they could count on the help of others or had to make their own way. Likewise the knowledge, standards, values, and traditions they brought with them were of great importance in the acculturation process.

To own one's own farm, to have enough land to feed one's family, to cultivate land that was fertile and not leached out, to raise cattle and perhaps be able to afford oxen for plowing or even a riding horse—those were the dreams of many emigrants leaving southern and southwestern Germany in the early years of the nineteenth century. The same hopes were harbored by those leaving Sweden and Norway a few decades later.

Oscar and Christine, the Swedish emigrants made famous by Vilhelm Moberg's novels, were pioneers in the 1840s, trying to clear a farm in what would later become Minnesota. More frequently it was the Yankees, as native-born Americans were called in the frontier regions, who had the money and the tools needed to clear the land and make it ready for farming. The immigrants followed afterward and bought land which had already been worked; if they had managed to sell their property at home at a decent price, they could sometimes settle down immediately with their family on a farm of sufficient size. More often, however, they had to earn and save the cash needed to buy a farm or send for the rest of the family. There were jobs available in the west of the 1850s, as hands or maids on farms; cutting timber or rafting it down river; cooking or washing in the lumber camps; building canals, roads, and later railroads; or working on the steamboats, carrying more and more people up the Mississippi to look for farmland.

Agricultural experience and skills were a form of capital immigrant farmers from Scandinavia and Germany could invest for a profit. Yet it was not possible to stick stubbornly to old ways: the settlers had to adapt to the new climate and soil characteristics, learn to appreciate the advantages of Indian corn or maize, and comprehend the structures and function of the American market. Their success in this adaptation was often

Chicago was founded in the mid 1830s and had 2 mio inhabitants by 1900

what determined their survival and future prospects.

Being a settler on the frontier demanded a high degree of planning, organization, and knowledge from the immigrants, and they also depended more on the help and co-operation of their neighbors than immigrants settling in cities. For this reason, families that had emigrated together often tried to buy land in the same area. Many had a particular destination in mind, having received detailed information in letters from friends and relatives; they traveled directly to the area in question and knew who to contact there. They met in front of the land office to decide together where to settle, often seeking to be near more experienced fellow-countrymen.

The pioneers had to save enough to buy food and tools for the first few months, during which a temporary log cabin or sod house could be built; with luck and the help of neighbors, they could survive the cold of the first winter and avoid sickness. The next spring they planted the crops they were familiar with, but new ones would be tried as well.

As the land was opened up to agriculture, towns were founded as well, and these turned out to be of equal importance for the development of the midwestern U.S. They sometimes expanded to become great metropolitan centers like Chicago, Mil-waukee, or St. Louis, but many remained small cities, which were urban in nature, with city life and culture, but still existed mainly to serve the needs of their agricultural hinterlands. In the period 1850-1880 these smaller cities offered many opportunities for skilled artisans emigrating from central and northern Europe. Set up to satisfy the needs and tastes of the farmers in the surrounding area, a baker, blacksmith, brewer, or cooper could earn a good living on the basis of his learned trade, which would have been impossible in Europe, with its oversupply of skilled artisans, or even in the industrial centers on the east coast.

Did the settlement of the midwest and the hard life on the frontier force immigrants to acculturate more rapidly, or did living in greater isolation, mainly among other immigrants and far from the centers of Anglo-American culture on the east coast, favor the preservation of an independent ethnic culture? These questions have not yet been answered conclusively by historical research. Both the climate and geological/ecological characteristics of the Great Plains and the agricultural market, which required maximum application of modern technology and scientific farming methods, demanded a high degree of adaptation of all settlers equally. We now know that there was relatively rapid acculturation in the areas of life dominated by the law of the market and modern technology. Other areas of human existence, however, escaped from these pressures and were able to resist rapid acculturation for a longer time. In the country, unlike the cosmopolitan cities, immigrants were still able to maintain their

mother tongues and religious practices, discourage marriage outside the ethnic group, and build political and social institutions which supported an ethnic culture of leisure-time activity, including their sons and daughters born in the New World.

The men and women who decided to remain in the large cities of the east coast or who traveled on to Chicago or San Francisco were confronted with a quite different reality. In 1890 about 41 percent of the population of New York City, 42 percent of that of Chicago, and 37 percent of that of Minneapolis were foreign-born, and three-quarters of the populations were either first- or second-generation immigrants. In the small highly industrialized towns of the east coast (such as Lawrence, Fall River, and Holyoke), where mainly textiles were manufactured, the proportion of inhabitants with parents born outside the U.S. (the official way of grouping first- and second-generation immigrants) was even higher—83-86 percent in 1900. Still no single ethnic group became strong enough there to dominate the culture of an entire city.

The immigrants from Great Britain, Scandinavia, Ireland, and Germany who settled on the land and especially in the cities in the 1870s and 1880s encountered a rapidly expanding economy in which there was demand for their labor and in which they could still play a part in determining the economic structure. In this period initiative, luck, and creativity, combined with skills, knowledge, and the necessary capital, might still lead to a successful career, sometimes even to the realization of the American Dream, where a dishwasher could rise to become a millionaire. Men and women with poorer chances, to be sure, could still face social crisis, poverty, and exploitation: if one was unable to work due to illness or an accident and lost his or her job, it took time to find a new one; if the rent went unpaid one month, one could be cast out into the jungle of the city.

In 1870 U.S. Census data were used to connect occupation and birthplace for the first time: of the approximately 12.5 million working people in the U.S. slightly less than 22 percent were foreign-born. The largest numbers were from Ireland and Germany, followed by those from England, Scandinavia, and British Canada. Although almost half of the total working population was employed in agriculture (47 percent), male and female immigrants were attracted by jobs in the city as well: 31 percent were in trade and in so-called »professional and personal services« (a broad category including such diverse occupations as doctors, domestic servants, judges, and unskilled female workers) and 22 percent were in manufacturing and mechanical pursuits.

Some details can be made out within these rough divisions. Immigrants from Scandinavia were mostly found in agriculture, especially in certain characteristic occupations such as dairying and gardening. The production of butter and cheese was also one of the most important agricultural sectors for German immigrants, and one of their major immigration areas, Wisconsin, became known as the »Dairy State«. Most immigrants in agriculture worked as independent farmers rather than as hired hands. Hardly any immigrants were to be found in the professions, although a few special niches were established by as early as 1870. Thus Germans were overrepresented, relative to their numbers in the population, among musicians, Irishwomen among nurses, and English and Welsh immigrants among the actors and architects. But these figures must be treated with caution, since the percentages are based on very small absolute numbers. At the opposite end of the occupational spectrum were the Irish and Scandinavian laborers working in canal and road construction and the Germans who dominated the restaurant, hotel, and boarding-house business.

In the trade and transportation sector Germans worked mainly as hawkers and peddlers—a job often done by women—and as shopkeepers. Few immigrants were found in the offices of the large business and manufacturing concerns at this time, with the exception of Englishmen, who had the advantage of knowing English.

Production work in the craftsmen's shops and factories offered the widest variety of jobs to immigrants. Germans were especially in demand for their skills in beer-brewing and distilling and were also dominant in food production, as bakers, butchers, and confectioners. Other valued skills in the mid-nineteenth century included cigar making, basket weaving, cabinetmaking, blacksmithing, barrel making, and tailoring. By 1870 the Irish were already more likely to be engaged in factory work, in steel, paper, or textile mills. The English were especially sought after for their skills in coal and iron mining and in making pottery and porcelain ware, but many of them, like the Germans and Irish, worked at the machines in the textile mills rather than at skilled jobs.

Forty years later, in 1910, the situation for immigrants had changed dramatically. Industrial production was now on a mass scale, and the work of industrial laborers was dominated by assembly lines, piecework, and manufacturing processes which were broken down into the smallest possible tasks. There was hardly any need for traditional skills and the ability to manufacture an article from start to finish. The immigrants arriving from eastern and southern Europe around 1910 found mainly two kinds of work available: giant factories with thousands of workers from all over the world on the one hand and work at home on the other. That meant apartments crowded with sewing machines, half-finished pieces of clothing, and women and children still speaking the language of the old country.

The workforce had almost doubled since 1870, with about 26.6 million working men and 6 million working women in 1910. During the peak years of immigration foreign-born workers made up one-fifth of the white workforce; including their sons and daughters brought the total to 45 percent.

The age structure of the group of male and female immigrants, who were generally between 15 and 35 years old when they left home, meant that immigrants made up a higher percentage of the workforce than of the total population. As in 1870, the ethnic groups were unevenly represented in the different occupational sectors and groups, relative to their numbers in the population. They were again overrepresented among the »laborers and operatives«, service workers, and craftsmen. Although more and more American women were employed as office workers (marking a significant change in the labor market), these occupations were for the most part closed to immigrant women; only young women of the second generation, schooled in the U.S., had good chances in office work.

In the following years immigrants found

work in the expanding iron and steel industry, the electrical industry, metalworking, and especially in automobile manufacturing and the clothing industry. The need for service workers—laundresses, scrubwomen, and maids—seemed insatiable as the middle class continued to grow in the cities. Theoretically there were still niches for small businesses, opportunities for opening a cigar-making shop or smithy to serve mainly immigrants of one's own ethnic group, but the chances for success were growing dimmer. The only exceptions were small businesses in the immigrant ghettos, the Italian greengrocers and Jewish fishmongers, for example, on Manhattan's Lower East Side.

The Everyday Life of Immigrants

One of the most difficult problems for immigrants was determining where and under what conditions work was available, but there were numerous other aspects of everyday life to take care of. Where could one live? With whom did one want to or have to share quarters, and who were the neighbors? What kinds of food could one buy in the neighborhood market, and could one make oneself understood to the clerk or salesgirl? The questions of what church the family should attend and what school the children should be sent to also required quick decisions.

Immigrant neighborhoods (i.e, areas with predominantly German, Irish, or Scandinavian inhabitants) had been part of American cities since the early nineteenth century. The families of immigrant workers lived in small houses near the city center, near factories, workshops, and stores. They needed to have a place to work near home and the chance of finding a new job in case they became unemployed; they tried to keep the walk to work relatively short.

No housing bureau had directed Irish families to the left and German families to the right, but nevertheless there were soon streets and blocks where members of a particular group would concentrate, where the old familiar language was still spoken on the street. Here merchants set up shops which carried products from the old

View of Milwaukee, 1898

country as well as the new, where it was easy to communicate one's needs. Neighbors who had been in the U.S. longer could recommend a store, could tell an immigrant where bread was still baked with pure grain and where he or she would not be cheated. In the local workshops articles were being manufactured to satisfy the needs of the neighbors, and immigrants could often find their first jobs there. Beer or whisky were served at the corner tavern, where there were newspapers available and back rooms for meetings of an amateur choral group, a mutual-aid society, or an ethnic club. In German neighborhoods women and children were to be found here as well on Sundays, when they joined their husbands and fathers for social events—a practice viewed with suspicion by Irish and Anglo-American observers.

German Catholics might hold services in one church, while there was a German Protestant church a few houses down the block and another Catholic church being built around the corer to serve the growing Irish community. The buildings were financed with contributions from the parishioners alone, and thus their size and furnishings reflected the prosperity of the community—ethnic groups often tried to outdo each other in this.

The halls of gymnastics and choral societies were used for meetings and events, serving the function of public community centers. Charity balls and theatrical performances could be held there, and they could be used for weddings or wakes as well as for political meetings.

Although the ethnic neighborhoods grew spontaneously with little central planning, they played an extremely important role in the acculturation of immigrants. The neighborhoods provided a protective sphere for new arrivals, where they could find people who spoke their language and understood their cultural behavior patterns and peculiar characteristics. Fellow-countrymen who had been in the U.S. longer helped the newcomers become accustomed to their new surroundings and acquaint themselves with the different political structures and social norms, without having to confront all of the new challenges at once.

Especially the female immigrants found

Log cabin in North Carolina

the neighborhood an excellent place to experience »America«. This was true for women who worked at home, organizing the household for their husbands, sons, and daughters, as well as for women (usually grown daughters) who worked outside the home, perhaps in a corner bakery or in a cannery two blocks away. The lives of these women were often led within the neighborhood, where they worked, shopped, exchanged information, learned about American customs, asked the neighbors for help watching the children, or even attended classes conducted by well-meaning American ladies to teach them home economics or modern child-rearing methods.

The ethnic neighborhood and existence of an ethnic community also made possible the rise of an ethnic middle class and ethnic leaders: successful merchants, journalists working for immigrant newspapers, politicians, priests, intellectuals, and charity workers. These people served a clientele consisting primarily of members of their own ethnic groups, and were supported and encouraged primarily by these immigrants; this gave the leaders the power base they needed to confront the dominant Anglo-American social structure.

The neighborhood was very important for the development of ethnic consciousness and an ethnic community, but it also pro-

vided a place where immigrants could learn to live side-by-side with people from other parts of Europe or from different ethnic groups. Ethnic neighborhoods were seldom as homogeneous, as completely dominated by a single group, as present-day black ghettos are. In the rapidly growing small cities of the midwest (Omaha, for example), each group made up only 10 or 20 percent of the population of a residential area. On the other hand, German-Americans still dominated some neighborhoods on Chicago's North Side, with up to 80 percent of the population in 1900. In both cases any citizen of the city could easily identify its »Little Sicily« or »German Broadway« neighborhoods; the degree of ethnic concentration or homogeneity was less important for this perception of an ethnic presence than the capability or possibility of occupying certain »strategic« points—the public hall on the corner, the church, or several stores. These symbolic points demonstrated to the outsider or passer-by which group had laid claim to the neighborhood.

In this way ethnic neighborhoods possessed greater continuity than the addresses of their immigrant inhabitants, who were typical mobile city-dwellers. A new job, a larger apartment, the possibility of buying a house, or even difficulties paying the rent could cause an immigrant family to leave the neighborhood and establish itself in another, perhaps better area; its place was taken by newly arriving immigrants. When the new arrivals began to come more and more from other ethnic groups, the neighborhood gradually began to change, becoming the center for a different community. Where church sermons were once preached in Polish, prayers are now in Spanish; the old Jewish quarter in Harlem is now occupied exclusively by blacks; the meeting hall of the Bohemian Sokol gymnastic club on Chicago's West Side is now used by Mexican immigrants.

Once an ethnic neighborhood had established itself and the group had reached a certain absolute size, a true *ethnic community* could develop. The ethnic neighborhood was a good starting point for the development of a community with an immigrant press, churches, clubs, and political parties. The organizations could live on long after the original neighborhood had broken up and disappeared. The communities did not have a single homogeneous structure but differed in various ways; the multiple layers are especially evident in the case of German-Americans, due to their relatively long immigration history and the heterogeneity of their culture of origin. Religion, regional differences within Germany, and class led to significant polarization within the ethnic group.

For all immigrant groups, the press and the church played important roles in the formation of an ethnic community and the articulation of an ethnic identity. This is especially clear for the German, Yiddish, and Italian newspapers: around 5000 German-language publications appeared during the first hundred years of German immigration to America, and the Italians produced 150 different labor newspapers although they did not begin to publish in the U.S. before the end of the nineteenth century. American publications offered immigrants from Austria-Hungary, like the Slovaks or the different Yugoslav ethnic groups, a first real opportunity to express their ethnic identity—not without implications for political development in the homelands. The German press, like that of other central European groups, was built to a large extent by educated and politically experienced refugees from the failed revolution of 1848; they founded the first newspapers, generally gave them a liberal slant, and used them to gain a degree of influence which was far out of proportion to their relatively small numbers.

The newspapers reflected the social, religious, political, and regional differences within the ethnic groups. There were dailies and weeklies; papers aimed at workers, union members and women; literary monthlies and almanacs; and church and club newsletters produced for small numbers of readers. They reported on events going on in the new culture in the language of the old, or they commented on Old World events from an outsider's perspective, with the experience of the new homeland as background. This contributed in complex and subtle ways to the acculturation process. Since the press was closely connected with the ethnic community, pro-

New York tenements, around 1900

143

Saw mill in Bogalusa, Louisiana 1912

duced by it and shaping it simultaneously, the existence of these newspapers, their success, continuity, and failure, depended closely on changes in immigration. The number of German-language papers remained high for a long time, but by 1900 it had sunk to about 700.

The church was similar to the press in that it, too, made possible the development of an ethnic intellectual elite which was visible outside the community. The church played a central role in the ethnic communities of the Irish, Catholic Germans, and Slovaks, but also for Orthodox Christians such as the Greeks and Russians. Churches preserved and transmitted traditional values and standards and also offered protection from anti-Catholic attacks, often motivated by racism, in Protestant Anglo-America. Churches were also the places where ethnic interests were formulated so they could be stated forcefully outside the group. Identification with Rome and the pope could be disadvantageous in the American context, but it also gave the Polish peasant or the Irish nurse (who was usually a nun) the feeling of belonging to a powerful international organization.

The internationalism of the Catholic church was no help, however, on the local level, where ethnic interests and contradictions often collided. Groups that had only arrived recently usually had to share a church building and attend services led by a priest of a different ethnic background until a priest from home could be recruited. Immigrants frequently had the feeling that priests from other ethnic groups did not really understand their needs and problems. As soon as they were financially able to construct a new church building and support their own priest, they moved out of the shared quarters and founded their own parish.

That was not the end of the conflicts in Catholic communities, however, where questions of power and hierarchy remained to be settled. In Boston, for example, the Irish bishops who controlled the church structure had to deal with a rapidly growing Italian community. In Chicago there were significant numbers of both Irish and German Catholics who had to seek some sort of compromise, often only at the cost of one group or another; there were many battles in the realm of church politics, but a split in the church was avoided for many years. The effort to »integrate« the Polish Catholics, however, was met with failure. In some cities a Polish national church was established as a reaction against what Poles called Irish-American Catholicism. Nor do they seem to have learned tolerance from their experience: today it is still hard for Polish Catholic parishes, who suffered under the dominance of the »older« Irish

and German groups, to accept the fact that new immigrant groups have followed after them. Only reluctantly do the gradually shrinking Polish parishes of Chicago's Northwest Side make room for their new Spanish-speaking Mexican neighbors.

Protestant immigrants had just as strong a need to found their own parishes, build their own churches, and hire pastors who spoke their language; they, too, often made the church the cultural and emotional center of their community. Frequently Protestants from Sweden or Germany had fled from the state church with its narrow dogma and hierarchical structures and practiced their own form of religion in the U.S. Protestant sects that built up large-scale organizational structures, like the Missouri Synod Lutherans, were continually faced with ideological struggles, schisms, and people leaving the church. Often conservative hierarchies and liberal thinking came into conflict over democratic forms of organization and the interpretation of religious doctrines. One central aim, however, was always the preservation of the German language in the service. The feeling was that the true faith and pure religion could only be practiced in the mother tongue, that changing to English would open the door to cultural and religious decline.

Religious groups in the U.S. could not depend on state-organized aid for their existence, and by the 1880s and 1890s they all had to realize that new immigrants arriving from Europe were no longer automatically seeking them out. Increasing secularization in Europe meant that immigrants did not necessarily bring religious faith or acceptance of church authority with them in their cultural baggage. Churches would have to do missionary work if they wished to maintain their influence over immigrants in the U.S.; missionary societies were founded in many congregations at this time to win over not only the »heathens« in Africa but also those in their own neighborhoods.

The churches often ran schools where

Bohemian cigarmaker in New York's Lower East Side around 1900

and collective responsibility for relatives supposedly played no part in modern nuclear families. Closer inspection revealed this hypothesis to be false, however. It has been shown that »the family« often organized and shaped the migration process. The ways this could happen are illustrated by the letters of the Klingner family. In 1848, a year of crisis and revolution, the eldest daughter Anna Maria Klingner applied for permission to emigrate, with the support of her 15-person family and received official certification that she had no expectation of inheritance from her father. Anna Maria reached New York in the same year, after a

classes were conducted in the mother tongue and where an attempt was made to preserve the culture and memory of the homeland for the children born in the U.S. At the end of the nineteenth century, the standards and curriculum requirements of the public schools were imposed on these private and parochial schools, which now had to conduct a significant portion of the classes in English. The demands of the labor market, however, had already made this step in acculturation necessary: if the immigrant girls and boys wanted to take advantage of the expanded job possibilities offered by their new home, they needed a solid English-language education. Church communities which had no all-day schools at least tried to teach the language of the home country to the second generation in Sunday schools. This was a special concern of the German churches, and even the Socialists in New York established a nondenominational Sunday school, where German-language instruction free of »harmful clerical influences« was offered.

Another important institution in the migration process was the family. For a long time historians and sociologists argued that the family broke down in the modernization process of the late nineteenth century: patriarchal structures, the extended family, care of the aged by the younger generation,

Welsh and Polish miners in Pennsylvania, 1900

145

Eduard Götz's Hotel

Goldnen Schwan

und Bairische Bierbrauerei,
No. 96 N. Front St., Philadelphia.

☞ Reisende finden billiges und freundliches Logis, nebst kalten und warmen Bädern.

long and arduous journey, immediately found a job as a domestic servant, and soon thereafter met her future husband. In the following years the couple quite systematically organized the emigration of the other Klingner siblings. Letters gave the family detailed information about the journey and what they needed to bring. Sometimes money was sent for the ticket, as and advance which the brother or sister had to pay off after arrival in the U.S. so that the money could be used to send for the next sibling. Careful consideration was given to which sibling with which job qualifications should come or stay home at a particular time. This clearly shows how labor-market strategies could play a significant role in the decision to migrate. Young women willing to work as domestics were unaffected by economic conditions, however, since maids were almost always in demand.

The family thus played a very important role in the organization of chain migration and in finding work for prospective immigrants. A man who had advanced to the position of foreman could easily help friends and relatives find jobs. Storekeepers, craftsmen, or businessmen could help newly arrived immigrants by hiring them as salesgirls, clerks, or apprentices. It is unclear whether fellow-countrymen or relatives made better bosses—there were frequently complaints of exploitation and low wages, and a maid could often find more respect and higher wages with a »Yankee« family. Immigrant survival strategies were developed in the context of the family. Only the work of all family members and their contributions to the family income made it possible to withstand crisis periods such as sickness, unemployment, births, and deaths, and only with the participation of all members could plans for the future be forged. The welfare of the family as a whole was taken into account when deciding who should stay in school, whether education was really useful, which daughter should stay at home, or which could or had to work for wages outside the home. The family thus appeared as an intermediary between modern capitalist society, dominated by the structure of the labor market on the one hand, and the individual family members with their needs, wishes, and hopes on the other.

It would be wrong, however, to assume that family life was always harmonious, especially during the migration process. Naturally the family had a stabilizing and protective function, but it was also the scene of generational and gender conflicts and power struggles. Here »traditional« and »modern« ideas about the role of women collided; here men and women had to confront them in their daily lives. The »American woman« was the aspect of life in the U.S. that immigrant men did not understand and had no appreciation for. They had difficulty accepting coeducation, the more informal relationships between young men and women, women's greater independence and mobility, their expanded employment opportunities, and their resulting desire for the right to vote. Immigrant women often had as little understanding for

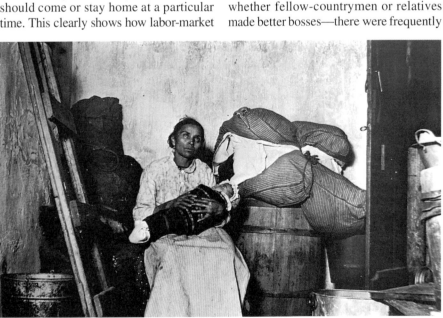

Italian ragpicker in Jersey Street, New York, around 1900

146

New York sweat shop around 1910

American women and the American women's movement as the men. Still many did consider the greater chances for self-improvement and the more favorable treatment they received in America to be a real gain for them. This fact may have been one reason why women had a significantly lower return migration rate than men.

The values of the »old« and »new« worlds collided especially frequently in generational conflicts. The children's desires for more school education or a free choice of occupation were often denied by their parents, and there were often family arguments about control of the money a child earned, a daughter's wish to choose her own husband, or even going to the movies or a dance. Nothing in the parent-child relationship was taken for granted or left unquestioned. If the father wanted to maintain his patriarchal status and authority in the family, he had to fight and win out against the rules and values in force all around him and against the acculturation process itself. The family was therefore like the other immigrant institutions and organizations in that it offered protection against too abrupt a confrontation with the new culture, but at the same time did not exist isolated from the society around it. For this reason it also underwent a continual process of change and accommodation.

The U.S. is as active today as a country of immigration as it was 300 years ago. People are still leaving home to work for a new way of life for themselves and their families, but the lands of origin have changed again. Most immigrants now come from Central and South America and from Asia. Chinatowns and Barrios, neighborhoods where only Spanish is spoken, Puerto Rican and Jamaican neighborhoods—these are as much a part of New York today as the Jewish, Italian, and German neighborhoods were 80 or 100 years ago. The new immigrants live as in earlier periods in the most dilapidated housing and work under the most insecure conditions; despite reform efforts and the labor movement, sweatshops are again part of daily life for immigrants, many of whom are in the U.S. illegally and therefore especially vulnerable to exploitation. Minimum-wage laws and other regulations are more or less meaningless for them. They are also confronted with the same racism, prejudice, and rejection as earlier immigrants over the last 300 years. The lands of origin have changed, and the social composition of the immigrant population has changed (for example, more women than men come to the U.S. today), but many of the current problems are familiar to us from the history of immigration.

References

Archdeacon, Thomas J.: Becoming American. An Ethnic History. New York/London, 1983.

Bodnar, John: The Transplanted. A History of Immigrants in Urban America. Bloomington, Indiana University Press, 1985.

Helbich, Wolfgang (ed.): »Amerika ist ein freies Land...«. Auswanderer schreiben nach Deutschland. Darmstadt.

Hoerder, Dirk; Knauf, Diethelm (eds.): Einwandererland USA - Gastarbeiterland BRD. Gulliver Bd. 22, Hamburg, 1988.

Keil, Hartmut (ed.): Deutsche Arbeiterkultur in Chikago von 1850 bis zum Ersten Weltkrieg. Eine Anthologie. Ostfildern, 1984.

Luebke, Frederick C.: Bonds of Loyalty: German-Americans During the First World War. University Press of Illinois, 1973.

Moltmann, Günter (ed.): »Germantown. 300 Jahre Auswanderung in die USA, 1683-1983«, in: Zeitschrift für Kulturaustausch. 32.Jg., 4/1982.

Raeithel, Gerd: »Go West«. Ein psychohistorischer Versuch über die Amerikaner. Frankfurt/Main, 1981.

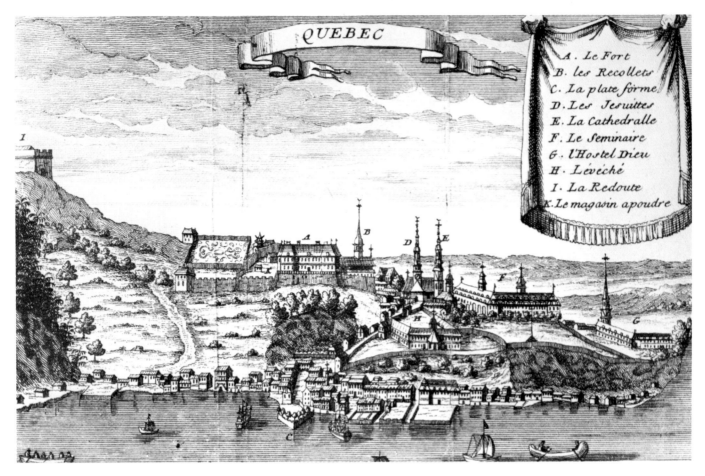

QUEBEC

A . Le Fort
B . les Recollets
C . La plate forme
D . Les Jesuittes
E . La Cathedralle
F . Le Seminaire
G . l'Hostel Dieu
H . Léveché
I . La Redoute
K . Le magasin apoudre

Quebec, 1722

Freedom in the North: Canada

Andrea Koch-Kraft

It seems surprising at first that Canada, as the second-largest country in the world, had a population of only about 25 million in 1981. The population density is 2.5 inhabitants per square kilometer, which means that there are about 100 times fewer people in a given area than in the Federal Republic of Germany (before reunification) and about 10 times less than in the neighboring United States. This disproportion is readily understood, however, if one considers the geography of Canada.

The surface formations and especially the cold climate produced by the latitude of the country are the primary natural constraints on development. Over 40 percent of the Canadian land is covered with tundra, and another 40 percent is covered with forest, mainly northern conifers. The growing season is short, even in the southern parts of Canada.

These unfriendly natural conditions have been a hindrance to humans since prehistoric times, when the ancestors of the Inuit and Indian populations now living in Canada entered via the Aleutians and Alaska. The land must have seemed just as forbidding to the legendary explorers of the historic period. It is assumed that »Markland« and »Vinland« of the Nordic sagas must have been in North America, probably in the present-day Canadian province of Newfoundland, although the existence of a Viking settlement founded by Leif Ericson, which is said to have existed around the year 1000, still remains to be proven.

The Rivalry between France and England in the East

While the discovery of America at the end of the tenth century was more or less accidental, the real impetus for the settlement of what is now Canada was the »discovery fever« stimulated by Columbus' success. Venetian captain John Cabot was authorized by King Henry VII to search for unknown lands and financed by Bristol merchants. He sailed west in 1496 seeking a northwest passage, a shorter sea route from Europe to Asia. He did not succeed in this ambitious undertaking, but he did discover rich fishing grounds off the coasts of Labrador, Newfoundland, and the Cape Breton Islands, satisfying his financial supporters in Great Britain. During the sixteenth century this important food source was exploited every summer by the French, Spanish, and Portuguese as well as the English, although only the English and Bretons founded fishermen's settlements, regularly frequented during the summer months.

Voyages of exploration continued to be sent out by the rival monarchs of Europe. King Francis I sent expeditions to explore North America, beginning with the Italian Giovanni da Verrazano in 1524, who took possession of North America for the French kings as Nova Francia, New France. More important for the later history of Canada than this formal claim were the expeditions of Jacques Cartier, a Breton sea captain. His three extensive voyages between 1534 and 1542 took him to the Gulf of St. Lawrence, Charleur Bay further upstream, and past the Iroquois settlement of Stadacona to Hochelaga, the present-day cities Quebec and Montreal. Attempts at agricultural colonization failed, however, after Cartier and his crew had spent five hard winter months at a site near Quebec. Disappointed, he returned to France.

Alongside fishing, which remained quite profitable, a new source of income for the Europeans developed and grew, slowly but steadily, to become the most lucrative and fought-over enterprise in the north. This was the fur trade, which was a determining factor in Canada's history until the mid-eighteenth century.

The French monarchy, strengthened under Henri IV, at first concentrated on developing the fur trade between New France and the motherland. The Crown and businessmen quickly recognized the profits to be made from the unequal trade of cheap metal products from France for the skins of the Native Americans. Following a typical mercantilist policy, Henri IV granted fur-trade licenses which guaranteed French merchants a monopoly, the exclusive right to buy furs in a specified region of New France. As the fur trade intensified, areas farther west and north were opened up, but settlements with agricultural colonists were not established.

Samuel de Champlain, who came to North America at the beginning of the seventeenth century not only as a representative of French merchants but also as a believing

Indian woman from the north of Alberta, around 1900

Catholic and colonizer, was the first to succeed in establishing a permanent settlement: Port Royal was founded in 1605 in the Annapolis valley of Acadia, a sheltered area near the Bay of Fundy in present-day Nova Scotia. Champlain also recognized that the area along the St. Lawrence River was better suited for both fur trading and agriculture than the coastal region, the present-day Atlantic provinces. In 1608 he established a permanent headquarters at Quebec, from where he undertook extensive canoe expeditions and opened up more and more new and more promising fur-trade areas in the interior; his trade partners included Algonquins and Hurons.

Lured by the profits to be made in furs, many young colonists abandoned their original plans for agricultural settlement and became traders. The French Crown required the trading companies to bring about

100 colonists per year to New France, but this measure was unsuccessful or was simply ignored by the companies. Thus ten years after Champlain founded Quebec there were only about 65 permanent settlers living in the area.

One factor discouraging settlement was the Counter-Reformation in France. After 1625 the Jesuits tried to carry out missionary work among the Native American population; only Catholic settlers were allowed to migrate to America; and the revocation of the Edict of Nantes in 1685, which had granted Protestants freedom of belief, meant that fewer French Huguenots could settle in New France. The practice of selecting colonists on the basis of their religious beliefs turned away from New France the very kinds of settlers that were to form the foundation of economic strength in the U.S.—settlers whose historic achievement is identified with the concept of a *Protestant ethic*.

The population of the colonies was counted frequently by the French administration, mainly to identify potential taxpayers. The first census in 1664 found the population of New France to be only 3125 people, mainly of French origin, but also including a few German colonists. Like most of the population of New France they settled near the banks of the St. Lawrence between Montreal and Quebec. The large rivers and their tributaries were the main travel routes of this period, connecting the single-family farms along their shores. The characteristic pattern of long strip fields which arose is typical of Quebec province today. Along with the Germans there were small numbers of English, Irish, Scotch, Italian, Spanish, and Portuguese settlers in New France, as well as some blacks.

The colonization of New France was stimulated and financially supported during the reign of Louis XIV (1661-1715). His desire to create a replica of the motherland in the New World is especially clear in the establishment of a feudal *seigneurial system* and in the rights granted to the Catholic church. The government subsidies provided and the institution of military bases to discourage attacks by the Iroquois resulted in an increase in the number of settlers or habitants, to over 6000 by 1672. The French population continued to increase even after the financial support of emigration was eliminated (the funds were needed for wars in Europe), but this was mainly due to high birth rates, stimulated to above-normal levels by the Catholic church and by special premiums paid to habitant families with many children. By the 1754 census, the last conducted by a French administration, the population of New France had reached 55,000; this should be contrasted with the fact that only about 10,000 people emigrated from France to New France between 1663 and 1760.

The English came to the northern part of North America as well, drawn by news of the plentiful furs available there. English explorers had landed at Hudson Bay, and in 1670 king Charles II declared the entire region drained by rivers flowing into the Bay to be part of the British realm, under the name *Rupert's Land*. The fur-trading monopoly for this territory was granted to the *Hudson Bay Company*, which still exists today. The British set up a series of easily accessible trading posts along the coast and became serious trade rivals to the French.

Conflicts between Britain and French populations in North America were thus inevitable, although the actual fighting usually ran parallel to events in Europe. The ethnic structure of the Canadian population was permanently affected by a series of his-

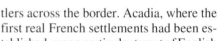
Buffaloes in Alberta, around 1900

torical events in the late seventeenth and eighteenth centuries.

In connection with armed actions at the time of the Great Alliance, an alliance against French dominance in Europe initiated by England (1689-1697), fear of British expansion starting from the New England colonies led to a number of attacks by French forces and their Native American allies on English settlements, answered in turn with counterattacks by English set-

tlers across the border. Acadia, where the first real French settlements had been established, was a particular target of English attacks by sea.

The peace treaty of Rysweik (1697) left Acadia in French control, but in the War of Spanish Succession (1703-1713) it became clear that France would have to make territorial compromises in the New World. In the Peace of Utrecht France ceded Acadia, thereafter known as Nova Scotia, Newfoundland, and Hudson Bay to the English. Now it was only a question of time, of how long the French could stand up to the superior British power in North America: by 1754 the 55,000 inhabitants of New France were outweighed by more than 2 million British colonists.

This imbalance is one reason why New France in North America and France in Europe were losers in the Seven Years' War of 1756-1763 (known in the U.S. as the French and Indian War). British and French troops in North America had already clashed in 1754, and as a result the British deported more than 6000 French settlers from Nova Scotia in 1755 and resettled them elsewhere along the coast of North

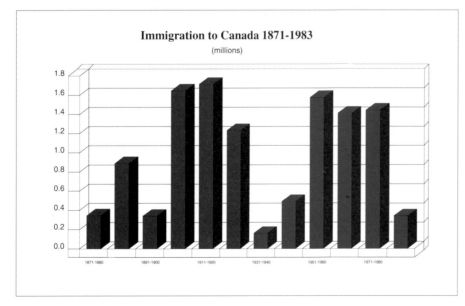

Immigration to Canada 1871-1983

(millions)

America—this is the origin of the present French-speaking population of Louisiana, while some who returned to the north were the basis of the French-Canadian population of New Brunswick province.

At first the political gains and losses of the two sides were about equal, but the fall of Montreal in 1760 sealed the fate of New France. Left in the lurch by the motherland, the colony could not withstand the better tactics and superior weaponry of the British, and the Treaty of Paris in 1763 granted all of New France to Great Britain. France lost all of its possessions and political power in North America, except for St. Pierre and Miquelon.

Contrary to the expectations of the British victors, that most of the French population of the former New France would leave their homes, most of the habitants chose to remain; a few French-born merchants returned to the mother country, opening up additional economic and trade opportunities for the British.

The British were also surprised that the French population remaining in the colonies showed no inclination to integrate itself into the dominant Protestant system. In the course of the 150-year history of New France, an identity and a feeling of belonging together had developed among the colonists, and these could not simply be abolished by decree. The influence of the Catholic priests was still strong, perhaps even stronger than before the war. Thus there were two population groups in the land that had been New France, clearly distinguished by both language and religion.

It is understandable that there was practically no more immigration from France after its defeat in North America, but no significant numbers arrived from Great Britain in the next few years, either. About 200 families migrated into the territory of New France during the first years after the war, constituting soldiers, administrative personnel, and merchants. The situation was similar in the other former French colony, now Nova Scotia, but the British Crown had already brought in about 2300 emigrants during the period 1750-1753—including almost 1500 German-speaking colonists from Switzerland and the Protestant regions of Lüneburg, Hannover,

Lumberjacks in Canada

Braunschweig, the Palatinate, and the upper Rhine valley. Among the towns they founded was Lunenburg, whose streets even today reveal its German origins.

Irish colonists and English families from Yorkshire founded their own settlements, but the largest group was made up of pioneers from New England. The rugged topography meant that the individual settlements were relatively isolated, making it possible for some immigrant groups to evade the control of the British administration. Present-day Ontario and the region to its west remained a wilderness whose potential value had been discovered only by the coureurs de bois and voyageurs, woodsmen and fur-traders.

In the Quebec Act of 1774 the British Crown granted several privileges to the French-Canadians. At this time, just before the American Revolution, the conquerors decided not to demand complete Anglicization; the seigneurial system and French civil law remained in force, and the Catholic church was allowed to collect tithes. Quebec's individuality and French character were officially recognized by the British authorities and could thus be preserved, and at the same time the loyalty of

these British subjects was strengthened. The struggle of the thirteen southern colonies for independence did not expand to Quebec or Nova Scotia.

British North America profited from the Revolutionary War in various ways. About 40,000 people who remained true to the Crown, the so-called United Empire Loyalists, fled north from the thirteen colonies. About 32,000 settled in Nova Scotia, presumably including German soldiers who had fought on the British side in the war. In recognition of their service to the Crown these Germans were given land to farm in the present province of New Brunswick.

The other Loyalists, who cut their way through the wilderness to the west of the province of Quebec, were true pioneers. Free land led them on into the Ottawa valley and across the northern shore of Lake Ontario. Germans, especially peasants from the Palatinate, were involved in this movement as well. To replace what they had left behind in New York State, they were given land, mainly in Williamsburg and the Kingston region. Along with the other pioneers they laid the foundations of the present province of Ontario.

Upper and Lower Canada

The legislative and administrative division of the former New France, now in British hands, took place in 1791 and was along ethnic lines. The eastern portion, now called Lower Canada, remained French, while the portion west of the Ottawa river, Upper Canada, was to be ruled and organized following English models. Until the early nineteenth century Upper Canada remained the destination of Loyalist latecomers from the U.S., and the British hoped that this steady immigration would lead to balance between the French- and English-speaking populations in Canada. It was soon realized, however, that continued immigration of British settlers to the Atlantic coast region would not lead to ethnic balance in Lower Canada: by 1812 the population of the coastal areas had not passed the 100,000 mark, whereas the population of the Lower Canada had tripled between 1783 and 1812, to about 330,000. The high birth rate was the determining factor.

Upper Canada remained the hope of the British. The population increased from 14,000 to 90,000 between 1791 and 1812, again not due primarily to the immigration of direct migrants. Clever advertising and the promise of free land lured part of the immigrant stream flowing westward toward the American frontier to Upper Canada, including the Mennonites, an ethnic-religious group which had been living in Pennsylvania for some time. Overall, however, the great stream of immigrants in the nineteenth century passed Upper Canada by. Those who did come included Scots and Irishmen, later some English, and limited numbers of immigrants from other countries; nevertheless, the population of Upper Canada increased from 70,000 to about 160,000 by 1825.

Some of these settlers were among those British who had felt the affects of the Napoleonic Wars most severely, and there was a general increase in emigration from Europe until about 1850 due to political in-

Trapping beaver, 1858-1860

stability. Most of the emigrants went to the U.S., but still about 800,000 people left Great Britain for Canada, known at this time as British North America.

American settlers were viewed with suspicion after the end of the war of 1812 between the U.S. and England, the North American counterpart of the Napoleonic Wars in Europe. The British drastically tightened the controls on land purchases by Americans, automatically reducing immigration from south of the border.

The destination of the immigrants was still mainly Upper Canada. That was where English families driven out by high grain prices ended up and where Irish colonists went to escape the great Potato Famine of 1846-1847; there was a noticeable population drop in the mother country. In contrast to the English emigrants the Irish often stayed to work in agriculture in the Eastern Townships, the area southwest of Montreal, and Montreal itself was the final stop for many members of the impoverished rural population of Ireland. They formed the beginnings of an urban proletariat, and even today there are Irish neighborhoods and an annual St. Patrick's Day parade in Montreal.

Although British North America inspired many dreams and plans in this period, reality often caught up with the immigrants even during the transatlantic voyage. The situation on board ship left a lot to be

desired, especially for the poor. They often traveled in freighters remade into passenger ships under catastrophic hygienic conditions. Of 109,690 emigrants from Europe in 1847, for example, over 16 percent died before reaching Canadian soil. In 1846 and 1847, over 6000 Irish emigrants died of »ship fever« (typhus) in the quarantine stations of Montreal harbor. Although British North America in principle encouraged immigration, there were complaints among the established Canadian population about the financial burden created by some of the people sent from the mother country. Canada did not wish to be looked on as a solution for problems which had their causes in Europe.

Immigration brought the population of Upper Canada up to 952,004 by 1851, so that what is now the province of Ontario surpassed Lower Canada (890,261) for the first time. The French language had already lost its dominant position by 1820, and there were 276,854 persons in Nova Scotia and 193,800 in New Brunswick. The government was concerned, however, that there was also significant emigration from Canada at this time as well. Rural people from Quebec were emigrating to the New England states to work in the textile mills.

The Canadian Pacific Region

In fact the decade from 1851 to 1861 was the last in which immigration to Canada was greater than emigration. Throughout the nineteenth century British migrants took advantage of the fact that fares to Canada were cheaper than those direct to the U.S. and were sometimes partially paid by the British government or emigration societies. Soon after their arrival they traveled on, crossing the border into the U.S. In the twentieth century, especially after World War II, Canadians with job skills migrated south for economic reasons. It is estimated that Canada lost no fewer than 7,750,000 inhabitants due to emigration between 1871 and 1971, mainly to the U.S.

The Canadian administration attempted from early on to work against this trend. The *Bureau of Agriculture*, opened in 1852, had the task of promoting immigration; emigration agents had already been sent to Europe the preceding year. Nevertheless, immigration from Europe averaged only about 20,000 per year before the passage of the Homestead Act of 1872. This period also saw the immigration of two groups which were clearly different from the previous immigrants and which had a lasting effect on the ethnic composition of the country: the blacks and the Chinese.

The ancestors of the present-day black population of Canada were mainly fugitive slaves seeking freedom in Canada. As early as the War of 1812 Canada had offered freedom to any black slave who would leave his master in the U.S. and join the British side; about 3600 people took advantage of this offer. In the decade before the Civil War (1861-1865) this moderate but continuous stream of blacks seeking freedom reached significant proportions. The Niagara peninsula, the southernmost point of Ontario province, was their destination. It is estimated that about 20,000 blacks came to Canada at this time.

The area that now makes up the province of British Columbia was claimed by the British since the landing of Captain James Cook in 1778; it was the first station for another minority, the Chinese. The first significant numbers of Chinese arrived in 1858, joining other fortune-seekers in the Cariboo Gold Rush, the first of its kind for Canada. These people had already been lured to the west coast of North America by the California gold rush of 1849.

When the gold deposits in British Columbia were exhausted, many Chinese moved on to the U.S. or returned home. Those who remained in Canada took up the trades they are known for in decades-old stereotypes: they operated laundries, grew vegetables, or worked as domestic servants. It is interesting that most of the Chinese immigrants who came to Canada (except those who had

lived in the U.S. first) were from Guang-Dong province, even as late as the 1960s; they were members of the subpeasant class fleeing poverty and overpopulation.

The very first Chinese did not come to Canada as permanent immigrants, however: like the early immigrants from southern Europe and the European »guest-workers« of today, they wanted to earn enough money abroad to build a more secure existence at home. From the Canadian perspective Chinese labor constituted a reservoir of workers who were more than ready to come to Canada when called on. When the job was finished, they were supposed to return home to China; since this expectation was not always fulfilled, it was inevitable that there would be conflicts between Canadian and Chinese interests. The result was discrimination, and the Canadian labor unions were also united in opposition to Chinese immigrants because they supposedly depressed wages.

Shortly before the turn of the century there was another spurt of Chinese immigration, about 15,000 laborers were recruited to build the transcontinental railroad line between the Atlantic and Pacific coasts of Canada in 1882-1885. As in the U.S., immigration from China was subject to special legal regulations. In order to slow down immigration the authorities imposed a tax of $50 per Chinese immigrant seeking work in Canada; this tax was increased to $100 in

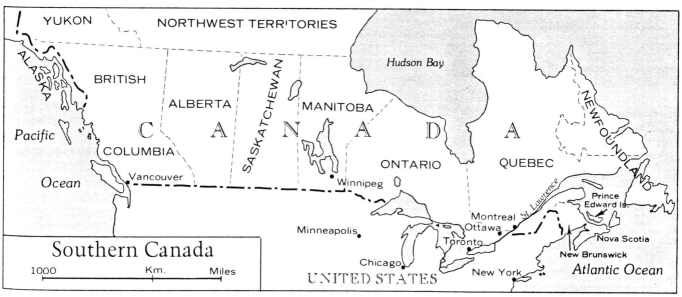

The Opening of the West and the Development of the Canadian Mosaic

Immigration to the west coast was rather modest in terms of absolute numbers, in contrast to that to the prairie region. The first immigration law was passed in 1869, two years after the foundation of the Dominion of Canada; in the same year Prince Rupert's Land was purchased from the Hudson Bay Company, which had administered it for trade purposes for over 200 years. The Homestead Act marked the beginning of the systematic settlement of the present-day prairie provinces of Manitoba, Saskatchewan, and Alberta. In the year the law was passed, immigration increased by about a third, to 36,578, and passed the 50,000 mark the following year; by 1881 it leveled off to an average rate of 34,000 per year.

Under the Homestead Act, any immigrant over 21 years of age could apply for a free quarter section of land, about 64 hectares. He became the legal owner of the land after three years if he had set up a farm and made at least part of the land arable. Additional farmland could be purchased at favorable prices.

Among the pioneers taking advantage of this opportunity were Mennonites of German origin living in Russia. They were easily induced to emigrate because they were suffering under a Russification campaign ordered by czar Alexander II. Catherine the Great had guaranteed the Mennonites a number of privileges to lure them to Russia in the 1780s, but in 1870 their exemption from military service and their language and school autonomy were revoked. Between 1874 and 1879 about 15,000 Mennonites settled in southern Manitoba, where they were granted the same privileges they had enjoyed in Russia.

This ethnic-religious minority was able to make its farms profitable in a short time. Where earlier settlements had failed because British immigrants were not used to the intemperate weather conditions, the Mennonites had farmed in Russia under conditions very similar to those in southern Manitoba. As in Russia, the villages they

Finnish cowboys in Ontario, Canada 1900

1900 and briefly to $500 in 1903. This drastic measure was only one aspect of the discrimination racial minorities were exposed to in the young Dominion of Canada.

The west coast of Canada, closest to Asia, was also a destination for other ethnic groups. Japanese immigration to Canada began toward the end of the nineteenth century in British Columbia. Typical jobs were in railroad construction, lumber, and fishing. Those who used savings in an effort to become independent played a significant role in establishing fruit and vegetable growing in the protected climate of the Okanagan basin.

British Columbia was also the province where Sikhs, an ethnic and religious minority from the Punjab state in India, were first registered as immigrants. As in the case of the Chinese and Japanese there was chain migration, as positive reports from emigrants caused members of their family clans or fellow villagers to emigrate as well.

built were strung out along the road, a characteristic structure which is still visible today. Considering the fact that the region between Ontario and the Rockies had generally been considered unsuited for agriculture or even uninhabitable a few years before, its cultivation should be seen as a major accomplishment.

From among the successful early pioneers were the Icelanders, a small ethnic group today (27,905 in 1970). They also came to what is now Manitoba in the mid-1870s and founded Gimli as the capital of their »New Iceland« colony, to be the starting point for future immigrants seeking a suitable piece of land. Winnipeg was the destination for those trying to make a living outside of agriculture; it grew to become the cultural and social center of the Icelandic population of Canada. Even today the movement to preserve Icelandic traditions all over North America is based in Manitoba.

Although the ethnic diversity of the prairie provinces began to develop in the 1870s, it was due to the active pro-immigration policy of the liberal Sir Wilfrid Laurier government (1896-1911) that the proportion of British settlers was smaller in the provinces of Manitoba, Saskatchewan, and Alberta than in the east (except for Quebec). Clifford Sifton, Laurier's Interior Secretary from 1896 to 1905, was responsible for immigration questions and therefore played a major role in bringing about the population increase in the prairies between 1881 and 1911.

The opinion in previous governments had always been that Canada should encourage immigration only among those groups in Europe which were similar in religion and way of life to the existing Canadian population and hence easier to absorb; Sifton now promoted the immigration of peasants from southeastern Europe. In his opinion they would best be able to cultivate the land under the harsh natural conditions prevailing in the prairies. Earlier efforts at recruiting British or French settlers to farm there had failed, and rapid settlement of the land with farmers loyal to Canada was an important aim for various reasons. For one thing, the U.S. repealed its Homestead Act, originally passed in 1862, in 1891. Illegal immi-

Picnic of the Ukrainian Social Democratic Party in Cobalt, Canada 1914

Greek immigrant family in Sudbury, ca. 1920

Wedding of Tot Yeng Lee and Peter Quan, 1921

grants began to cross the border into Canada. A large uncontrolled stream of American settlers, Canadians feared, could lead to annexation of the prairie region by the U.S.

Sifton's term of office also coincided with a period of great economic optimism. Industrial capacity was growing in the cities, and with it a population that had to be fed. Increasing grain prices seemed to promise substantial profits from agriculture, and the operators of the transcontinental railroad also hoped to gain new customers for their just-completed lines. As in the U.S., they had also been granted large tracts of land for construction, which they now wanted to sell.

Massive advertising campaigns in Europe led to a continual increase in the number of immigrants from 16,835 in 1896 to 400,870 in 1913, the largest total number ever registered for Canada. The group targeted by Sifton, the southeastern European peasants, thankfully accepted the offer of free land to farm.

Although a few Ukrainians had migrated to

Canada before, between 1891 and 1914 a total of about 170,000-200,000 settled there. They came almost exclusively (97 percent) from Galicia and Bucovina, territories ruled by Austria-Hungary. The land-hungry peasants were seeking a way out of confining social and economic conditions. As late as the 1930s their settlements in Canada had the traditional appearance, with whitewashed thatched-roof houses; even today onion-domed churches in small prairie towns remind the visitor of the Ukrainian origins of the communities. The first Ukrainians settled in the province of Alberta, east of Edmonton, and a large number came to Manitoba and Saskatchewan in the years before 1921. Today most of the Ukrainian population of Canada, like the population in general, lives in cities; the largest concentrations of Ukrainians are in Winnipeg and Edmonton.

Poles had migrated to Ontario even before the great wave of immigration in the nineteenth century. Sifton's campaign caused about 115,000 Poles to join their Ukrainian

neighbors in seeking a better life in Canada. Overpopulation and undernourishment were major factors leading Poles, especially from Galicia, to Canada.

The number of Germans migrating to Canada up to the outbreak of World War I was smaller than those of Poles or Ukrainians; for the decade 1901-1910, for example, there were only 18,302 immigrants of German origin. On the other hand, the German Empire registered only 3209 persons emigrating to Canada during the same period. Estimates based on the total number of immigrants of German origin settling in the Canadian prairies before 1914 can help explain this difference: 44 percent of them came from Russia; 18 percent had been living in Galicia, Bucovina, or the Banat; and 6 percent were Germans from Rumania. Another 18 percent had been living in the U.S., and 2 percent were from Ontario, leaving only 12 percent immigrating directly from Germany. Nevertheless, there were a significant number of German settlements in the prairie provinces.

German Catholics from southern Russia established St. Peter's and St. Joseph's colonies in Saskatchewan as group settlements based on their religion. Many times the religious confession of an immigrant played a greater role in choosing a place to live than his ethnic origin. Where immigrants of differing origin but the same religion settled together they unavoidably stopped using their native languages rather quickly, paving the way for integration into Canadian society.

Along with the Mennonites, Catholics, and Protestants there were about 7000 members of the Dukhobors sect, a minority group from Russia which came in 1899 to seek refuge in Canada, as part of the Sifton campaign. Their pacifist and community-oriented way of life was threatened in Russia but was at first guaranteed protection, along with school autonomy, in Canada; disagreements soon arose between this group and the Canadian administration, however. The Dukhobors refused to swear the oath of allegiance because it meant they could be drafted in case of war. When school autonomy was revoked they refused to send their children to the public schools. The administration favored single-family farms, hoping that speedy acculturation would result, whereas the Dukhobors preferred community settlements. Confrontations led to the repeated imposition of sanctions against the Dukhobors, continuing into the 1970s, because they did not feel bound by national and provincial laws. Frequent jail terms for their spokesmen accelerated the breakup of the group.

Events in Europe led to a sharp increase in the Jewish population of Canada between 1881 (667 people) and 1911 (76,199). Individual Jews had been active as merchants in the eastern cities, mainly Montreal, as early as the eighteenth century, while the opening up of the Canadian west and the mass emigration of Jews coincided in the later nineteenth century. Hundreds of thousands of Jews fled the pogroms in Russia, Rumania, and Poland, and land in the prairie regions was obtained for them by Jewish aid societies. About 30 percent of the Jewish immigrants settled in the west, with another 30 percent in Ontario and about 40 percent in Quebec.

After 1900 the Canadian census begins to note significant numbers of immigrants from other groups such as Belgians, Finns, Austrians, Rumanians, Hungarians, Greeks, and Italians. The lands of origin still lay mainly in Europe, but with a definite shift to the east and south. Immigration from Asia was for the most part directed to the Pacific coast and still comprised mainly Chinese, Japanese, and Sikhs.

Immigration to Canada continued at a reduced rate during World War I and the years immediately following it. The Canadian economy had enough to do reintegrating the returning soldiers into the labor market. When the situation had eased somewhat, measures were taken to control immigration; in 1928, for example, the number of Japanese immigrants was limited to 150 per year by a so-called Gentlemen's Agreement with the Japanese government.

In 1923 Canada began to differentiate between preferred and nonpreferred countries of origin for immigrants. Northern and

»German Oktoberfest« in Edmonton, Canada

western European lands belonged to the first group, while immigrants from central and eastern European lands had to meet special requirements. During the Great Depression of the 1930s the government extended these requirements to all immigrants: they could enter Canada if they had the money to buy a farm or planned to take some other job in the agricultural sector.

Compared to the previous years, immigration in the 1930s decreased sharply, from about 100,000 to about 15,000 per year, and continued to drop during World War II. Germans were »enemy aliens« during this period, and they were not permitted to immigrate. One exception was a group of Social Democratic refugees from the Sudetenland who came via England to British Columbia, where the former artisans became farm workers.

New Immigrants from Postwar Europe

Refugees from Europe were among the first to find new homes in Canada after World War II. Contrary to expectations Canadian industry made a smooth transition from war production to peacetime production, and returning soldiers had no trouble finding jobs. There were even labor shortages in agriculture, with the sudden lack of prisoners of war and internees to help out. A need for workers was felt in other parts of the primary sector as well. This aroused the farmers, who put pressure on the government to encourage the immigration of farmers and agricultural workers. There were plenty of potential immigrants in Europe, where there were five million refugees in war-damaged Germany alone.

A proclamation by Prime Minister Mackenzie King in 1947 defined the goals of the new Canadian immigration policy. The population of Canada was to grow; immigrants who could be integrated without problems into the Canadian economy

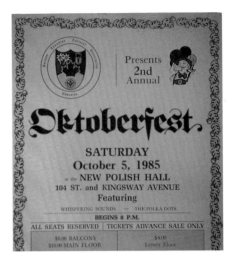

would be selected; and (as a third new principle) refugees and homeless persons would be accepted.

Working together with the International Refugee Organization about 166,000 so-called displaced persons immigrated to Canada between 1947 and 1952. A large number of these were of German origin. In prearranged work contracts they agreed to take jobs in agriculture for two years. After this time only a few remained in these occupations; most went to the cities, where money could be earned more quickly and easily. German citizens, on the other hand, were still considered enemy aliens and not permitted to immigrate at this time.

The new open-door policy led to a doubling of the number of immigrants (compared to the previous year), to 125,414 in the year after the proclamation. As before, the greatest numbers came from England, Ireland, Scotland, and Wales.

Immigration from the Netherlands was substantial, with over 10,000 persons, and the rural areas of Holland were stricken with a virtual »emigration fever«. Entire villages decided to leave, and the process was made easier by a bilateral emigration agreement between Canada and the Netherlands. The after-effects of German occupation had almost completely destroyed the economy, and emigration was also driven by rapid population growth, a growing land shortage, and continuing conflicts between government troops and guerrillas in the Dutch colony of Indonesia. In 1950 the enemy alien label for Germans and Italians was removed, and potential immigrants from these countries were treated the same as others. This action had a direct effect on immigration from Germany and Italy, especially when combined with the Assisted Passage Loan Scheme of 1951, whereby the Canadian government loaned money for or even partially paid the transatlantic passage of prospective immigrants. The numbers of immigrants quickly increased, from 5800 Germans and 9000 Italians in 1950 to 32,400 Germans and 24,350 Italians in 1951.

Conditions in Germany, characterized by destroyed industries, a housing shortage, and high unemployment, drove emigration. The Canadian authorities also took care of immigration formalities more quickly and less bureaucratically than U.S. officials. In contrast to the immigrants before the War, relatively few sought work in the agricultural sector; those with solid training were glad to take jobs in industry or the trades. About 160,000 persons of German origin had immigrated to Canada by 1961. Their preferred destinations were in Ontario, Alberta, and British Columbia; few Germans went to Quebec or the Atlantic provinces.

Italy, suffering from chronic unemployment, had state-subsidized emigration to Canada. People renewed their ties to relatives in Canada, and a kind of delayed chain migration developed, bringing 285,720 persons of Italian origin to Canada by 1961. Toronto is home to by far the greatest number of Italians and still has its Little Italy today, although Montreal is the traditional Italian center. There the Italians have become integrated into a French-speaking rather than an English-speaking culture, in contrast to most of the pre- and postwar immigrants from the major countries of origin. During the 1950s there was little change in the pattern of countries of origin, although there was some increase in immigration from the agriculturally oriented countries, such as Portugal, Yugoslavia, and Greece. Bureaucratic formalities were set aside to accept over 30,000 refugees from Hungary after the bloody repression of revolt in that country in 1956.

The Canadian government still had reservations about immigration from Asia in the 1950s, as expressed in agreements with India, Pakistan, and Ceylon (Sri Lanka) establishing immigration quotas. A negative attitude toward Japan, reflected in a quota of only 150 immigrants per year on average, continued until the end of the decade.

The New Immigration Policy: Occupational Criteria versus Humanitarian Goals

When immigration from the traditional lands of origin continued to decrease, there was a change of opinion among those responsible for policy. Now the education and training of potential immigrants were to be the most important selection criteria, whereas the previous practice of discriminating against particular countries or ethnic groups was considered no longer appropriate and contrary to the liberal image the country was trying to develop. A new law to this effect was passed in 1962, and in the same year Canada accepted 100 refugee families from Hong Kong.

The countries of the British Commonwealth, primarily those in the Third World, were »discovered« as lands of emigration. Whereas craftsmen had been especially sought-after in the 1950s, members of the educated elite were now recruited in the Caribbean and in Asian and African countries. The province of Quebec was attractive for Haitians who spoke French as their official language, and Montreal soon became a center of activity for these immigrants. Students from the so-called developing countries attending university in Canada often took advantage of the possibility of applying for immigration after completing their studies. This is the probable origin of the Filipino and Indonesian communities in Canada.

Canada now also gave prominent consideration to humanitarian factors in admitting immigrants. After Soviet troops marched into Czechoslovakia in 1968 Canada took in over 12,000 refugees, easing entrance requirements and providing special language courses to facilitate their integration. Less spectacular but following the same general policy direction was an offer of asylum to the Dalai Lama and his small group of Tibetan refugees fleeing Chinese repression. About 6000 refugees of Indian origin expelled from Uganda under an Africanization policy were accepted as immigrants in Canada, as were Chileans fleeing their homeland for political reasons after the fall of the Allende government in 1973. Immediately after the end of the Vietnam War Canada declared its willingness to accept refugees from that country as well. Special programs were set up to help those fleeing in boat across the South China Sea, and in 1979 alone 24,573 of these so-called »boat people« arrived in Canada; the following year the number increased by over 10,000. In 1970 there were about 1200 Vietnamese living in Canada, mainly in the province of Quebec. In the census of 1981 the total number of new Canadians born in Vietnam had increased to 50,710.

In the 1960s and 1970s immigration to Canada varied between 71,689 and 222,876 people per year, with an average value of about 130,000 per year. Official statistics for the mid-1980s list immigrants from almost 190 different countries and territories, mainly in small groups.

Clearly recognizable is a shift in the countries of origin, away from Europe. In 1965 about 75 percent of all immigrants came from Europe, but the proportion was 50 percent in 1975 and only 22 percent in 1985. Asia assumed the leading position, and South America and the Caribbean were also important areas sending immigrants.

This new constellation is closely linked to the new Canadian immigration policy, but also to the economic situation in the lands of origin. In terms of average income, Canada is now less attractive to university graduates from Europe than to those from countries where wages are low.

Canada has, however, managed to attract some new immigrants from wealthy industrial nations: investors wishing to establish new mid-sized business enterprises. In recent years, Germans and Chinese from Hong Kong have been overrepresented in this group of immigrants. Retirees are also welcome immigrants, at least as long as they have sufficient funds. In addition, permission to immigrate is granted to citizens' family members as long as their means of support are guaranteed by a sponsor.

Despite the selectivity of its immigration laws and current economic conditions, Canada today receives a relatively large number of applications for immigration. The country's liberal image has made it a favored land of immigration for people from all over the world.

References

Anderson, Alan B.; Frideres, James S.: Ethnicity in Canada: Theoretical Perspectives. Toronto, 1981.

Census of Canada 1871-1981. Ottawa.

Creighton, Donald G.: Dominion of the North. A history of Canada. Überarbeiteter Wiederabdruck, Toronto, 1977.

Driedger, Leo (ed.): Ethnic Canada. Identities and Inequalities. Toronto, 1987.

Kalbach, Warren E.: »Growth and Distribution of Canada's Ethnic Population, 1871-1981«, in: Driedger, Leo (ed.): Ethnic Canada. Identities and Inequalities. Toronto, 1987, S.82-110.

Koch, Andrea: »Deutsche in Kanada - Einwanderung und Adaptation. Mit einer Untersuchung zur Situation der Nachkriegsimmigranten in Edmonton, Alberta«, in: Kanada-Studien. Bd. 7, Bochum, 1990.

Krauter, Joseph F.; Davis, Morris: Minority Canadians: Ethnic Groups. Toronto, 1978.

Lehmann, Heinz: Das Deutschtum in Westkanada. Berlin, 1939.

Lenz, Karl: »Die Prärieprovinzen Kanadas. Der Wandel der Kulturlandschaft von der Kolonisation bis zur Gegenwart unter dem Einfluß der Industrie«, in: Marburger Geographische Schriften. Heft 21, Marburg, 1965.

Lenz, Karl: Kanada. Eine geographische Landeskunde. Darmstadt, 1988.

McNaught, Kenneth: The Pelican History of Canada. überarbeiteter Wiederabdruck, Harmondsworth, 1978.

The Canadian Family Tree: Canada's Peoples. Don Mills, 1979.

Canadian Mohawk Indians fight for their land, 1990

To Govern is to Populate! Migration to Latin America

Diethelm Knauf

When in 1492 Spanish boots were first planted in the sand of the island of Guanahani in the Bahamas, later called San Salvador by the new arrivals, immigration to Latin America had begun. After the discoverers came the conquerors, lured across the Atlantic by gold, silver, and storied treasures to fill the empty coffers of the government in Madrid, and soon also in Lisbon. The power politics of the European countries, constant warfare, and extravagant court life required new sources of income.

Early European Expansion

The treaty of Tordesillas in 1494, arbitrated by the Pope, divided the newly discovered and even the not yet discovered lands of the New World, by Apostolic Grace, between Spain and Portugal: a line of demarcation was drawn from north to south 370 miles west of the Cape Verde Islands; it separated the Spanish possessions and sphere of influence to the west from the Portuguese areas to the east. Africa and the northeastern corner of what is now Brazil was granted to the Portuguese Crown, while the rest of America was granted to the Spanish. The Conquistadors encountered many different native peoples, Indians as they called them, who were living at widely varying levels of cultural and technological development. Practically anything was possible among the Native Americans: astronomers and engineers, but also people living under stone-age conditions. The conquest was first directed against the great empires, the Aztecs and Mayas in Central America and the Incas in northwestern South America. These areas were linked to the legend of *El Dorado* and did indeed possess vast treasures, undreamed-of riches, gold and silver mines. All too soon it became clear that plans for economic exploitation here could be realized only by

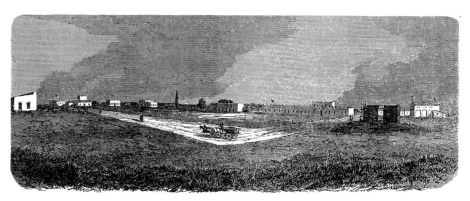

Swiss colony »Esperanza« in Santa Fé province, Argentina

force, against the resistance of the native population. A campaign of genocide began, with the weapons and instruments of torture blessed by the Catholic church, which had no understanding for the native cultures and regarded the Indians only as the targets of their missionary work, as mere heathens, despite the obvious achievements of the native civilizations. There were also critical voices, like that of the monk Bartholome de Las Casas, who wrote a description of the criminal behavior of the whites toward the Indians in order to preach against it. But these reports had practically no effect on the colonial policy of the state.

It is estimated that North and South America had 40-60 million inhabitants at the time Columbus arrived, although estimates as low as 10 million and as high as 90-110 million (with 60 million in Mexico and Peru alone) have been put forward as well. A population of 25 million seems reliable for the present-day territory of Mexico, nor is there any doubt that large numbers were systematically wiped out as a result of wars, epidemics, and slavery. In Mexico between 1519 and 1532 more than 8 million people lost their lives. Thirty years later only 3 million of the original population of 25 million remained, and by the beginning of the seventeenth century the population had been reduced to 4 percent of its original size. Brazil had about 22 million native inhabitants; today the number is 220,000. When Columbus landed on Hispaniola, the island holding the present-day

Trade routes during the colonial period: triangular trade

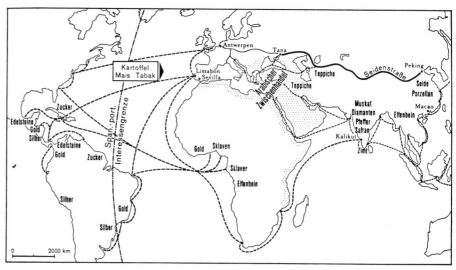

countries of Haiti and the Dominican Republic, about 1 million Indians lived there, but by 1520 the number had shrunk to 25,000.

The white man's appropriation of the Americas was characterized by the plunder of advanced civilizations, the exploitation of gold and silver deposits, and the decimation and enslavement of the native population. In fact a significant and continuous stream of immigrants from Europe (as soldiers and military officials, bureaucrats, monks and missionaries, merchants and tradesmen, craftsmen, or farmers) was necessary in order to take possession of the large land area; build the economy, government, and bureaucracy; and establish functioning colonies.

From the beginning migration from Spain to the new colonies was strictly regulated by the state. Emigration matters were handled by the *Casa de contracion de las Indias* (House of Trade) in Seville and later by the *Consejo de Indias* (Council of the Indies), in Madrid. These offices evaluated applications to emigrate and enforced a strictly exclusive emigration policy which kept non-Spaniards and non-Catholics out of the colonies.

Brazil was claimed for Portugal by Pedro Alvares Cabral in 1550, but the first settlers there were mainly *degredados*, exiled criminals. There were no Indian cultures there with gold and other riches to be plundered, nor even any known deposits of valuable minerals. For this reason Portuguese colonial policy was less restrictive, and Dutch and French merchants established trading posts on the northeast coast. This situation changed when gold was discovered in the province of Minas Gerais around 1700: new regulations prohibited the immigration of foreigners. Even Portuguese subjects were forbidden to travel to Brazil in 1720, in an effort to stop the depopulation of the northern provinces of Portugal, a region where emigration had become a tradition.

In 1550 there were about 220,000 Spanish colonists in Latin America, concentrated mainly in Mexico, and about 30,000 Portuguese on the coast of Brazil. Over the following 200 years the Spanish population rose, to about 500,000 by the year 1700.

View of Lima

This increase was due primarily to a high birth rate, especially in mixed marriages linking a Spanish husband and an Indian wife, and a low mortality rate (relative to that among the native population). On the other hand, immigration also played a certain role. Using records of ship traffic between Spain and America it can be estimated that about 450,000 colonists left Europe for the Spanish colonies between 1500 and 1650, a sizeable number considering that the total population of Spain in 1600 was only about 8 million. Purely theoretical estimates put emigration from Portugal during the same period even higher, at 580,000, followed by 600,000 more during the Minas Gerais gold rush between 1700 and 1762.

During the period of conquest the proportion of women among the immigrants was only about 8 percent, but by the middle of the sixteenth century it was 25 percent and later rose to 33 percent. These figures serve to correct the erroneous assumption that the early emigration was a purely masculine enterprise.

There was also return migration, although this is only documented for the conquistadors and their troops. Since these were soldiers rather than colonists, return migration for this group is really to be expected.

With the consolidation and development of a new society the immigrants, both Spanish and Portuguese, became the ruling class in the American colonies, the source of the military, administrative, economic, and political elite. The majority of the population still consisted of Native Americans, al-

CHRISTOPH COLUMBUS.

Columbus erklärt seine Pläne den Granden Spaniens.

COMPAGNIE LIEBIG.

CHRISTOPH COLUMBUS.

COMPAGNIE LIEBIG.

Erste Landung in der neuen Welt.

CHRISTOPH COLUMBUS.

Rückkehr, mit Erzeugnissen der neuen Welt.

COMPAGNIE LIEBIG.

Christopher Columbus' discovery of America, as portrayed on trading cards, 1888

162

A Mexican scene from before the destruction of the Aztec civilization by the Spanish conquistadores (part of a fresco)

though these continued to be decimated, and an increasing number of African slaves. The deportation of slaves by force from Africa constituted a second inglorious chapter in the white history of the Americas. Even the most conservative estimates indicate that 500,000 slaves were imported between 1500 and 1650, and the trade reached a high point in the period 1760-1810, when over 1.3 million people were shipped as freight to Latin America. A total of 4 million blacks were taken to Brazil alone, where they constituted over half the population by the beginning of the nineteenth century. In 1816 there were 1.9 million slaves in an overall population of 3.5 million, and whites made up only 23 percent of the total. Around the same time Spain's weakened position in Europe (as a result of the Napoleonic expansion) and a feeling of common identity among the colonists led to independence for most of Central and South America: Argentina in 1816, Chile in 1818, Mexico and Peru in 1821, and Brazil in 1822. These new states abolished first the slave trade and later slavery itself; nevertheless, by 1860 almost 1.7 million black slaves had reached Brazil, Cuba, and Puerto Rico alone.

Slaves were used as laborers in the mines and also on the large farm estates, for the private acquisition of vast areas of land and their agricultural exploitation in the form of single-crop plantation farming played just as important a role as the hunt for gold, silver, and jewels. Plantation agriculture began around the middle of the sixteenth century, only a few decades after Columbus made his discovery, and involved mainly sugar cane, cattle, and natural resources such as lumber. Alongside the large plantations (similar to the latifundia of ancient Rome) and the extensive cattle ranches there were also small peasant holdings granted to colonists or resident soldiers. The urban settlements were dominated by the offices of trading companies and factories for processing raw materials and agricultural products; e.g., sugar refineries and tanneries.

Colonization Programs and Labor Recruiting

In the 1840s the liberal Argentine writer Juan Alberti characterized the Latin American governments' new thinking in immigration policy with the slogan, »In South America to govern is to populate«. The progressive approach seemed to be to recruit immigrants from all the developed countries of Europe. There were vast land areas to be explored and made ready for cultivation, and immigration also seemed to be a way to alleviate the chronic labor shortage on the plantations.

In the first half of the nineteenth century migration to Latin America was quite heterogeneous. Large numbers of merchants, artisans, and sailors established themselves in the coastal towns and port cities to seek their fortunes. British and Irish soldiers fought in Simón Bolívar's armies of liberation, and many political refugees and exiles found new homes in Latin America—including Giuseppe Garibaldi, who arrived in South America in 1820 with his band of Italian revolutionaries.

The characteristic activities for this period, however, were colonization projects and the foundation of agricultural settlements, frequently initiated for economic reasons by European entrepreneurs and travel agents, who hoped to use the pro-immigration policies of the Latin American governments for their own purposes.

Most of the countries made great efforts to recruit European emigrants to found settlements. The prospective immigrants were promised free land, exemptions from taxes and military service, and sometimes even free equipment to start up—tools, cattle, a place to live—and other advantages. Settlers from Germany, Ireland, and northern Europe were especially attracted by these offers, but they were joined mainly by Spanish, Italian, and French immigrants. Two popular destinations were the Rio de la Plata region and southern Brazil. One of the most spectacular settlement projects was started in 1819 by 2000 Swiss, mainly in family groups, who founded the colony Nova Friburgo in the highlands of Brazil's Rio de Janeiro province. Many were willing to emigrate because of failed harvests, famine, and unemployment in Switzerland, explaining the relatively large number of colonists and the positive stance taken by the Swiss authorities. This enterprise ended tragically: almost 19 percent of the settlers died during the voyage, mostly from malaria, which they had contracted during an unnecessarily long layover in a swampy area of the Netherlands. The site

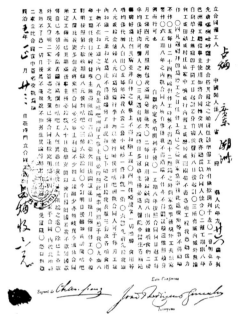

After slavery was abolished Chinese coolies were recruited. Work contract

chosen for the settlement turned out to be very poorly suited, and the hard work, many deprivations, poor food, and unaccustomed climate and geological conditions kept the death rate very high at the beginning. Nova Friburgo was a catastrophic failure, and most of the colonists left to try their luck at establishing a new home elsewhere.

Baja Verapaz, in the northeastern part of Guatemala, was another ambitious European colonization project. It was initiated by President Mariano Galvez, but its implementation was in the hands of English and Belgian entrepreneurs who had little understanding of how to organize travel or set up a colony. Like Nova Friburgo, Baja Verapaz demonstrated how hard it is to practice European-style agriculture in a tropical or subtropical climate.

The colonization projects in the temperate zone had better initial conditions for success; the German settlements in southern Brazil, for example, relatively quickly enjoyed a certain degree of prosperity. So Leopoldo, founded in 1824, was the first of numerous German settlements in Rio Grande del Sul. In the following years over 5000 Germans migrated to this area, most of them signed up by the notorious adventurer Georg Anton von Schäffer and his unscrupulous recruiters. Sao Leopoldo was a colony of small farmers, sharing the land in equal plots of 24 hectares per family.

There were also successfully functioning German settlements in Chile, in the forests of Valdivia and Llanquihue; by 1850 there were about 3000 pioneers living there. Swiss and French colonists settled in Argentina, and in Uruguay a native entrepreneur was able to recruit 850 Spanish settlers from the Canary Islands.

All Latin American governments tried to establish colonies of this type. Despite the successes mentioned above the overall results of these colonization projects, however, were disappointing. All too often the natural obstacles proved insurmountable, the settlers were poorly organized, or the governments broke their recruiting promises. The land that was granted the colonists was unsuitable for farming; the promised housing, tools, or bank credit were unavailable; there were no means of transportation to the site; etc. When the projects failed, the settlers were in dire straits; many paid with their lives.

Despite the repeated failures of immigrant colonies, the Latin American governments maintained a policy of opening their borders to new settlers. In the course of the nineteenth century the global economy and world politics played an increasingly important role. The progress of industrialization in Europe and North America drew Latin America into world trade as a source of raw materials, an exporter of agricultural products, and a market for industrial products. Many workers were needed to build up the infrastructure, settle the land, and operate the plantations. Because the population had grown only gradually over the preceding decades, these needs could not be met with native resources alone. Policies favorable to immigration were designed to bring in not only workers and know-how but also capital.

The labor shortage was even more intensely felt when the Latin American states which were still practicing slavery came under international pressure to abolish it in the 1830s. Cuba (still under Spanish rule) and Brazil, two major slave importers, had to close the slave trade in 1855 and 1865, respectively, although slavery per se was only completely abolished in Brazil in 1888 and in Cuba in 1886. But even earlier there were signs that the institution of slavery had become economically obsolete, primarily due to the low birth rate among the slaves and their low life expectancy—in British Guyana, for example, it was about 28 years in 1830.

A potential solution for this problem was to recruit technically free contract laborers. A worker was loaned the price of a passage ticket by the owner of the plantation or business or by a professional emigration agent; to pay it back, these poorest immigrants contracted to serve their creditor for little or no pay for a certain number of years. Contract laborers were recruited mainly among Chinese coolies, 142,000 of whom migrated to Cuba alone between 1847 and 1874, mainly to work on the sugar plantations. Peru recruited about 75,000 Chinese during the same period, for plantation work and also for railroad construction. Chinese laborers also had a significant role in building the Panama Canal. Contract laborers for the British colonies in Latin America were recruited mainly from India.

Living conditions for contract laborers scarcely differed from those for slaves. Over 10 percent died during the sea voyage—as a Cuban merchant cynically explained: »Supposing that 600 men were shipped from China, and that only 300 arrived in Cuba, these would cover all the losses and still leave a brilliant profit«. At their workplaces they were subjected to inhumane treatment, housed in isolated camps without their wives and families, abused, cheated of their wages, and often forced to sign oppressive new contracts. Only a few were able to return to China or lead an independent life after their contracts ran out.

The Period of the World Wars

Until the second third of the nineteenth century immigration to Latin America was a constant phenomenon but involved only a few thousand people; in general the ambitious plans of the Latin American govern-

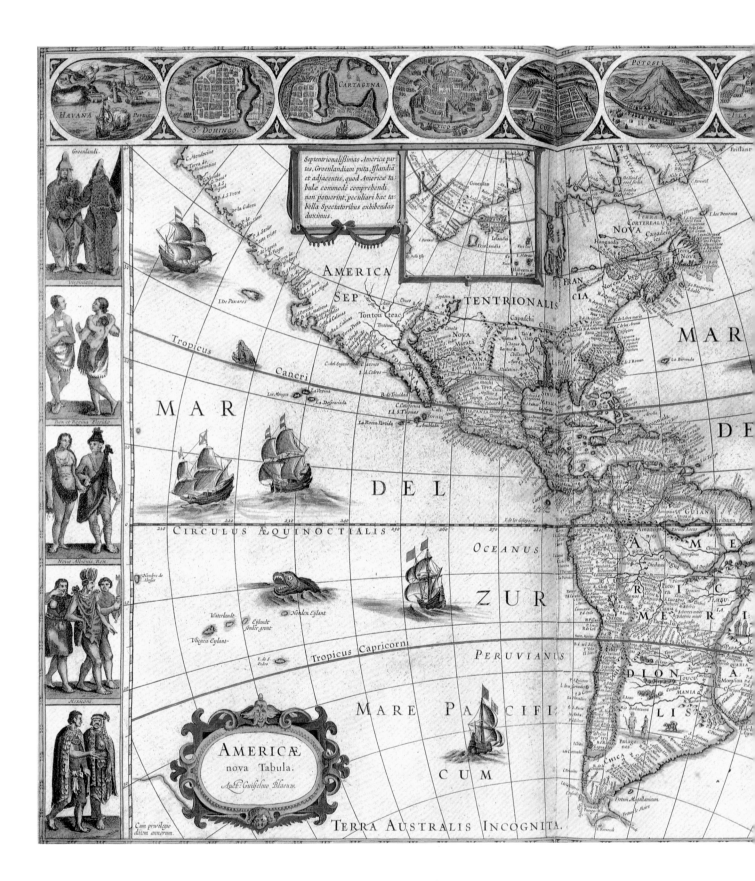

Map of North and South America, published around 1630 by Wilhelm Blaeu

167

»Favelas« in Rio de Janeiro, Brazil. Poverty has increased tremendously since the end of World War II

ments could not be realized. This was due primarily to conditions in the different countries, to climate and geography and to a lack of economic development and political stability. From the time the Latin American countries became independent it took until the last decades of the nineteenth century for their border squabbles and internal political conflicts to be resolved, for the process of state formation to be completed and the political and economic structure consolidated. In southern Brazil and the Rio de la Plata basin the climate and soil were such that European colonists could live, grow crops, and raise farm animals using the methods they had brought from home. In these areas it was also possible to produce goods that were in demand in Europe: meat, grain, leather, coffee, and certain wood and fiber products. After slavery was abolished there was no satisfactory answer to the labor shortage, and as living conditions in Europe worsened and the cost of a transatlantic passage grew cheaper, all the necessary conditions for a wave of mass migration to Latin America were in place.

It is well known that the greatest number of transatlantic migrants went to North America. Nevertheless, about 11 million people, about one fifth of the total number of migrants, chose Latin America. It is surprising, for example, that 68 percent of the Italian transatlantic migrants, 70 percent of the Portuguese migrants, and a great majority of the Spanish emigrants between 1875 and 1898 came to Latin America.

In the latter cases linguistic and cultural affinities may have played a role, although at this time the former colonial powers and their one-time colonies were not on the best of terms politically; other factors must be taken into consideration. For the individual migrant, the choice of destination was based on a number of criteria: the need to avoid a financial or social step downward in times of economic or political crisis; the desire to maintain one's standard of living or earn a small step upward in the social hierarchy; travel subsidies from the country of immigration; chance occurrences (like which emigration agent or shipowner one happened to meet); the sources of information one had access to; and where friends

Italian immigrant family in Argentina, around 1920

and relatives had gone previously. In terms of expense it was significant that Argentina, Uruguay, and Brazil subsidized the travel and transportation costs. In So Paulo around 1890, when the need for workers on the coffee plantations was especially high, the proportion of immigrants arriving on subsidized tickets varied between 82 and 99 percent. The living costs in Latin America were also relatively low: around 1900 they were only 25 percent of wages in Argentina, compared with 33 percent in the U.S. and 60 percent in Spain and Italy.

The shipping lines and most of the emigration agents used all available means to lure potential emigrants to the country they represented. Priests were sometimes agents, taking advantage of their positions to convince the emigrants, and agents would take young men out of the country illegally in order to avoid military conscription. In the 1890s an agent from Udine, northwest of Venice, was able to stir up a »Brazil-fever« among the very poor and economically exploited peasants of western Galicia. Workers were needed to build the railroad line from Madeira to Marmoré, and thousands signed up. Many became ill in the jungle—for them »fever« became terrifying reality. Emigration agents had a significant influence on which country people decided to migrate to; as one Italian historian dis-

covered, many Italians simply left the choice of destination to the shipping-company agent.

The more personal reasons given for emigration sometimes seem less than serious. A Catalan woodworker left for America because he could not endure constant arguments with his mother-in-law. A Syrian living in Chile claimed he had been sent away by his family because he had a passion for raising pigeons. Two Swedish engineers selected their destination by sticking a pin into a globe, ending up in Peru.

Intercontinental migration between 1824 and 1924 involved 52 million men and women, of whom 72 percent went to the U.S., 21 percent went to Latin America, and 7 percent went to Australia. Of 11 million emigrants who went to Latin America, about half (5.5 million or 10 percent of the global migration) went to Argentina; 36 percent went to Brazil (mainly to the temperate south); 5 percent went to Uruguay; and the remaining 9 percent were divided among the other countries.

Toward the end of the 1860s the number of immigrants attained significant numbers,

surpassing 50,000 per year. The peak immigration period, with over 250,000 per year, began after about 1850 and continued until World War I. After the war immigration reached almost the same level, but dropped sharply during the worldwide depression of the 1930s.

The immigrant population was concentrated in the areas of production for export, as wheat-growing tenant farmers in Argentina, for example, or as wage workers on the coffee plantations in Sao Paulo. With time many of the rural migrants returned home to Europe or moved on to the cities. By 1895 only 16 percent of immigrants to Argentina were employed in agriculture, with 17 percent craftsmen and skilled workers, and 14 percent in business, trade, and transportation.

Naturally the agricultural workers and tenant farmers settled in the more fertile regions; in the later phases of the migration their numbers were far surpassed by those of unskilled workers, who tended to go to the urban centers, hoping to find work in the industries being established there. An especially characteristic example of urbanization is Montevideo, which grew from a small provincial town to the fourth-largest city in Spanish-speaking America during the nineteenth century.

Sao Paulo also experienced rapid urbanization. At the end of the nineteenth century it developed into a center of agricultural industry for coffee production, and then a powerful and comprehensive industrialization process made it the second-largest city and most important industrial region of Latin America. Overall immigration to Latin America had an urban character. The census of Argentina in 1914 showed that 68 percent of the foreign-born population lived in cities, with only 10 percent in the interior or southern provinces.

Along with Brazil, Argentina was the primary country of immigration in Latin America. Between 1881 and 1935 about 3.4 million people settled there, while about 3.3 million chose Brazil between 1872 and 1940 and Uruguay definitely had fewer immigrants, about 600,000 for the same period. The high point of immigration was between 1880 and 1900, but the rate of return migration was also very high. In the

Immigrant monument in Sao Leopoldo, Brazil - 100 years of German immigration 1824-1924

came to Argentina, along with 200,000 French, including some refugees from the Paris Commune of 1871. The following figures show how important this immigration was for Argentina: according to the 1914 census 30 percent of the population of the country was foreign-born. In the period 1840-1940 about 29 percent of the population growth in Argentina was from direct immigration, and another 29 percent was second-generation immigrants. These figures are twice as high as the corresponding values for the land of immigration par excellence, the U.S., where the maximum was reached in 1910 with 14.7 percent foreign-born. Without mass migration the population of Argentina in 1940 would have been 6 million, instead of the actual value, 13 million.

In Cuba the situation was determined by the lateness and long duration of the war of independence, which ended only in 1898 with the defeat of the Spanish colonial power. Before that time population growth stagnated and even decreased (because of the war) in the decade before independence. The new republican government had an open-door policy, needing immigrants in order to stabilize the economy, especially the sugar industry. Large numbers now immigrated, especially from Spain (about 800,000 between 1902 and 1930), securing Spanish dominance in Cuban society. However, the immigrants were now more likely to be employed in the productive sector than in administration or the military jobs typical of the colonial period. Another major source of immigrants to Cuba was the West Indies, especially Haiti and Jamaica; about 300,000 came to Cuba, most of them after World War I. The return migration rate was probably relatively high for this group, with only a fuzzy distinction between immigration and the migration of harvest workers among the sugar plantations of Cuba and the neighboring islands.

1880s about three-quarters of the immigrants remained, which was considered the best percentage attainable—in the previous decade the proportions were reversed, and three-quarters emigrated again. In years of crisis (1890 and during World War I) the number of emigrants was greater than that of immigrants. Between 1857 and 1926 5.7 million immigrants came to Argentina, and 2.3 million left; the proportion of returners was thus almost 50 percent. In the period immediately before World War I Argentina became known as the land of »swallows« or »birds of passage«. The farming regions had fallen into the hands of a few great landowners, by direct seizure and through legal machinations tolerated by the government, and thus

there was little usable land available and few opportunities for immigrant settlers. Many had to take jobs as agricultural laborers. As soon as the harvest season was over, the workers traveled back to Spain or Italy, where they arrived just in time for the European harvest. This cycle was interrupted by World War I; when the war was over and the U.S. tightened immigration restrictions, it seemed as if immigration to South America might reach prewar levels again, but the Depression ended this trend and with it mass migration to South America.

The largest fraction of immigrants to South America came from the Iberian peninsula and Italy. Between 1857 and 1924 about 1.8 million Italians and 900,000 Spanish

Brazil's main exports since 1500

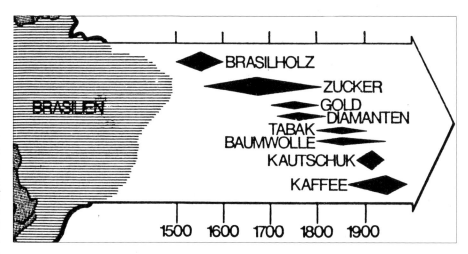

The Example of Brazil

Next to Argentina Brazil was the most important country of immigration in Latin America, including—in contrast to the other destinations—a significant German component. The original inhabitants of Brazil were stone-age Indians, and the Portuguese were the pioneers and dominant force in colonizing the land and establishing a nation and a state. The main groups represented in the mass migration of the nineteenth century were Italians, Spanish, Germans, and Japanese. In addition, Brazil was a major importer of black slaves well into the second half of the century.

The different raw materials and agricultural products of Brazil reveal the relationships between colonial exploitation, export trade, settlement of the land, and immigration. Brazilwood, which gave the country its name and was used to produce a sought-after dye in Europe, attracted the first Europeans, who established military and trading posts. The introduction of sugar cane led to the first permanent settlements, where an agricultural aristocracy grew rich on the plantations, and millions of slaves were shipped in to provide labor. The sugar industry also drove territorial expansion, as more and more land came under cultivation. With single-crop agriculture there was also a market for cattle, and the leather trade fueled expansion of the settlement area to the south, down to the Rio de la Plata. The discovery of gold brought the first wave of mass migration from Europe and the permanent settlement of the interior. A new generation of planters profited from rubber, and new areas were cleared to grow cotton and coffee. Coffee was the primary basis for the industrialization of the important So Paulo region and provided jobs for millions of European labor migrants.

After Pedro Alvares Cabral claimed Brazil as a domain of the Portuguese Crown in 1500, the land was divided into 15 inheritable fiefs (*capitanias*) to ensure the economic exploitation of the colony and promote settlement of the coast of the Amazon region, the south down to the Rio Grande do Sul, and some of the interior; the holders of the fiefs (*donatários*) were granted complete authority. Once the Portuguese had fended off Dutch and French attempts at conquest and solidified their

Alemannic settlement Tovar, Venezuela

power in Brazil, they could expand the borders of the territory to the west, southwest, and northwest, far beyond the line agreed to in the treaty of Tordesillas. An especially strong reason for expansion and the establishment of Brazil as a colony of the Portuguese Empire was the discovery of gold in Minas Gerais province, which motivated the government to close the colony, limiting trade and transport and prohibiting immigration or even internal migration—to make sure the gold went exclusively to the state treasury. The result of this policy was that the original Portuguese

171

immigrants were the dominant force in colonization, settlement, and the establishment of a government. In 1816 there were about 850,000 Portuguese immigrants and their descendants living in Brazil, making up the economic, political, military, and administrative elite.

When Napoleonic troops invaded Portugal, Prince Regent Joo VI fled to Brazil, and in 1815 he transformed the Kingdom of Portugal into the United Kingdom of Portugal, Brazil, and Algarve, giving Brazil a status equal to that of the motherland. When the Portuguese parliament tried to declare it a colony again, Brazil broke its ties to Portugal and declared independence with Dom Pedro I as its Emperor.

The increasing need for raw materials and agricultural products in Europe had forced Portugal to give up its exclusive and protectionist colonial policies and open the Brazilian ports in 1808. The government's new recruitment policy was supposed to lure European immigrants to Brazil, with promises of a right to grants of free land (sesmarias). In addition, settlers were exempted from fees and taxes for ten years and supplied with money, cattle, and equipment to get started.

According to calculations using data from the Brazilian Institute for Geography and Statistics, about 5 million immigrants came to Brazil between 1800 and about 1950, the main phase of immigration. Among these were 2 million Portuguese, 1.5 million Italians, 600,000 Spanish, 300,000 Germans, and 190,000 Japanese. The Portuguese and Spanish immigration came in spurts over the entire 150-year period; the first Germans came in 1818, while the Italians began coming in 1870 and the Japanese started in 1908. The European and Japanese immigrants preferred the southern areas because of the climate. The proportion of return migrants was about 20 percent. The dominance of the Portuguese in economy, politics, and society is explained by the colonial ties between Portugal and Brazil, which guaranteed this group linguistic, economic, and cultural advantages and thus a better starting position for integration into Brazilian society and improvement of their status.

German emigration to Brazil seems insignificant compared with that to the U.S. (about 6 million), but it is different in that settlements there were more closely knit than was possible in the U.S. Settlement colonies like Sao Leopoldo or Blumenau were typical, and between 1820 and 1830 about 50 percent of the German emigrants chose Brazil. Most came from southwestern Germany, especially the Saar-Hunsrück area. Only after 1830 did German emigration settle into a general pattern with over 90 percent heading for the U.S.

Over the years Brazil's economy, culture, and politics were influenced by immigrant groups of varying ethnic background. They explored and settled the land, cleared the jungle, built railroad lines and formed the working class of the cities, were responsible for economic and technological progress, won riches as industrialists and attracted foreign capital for Brazil. Although substantial immigration was advantageous for the Brazilian government, it did not pursue a policy of integration but instead acted to secure the dominance of Portuguese-Brazilian culture. Because of the close ties between church and state belonging to the Catholic religion was necessary to achieve advancement in government and society during the early centuries, when Protestant faiths were tolerated but not really treated fairly. Later, after the global depression of the 1930s, a quota system was introduced, mainly to keep working-class people from immigrating but also to favor certain ethnic groups (from southern Europe) over others (Japanese and Jewish immigrants). Laws were also passed to regulate the way the members of different ethnic groups lived together. For example, these laws could prohibit the sale of land in existing colonies to immigrants if one ethnic group would become dominant as a result; a 1940 law prescribed a proportion of 50 percent Brazilians and no more than 25 percent of any other nationality. All schools had to be headed by Brazilians; the language of instruction was exclusively Portuguese; and pupils under 14 were not to be taught foreign languages. Companies and clubs were not allowed to have foreign names, and foreign-language publications required special government approval. Eighty percent of the immigrants admitted under the quota system had to be farmers. These restrictions of the rights of immigrants were loosened somewhat in 1957, but they were not completely abolished.

Migration and the Receiving Culture

An unfriendly attitude toward immigrants on the part of officials and the general population is well known from other countries and during earlier periods. In Argentina, for example, there was already a tendency to see immigration as a threat to material well-being and progress in the years after World War I. These ideas came mainly from certain members of the political and intellectual elite and from their opponents in the same social groups. Especially successful »Turkish« and Jewish merchants were the targets of attacks; in 1919 a pogrom was stirred up in Buenos Aires, and 150 Jews were injured. Asians were also the victims of hostility: during the revolutionary upheaval in Mexico in 1910 Chinese immigrants were brutally persecuted; their property was confiscated, and they were expelled from the country. Discrimination and persecution were part of the immigrants' history just as they influenced the history of all the Latin American countries. Immigrants were responsible for the growth of agriculture in Argentina, Uruguay, Cuba, and southern Brazil; they made possible the expansion of industrial production in Buenos Aires, Sao Paulo, Santiago de Chile, and other economic centers; they were the driving force behind the development of trade, culture, science, and general education; they brought about the professionalization of the armed forces. Immigrants introduced barbed wire, more effective farming methods, different kinds of food and clothing, new customs and a new work ethic. As poor tenant farmers and capitalist wage workers immigrants produced the wealth of the great landowners and barons of industry; they also organized the labor movement and fought for a better way of life.

The history of immigration recalls such men as Francesco Matarazzo, who came from near Naples and arrived almost penniless in Brazil in 1892. He worked hard as a stevedore and street peddlar and lived frugally. Soon he had saved enough to buy a small grocery store, where he put his entire family to work, and a few years later he was the head of a blossoming business that continued to expand rapidly. Today the Matarazzo organization is one of the largest businesses in all of South America, controlling over 300 smaller companies with a total of 35,000 employees. It is said that the Matarazzo factories used more electrical power than all of Peru.

There are even fairy tales about immigrants. In 1849 a young Irishman named Patrick Mullins, soon changed to Patricio Milmo, came to Nuevo Leon in northern Mexico. He married the daughter of the governor and founded an economic empire based on cattle, trade, and banking; his daughter even married a Polish prince. The happy ending was missing, however, because the family had to flee during the Mexican revolution.

Most immigrants, of course, had no such

The Italian immigrant Fernando Maria Perrone in Argentina, 1890

success stories to tell—as reflected by the high rate of return migration, about 50 percent for Latin America as a whole. This number includes the so-called Indianos of the Mediterranean countries, who made their fortunes in the New World but returned to spend their retirement years in their homelands; it also encompasses temporary labor migrants such as the »swallows« of Argentina, who had never intended to remain abroad. But it is also clear that many who returned had not intended to do so but rather gave up in the face of difficult conditions in the new homeland. Above all, land ownership in Latin America was already clearly established: if immigrants had come from a rural area dreaming of owning their own farms, they were disappointed when they found an agricultural economy dominated by large estates. For a worker on one of Sao Paulo's coffee plantations, for example, it was much easier to save up the 300 milreis needed to transport the entire family back to Europe than to get 6000 milreis together to buy a small farm. Sometimes the Latin

American governments were disturbed by the high rate of return migration: in 1911 Argentina forced the shipping companies to double the price of a return steamship ticket.

The stream of transatlantic immigrants almost completely dried up during World War II, but in the period 1947-1950 about 12 percent of the world's »displaced persons«, refugees and former forced laborers, found their way to Latin America, especially to Argentina, Brazil, and Venezuela. Many Nazi War criminals found hiding places in South America as well. In the 1950s the immigration rate rose again, and again Argentina and Brazil were the most popular destinations (with 600,000 and 450,000 immigrants, respectively, between 1946 and 1957). After 1960, however, the rate dropped off; for 1970, for example, Brazil reported only 6900 immigrants. Many potential emigrants from southern Europe were now being recruited to work in European industrial countries such as Germany.

The oil boom in Venezuela spurred immigration in the 1960s, luring laborers from the rural areas and from Colombia and skilled workers, engineers, managers, businessmen, and bankers from Europe.

This example shows how most transatlantic migration today has become the labor migration of an intellectual or technological elite: people come for a limited time to perform tasks such as building up a new branch of industry.

After the 1960s, the historical direction of migration was reversed, as Latin America became a land of emigration. First of all, the oppressive conditions in many countries forced people to seek out the more prosperous lands of North America, legally or illegally. While the U.S. census of 1920 already registered 500,000 Mexicans living in the southwestern states, today about 750,000 people are arrested for illegally crossing the border each year, and the numbers continue to grow rapidly. Spanish is becoming the second language of U.S. business.

Second, the so-called »brain drain« takes the same general direction, representing a further loss to the poor countries of Latin America. Well educated and highly skilled people leave for the industrial nations of North America and Europe, where the jobs and pay are better; the costs for educating them, on the other hand, are still paid by their impoverished Latin American homelands. The term brain drain was coined to show how the skills and potential sorely needed by the poor nations are drained away by the rich nations.

The third component of this migration stream is made up of political refugees who have sought and continue to seek asylum from the brutal dictatorial regimes of Latin America.

In addition to this continental movement there is a complementary interregional migration, from sparsely populated, underdeveloped rural areas to the large cities and developed industrial areas. Between 1960 and 1980 the population of Mexico City shot up from 5 million to 15 million, and every sizeable city of Latin America has its *barrios, conventillos,* or *favelas*—miserable strips of temporary huts made of earth, corrugated metal, and cardboard, without water or sanitary facilities, without schools or any infrastructure at all, and without a future.

Migration to the cities is not new, of course. Even in 1900 the poor development status of the rural regions forced European immigrants to settle in the cities. But there are significant differences. At the beginning of the twentieth century the cities seemed to offer unlimited possibilities. The expansion of industry was underway, so there was work; social advancement, even if limited, was still possible; immigrants seldom lived in the slums for more than one generation—no such hopes exist for the residents of today's *villas miserias.*

Considering the overall demographic trends in Latin America over the last 200 years, we find three main tendencies. First, the population doubled between 1850 and 1900, from 30.5 million to 51 million. There was rapid population growth, especially in the temperate regions and later in Cuba, and mainly due to immigration from Europe. These immigrants favored a moderate climate. In Argentina and Brazil first-generation immigrants accounted for 30 percent of the population increase, and their children made up another 30 percent. Mass immigration from Europe is thus responsible for the rapid population growth around 1900.

Second, there was only relatively slow natural population growth in the areas settled the earliest, such as Mexico and Peru. Immigration to these countries during the nineteenth and twentieth centuries was negligible. The population in the tropical areas rose only about one-third as fast as that in Brazil, and there, too, there is no rapid jump around 1900. Mexico had especially slow growth, due to the Mexican revolution and to several epidemics, which hit harder there than in other countries. The population actually decreased by about 885,000 between 1910 and 1921. When internal stability was restored toward the end of the decade, the population began to rise again.

Third, there was a significant if not spectacular population increase in Central America and the Caribbean which was due less to immigration than to natural factors such as higher birth rates and lower mortality rates. The countries to the west of the Andes, which had been important in earlier centuries, lost out to those on the Atlantic coast.

Mass immigration from Europe left permanent economic, social, and cultural marks on the receiving countries. It also speeded up the demographic development of the most popular destinations and had a decisive influence on the growth and political formation processes.

References

Fouquet, Carlos: Der deutsche Einwanderer und seine Nachkommen in Brasilien 1808-1824-1974. Sao Paulo, 1974.

Galeano, Eduardo: Die offenen Adern Lateinamerikas. Die Geschichte eines Kontinents. 1971, Wuppertal, repr. 1988.

Mörner, Magnus: Adventurers and Proletarians. The Story of Migrants in Latin America. Paris, University of Pittsburgh Press, 1985.

Sanchez-Albornoz, Nicholas: The Population of Latin America. A History. Berkeley/Los Angeles, California University Press, 1974.

Schneider, Robin: »Die Lage der Indianer Lateinamerikas«, in: Komitee für Grundrechte und Demokratie. Jahrbuch 1984, S.173-180.

Indians fight against the destruction of their land by a power company. Rio Xingu, Brazil, 1989

The Legendary Southern Continent: Australia

Diethelm Knauf

From Discovery to the Founding of the Colony

Man's history on the Australian continent began with migration, although it came relatively late because the island is so isolated geographically. It was probably during the last ice age, about 40,000 years ago, that dark-skinned people from Asia settled the land, at a time when the level of the sea was much lower and land bridges joined many of the islands of the present Indonesian archipelago. Nevertheless, the voyagers did have to cross many deep and dangerous straits. It is assumed that they were not very experienced sailors and did not possess any sophisticated navigation skills; thus it was probably more by chance than by carefully steered courses that small groups of them reached Australia on rafts. These first migrants, the aborigines, were nomadic hunters, fishermen, and gatherers, and they spread gradually over the entire Australian continent, including the southern island of Tasmania, which was joined to the mainland at the time. As the great ice masses of the Northern Hemisphere melted about 16,000 years ago, the level of the seas rose and many of the land bridges disappeared. Now any migration through the Indonesian archipelago required seafaring skills, and only peoples with substantial knowledge of navigation dared to venture out onto the unknown open sea. Until the eighteenth century the culture and economy of the aborigines developed without contact to other peoples, although ships from Papua-New Guinea and other nearby islands sometimes landed on the Australian coast. Australia was colonized not from the adjacent Asiatic culture area but from white Europe.

The ancient Greek legends of a fantastically rich southern continent had survived through the middle ages, and with the dis-

Mythical creature carved by native Australian Aborigines

covery of America and the opening of new sea routes to the Far East these legends experienced new growth. Magellan's circumnavigation of the world (1519-1521) established its spherical shape and the connection between the Pacific and Indian Oceans; people now assumed that, somewhere in these seas, there must be a southern continent, a *terra australis*, to balance the great land masses of the Northern Hemisphere. In the sixteenth century Spanish and Portuguese explorers tried to find the mysterious *terra australis* by sailing west from South America, but unfavorable winds and ocean currents drove them too far to the northwest, to the Spice Islands. The Spanish navigator Luis Vaez de Torres discovered the strait between Australia and New Guinea which was named after him, but without sighting the Australian coast. The Netherlands, having established their dominance over the Spice Islands with the founding of the Dutch East India Company in 1602, also joined the search for *terra australis*. The Dutchman Willem Jansz landed in 1606 on the west coast of Cape York, the first European to set foot on Australian soil; others followed to sail along and map the coast of Australia, which they named New Holland. But since they saw none of the expected wealth and riches, since they found the coasts barren and deserted, and since they considered the natives brutish, menacing, and completely uncivilized, the Dutch rather quickly lost interest in Australia.

Great Britain began to show interest in the Pacific area only in the second half of the eighteenth century, when the discovery of Tahiti by the Englishman Samuel Wallis (1767) again fueled hopes of finding the legendary southern continent with its riches. In 1768 the British government equipped an expedition under the leadership of Captain James Cook; the secret aim of the mission was to find *terra australis*. After months of fruitless searching Cook gave up on this plan and sailed to New Zealand, which had been discovered by the Dutchman Abel Tasman in 1642. From here he intended to explore the unknown eastern coast of New Holland. This decision led to the discovery of the attractive, fertile, thickly forested, and well watered

English female emigrants waiting for their departure to Australia, Hatton-Garden 1853

coastal areas of eastern Australia, which Cook claimed as British territory and named New South Wales. Cook did not find *terra australis* on any of his following voyages across the Pacific, from South America to New Zealand, from North America to China, and from the Bering Strait to Antarctica—apparently there was no such continent.

The history of white Australia begins with the American War of independence, for at first the areas discovered by Cook had little interest for the British. People only remembered the far-off land of New South Wales after Britain had lost its American possessions (and with them both profitable trade relations and penal colonies), when the prisons of English cities and even the prison ships in the Thames were completely overfilled, and when prison revolts and protests in the liberal press led to a politically dangerous situation. In 1787 the King declared that from then on convicts were to be deported to Australia, where a penal colony was to be established. Arthur Philipp, the future governor of New South Wales, became Commandant of the first fleet of ships, which in January 1788 brought over 1000 men and women, over

three-fourths of whom were convicts, to Australia. The settlement they founded lay somewhat north of Botany Bay—which soon became a synonym for convict deportation—and was called »Sydney Cove«.

Convicts and Free Settlers

Australia, too, has its myths: one persisted well into the 1950s and claimed that the convict-settlers were actually innocent and courageous men who fought for freedom and against social injustice and political oppression. Many of them were supposedly small farmers and poor rural workers, driven to poaching and other criminal acts by the poverty which resulted from the capitalistic enclosures, consolidations of tenant farms and pasture lands to form large estates. This myth was a way to hide that the history of white settlement in Australia did not begin with the intrepid free pioneer, forcing nature to his will by honest hard work, but with the convict, a criminal who only came to Australia to pay his debt to society—a flaw in the self-understanding and self-image of the country.

This nationalistic interpretation of history was called into question in the 1950s and replaced with a new view, that the deported convicts were neither workers forced to steal by economic necessity nor victims of cruel British society, but rather members of

a criminal class which included thieves, pickpockets, robbers, and prostitutes and which was different from the working class, the source of most of its members. This group was described as a criminal subculture distinguished by particular types of upbringing and psychological characteristics. In this view, those who were deported were the scum of humanity and raised from birth to be criminals.

But this view is one-sided as well. Studies of the ships' documents, which recorded up to 18 pieces of information (age, sex, education, marital status, height, occupation, place of birth etc.) for each convict, show that the majority of deportees were young, strong, healthy men, and that about 16 percent were women. Before deportation they were highly mobile, and thus had migration experience. The occupational distribution corresponded roughly to the general figures for the British urban working class and included brass founders from Warwickshire, stocking weavers from Nottingham, potters from Staffordshire, and cotton-mill and factory workers from Lancashire, as well as watch-chain makers, mule spinners, and button polishers. The learned professions and agricultural workers were underrepresented, but the majority of the convicts had some training, specific job skills, or qualifications to offer. The ability to read and write was also surprisingly common: only 65 percent of the population in England could read and/or write in the second quarter of the nineteenth century, but among the convicts the number was 75 percent. Those who were sent out to establish a penal colony on the other side of the world were well equipped for the task of transforming an open prison into a capitalist economy.

A total of about 160,000 convicts were shipped to Australia, 80,000 to New South Wales and almost 70,000 to Van Diemens Land, which because of its miserable reputation as a penal colony was later renamed Tasmania. New South Wales also had a bad reputation: Peter Cunningham, a medical doctor on the convict ships and a landowner in Australia, complained in 1827 that even a very friendly conversation partner in a British coach moved farther away on learning that he was from New South

Wales, pretending to look for a toothpick in order to check that nothing had been stolen from his bags.

According to the census of 1828, New South Wales had a population of 36,598, of whom only 5000 had come voluntarily—and these free settlers included members of the military organization, supervisors, and administrative officials stationed there. In the decade 1830-1840 the ratio began to change, with 65,000 free settlers as well as 50,000 deportees. The British government had to offer considerable subsidies to prospective emigrants, because Australia had no real advantages over North America; it was thousands of miles farther away, and the passage cost three or four times as much. Australia did have attractions for businessmen with capital to invest however: free land and the cheap labor of the convicts. At first the convicts worked on state-owned farms or in other state operations, felling trees, clearing pasture land, building roads, slaving in stone quarries, or firing bricks and lime. As the number of free settlers increased, more and more convicts were assigned to private employers, who had to provide food and shelter in exchange for their forced labor. Wages were

Aborigenes, around 1850

German family in Rosewood, Queensland, around 1890

not permitted and seldom paid. This system was very economical for the government, which was no longer financially responsible for keeping and housing the convicts, their supervision, and administrative handling. However, since most of the convicts came from the working-class neighborhoods and slums of the British cities, their knowledge of farming, cattle-raising, and agriculture in general was very limited. For this reason there was still a great demand for free settlers who would clear the land and build up the economy on their own initiative, with energy and motivation. In order to arouse interest for agriculture among the convicts as well, Governor Philipp quite early on issued a proclamation which pardoned deportees with good behavior and granted free farmland to »those convicts so emancipated«, known as »Emancipists« because of this formulation. The settlers in the early colonial period were thus free immigrants, military or administrative personnel who had decided to stay in Australia, and convicts who had been pardoned or completed their sentences; all of these were given land by the British government.

This procedure was discontinued by the government in 1831, and land was now

Advertisement for the »Gulf of Siam«, 1892

sold for not less than 5 shillings per acre. The money collected was to be used to pay for an Assisted Immigration Scheme, in which the government paid for the passage tickets of immigrants who could not afford it themselves. The aim was to release population pressure in Great Britain and at the same ease the chronic labor shortage in Australia.

Australia now became a country for emigrants as well as for convicts. Many of the emancipated convicts viewed the free immigrants as intruders. When a group of Scottish craftsmen docked in Sydney in 1831, they were greeted with angry cursing: »There are these bloody emigrants come to take the country from us«. In 1825 the free immigrant Alexander Harris was told, »One of the free objects—bad luck to 'em. What business have they here in the prisoners' country?«.

Toward the end of the 1830s there was increasing pressure on the deportation system and forced convict labor. Many cattle ranchers still saw the deportees as a source of cheap labor, which could be replaced by Indian and Chinese coolies if the number of subsidized free workers (»bounty migrants«) was insufficient. Others saw the deportations as an obstacle to eventual political independence and/or as a depressive force in the free labor market. Probably the strongest protests were heard at home in England, especially from those who believed that deportation was too mild a punishment to deter crime. There was dissatisfaction with the amount of freedom convicts enjoyed in Australia, displeasure with the economic success emancipated convicts often achieved, and shocked surprise that deported criminals seemed to have a much higher standard of living than poor workers in English cities.

In fact, many Emancipists were able to earn a decent living or even achieve a degree of prosperity. George Howe, sentenced for shoplifting, was immediately given the task of publishing the only newspaper, the Sydney Gazette and New South Wales Advertiser, and Edward Wills, deported as a highwayman in 1799, was a rich merchant and dock owner at his death in 1811, and his widow married George Howe. Daniel Cooper, deported for theft and pardoned in 1821, entered a partnership with Solomon Levy and made a fortune in trade; they were the most famous example of a rapid rise from disgrace to prosperity. Women had success as well: Mary Haydock, deported for horse-stealing in 1790, married Thomas Reibey, a free settler and partner of Edward Wills. After his death Mary Reibey further expanded his business and became one of the richest people in New South Wales. As the deportation system grew more and more discredited in the 1840s and 1850s, the number of convicts transported to Australia dropped; the system was abandoned in 1868.

The Myth of the Bush

The second important Australian myth is the bush myth. The bush is the vast hinterland which began where the fertile strip of coastal land ended and contained the frontier, the borderline between the settled land and the wilderness. The bush was the stage for many of the heroic deeds and tragedies of Australian pioneer history, a hard land for hard men. Part of the myth was the mythical Australian or »working bushman«, whose ethic was based on independence, egalitarian collectivism, and the concept of »mateship«, loyalty to his companions through thick and thin, complemented by hate for the authorities and standing up for the underdog. Especially the elements of egalitarianism and solidarity show that this myth has its origins in the penal colonies and the working-class milieu.

Around 1900 the Australian cities lost their image as examples of British business sense and material prosperity. Among the intellectuals in particular there was heated sociopolitical discussion of the Australian national character. In the outside world many considered the city a place of decadence; the high degree of urbanization and the fact that the majority of the population lived in cities were surprising for such a young nation. The city no longer demonstrated the vitality of the colony but rather stood for racial degeneracy, and its apparently uncontrolled growth proved that Australia had lost its pioneer spirit. The vision of the parasitic city absorbing the valuable energy of the nation was contrasted with the fascinating picture of rural Australia and its inhabitants, especially the bush workers.

Industrial-scale agriculture and cattle-raising were and still are the most important branches of the Australian economy. The agricultural sector produced a special kind of rural proletariat characterized by very high mobility. The extreme conditions in the Australian hinterland, the »outback«, and the chronic shortage of women produced the mythical bushman with the traits described above. After the »squatting rush« for land which began in the 1820s and led to occupation of the continent over the following decades, there was an army of unemployed cattle drivers, riders, shepherds, shearers, oxcart drivers, cowboys, and farm hands constantly on the move. The extent and intensity of internal migration movements can be seen in the following examples: a convict might have spent months or years working on road construction in the cities before being assigned to a landowner as a farm worker, and the opposite path from years »up the country« to the city was also possible. Small farmers and hands often looked for work as shearers in the west to improve their incomes, and many urban wage-earners did the same, especially when there were economic crises on the coast. Teamsters, driving their oxen back and forth on a regular basis from the colonial centers and port cities to the interior of the continent, were important before the railroads were built, reaching into the interior by the 1870s. Along with their loads of wool and hides they brought news, gossip, songs, fashions, customs, and attitudes. Cattle drivers not only delivered the sheep and cattle to the city markets; they also spread curious clothing, a special language, and unusual behavior. The myth traveled with the men.

In reality, however, the typical Australian is more a city-dweller than a wild, sunburned bushman. Australia is one of the most urbanized nations in the world, and this is no new phenomenon, but has been typical of the country since the first convict settlements. The 1921 census found that the urban population outweighed the rural by 61 to 39 percent; among immigrants, 70 percent lived in cities. Today the urban population is 86 percent of the total, with half concentrated in the two cities of Sydney and Melbourne; Sydney's population increases by 75,000 every year. Only 7.5 percent of the working population is in agricultural occupations, and the number is continuing to fall.

North German Lloyd poster, around 1900

The Gold Rush

By the middle of the nineteenth century about 220,000 free settlers had immigrated to Australia, so that they already outnumbered the convicts by 60,000. When gold was discovered in New South Wales in 1851 and a few months later in Victoria, there was a dramatic increase in the number of free immigrants. Within ten years the population almost tripled, from 400,000 to almost 1.2 million. The influx of immigrants was of great significance for the economic development of Australia, because it included people with job skills in the crafts, business, and commerce, thus closing some gaps in the occupational structure. Among the gold-diggers were not only Britons but also members of other ethnic groups such as Germans and especially Americans (who came to try their luck in Australia after failing to find gold in California). Their absolute numbers were not great, but they did bring new cultural practices and political ideas. Some later played a big part in conflicts with the police and government officials. In 1854 there were armed confrontations in Ballarat, the so-called Eureka Stockade. The gold prospectors were dissatisfied, because the deposits were not as rich as they had expected; big corporations and wealthy entrepreneurs had already taken out large amount; and the government also tried to get its share by imposing high license fees for prospecting. When the police were too vigorous in collecting taxes and license fees, the gold miners armed themselves, set up barricades, and traded shots with the police, but their resistance was broken after two days. A Reform League founded by the miners also made radical political demands for things such as general elections with a secret ballot.

The gold fever had a strong negative effect on the traditional Australian economy, because the farmers were suddenly left with no workers. Workers, businessmen, salaried employees, and even policemen left their jobs and hurried to the gold fields. On closed shop doors in the cities hung signs saying, »Gone to look for gold«.

In 1891 gold was found in Western Australia, but despite this discovery immi-

View of Adelaide, Australia, around 1920

gration did not increase significantly. In the previous decade about 175,000 new immigrants had come, the highest number so far. The proportions of European and Asian immigrants began to shift in favor of Asia, mainly because Australia was not attracting enough immigrants from countries with relatively high standards of living. The worldwide depression at this time probably had an effect as well, since poorer potential migrants could not afford the trip. The most important component of the gold rush to Western Australia was internal migration from the east coast. Another factor was the fact that claims were staked and ownership rights to the gold mines transferred more quickly than had been the case in New South Wales and Victoria. By the time gold was discovered in Coolgardie and Kalgoorlie, the lonesome prospector patiently working his small claim was the exception, and most gold-seekers had to take jobs working as miners for large companies. In this situation the police had their hands full keeping gold theft under control: it wasn't enough to watch the miners, and gold was smuggled out of the mines in blankets, candles, and water bottles, and sometimes transported out of town in coffins. In 1970 Australia was still the world's fifth largest gold producer, with about 70 percent coming from the fields of Western Australia; more recently the cost-intensive operation of the mines and a fall in the price of gold on the world market have made things more

difficult. The former El Dorados on the edge of the Great Australian Desert threaten to become ghost towns.

Gold fields and gold-mining camps have traditionally attracted Chinese immigrants; they came in great numbers to Victoria in 1855-1857, as the amount being mined was already noticeably decreasing. In 1857 there were 24,000 Chinese working in the gold fields of Victoria, or about 12 percent of the population there. From the very beginning whites viewed their arrival with distance and skepticism. The Chinese kept to themselves and spoke no English, and there was hardly any contact between them and the other miners. Many of them were contract laborers tied to wealthy Chinese employers, who had paid their passage, or to white farmers and entrepreneurs. They worked for extremely low wages and were seen by white miners as a threat to their standard of living. Although they were hardly ever in direct competition with whites, working mainly on the slag heaps and tailings piled up by other miners, in abandoned mines, or at poorly paid jobs in laundries and kitchens, they were blamed for the economic decline of the gold fields. As early as 1843 skilled workers in Sydney fearing depression of wages had voiced opposition to the import of Indian coolies. They were vehemently opposed to the resumption of convict deportation and the subsidization of free immigration. Anti-Chinese feelings culminated in pogroms, the worst in Buckland, Victoria (1857) and Lambing, New South Wales (1861); Chinese workers were the victims of violent attacks, robbery, looting, and arson. Some were murdered, others scalped, and others died as a result of their injuries. »Patriots« told their children to stone the Chinese, who were mocked in countless stories, songs, and newspaper articles. Their persecutors were seldom arrested by the police or convicted by the courts, and the racist feelings and pogroms obtained official state sanction in the *White Australia Policy*, as embodied by the *Commonwealth Immigration Restriction Act* of 1901, a law passed by the Australian government to prohibit the immigration of non-Europeans. This law was not replaced by non-discriminatory legislation until 1973.

After the various spells of gold fever sub-

Wedding party in Hatton Vale, around 1900

sided, the immigration rate sank significantly, and the population born in Australia soon surpassed that of immigrants. At the beginning of World War I only one in ten was born outside Australia, and the 1921 census found 85 percent natives, even though another 286,000 immigrants had arrived between 1911 and 1920—the highest number ever attained in a decade. Of the foreign-born, 80 percent came from the British isles, 8 percent from the rest of Europe (2.7 percent from Germany), 4.5 percent from New Zealand, and 3.5 percent from Asia. These figures also show that Australia, unlike North America, never became a destination for mass European emi-

gration; instead it remained, at least until after World War II, a country with a predominantly British population and strong cultural, economic, and political links to the motherland. The social and political environment encountered by the new arrivals was familiar to most of them, whereas the natural environment was new. Unlike typical immigrants to North or South America, who were strangers at first, had to learn a new language and come to terms with a new cultural milieu, immigrants from

Great Britain, setting foot for the first time on Australian soil after a long sea voyage, remained subjects of the same monarch and settled among people who spoke their own language. Here, as in New Zealand, colonists seldom had to share the land with people from other European countries, and the resistance of the native population was also weaker than in North America or New Zealand. Although the journey was longer, people came to areas that were familiar to them, that they could easily consider provinces of Great Britain.

The Irish formed one easily distinguishable group that did not share the pro-English sentiments of the Australian majority. Irish immigrants were not only ethnically different, they were also Roman Catholics and mostly members of the lower classes. Their numbers among the convicts were disproportionately high, and among the free Irish immigrants were many poor agricultural workers who came as contract laborers with long terms of service to serve before their passage money was paid off. For this reason the Irish element was always strong in the working class, and it is not surprising that the labor and trade-union movement had strong links to Ireland and the Catholic church.

The marks left in Australia's history and present-day culture by German immigrants are also notable. Individual migrants took part in the settlement of Australia from the very beginning—for example, the German-born navigator of the first English fleet or Ludwig Leichhardt, who led one of the expeditions to explore the interior, successfully charting the land between Darling Downs and Arnhem Land in 1844-1845. When Leichhardt set out to cross the continent from east to west, he never returned, and no trace of him was ever found. The Lutherans from Silesia, however, who arrived in Adelaide in 1838 were emigrants rather than adventurers, having defied the order of King Friedrich Wilhelm III. of Prussia to worship together with their Reformed religious opponents in a unified state church at home in Germany. Although they settled near the town at first, most of them moved on into the Barossa Valley and planted vineyards; Barossa today is synonymous with good wines and German traditions. German villages were also founded in Queensland in the middle of the nineteenth century; the emigration movement was preceded by the work of five missionaries, who had come to preach Christianity to the native population near present-day Brisbane. A few years later a German merchant sailed from Brisbane to recruit new settlers in his homeland, promising free passage to farm workers, vintners, mechanics, and domestic servants, or a free piece of land on arrival in Australia to emigrants who could pay their own way. German family names in the sugar-cane-growing areas and country towns with names like Minden and Marburg recall this early

settlement period, although not much more is left. No German settlements remain in Victoria or New South Wales, either: although there were about 10,000 Germans living in Victoria in 1861, only a few small groups founded new villages. About 6000 of the immigrants lived in the gold-mining camps, and many moved on to New South Wales when gold was discovered there. Two Germans, Bernhard Otto Holermann and Ludwig Beyers, found the largest known single piece of gold ore at Hill End, near Sydney, in 1872. It was almost 5 feet high and 26 inches wide and weighed 570 pounds. Beyers retired on the money he got for the ore, whereas the Hamburg native Holtermann built shops and hotels, set up factories, and invested in a railroad line.

The settlements of Germans in New South Wales, Queensland, and Victoria adapted to their Anglo-Saxon environment in only a few years; only in the Barossa Valley did German customs and traditions remain unchanged for over a century. Most of the Lutherans there had brought their families with them to South Australia, and Adelaide, the nearest city, was 40 miles away: the settlers lived in voluntary isolation. Only a few applied for Australian citizenship. The unifying element for this community was the Lutheran religious faith, and the Luther Bible was the most popular book. In 1891 there were 25,000 first- and second-generation Germans living in South Australia, and at the turn of the century there were 46 Lutheran schools in that province alone. Members of the Lutheran community in Adelaide also founded the Herrmansburg mission station on the Finke River in central Australia. For them basic aid for the aborigines was more important than religious conversion. In 1875, only thirteen years after the John McDouall Stuart expedition crossed the continent in the north-south direction for the first time, a small group set out on an overland journey which almost cost many of them their lives. Their destination was the area around the present-day city of Alice Springs, and the trek through the desert lasted 18 months. The members of the expedition suffered from scurvy, and many of their animals died of thirst before the group reached its destination in June 1877. Today about 600

aborigines live at the station, near the border of the Arunda tribal reservation. There is a school and a hospital to help the sick. A cattle ranch provides jobs, so that the aborigines are not solely dependent on welfare.

Populate or Perish - Immigration after 1945

By the end of World War II the population of Australia had reached 7.5 million. The war and the threat of invasion by Japanese troops not only caused Australia to change its political orientation from Great Britain to the U.S., it also led to a new attitude toward immigration. The belief was, at least until the end of the 1960s, that only a continually growing population could discourage Australia's northern neighbors from making territorial claims. In addition, the country needed a strong labor force to fulfill its economic potential. As at the end of the nineteenth century, it was considered important to populate the vast empty continent and strengthen its economy, and thus to take permanent possession of it for the white race. In 1946 the government announced plans for promoting and financially subsidizing immigration from Europe at unprecedented levels. Immigration would be open to all Europeans and not just to British subjects. At first the recruitment strategies and immigration programs were aimed at the many refugees and displaced persons in postwar Europe, but soon they were extended to all countries. Up to today about 3 million new immigrants have come to Australia, including 1.1 million from Great Britain and about the same number from the rest of Europe before 1971. After the British the largest groups are the Italians (26 percent), the Greeks (18 percent), the Germans (10 percent), the Dutch (9 percent), and the Poles and Maltese (5 percent each). Today every fifth Australian is of non-British ancestry in the first or second generation, and almost half of the population is a direct or indirect descendant of the postwar immigrants. But one-eighth of present-day immigrants remain only a few years in Australia before returning to their homelands.

Ethnic Composition of the Australian People (percent)						
Ethnic origin	**1787**	**1846**	**1861**	**1891**	**1947**	**1988**
Aboriginal	100	41.5	13.3	3.4	0.8	1.0
Anglo-Celt	-	57.2	78.1	86.8	89.7	74.6
Other European	-	1.1	5.4	7.2	8.6	19.3
Asian	-	0.2	3.1	2.3	0.8	4.5
Other	-	-	0.1	0.3	0.1	0.6*
Total	100	100	100	100	100	100
Nos (000s)	500	484	1328	3275	7640	16300

Includes black Africans and West Indians, Pacific Islanders and American Indians. More than half this total are Pacific Islanders

References

Clark, C. M. H.: »The Origins of the Convicts Transported to Eastern Australia, 1787-1852«, in: Historical Studies of Australia and New Zealand. Bd. 7, Nr.26 und 27, 1956.

Günthner, Ulrich: Australien heute. Wien/Düsseldorf, 1973.

Inglis, K. S.: The Australian Colonists: An Exploration of Social History 1788-1870. Melbourne, 1974.

Löffler, Ernst; Rose, A. J.; Warner, Denis: Australia. London/Melbourne, 1977.

Mc.Phee, E. T.: »Australia - Its Immigrant Population«, in: Willcox; Ferenzci: International Migrations. Vol. 2, New York, 1929/1931, S.173ff.

Nicolas, Stephen; Shergold, Peter R.: »Sträflinge als Migranten«, in: Gulliver. Bd. 23, Hamburg, 1988, S.13ff.

Walker, David: »National Identity: Aspects of its History in Australia«, in: Gulliver. Bd. 23, S.27ff.

Ward, Russel: The Australian Legend. Melbourne, 1958.

After 1971 immigration policy took a new turn. Series of full-page advertisements in European newspapers were canceled, and a rest was ordered for the embassy recruiters, who had been traveling across Europe, using film presentations to interest hundreds of thousands in Australia. The immigration quotas were lowered, so that in 1971-1972 only 140,000 instead of 170,000 migrants were granted visas. The Assisted Immigration Scheme had put a big hole in the budget—according to the estimates of government critics, the state hired two employees and spent almost 8000 dollars for every immigrant who came. Most of the new arrivals traveled free, with the Australian taxpayers paying the fare. In 1971 it was said that Australia spent almost twice as much for the immigration program as the budgeted amount, 74 million dollars. Increasing unemployment and high inflation rates have led to a further reduction in immigration, and today regulations are relatively strict. Relatives of people already living in Australia have a good chance, but otherwise prospective immigrants must show their economic potential, personality, and strength of character and demonstrate, as the regulations stipulate, the intention to settle permanently in Australia and apply for citizenship after several years. The country is mainly interested in attracting companies with capital to invest, skilled workers, innovative know-how, and immigrants who will strengthen the Australian economy. Capital and know-how are much in need for the exploration and exploitation of Australia's vast natural resources, including coal, copper, lead, and especially gold, silver, and uranium. Companies from the U.S., Great Britain, and now Japan have opened branches in Australia, and German firms have been building production facilities, mostly in Melbourne and Sydney, since the 1960s. Chemical firms like BASF and Hoechst and the Volkswagen corporation have invested over 1 billion DM, often bringing in specialized workers and management personnel from Germany as well. There are about 15,000 new arrivals with German passports living in Melbourne today, with 7000 more in Sydney; overall about 70,000 immigrants from the Federal Republic of Germany have found new homes in Melbourne since the 1960s, and most have already taken Australian citizenship. Emigration to Australia became more interesting for Germans at the beginning of the 1980s, when the stationing of intermediate-range missiles increased the fear of war, and dramatic climate changes and forest damage due to acid rain caused anxiety about an impending ecological catastrophe. For many who felt fearful or insecure about the future because of political or ecological developments, the fifth continent seemed an attractive refuge. Of course, this is not always true—as evidenced by newspaper reports in summer 1989, when the Australien government warned people to stay indoors to avoid excess ultraviolet radiation due to the ozone hole.

»A Working Man's Paradise«: New Zealand

Diethelm Knauf

»The land of the long white cloud« is what the two islands now known as New Zealand were called by the first Polynesian migrants, whose descendants were the Maori found by the white explorers in the seventeenth and eighteenth centuries. Little is known for sure about the first settlement of New Zealand. The first migrants came from eastern Polynesia and probably had the Society Islands as their home base. About 1000 years ago they landed on the coast of New Zealand, either by chance, as a result of violent expulsion from their homeland, or as voluntary exiles fleeing economic or political troubles at home. Maori legends still tell of the original immigrants and especially their leaders, Kupe and Toe, who came in a fleet of long outriggers. Many Maori trace their origin to this first settlement, and scholars have learned that the early settlers even brought dogs and a supply of food, which suggests planned emigration rather than a chance landing.

Polynesian settlement sites from the eleventh and twelfth centuries have been found all over New Zealand, especially near protected natural harbors on the northeast coast of the North Island, but also at river mouths and in bays on the South Island. The settlers were a peaceful people at first, living in open villages and basing their economy on locally available foods. When the Europeans arrived, however, war bands were already part of Maori life; rivalries and violent conflicts arose especially over favorite settlement sites. Fortified villages were the typical settlement form at this time.

In 1642 about 260,000 Maori were probably living in Aotearoa, the land of the long white cloud, when the Dutch explorer Abel Tasman touched the western coast on his search for gold and spices—neither of which he found there. The island of New Zealand were soon forgotten in Europe and remained so until James Cook claimed them for Great Britain in 1769. Settlement by white colonists began only sporadically: in the late eighteenth and early nineteenth centuries there were only short visits by official representatives of the penal settlements in Australia, and from time to time ships stopped to take on food and water. Then the first small settlements were founded, and missionary stations soon followed. Gradually the continuing search for new trade goods and a certain amount of population pressure in New South Wales made New Zealand a permanent part of British businessmen's financial calculations. Several whaling bases, financed by merchants from Sydney, were set up on the south coast of the South Island; lumber camps were established in the forests of kauri trees, related to European firs; and the Bay of Islands developed into a provisioning center for trading ships, whalers, and seal hunters in the South Pacific. The mission stations grew, but by 1839 there were still only about 2000 Europeans living in New Zealand.

The first significant immigration of European settlers began in the 1840s, after Great Britain had formally declared its sovereignty over New Zealand in the Treaty of Waitangi, concluded with 500 Maori chiefs. A long time had already passed since the first colonization companies, the best known of which was the New Zealand Company, had been established to acquire land, to recruit and settle colonists, and to open up the interior of the islands economically and make it usable. The New Zealand Company had several divisions and was supported by the Scottish and Anglican churches. The colonization companies brought in over 15,000 settlers, who founded the towns of Wellington, Canterbury, and Otago, among others.

At first the goal of the companies was to interest people of all British social classes in their project, including investors and rich landowners. In reality, however, it was mostly artisans, farm hands, unskilled factory workers, and domestic servants who joined the companies. After some early disappointments, most of the colonists were able to establish themselves as farmers or sheep ranchers, or more likely practicing the trades they brought with them in the growing cities.

Among the New Zealand Company settlers there were also two German groups. There were Lutherans from the Rheinland, mostly agricultural workers, and artisans from Bremen and Hamburg. They settled in the area near Nelson and started farms. They maintained their own churches and schools until the 1870s.

The *Native Land Acts* of 1862 and 1865 did away with the royal monopoly on land ownership, and settlers could now buy land from the Maori without restriction. After the natives' resistance had been broken in the Maori Wars, both the colonization companies and the provincial government made new efforts at recruiting settlers. On the South Island there were fertile farms and vast pasture lands, and therefore a need for many agricultural workers, who were to be recruited overseas. They, like domestic servants and artisans, were given financial aid to pay for the passage, and there were also grants of free land to those who could

Maori chief, engraving from 1820

pay their own way, as in Australia. The Sudetenland Germans who settled at Puhoi, near Auckland, are an example of the latter type of migrant. They arrived in 1859 and had to fight for survival for several years because of the poor soil.

These migrations were insignificant in terms of absolute numbers, compared with the major influx to the South Island which began in 1861, when gold was discovered in the river beds and valleys of Otago. At the beginning of the gold rush the population of Otago was 12,000, but by September 1863 it was already about 60,000. From the gold fields of California, from Victoria in Australia, and from other areas of New Zealand miners, shopkeepers, clerks, innkeepers, and businessmen joined the search for gold. In a single month, March 1863, over 14,000 people arrived at Dunedin. Most of the new arrivals were men—the ratio of women to men in the gold fields was 1:100 in 1863 and still only 18:100 in 1864. The majority of the prospectors came from Australia and moved on when they heard about new finds farther north, but a fair number remained. At the end of the 1860s Otago province was the most populous and prosperous in New Zealand. In total 132,000 people came to New Zealand during the gold rush between 1860 and 1864.

Westland province profited from gold as well. Beginning in 1864, thousands streamed into the almost uninhabited province, mainly from Australia and Otago. As in Australia, Chinese immigrants arrived when the gold deposits were beginning to dry up, and here, too, they encountered prejudice, discrimination, and efforts to limit their immigration through taxation, language tests, special permission forms, and after 1881 with quotas. In 1971 there were about 12,000 Chinese living in New Zealand. The government of New Zealand passed the *Undesirable Immigrants Exclusion Act*, discriminating against Chinese, Indians, and other Asians, in 1919.

In 1870 the gold rush was over, and immigration came to an almost complete stop in all the provinces; the central government now decided on an ambitious program to support immigration, construction, and settlement. These measures helped the population double during the 1870s. Of the over 190,000 immigrants, most received government financial support, while the others were attracted by good-paying jobs in government-sponsored construction projects and by favorable economic factors, such as the availability of government and private loans.

By far the most immigrants came from England, Scotland, and Ireland and thus assimilated easily into the existing ethnic and cultural structure of New Zealand. There were also small groups of Germans (about 3000), Danes (2000), French, and Italians. Otago and Canterbury had the most immigrants, with 29,000 and 27,000, respectively. The largest occupational groups were agricultural workers and domestic servants.

The year with the greatest number of immigrants was 1874, when 44,000 entered New Zealand. After that the figures decreased, although in 1879 there were still 24,000 immigrants. In the early 1880s the Long De-

pression began, a severe economic crisis brought on by excessive dependence on exports, speculation, and high public and private indebtedness. The Depression lasted almost 20 years, and New Zealand became a land of emigration: between 1886 and 1890, for example, the number of emigrants was about 9000 higher than that of immigrants. A comparison of immigration and emigration figures for 1900 shows that many arriving in New Zealand were not settlers who planned to remain for a long time; similarly, in the period 1921-1924 only 36 percent of new immigrants indicated a desire to settle permanently. These data suggest that many emigration decisions were not definitive. New Zealand had significant emigration beginning in the 1870s, about 121,000 between 1870 and 1880 alone. In the following decade the number was 172,000, or 90 percent of the immigration rate, and for the period 1900-1910 it was 250,000, or 75 percent of the immigration. The main destination of these emigrants was Australia.

In the period from 1870 to 1924, the net immigration to New Zealand, with emigration subtracted, was 357,000. In 1879 the population included 450,000 whites, of whom 42 percent were native born; after 1875, however, only 25 percent of New Zealand's population growth was due to immigration. For the period 1869-1919, the total immigration was 1.36 million, 30 percent from Great Britain and Ireland, 66 percent from British possessions, especially Australia, and only 4 percent from other countries.

After 1880 natural causes of population growth outweighed immigration, and settlement patterns were determined by internal migration. There was a rapid jump in economic development in the farming and agricultural processing industries of the North Island as the bush was cleared for new pasture land, and as new refrigeration technology made it feasible to export meat and milk products as well as wool to distant markets, mainly Great Britain; this was naturally accompanied by a northward movement of the population. A number of small towns were founded, service and market centers where agricultural businesses had their headquarters, attracted migrants as well. Today more than 2 million people live on the North Island, while only about 800,000 live on the South Island.

Immigration in the twentieth century depended for the most part on the economic situation. The government promoted limited immigration from 1906 to 1927, and in 1947 subsidized passages for immigrants were reintroduced to fill labor shortages in certain occupational and age groups. This program was limited to immigrants from Great Britain until 1950, but then it was extended to other countries; the principal beneficiaries were about 7000 Dutch migrants. Another group of over 4500 came under an agreement with the International Refugee Organisation after World War II, mainly from Poland and Rumania.

Most of the new immigrants settled in the cities, although urbanization in New Zealand had already begun decades earlier and continued at an increasing rate. In 1874 two-thirds of the population still lived on the land, but by the census of 1926 the ratio had virtually reversed itself, with 63 percent living in cities, and by 1966 the number was over 77 percent. The urban population grew from 740,000 in 1926 to 1.4 million in 1961, and increase of 95 percent,

A Kiwi. This bird is native only to New Zealand

and in 1965 43 percent of the total population lived in the five largest urban centers. The proportion of immigrants living in cities is even higher, 60 percent, complementing the continuing internal immigration trend to the north and the cities.

The Maori have become an urban people as well, and in 1971 almost half were living in cities, especially Auckland with over 50,000 Maori. They have to put up with the poorest-paying jobs and worst living quarters, although their living conditions are reportedly better than those in the slums of Australian, British, or North American cities. At first young Maori men were lured to the cities by the availability of jobs, and later their families followed. Farming the Maori land, commonly owned by the tribes, was not profitable enough to feed all of their members, and so younger Maori had to seek a way of life elsewhere.

The bonds linking New Zealand to Great Britain were stronger than in almost any other former colony. This is especially true of economic ties, and Great Britain is still the primary recipient of New Zealand's agricultural exports. The fact that almost 100 percent of the white population of New Zealand is of British origin explains why society, culture, and public life are dominated by British traditions. Other European ethnic groups have been almost completely assimilated, although some preserve their cultural heritage in ethnic clubs.

The ethnic composition of the New Zealand population has changed since the

1970s due to increased immigration of unskilled workers from Polynesia. In 1956 there were fewer than 9000 people born on Pacific islands living in New Zealand, in part because strict laws and regulations had limited their immigration, but the 1971 census registered over 45,000 Polynesians, most living on the North Island and half of those in Auckland alone. Many of them are skilled or unskilled workers in the industrial and service sectors, hoping to escape at least temporarily the failing subsistence economies of their homelands and to support their families at home with remittance payments. To be sure, the arrival of these labor migrants has given rise to a series of legal, social, and economic problems. Many of them are from the Cook Islands, Niue, and the Tokelau Islands and therefore citizens of New Zealand, who can enter freely. People from other islands such as Samoa, Fiji, or Tonga, need entrance visas, but this regulation is often circumvented by migrants who enter legally on a tourist visa and then work illegally in agriculture. This is one reason for racial discrimination and prejudice. The Polynesian immigrants are on the bottom rung of the social and job hierarchy and are also discriminated against in the housing market. They are the inhabitants of large ethnic neighborhoods in the urban centers, and Auckland especially is becoming a multiethnic city. On the other hand, differences in citizenship status and origin have also led to cultural and ethnic conflicts among the Polynesian population. The new immigrants are welcomed by the New Zealand government as a reserve labor force because of their age structure and their willingness to take on any kind of work.

New Zealand remains an attractive destination for residents of the Pacific islands and many Europeans, although economic problems have intensified since the mid-1970s, with increased unemployment and inflation, relatively low industrial capacity, and few jobs available. These factors led to a new change in immigration policy in 1974. There are now quotas for all ethnic groups, and even British citizens do not have an automatic right to enter New Zealand; all prospective immigrants must now have a visa. The quotas are based not only on numbers but also on occupational requirement. Liberal laws passed at the end of the nineteenth century, including provisions to help small farmers buy land, guarantees of workers' rights to representation in the workplace, and social-security measures, gave New Zealand the reputation of a »working Manitoba's paradise«. No such claims could be made today, although the standard of living for the vast majority of the population is relatively high.

References

Cruickshank, D. J.: »New Zealand - External Migration«, in: Ferenzci; Willcox; International Migrations. Vol. 2, S.179ff.

Dalziel, Raewyn: »Patterns of Settlement«, in: Ward, Ian (ed.): New Zealand Atlas. Wellington, 1976, S.53ff.

Foster, John: »The Structure of New Zealand Society«, in: Osborne, Charles (ed.): Australia, New Zealand and the South Pacific. A Handbook. Belfast, 1970.

Johnston, R. J.: The New Zealanders. How They Live and Work. New York, 1976.

Osborne, Charles, ed. Australia, New Zealand and the South Pacific. A Handbook. Belfast, 1970.

New Zealand landscape

»Africa in chains« - The survivors of the Herero uprising of 1907

»...and divide the spoils«: Africa

Helga Rathjen

Before the colonial period Africa was for Europeans the dark, wild continent, too dangerous to settle. Adventurers journeyed across it: businessmen like Bremen-born Adolf Lüderitz, or researchers who wanted to satisfy their scientific curiosity and make great discoveries on the great expeditions of the eighteenth and nineteenth centuries. Their predecessors were the explorers of the fifteenth and sixteenth centuries, searching for the new and profitable, who had »opened up« the coast of the continent piece by piece and thereby laid the foundations for 500 years of exploitation of the riches of Africa. Once the Americas had been conquered, the hunt for »ebony« began. The Portuguese began with the systematic abduction of African people to slavery in America, and all the great European trading countries eventually took part in this enterprise. European settlement was not necessary to maintain the slave trade; all that was required was military control of the seas off the coasts, supported by a few forts and trading posts.

The African continent itself experienced the slave trade as a large-scale and violent migration movement, however, with between 50 and 200 million Africans shipped off in the period from the fifteenth to the nineteenth century.

For 400 long years the population was robbed of its most able-bodied and productive members; violent changes took place among those who remained. The pressure of slave-hunting brought about a permanent state of war, and not only in the coastal regions. Entire peoples fled to other areas or retreated to hard-to-reach territories, where they were often forced to change their whole way of life.

The Scramble for Africa: The Colonial Period

The industrial revolution changed Europe's interest in Africa. Slaves for plantations were no longer the main target, and the British Navy imposed abolition, ending the slave trade, and replaced it with a »peaceful« trade in tropical agricultural products for the home market. This marked the beginning of a European race to gain raw materials and markets for industrial products, which reached a peak at the Congo Conference in Berlin in 1884. Africa was divided up among the European powers, in part by drawing straight lines which broke up the existing ethnic, economic, and geographic structure of the continent.

Under the protection of colonial armies and administrations, a modest European infrastructure of settlements and roads arose; the land was »civilized«; i.e., made inhabitable by Europeans. Wars of subjugation took the land from the Africans and made it available to Europeans for large-scale plantations or farms. While the infrastructure of the French colonies in the northern half of Africa was set up primarily to foster trade, settlement colonies were established in the British, German, and Portuguese possessions of southern Africa, and the colonies founded in West Africa used both trade and plantations to exploit the conquered land. Still, decades passed before the European powers were able to improve conditions in the colonies enough to make them profitable for investors and safe for permanent settlement by European emigrants. There was strong and persistent resistance to the colonizers from the hinterland, the areas beyond the conquered coastal strip, and only so-called »wars of pacification« were able to bring these peoples under European jurisdiction and control.

Once colonial rule had been stabilized in the first decades of the twentieth century (except in the German possessions), the stream of European emigrants coming to Africa grew. By 1960, on the eve of independence for many African colonies, it had reached a peak of about 3 million Europeans living in Africa. The trend reversed itself during the following period of decolonization: except for the few British settlers who migrated to Rhodesia and South Africa, most found their way back to Europe. Hundreds of thousands of French and Portuguese settlers had to leave the colonial areas that had been their homes for generations.

German Interests in Africa: A Case Study

The Bible and the musket
What are we Germans up to in Africa?
Listen, listen!
We'll destroy slavery everywhere!
And if some natives complain,
we'll silence them quickly and permanently.
Bang, bang! Bang, bang! Hurrah!
O blessed Africa!

We preach Christianity to the heathens.
How noble!
And those who won't believe, we kill.
Bang, bang!
Blessed are the wild ones we can teach
Christian love with fire and sword.
Bang, bang! Bang, bang! Hurrah!
O blessed Africa!

We've got some missionaries with real »punch«
Brandy, Krupp, and the Mauser machine gun!
Those three!
With them we can bring »culture« to Africa.
Load! Fire! Hallelujah!
Bang, bang! Bang, bang! Bang, bang! Hurrah!
O blessed Africa!

from the *Democratic Reader*

A climate of economic expansion, middle-class fear of socialism, and nationalistic dreams of great-power status favored the growth of hopes for a far-flung German Empire led by German colonists. This aggressive vision of the German people, caught up in the struggle for survival and filled with a drive for expansion of the race (for whom the homeland is too confining) reveals both its intellectual connection with the later wars of expansion and its real motive: behind all of the ideological phraseology lies a desire to make a profit from economic exploitation of the colonies.

Hence German emigration to Africa was linked from the very beginning with colonialism, exploitation, and racism. For those leaving Germany, membership in the »master race« was guaranteed by the chauvinistic colonial propaganda as well as by the power structure of the colonies. Emigration to the colonies was praised to nervous

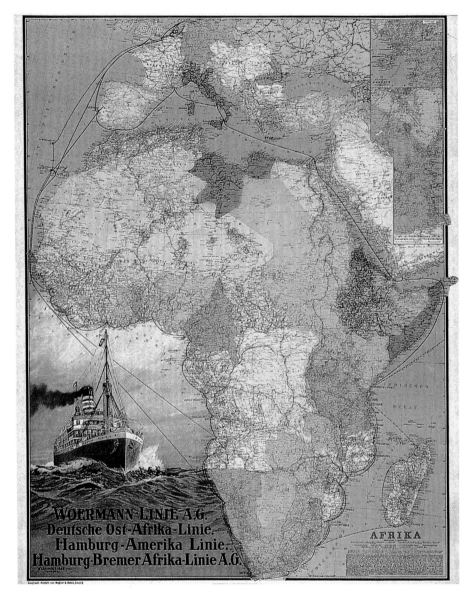

Woermann Line poster, 1927

of colonial economics, Togo was mainly a source of palm kernels for the extraction of palm oil, needed for the machines of heavy industry. African farmers could gather palm kernels or grow palms on very small plantations; for this reason the colonial administration wished to maintain the native small-scale agricultural producers and pursued a very restrictive policy vis à vis potential German emigrants. Anyone coming from Europe had to have a work contract or else pay a security deposit for the return fare before he was allowed to enter Togo. The few efforts made to establish a plantation economy were unsuccessful, with only 2 percent of the German population registered as plantation owners. By 1913 there were only 320 Germans living in Togo.

Cameroon (now the Federal Republic of Cameroun) became Germany's most important plantation settlement in only three years, specializing in rubber, but emigrants were not attracted by this colony.

Settlement companies, owned by large investors with capital, divided the extensive land grants made by the colonial bureaucracy among themselves, and small- or mid-scale plantation owners could survive economically only in a few specialized niches. Again the German population before the outbreak of World War I in 1914 was very small.

Even the class of German colonial bureaucrats and army officers remained tiny: in order to limit the cost of administration, which consistently surpassed the income of the colonial government, all subordinate positions in the military and administration were filled with poorly paid Africans.

At any rate most of the Germans working in the colonial administrations or armed forces were a special group of temporary labor migrants, bureaucrats, officers, missionaries, plantation managers, and businessmen served their terms with no intentions of emigrating.

Only in the agriculturally usable areas of »German Southwest Africa« (Namibia) and to a lesser extent in »German East Africa«

middle-class citizens as a »safety valve« which would reduce pressure in the »steam boiler« of class struggle in Germany.

The settlement companies and the colonial societies which were springing up all over Germany used this sort of propaganda in an effort to build popular support for expanding the rather hesitant colonization policy of the Bismarck government. European power politics and a free-trade strategy opposed to protectionist control of raw-material markets prevented the development of a colonialist foreign policy under Bismarck. Economic interests hoping to make a profit by exploiting overseas areas annexed by the state joined together in the settlement societies. Their policies and propaganda fed fears that the German Empire would »come too late« to a world already divided up among the other powers. They were able to set up German »protectorates« in those parts of Africa which were still »left over«.

The hopes of colonial propagandists for flourishing German settlement colonies were disappointed. From the point of view

"All among the Hottentots Capering ashore"!! or the Blessings of Emigration to the Cape of Forlorn Hope (sic) To be half roasted by the Sun & Devoured by the Natives!!!

»Blessing of the emigration to the Cape of (the lost) Good Hope. Half roasted by the sun and eaten by the Hottentots«. Anti-emigration cartoon, ca. 1819

(Tanzania) did real emigrant settlements arise. In 1913 there were 5300 Europeans registered in German East Africa, plantation owners making a clear profit from the export of coffee, cotton, peanuts, and sisal grown on the fertile land to the north, where the native Moshi lived. Here, too, large investors dominated the scene, and the resulting disappointment among colonial-society members from the petite bourgeoisie and upper middle class led to heated confrontations with the big investors. Fewer than 900 of the over 5000 white colonists were planters, settlers, or plantation employees, and the majority of these did not bring families with them to Africa. The only fully developed settlement colony was German Southwest Africa, now Namibia, which was claimed for the German Empire by the ruthless Bremen merchant and adventurer Adolf Lüderitz in 1884. A barbarian war of annihilation against the native Herero and Nama populations, requiring at times as many as 10,000 German »protection troops«, had »liberated« the relatively fertile land for German farmers and cattle ranchers.

The native population in the colonies had no need for the colonists; but from the opposite perspective there is no advantage in seizing colonies without gaining complete control over the labor force of the natives as well. The relationship of Germans to Africans was characterized by military control and violence and was a necessary component of the colonization process.

The »Negroes« were described as dumb, lazy, deceitful, and bad-smelling or (more charitably) as primitive children; this implied a duty to educate them—to be good workers, of course—with a hippo-leather whip. The unscrupulous exploitation of the natives to serve the whites was carried out in the name of civilizing them, a task for which the German proponents of colonialism felt a special calling, as members of the »master race«.

Wherever the German flag flies in far-off Africa,
And the palm trees grow tall in the blazing sun;
Wherever the German eagle, free and true,
Freely spreads its mighty wings
There we are the defenders,
Bearing German honor
And German culture.
(Friedrich Clark)

Violence and its ideological justification were the determinants of the consciousness and existence of the German colonists, bridging all class differences among them. Ardent nationalism was combined with racist arrogance and cruelty; German cultural chauvinism was paired with idyllic middle-class family life in the midst of so-called »African hordes«. For emigrants of lower-middle-class origin, having white skin and belonging to the colonizing nation provided the illusion of sharing power: although they were in reality cut off from power by the sharp class differences within colonial society, they belonged to the elite when compared with the army of Africans in de facto slavery.

For this reason, these »masters« felt especially threatened by what they called Verkafferung and »miscegenation«. Verkafferte Germans were those who broke with the racist code of behavior and treated the Africans as human beings or even married them (instead of raping them), undermining the racially based unity of the colonial ruling class. Only if the image of inferior »Negroes« could be maintained could their brutal exploitation be justified. Anyone who, through his behavior, granted human rights to blacks had to be excluded as well. Colonial exploitation of Africa included as a matter of course the right to command not only the labor but also the sexuality of the African population. Within the patriarchal structure of colonial society this meant that German men took Africa wives.

The children of such forced relationships (which often resembled marriage in many ways) threatened the German claim to dominance. The same patriarchal structures, in which rights were derived from the father, seemed to demand equal legal status for the so-called »mixed-race children« (who were otherwise discriminated against). But, as the Superior Court in Windhoek ruled in 1907, »If descent from even one member of a primitive race can be proved, then the descendent is by blood a native«.

German colonial society, especially its women, came to the rescue in this dilemma by organizing a special sort of emigration campaign. »To maintain the purity of the German race«, the (mainly single) men of the German colonies were to be granted the blessings of hearth and home and placed under the watchful eyes of German wives. Fiancees and wives were sent for, and brides were recruited among German women willing to emigrate and marry. These »Christmas packages« (as they were actually called) were mainly sent to German Southwest Africa. It was primarily domestic maids who were eager to put their names on the German Colonial Society waiting lists. For them the colonies opened up paths to social advancement which were closed in the poorly paid and completely dependent jobs they held in Germany.

When German colonial rule came to an end in 1918, the German inhabitants of the colonies were interned by the victorious colonial powers and deported to Germany. Parts of Togo and Cameroon went to France, while German East Africa and southwestern Togo came under British rule. Southwest Africa was placed under the League of Nations mandate of South Africa and achieved independence only in the 1980s.

In the 1920s missionaries and merchants were allowed to take up their old activities in the formerly German areas, and in Southwest Africa German colonists were allowed to keep their farms and businesses. In 1944 a large number of them were deported because of their demonstrative support for Fascism, but in 1948 they were readmitted. South Africa guaranteed them, like any other whites in the colonial population, a dominant and privileged position in the apartheid system of Namibia, which had been created with significant German participation.

The Labor Question: Colonial Labor Migration

Whether it was for agriculture or for the creation of an infrastructure, one of the most pressing problems facing colonial bureaucracies was the question of workers, of comprehensive control over the labor of the African population.

The colonial administrations applied coercion and violence; taxes were introduced:

> There is another means at our disposal for educating the Negro. One must instill in him the desire to earn money, by imposing a head tax. Every adult Negro will have a similar sum to pay. In order to earn this money, the Negro must sell his labor in a market where only the white man has need of it«. (Graf Pfeil, 1886)

Since »the white man« tended to need workers far from native settlements and mainly during particular agricultural seasons, the Africans were brutally severed from their traditional economic patterns and their traditional homelands.

Eighty years after the abolition of the slave trade in the British Empire (1808) so-called contracts made workers into forced laborers and hence into de facto slaves. Without any social protection whatsoever they were subject to the total control of their employers for the duration of the contract; anyone who resisted was whipped or even hanged.

If the military power of the plantation owner or other employer was insufficient, the armed forces of the colonial administration were ready to help. Since the exploitative relations were legally sanctioned, the colonial government itself organized the forced labor. The population was called to forced labor by decree, for example to build roads. The court system also helped to find workers, condemning Africans to chaingang labor for minor offenses.

In East Africa villagers were required to work 24 days per year in the fields of German farmers, recalling the customary services of medieval feudalism.

Administrative action also had the effect of destroying the natural foundations of the African way of life: land was cleared for settlers or plantations, and the Africans had to look for wage work to survive. In German Southwest Africa natives were not allowed to buy land or cattle after 1907. A comprehensive system of laws, the immediate forerunners of the later apartheid system, limited the mobility of Africans and created black ghettos as labor pools. A predatory mentality and a thirst for quick profits made most colonists reject the arguments of more farsighted whites, who wanted to maintain a work force for long-

Dividing up the earth. Zeus to Germania: Where were you when the earth was divided up? Drawing from the Kladderadatsch

term exploitation and thus sought to protect black workers from the physically destructive effects of catastrophic working conditions.

African Labor Migrants Today

There was migration before the onset of European and Arab intervention in black Africa, but the nomadic peoples of that time could choose their new settlement areas themselves and developed well adapted ways of life on their own. In this way balance was established, on a long-term basis, between the natural environment and the human population, assuring the survival of all the different tribal groups.

The European conquest of Africa created structures in which this equilibrium suffered lasting destruction. Since the beginning of colonization the continent has been splitting up into two economic systems, an underdeveloped agricultural hinterland and a Europe-centered export economy. The underdevelopment of the rural areas forces people to seek money income elsewhere; even when the desire for a higher standard of living, or the need to escape the social constraints of village life seem to shape the individual decisions of migrants.

One characteristic form of labor migration in Africa is seasonal migration in the agri-

The troop of Hendrik Witboi, Nama chief, 1894, before the attack on German troops

Cutting sisal in German-East Africa (Tanzania), around 1900

cultural sector. Farm workers spend most of the year outside their villages as wage workers or sharecroppers in export agriculture (mainly on plantations) and return home at harvest time to gather their own crops and prepare for the next year's planting.

Areas where African natural resources are being exploited also attract seasonal workers.

Another form of migration is the move into the large urban centers. This often begins with the gradual development of seasonal migration to smaller regional centers, where Africans are separated from the subsistence economy of their home villages for the first time. The length of time between trips back to the village grows longer, and the burden of supporting the family is shifted more and more, and finally completely, to the backs of the women.

The decision to settle permanently in the city often comes when migrants no longer depend on help from the village. At this point families are sent for. Traditionally close family ties to the village are not necessarily broken, but instead remain a form of important social and economic insurance in times of crisis.

The labor pool in the rural areas is in many

cases so large that the need for seasonal workers can be completely met and there are no jobs for migrants.

Both geographically and demographically there is a clear distinction between immigration and emigration regions: the traditional agricultural areas serve as a source of workers for the export-oriented wage-labor areas. Unskilled young men between 18 and 30 years old make up the vast majority of the labor migrants. In the urban centers there are also numbers of unskilled women, often wives who have followed their husbands. The average age in the villages increases, as the younger working population moves to the cities, returning only if they need to be supported or cared for.

This type of labor migration has been institutionalized in a particularly crass way in South Africa, where the apartheid laws prevent families from following wage-earning husbands or wives and moving to the towns where they work.

Since families are left behind to earn a living from subsistence agriculture, the wages of the migrants can be kept very low. When these workers are no longer needed they can be sent home to the reservation-like »homelands« or to their own countries, avoiding any claims on the employer for support.

Geographically the main migration is from the interior to the coastal areas; for example, from the savannah areas of western Africa to the coastal areas to the south. The towns which have become large cities were begun as European settlements on the coasts, following the chronology of the conquests. In west Africa rural areas near the coast were also occupied to establish plantations, and the centers of the cash economy are still to be found there.

Migration in Africa is international; neither the arbitrary national boundaries inherited from the colonial period nor differing citizenship or ancestry seem to impede migratory movement, except in times of political conflict. Then, to be sure, migration is often forced and takes the form of a mass exodus of refugees of a particular tribe or nationality.

Also international in character is the »brain drain« of the African (technological) intelligentsia. Skilled personnel are needed mainly in the production industries, but the nature of most African underdevelopment is such that this sector cannot get off the ground; finding no jobs at home, skilled workers migrate to the cities of Europe and North America.

Unskilled workers leave Africa as well; in the past it was mainly North Africans seeking work in France or in the oil fields of the Arab countries and Libya.

Besides the continuous flow of migrants from the countryside to the cities, there are regional and temporary patterns of involuntary migration, such as the politically motivated expulsions mentioned above. Political or development programs to resettle nomadic populations, to open up new agricultural areas or to preserve the environment in threatened regions, have again and again shifted large numbers of people.

In 1983, for example, political or ecological factors made refugees of over 6 million people in Africa.

Ecological catastrophes sparked by economic factors lead to severe famines and force millions of people to leave their traditional homes with nowhere to go. All too often anticolonial wars of liberation and intra-African political strife caused or exacerbated by colonialism (and nevertheless denounced by us as »tribal wars«) develop into civil wars and drive millions of Africans from their homes. Even before decolonization not a year passed without some incident involving large numbers of civilian refugees: the Sudan, the Belgian Congo (now Zaire), Nigeria, West Sahara, the Horn of Africa, Chad, southern Africa, and Liberia are the best known cases of mass exodus due to war. The environmental crisis in the Sahel continues; Uganda, Rwanda, Burundi, and Nigeria are by no means the only examples of the forcible expulsion of former immigrant minorities; and in southern Africa the choice between the destabilization policy and true reforms still remains.

References

Hinz, Manfred O.; Meier, Arnim; Patemann, Helgard (eds.): Weiß auf Schwarz. 100 Jahre Einmischung in Afrika. Deutscher Kolonialismus und afrikanischer Widerstand. Berlin, 1984.

Höpker, Thomas; Petschull, Jürgen: Der Wahn vom Weltreich. Die Geschichte der deutschen Kolonien. Hamburg, 1984.

Hücking, Renate; Launer, Ekkehard: Aus Menschen Neger machen. Wie sich das Handelshaus Woermann an Afrika entwickelt hat. Hamburg, 1986.

Mayer, Hans; Weiss, Ruth (eds.): Afrika den Europäern! Von der Berliner Kongokonferenz 1884 ins Afrika der neuen Kolonisation. Wuppertal, 1984.

The struggle to survive - a 3000 year old tree in the Sahara desert

Prospects

The 19th century is often called the century of mass migration. The world had been explored and divided up according to the economic and political interests of the European powers. A worldwide economic system developed in the wake of the industrial revolution which was characterized by dominant industrial centers with dependent, mainly agrarian peripheries. This structure is still prevelant today. In hitherto unknown numbers people from backward regions set out to find a better life. The continental and transatlantic migration system was directed from east to west. Today we are facing a similar and historically, possibly more, significant situation. Around World War I the east-west migration system was superseded, at first slowly and after World War II distinctly, by a global migration system which is orientated towards the rich industrial North. Next to peace, worldwide disarmament and ecology, migration will be a key issue in the future. 50 million migrants from Europe to the New World in the past, according to UNESCO figures 500 million refugees worldwide at present: We are hardly confronted with an exclusively historical phenomenon.

Migration Processes after World War I: The German and European Experience

Klaus J. Bade

The shift from emigration to immigration questions has been a common tendency in the developed European countries since the late nineteenth century. The beginning point was the massive transatlantic migration from western and northern Europe which started in the 1830s and then declined toward the end of the century, when it was overtaken by the exodus from southern, eastern, and southeastern Europe, known in North America as the »new immigration«. In the course of the nineteenth century the industrializing states of western and central Europe also became »labor-importing countries« (I. Ferenczi). The European periphery (Ireland, Italy, the Ukraine, and Poland) exported people not only to America but also to western Europe: from Ireland to England; from Italy to France, Switzerland, and Germany; from the Russian part of Poland to Germany (especially Prussia), France, and Denmark; and from Austrian-controlled Galicia (Poland and Ruthenia) to Germany. At the turn of the century, when the U.S. was recording record numbers of immigrants, heated opposition to further immigration arose. Reading and writing tests for immigrants were introduced in 1917, and in 1924 a quota law was passed which, after some legal clarification, became fully effective in 1929. This law led to certain changes in the direction of mass migration. Canada became more attractive and even advertised for eastern European farmers to populate its western provinces and work in its cities.

Overall the volume of transatlantic migration decreased in the 1930s, after a short upswing in the early 1920s, as a result of slower economic growth and the negative attitude of the U.S. toward immigrants from southern and eastern Europe. The flow almost completely stopped during the Depression and at times even reversed itself—in some ethnic groups, such as the Italians, return migration from North America to Italy was greater than Italian immigration.

At the same time new migration streams from south to north arose. In the U.S. the need for workers in northern cities was met by blacks migrating from the southern states and some immigrants from Mexico. In Europe the migration from Italy to the north was limited at first, reaching mass proportions only in the 1950s. Like Mexico, the European Mediterranean basin, including the North African coastal states of the former French Colonial Empire, became an emigration region. Here low wages in the southern areas and active recruitment by the northern industrial states worked together. As a result of this migration there were almost 12 million people living as resident aliens in the principal industrial countries in 1981.

Beginning in the 1970s there were even signs of migration processes in the socialist countries west of the Soviet Union, from Poland to Hungary, and from Yugoslavia to its neighbors and to the north. Polish emigration to the west and once again to the U.S. and Canada increased steadily. East-west immigration pressure has grown since the borders were opened and may even reach the proportions of that from south to north. Because of technological change and global differences in development, however, there are not enough jobs available to absorb the surplus labor force.

Grandma Aukzemas, the 15,000th emigrant after 1945, with her daughter before departing for Canada 1951

The freedom of movement for workers within the European Community planned for 1993 will bring further changes for migration patterns. In North America, changes already began in the 1908s, with a significant increase in immigration from the Pacific accompanied by closer economic ties to that region. Some have asked whether the past »Atlantic century« will be followed by a »Pacific age«.

Germany went from mass emigration in the nineteenth century to mass immigration in the twentieth century; it is thus, although unique in many respects, an especially noteworthy example of the European experience.

The End of the Mass Transatlantic Exodus from Germany

Between 1816 and 1914 about 5.5 million Germans emigrated to the U.S., and since 1914 about 1.5 million more followed them. German-born immigrants made up 30 percent of the U.S. population in the period 1820-1860 and were thus the second most important group, after the Irish. Between 1861 and 1890 they were the largest immigrant group in the U.S. Considering the total European immigration from 1820 to the present, Germans were again the largest group, making up 15 percent of the total of 47 million. A survey conducted in 1979 found that more Americans can trace their ancestry back to Germany than to any other single country. This fact also points to the importance of German transatlantic mass emigration.

The mass transatlantic exodus of the nineteenth century was primarily socioeconomic in origin, caused by the fact that the economy and the number of jobs available grew more slowly than the population during the crisis-plagued transition from an agricultural to an industrial state. As the industrialization process continued, population increase was balanced more and more by rapid jumps in the number of job opportunities, as a result of the phenomenal economic growth of Germany. Germany, however, remained a country of emigration. Economic growth was continuous, except for two short recessions, during the

period from the mid-1890s until just before World War I; the attractions of the main transatlantic immigration country became less appealing than the expanding job market in the home country. Mass transatlantic migration after about 1890 blended with the stream of internal migration from rural areas to urban and industrial ways of life and work. The drop in transatlantic emigration was roughly the inverse of a rise in the number of foreign migrant workers from Prussian Poland, Galicia, and Italy, which reached massive proportions and changed Germany under the Kaisers from a land of emigration to a labor importing country in the course of a single decade.

Emigration from the Weimar Republic, Nazi Germany, and the Federal Republic of Germany

After World War I and especially after the Treaty of Versailles a big new wave of emigration from Germany was expected. The predictions were wrong, however, and emigration in 1919-1920 remained insignificant. It did increase markedly as the restrictions imposed after the war were gradually loosened, but it took until 1923 to reach a sharp, short-lived peak. This was due on the one hand to the realization of plans made earlier but delayed because emigration was impossible during the war and immediately thereafter. On the other hand, some were fleeing from the inflation crisis, as a form of economic speculation: they had been planning to emigrate later but took action now in order to save at least some capital and make a new start overseas. Another group of emigrants consisted of those uprooted or displaced by Germany's defeat in the war, the losses of territory called for in the Treaty of Versailles, the collapse of the Imperial government, their experience in revolutionary movements of 1918-1919, or mistrust of the new Weimar Republic. When the economy was stabilized in the mid-1920s emigration decreased somewhat and then dropped precipitously during the Depression (after 1929), as it had during the economic crisis of the mid-1870s.

The end of World War I and the new politi-

cal structure of Europe were important for Germany in another way: before 1914 Germany (especially Prussia) was the primary transit land for emigrants from eastern and southeastern Europe as well as an »importer« of Russian-Polish and Galician agricultural workers and Prussian-Polish (Ruhrpolen) industrial workers. Political factors (the creation of new countries after the destruction of the multiethnic Ottoman, Habsburg, and Czarist Empires) and economic factors (increased industrialization and the growth of industrial centers) led to the disappearance of some causes of emigration, a substantial decrease in the number of emigrants from these areas, and significant changes in the European and transatlantic migration system. This trend was reinforced by political measures in the lands of immigration (such as the U.S. quota system) which were especially disadvantageous for eastern and southeastern Europeans, and by the effects of economic crisis. On the other hand, the accelerated industrialization of the Soviet Union in the late 1920s and early 1930s acted as a magnet for workers and technical experts, especially engineers, with socialist class consciousness. This west-east migration from Europe and North America soon came to a stop, however, with the Depression and the Soviet purges of the 1930s.

Political emigration and the flight of Jewish refugees from Nazi Germany began a new chapter in German migration history, quite different from the past hundred years of transatlantic migration and comparable only with the political emigration after the revolution of 1848-1849 (the »Forty-Eighters«) and at the time of Bismarck's anti-Socialist law. This is especially true of the Nazi racist policies, which were grounds for persecution and the reason for many to flee the country: the total number of people who left the German-speaking area for other European or non-European countries between 1933 and 1945 must be much higher than half a million, the group of emigrants considered (in the broadest sense) to be of Jewish origin was larger than 500,000 by itself.

The emigration routes led to about 75 different lands, with those lying on Germany's borders serving mainly as transit

War I, people predicted mass emigration from post-World War II Germany, which was divided, for the most part destroyed, economically ruined, and overpopulated. In the first years after the war, however, emigration was open only to a limited group of people and only for special reasons. Otherwise the Allies prohibited emigration, and the transatlantic countries which had been primary destinations for emigration previously refused to take German immigrants at first. Only in 1948 did transatlantic migration take on significant proportions (about 27,400); it peaked at about 90,000 in 1952 and then fell continuously after 1956 (82,000), reaching 47,700 in 1960, the first year of full employment in Germany. Among the countries of destination the U.S. was first, followed by Canada, Australia, and Brazil. Until the mid-1950s, a high proportion of the emigrants was made up of refugees.

As the labor market became more international after 1960, the term »emigration« became a »nineteenth-century concept« for most migrants. Instead of firm decisions to emigrate there were simply moves to take jobs in foreign countries for an indefinite period, and the corresponding labor statistics recorded not »emigration« but rather »departures«—temporary migration, which often enough became permanent if the stay abroad lasted longer than planned. It is therefore hard to estimate the proportion of real emigrants in the annual rate data (for example, 53,728 in 1980).

In the late 1970s and early 1980s, there was a new wave of transatlantic emigration, especially among young people, as a kind of fundamental rejection of their homeland. There was talk of a »new emigration« from West Germany, and destinations other than the U.S. gained in importance. Hundreds of thousands of inquiries were directed to the information offices operated by Australia and New Zealand. The results of emigration counseling sessions indicated, however, a greater increase in the

countries until the war crossed their borders. The U.S. was by far the most important final destination, followed by England, Palestine, and Switzerland. Between 1933 and the U.S. entry into the war in 1941, a total of 104,098 Germans and Austrians entered the U.S., over 80 percent of whom were Jews. Half arrived in the years 1938-1941, since at first many had hoped they would have to leave only temporarily and remained in neighboring European countries, leaving from there to come to America as the threat of German military expansion increased. For many, especially for the Jewish emigrants, flight into exile meant rescue from mortal danger. Most intended to leave temporarily, but many remained permanently. Refugees became real emigrants.

To an even greater extent than after World

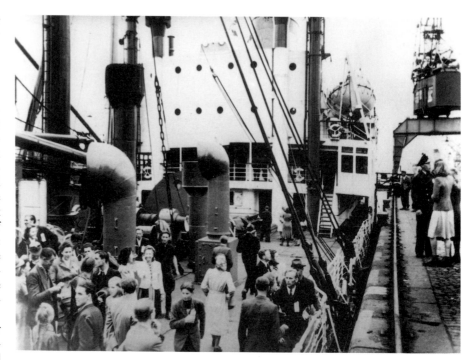

In the early years after World War II it was mainly displaced persons who emigrated from Europe, followed by many Germans in the 1950s

number of Germans with a »desire to emigrate« than in actual emigration. In many cases people were motivated by general adjustment problems, criticism of European civilization, cultural malaise, anxiety during political crises, and poorly defined needs for room to develop personally; the emigration advisors naturally had to cast cold water on their idealistic dreams of emigration. In a way, the »new emigration« from West Germany as a response to the crises of the 1970s was a brief episode reprising some of the classical themes of the great transatlantic migration, with its idealized vision of the New World.

Today transatlantic emigration is no longer an issue in the FRG; the patterns and problems of migration in Germany have reversed themselves in the last hundred years, especially after World War II. The first signs of the change from a country of emigration to a country of immigration appeared in the late nineteenth century.

From Emigration to Labor Importation: Foreign Workers in the German Empire, the Weimar Republic, and Nazi Germany

The great economic upswing in the two decades before World War I brought a shortage of workers to German agriculture and industry, instead of the oversupply which had existed before and constituted the most important driving force behind transatlantic emigration. Beginning in the 1890s, the migration of European workers into Germany (especially Prussia) grew into a mass movement, rapidly approaching the million mark in the decade before the war and peaking at 1.2 million in 1914, the year the war began.

The largest immigrant groups were Poles from the Russian part of Poland and Poles and Ruthenians from Austrian-ruled Galicia. They worked for the most part in agriculture, particularly in eastern Prussia. The

second, much smaller immigrant group was made up of Italian workers, primarily employed in brickyards and mines.

The shift in the balance of German transnational migration from emigration to immigration which began to appear in the statistical data was at first opposed by Prussian government decrees for political reasons, to assure the security of Prussia's eastern border. The aim of Prussia's restrictive policy (*Abwehrpolitik*) was to make sure that the influx of workers across the border from Russian Poland was limited to seasonal transnational migration and did not become immigration. To achieve this aim a set of laws and regulations (requiring people to carry identity papers) was set up in Prussia around the turn of the century to prevent immigration from the east. There were numerous holding camps, monitoring stations, and government-agency offices along the Prussian border. The result was an annual pattern resembling a fever chart, with the curve representing labor migration from eastern Europe to Prussia/Germany climbing rapidly in the spring to a peak in the summer and then falling just as quickly at the beginning of the winter season when entrance was prohibited.

Germany, now both a country of emigration and a labor importing country, experienced internal conflicts of interest with respect to the admission of aliens, beginning in the 1890s and continuing even after World War I—conflicts of a scope and intensity usually encountered only in immigration-policy discussions in the traditional countries of immigration. The tension between emigration and the employment of foreign workers is seen in the contrasting aims of German migration policy as well: protection for German transatlantic emigration and protection against immigration from other European countries.

In the Weimar period the employment of foreign workers continued to exhibit the characteristic pattern of the prewar years, with its annual fluctuations, although at a much lower overall level. Government efforts to control the admission of foreigners no longer followed the Prussian restrictive policy but instead were part of a rational labor-market strategy. Foreign workers could only get visas if the newly established Labor Exchanges (»*Arbeitsnachweise*«) certified that no German workers suitable for the job were available. For this reason the number of foreigners employed remained relatively low and then decreased sharply during the Depression.

The 1,000,000th guest worker in Germany, 1964 - then he received a gift, is he now a threat?

This relatively low employment level in Germany is especially noteworthy in comparison to other European countries, considering the ratio of foreigners to the total population. In absolute numbers the German census of 1925 counted just under 1 million foreigners, well behind France, which had 2.5 million. The proportion of foreigners was 6.2 percent for France, but only 1.5 percent for Germany. Among the countries with higher proportions were Luxembourg (33,500 foreigners or 12.8 percent) and Switzerland (402,000 or 10.4 percent), while the Netherlands (112,000 or 1.6 percent) and Belgium (153,000 or 2.1 percent) were closer to Germany. Great Britain had only 0.6 percent (250,000), and Italy only 0.3 percent (110,000). The eastern and southeastern European countries also had significant numbers of foreigners, for example 3.5 percent (65,000) in Lithuania and 1.8 percent (238,000) in Czechoslovakia—although there cases of unclarified nationality were probably a greater factor than actual migration. These numbers are for the period 1920-1926, depending on when census data were taken in the different countries; an exact comparison of countries is not possible, but it is clear enough that immigration was a common phenomenon in most of the western and central European countries between the wars, and that Germany's position in this regard was not nearly as exceptional as in the case of transatlantic emigration before World War I.

In 1933 a new and (especially during World War II) tragic chapter in the history of foreign workers in Germany began with the alien worker (*Fremdarbeiter*) policy of the Nazi government. To be sure, the basic principles followed between the Nazi takeover and the outbreak of World War II were still in the tradition of the Empire and the Weimar Republic. Only in the war economy were the rules completely rewritten in the spirit of the Nazi policy of »deploying foreigners«. In contrast to the high proportion of foreign workers in Germany

at the beginning of World War I, there were fewer than half a million in the late 1930s and even in the last year before World War II, despite an extreme labor shortage. This was due to the goal of self-sufficiency underlying Nazi economic policy and to restrictive currency laws which made it difficult to transfer wages earned in Germany to the worker's homeland. But when the state gained direct control over the labor force of the occupied areas during the war, the number of foreigners recruited to work shot up into the hundreds of thousands. The work relationship was frequently based on coer-

cion and violence, especially in Poland, where at total of 1.8-2 million forced laborers were deported. Estimates are that at war's end there were 10.5-11.7 million »displaced persons« (DPs), of about 20 different nationalities and speaking more than 35 languages, living in the areas which had been occupied by Hitler. Most of these people had been *Fremdarbeiter*, slave laborers in the Nazi War economy.

Between the end of the war in May 1945 and September of the same year over 5 million DPs were »repatriated«, voluntarily in most cases but by force in the case of the

Soviet DPs, as called for by the last wartime Allied conference at Yalta in February 1945. At the end of 1945 there were still 1.7 million DPs living in camps in the western occupation zones; these were mainly Poles, Ukrainians, Estonians, Latvians, and Lithuanians who had lost their homelands or their connections to them as a result of the expansion of Soviet territory and the westward shift of Poland's borders agreed to at Yalta. Another 500,000 of these returned home in 1946, but then efforts at further repatriation were abandoned. The DPs became »homeless aliens« and had a distinct legal status which was reaffirmed by a German law when jurisdiction was passed from the Allies to the authorities of the Federal Republic of Germany in 1950. After 1947 repatriation was replaced with an international campaign aimed at resettlement overseas or in other western European countries. Under this program about 712,000 DPs left the western zones of Germany in 1951. Relatively few of these people (about 110,000) sought new homes in western Europe; most went to the classical overseas destinations, the U.S. (about 273,000), Canada (83,000), and Australia (136,000). This migration resulted in a temporary increase in transatlantic migrant traffic from German harbors, although German overseas emigration grew only gradually at first.

Immigration Processes after World War II

The population, economy, and society of the Federal Republic of Germany were influenced more than in any other industrial country in the second half of the twentieth century by international mass migration. A total of over 15 million displaced persons (expelled from their homes in eastern Europe), refugees, *Übersiedler* (people moving from East to West Germany), and *Aussiedler* (ethnic Germans whose ancestors emigrated from Germany to Eastern Europe centuries ago and who are now intending to return to Germany or have done so) came to the western occupation zones and later West Germany. This influx of new citizens made up more than a quarter of the total population of German citizens living in the »old« FRG before reunification in October 1990.

By the mid-1950s the integration of the refugees and displaced persons had been accomplished on a superficial, social and occupational level, and the German »economic miracle« (*Wirtschaftswunder*) was in full swing. It was at this point, in 1955, that a German-Italian agreement marked the beginning of government-organized recruiting of foreigners, soon known as »guest workers« (*Gastarbeiter*). Between 1955 and 1973, when advertising was stopped, about 14 million foreign workers came to West Germany, of whom about 11 million returned to their homelands. At present the foreign population in West Germany is about 4.8 million, including almost 3 million belonging to the *Gastarbeiter* population, immigrants recruited in the advertising campaign or their descendants. If one includes this minority *Gastarbeiter* population, almost one third of the people living in the »old« FRG in 1990 has its origin in immigration since the end of World War II.

Throughout Europe the period of economic growth after the war triggered a migration from South to North which was economically motivated and crossed over the boundaries of countries, continents, spheres of influence, and stages of economic development. This migration developed over thirty years into a mass movement of workers and families from the peripheral areas to the centers of concentrated economic activity. The countries of origin were mainly Turkey and the Mediterranean lands, although England also attracted people from the former colonies in the Caribbean and the Indian subcontinent. As a result significant numbers of migrants were living in Europe (with their families and descendants) in the early 1980s: 4.6 million (7.5 percent of the population) in the FRG, 4.2 million (8.5 percent) in France, 2.1 million (3.9 percent) in Great Britain, 0.9 million (8.6 percent in Belgium, 0.5 million (3.8 percent) in the Netherlands, 0.2 million (3.9 percent) in Austria, 0.4 million (5.1 percent) in Sweden, and 0.9 million (14.5 percent) in Switzerland.

For the historical development of the FRG since World War II it is possible to distinguish three different, chronologically overlapping phases of integration:

1. The first process was the integration of the refugees, primarily of German descent. Many of them still held out hope for a return to their former homes, which was an obstacle to integration until they came to understand that they had to accept the west as their new homeland or at least a long-term residence. Except for those who traveled on overseas, immigrants in this group typically aimed for permanent integration, from the very beginning or at least from the time of their disillusionment with chances for return to the east.

2. The second major integration process was determined by changes in the recruitment of foreign workers, from active advertising in the 1950s to the »*Gastarbeiterproblem*« of the 1960s and 1970s to the immigration problem of the 1980s. In the 1950s and 1960s the dominant conception in the receiving society and among the foreign workers themselves was of temporary residence, although in fact the stays were becoming longer and longer. The end of officially sanctioned recruiting in 1973 strengthened the tendency toward long-term residence and the immigration of family members. Increasing integration led to a paradox: by the early 1980s most members of the alien minority with origins in the original *Gastarbeiter* population were living as true immigrants in West Germany, which officially still denied being a country of immigration.

3. The immigration and integration problems facing West Germany since the late 1980s seem to be even more complex than those of the two preceding phases, since five essentially different problem areas are involved: a) the above-mentioned immigrant situation without a country of immigration for the minority population of former *Gastarbeiter*; b) the special problems of refugees living in the FRG as recognized or unrecognized applicants for asylum or asylum-seekers (or rejected applicants who are still allowed to stay under the provisions of the 1951 Geneva conventions on refugees, signed by West Germany); c) the integration problems of *Aussiedler* from eastern, east-central, or south-

eastern Europe, especially severe for those with poor knowledge of the German language; d) the identity problems of *Übersiedler* from the former German Democratic Republic (GDR), who apparently migrated from Germany to Germany but learned once in West Germany how far apart the two economic, social, and political systems and even the values and collective mentalities had become; and e) the identity problems of people now living in what was the GDR before German reunification in 1990—because of the one-sided way in which the economy, society, and political culture of their country were focused on ideological opposition to the archenemies »capitalism« and »market economy«, they have temporarily become foreigners in their own country.

Aussiedler and German-German identity problems are specifically German phenomena in the European and international migration process. Refugee problems and the question of political asylum naturally affect other countries as well. On a global scale, 90 percent of migration takes place in the third world. A problem which is common to most western industrial countries is that of integrating foreign minorities which were recruited earlier for economic reasons but now live as de facto immigrants, regardless of whether the receiving culture considers itself an »immigration country« or not. England and France in particular, but also the Netherlands, have to resolve the conflicts of a postcolonial era within their own borders.

In general the scenario of integration problems faced by Germany in the last decade of the twentieth century includes many tensions (or fears of tensions), between the native population and immigrant minorities taken together and between native groups and specific immigrant minorities (for example pitting »native foreigners«—or »alien natives«—and FRG Germans against foreign-language-speaking *Aussiedler* or asylum-seekers). Finally, there are group tensions among the different immigrant minorities themselves.

The most dangerous tensions are those involving a cultural or ethnic pecking order: for example, *Übersiedler* from the GDR (»pure Germans«) against German *Aussiedler* from the Soviet Union (»Russians«)

Refugees in Ethiopia

or especially from Poland (»Polacks«); *Aussiedler* against »foreigners« and especially against asylum-seekers from the third world (»blacks«, »economic refugees«, or »drug dealers«); etc. Beneath all of these in the hierarchy—although the boundaries are often unclear—are the illegal aliens, whose numbers are difficult to estimate but definitely significant, and who lack any protection under the law.

The political decay and economic collapse of the moribund »East Bloc« (resulting in east-west migration pressure) and the economic, ecological, and political crises in the third world (leading to the migration of very large numbers of refugees)—such developments put fear in the hearts of many people. The internal German, European, and global migration patterns with their highly complex and hard-to-grasp development tendencies give people a vague sense that migration itself is a general and omnipresent threat. These feelings range from the nightmare of an invasion led by the starving masses of the third world, to the possibly self-fulfilling prophecy of a flood of millions of labor migrants and refugees fleeing the economic misery of eastern Europe, to a skeptical view of all »strangers« in the concrete day-to-day life of the immigrant situation.

Xenophobia and the confusion between immigration and a threatening invasion of starving people from underdeveloped parts of the world are not unfamiliar to historians of the classical immigration countries. Despite sometimes vehement discussions of immigration restrictions, despite diverse types of ethnic prejudice, day-to-day discrimination, and xenophobic tendencies in the U.S., Canada, and Australia, it was

eventually possible to develop concepts of ethnic pluralism or multiculturalism there. Although there were many social imperfections, these concepts at least opened up the possibility that different ethnic groups could coexist peacefully, with equal rights and tolerance for one another. In Europe the discussion of ethnocultural pluralism has only begun recently, and it is not yet known what, if any, of the American, Canadian, and Australian experience is applicable.

Migration and Integration Policy: Future Tasks and the Historical Experience

In confronting the already very complex hierarchy and constant changes of the immigration situation within Germany as well as the increasing immigration pressure from outside, politicians, legislators, and administrators need to reconsider their choice of options and the possibility of creative solutions. As a basis they need a comprehensive migration and integration policy, based on clear legal principles, which can be applied to all sorts of migration problems and their possible consequences and to all the different groups of immigrants as well—from Aussiedler and Übersiedler to temporary labor migrants, long-term resident aliens, and true immigrants, to the many political and economic refugees. In the latter case, the German asylum laws, uniquely generous to the asylum-seeker in theory but sharply limited in practice, are hopelessly inadequate to handle the numbers of people now entering the country. With such a comprehensive policy the country would be legally prepared for the challenges of future migration processes, both within and outside the borders of the European community.

Such an initiative would include both a domestic immigrant and minority policy, immigration laws, and an immigration policy which foresees new developments and plans to meet them; i.e., which actively attempts to shape the process rather than simply passively administering it. In emergency situations there may have to be quotas for immigrants and labor migrants as well as international agreements regulating the migration of refugees—beyond the constitutionally guaranteed individual right of the politically persecuted to asylum. Also needed is a graduated, flexible integration plan, building an institutional network to provide a wide variety of different services to inform and help people through all the stages and transitions of immigrant life.

The prerequisite for all of this is a well-founded overall conception of migration and integration policy based on sound socio-political principles. It must address the complex and highly differentiated problems of the immigration situation as a whole, and it must be sufficiently coordinated with other economic, social, and cultural policies. And it must have balancing and mediation functions which help prevent individual groups from colliding or even being played off against each other.

In this process the Germans can learn from their own history that encounters with »strangers« may well produce tensions, but in most cases are still to the advantage of both parties. In the past millions of Germans were just as much strangers in foreign countries as the present-day aliens are in Germany. With this kind of history as a background it is possible to see tensions in the immigrant situation as a potential learning experience, to admit their existence and try to relax them, without overoptimistic expectations, without crippling stereotypes, and with the necessary insight and patience.

An acute need for action exists, however, not only at the national level but also at the European and global levels. On a European scale, it should be pointed out that the integration of Europe and the establishment of a single market will have two different effects on the international migration process. On the one hand there will be increased mobility within Europe, but on the other hand a »fortified Europe« will be more tightly closed to the outside world. This closing does not affect only the flow of goods, arousing mistrust of the growing power of Europe in the other great trading nations, the U.S. and Japan. It also affects the flow of migrants and migration policy—factors which, for the third world, are just as important as economic and trade issues.

The great questions for the future of global population are still unanswered: are population growth and decline like a self-regulating system of connecting pipes? Is Europe, with lower birthrates and increasing life expectancy leading to population decline and higher average age, to be a bunker fortified against population explosion in the surrounding third world, closed to third-world immigrants but insisting that third-world markets be open to its manufactured goods? Can the world survive if it is divided into industrialized centers (Europe, Japan, and the U.S.), »threshold« countries, and non-industrialized, mainly agrarian peripheral countries which make their material and labor resources available to the industrialized centers and serve as markets for their products?

In the nineteenth century people had to leave their homes in eastern and southern Europe to seek work and bread; in the most recent decades labor migration patterns have covered the globe. Labor migrants have come from Italy, Greece, Spain, Portugal, Yugoslavia, and then especially from Turkey to Germany; from the Caribbean and Pakistan to England; from North Africa to France and more recently to Italy; from the Philippines and Korea to Japan; from India, East Africa, Egypt, and Indonesia to the Arab oil-producing countries; and from Latin America to the U.S. In addition to migration between countries there has also been intraregional migration: outside Europe, the U.S., and Japan massive migration from the countryside to urban centers has produced monstrous concentrations of slums. The industrialized centers have become crystallization points for the hopes of millions of people for a better life, and the boundary separating labor migrants from refugees has become fuzzy. In the worldwide migration process, Europe must find answers to the global challenges raised by its very existence—not only in its trade policies, but also in its foreign-aid and migration policies.

This brings us to the global questions. The crisis of growth and the population explosion, the acceleration of underdevelopment, the continuing destruction of the environment and the greenhouse effect on the climate—all of these factors make it harder and harder to distinguish between political refugees on the one hand and crisis, economic, ecological, and climatic refugees on the other. After all, the type of death (by torture, war, or starvation) refugees are trying to escape cannot really be considered as an argument for or against rescuing them. It is important to remember that migration policy is always a way of treating effects, not causes. Humane treatment and charity are necessary, but not sufficient.

To react to the flow of refugees, which according to UNESCO estimates now encompasses about 500 million people and could reach 1 billion by the year 2000, by admitting refugees, by helping them to assimilate, or by means of migration policy would be trying to cure the disease by treating the symptoms. The treatment must address the causes of the problem on a worldwide scale. In order to achieve a peaceful international balance of burdens between north and south, but also between east and west with respect to the global refugee problem, a foreign aid policy which alleviates the need for migration is required. For the immediate future a humane migration policy is needed.

References

Bade, Klaus J. (ed.): Deutsche im Ausland - Fremde in Deutschland. Migration in Geschichte und Gegenwart. München, 1992.

Bade, Klaus J.: Deutschland. Vom Auswanderungsland zum Einwanderungsland. Berlin, 1983.

Bickelmann, Hartmut: Deutsche Überseeauswanderung in der Weimarer Zeit. Wiesbaden, 1980.

Tichy, Roland: Ausländer rein! Warum es kein Ausländerproblem gibt. München, 1990.

Refugee camp in Africa

Credits

Arno Armgort,private collection, Bremen: 85, 97, 149, 150, 151, 189
Black Star, Claus Meyer, Essen: 175
Archiv Beck & Co, Bremen: 5
Ellis Island Museum, National Park Service, New York: 2, 7, 8, 19, 28, 31, 55, 65, 115, 116, 118, 122, 129, 131, 132, 134, 135
Förderverein Deutsches Auswanderermuseum, Bremerhaven: 10, 15, 26, 32, 33, 82, 83, 92, 108, 128
Christiane Harzig, private collection, Worpswede: 11, 13, 14, 34, 39, 42, 43, 44, 52, 57, 60, 61, 62, 68, 77, 78, 79, 87, 101, 110, 111, 137, 144, 192, 193, 194
Labor Migration Project, Bremen, Bildarchiv: 6, 20, 21, 22, 23, 25, 29, 36, 37, 38, 41, 45, 47, 49, 54, 55, 56, 58, 59, 63, 67, 69, 70, 71, 75, 76, 84, 86, 89, 91, 93, 94, 95, 96, 100, 103, 104, 105, 107, 109, 111, 112, 113, 114, 125/26, 127, 128, 133, 136, 138, 139, 140/41, 142, 145, 146, 148, 152, 154, 155, 156, 157, 159, 160, 162, 163, 164, 165, 168, 169, 170, 171, 172, 173, 177, 178, 179, 180, 183, 187, 190, 195, 196, 198, 202, 203, 205, 206
Library of Congress, Washington: Umschlag S. 1.
Náprstek Museum Library, Prag: 24, 129
Jacob A. Riis Collection, New York: 143, 145, 146, 147
Deutsches Schiffahrtsmuseum, Bremerhaven: 80, 98, 117
Staatsarchiv Bremen: 16, 86, 88, 93, 102, 181
Jochen Tholen, Bremen: 197
Verlagsarchiv: 35, 53, 120/21, 161, 167, 176, 179, 182, 186, 188, 201
Volkskundliches Museum, Krakow: 50, 74

Acknowledgements

Christiane Harzig had the idea for this book.
The following persons contributed to its completion:
Hans W. Petersen, Stefan Knobloch and Karin Schulz from the Förderverein Deutsches Auswanderermuseum (Friends of the German Migration Museum), Bremerhaven;
Wiebke Skalicky and Horst Temmen from Edition Temmen;
Renate Dirks, Birgit Nahrmann, Natascha Apmann and the members of the Labor Migration Project at the University of Bremen.
The Förderverein Deutsches Auswanderermuseum let us have use of the engravings and photographs in its archives, and Christiane Harzig and Arno Armgort gave us free access to their private collections.
The captions and selection of illustrations have been done by D. Knauf.
Thomas Kozak, New York, translated the German text into English. Mia Katz, Bremen, helped us out with ad hoc translating.
This book is sponsored by Beck&Co, Bremen.
A warm thank you to all of them.

Diethelm Knauf / Dirk Hoerder